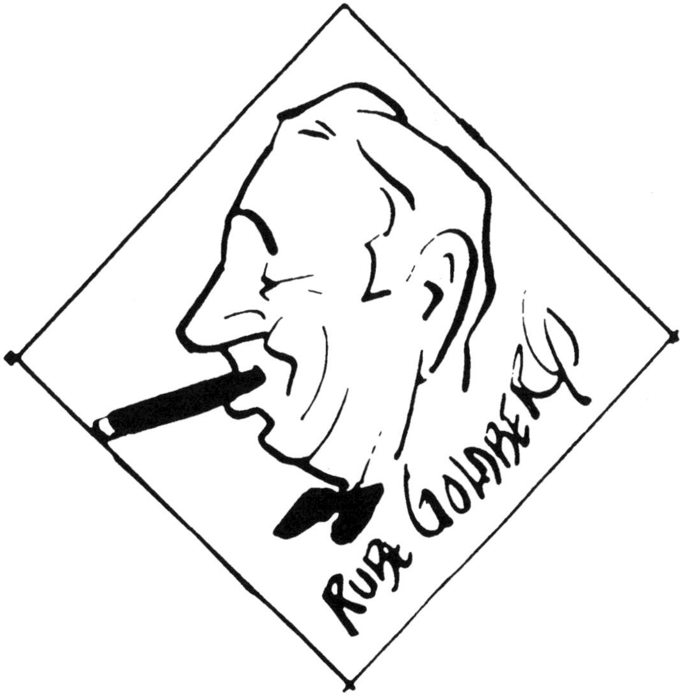
RUBE GOLDBERG

RUBE GOLDBERG

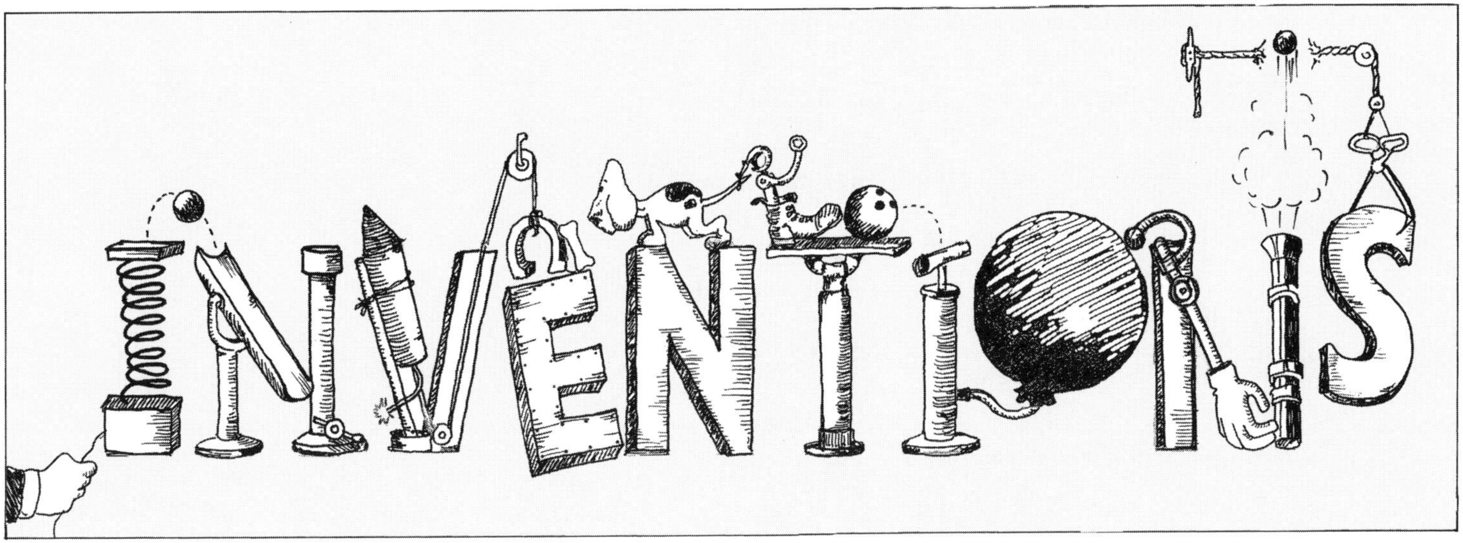
INVENTIONS

Maynard Frank Wolfe

Simon & Schuster
New York London Toronto Sydney Singapore

SIMON & SCHUSTER
Rockefeller Center
1230 Avenue of the Americas
New York, NY 10020

Produced by: **David Kaestle, Inc.**
Design by: **Rick DeMonico**
Design and Production Assistants: **Theresa Venezia** & **Masha Kroshinskaya**
Digital Imaging: **Richard Stokell**

Front jacket drawing by David Kaestle and back jacket collage by Rick DeMonico
using drawings by Rube Goldberg.

Manufactured in the United States of America

10 9 8 7 6

Library of Congress Cataloging-in-Publication Data
Wolfe, Maynard Frank
   Rube Goldberg : inventions / Maynard Frank Wolfe.
      p. cm
   Includes biographical references.
   1. Goldberg, Rube, 1883–1970—Catalogs. 2. Inventions in art—Catalogs. 3. American
wit and humor, Pictorial—Catalogs. I. Goldberg, Rube, 1883–1979. II. Title

NC1429.G46 A4 2000
741.5'973—dc21

00-055612

ISBN 0-684-86724-9

With my thanks for their inspiration and support,
this book is dedicated to
my daughter, Jessica,
my son, Alexander,
my friend Margo Astrachan,
and to the memory of my mother, Mabel Lewis Wolfe

Eating & Drinking 54

Contents

Sports & Games 72

Good Grooming 94

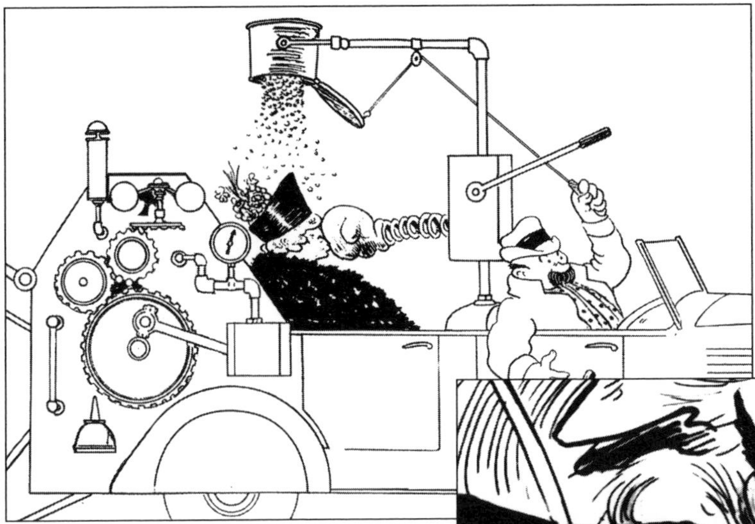

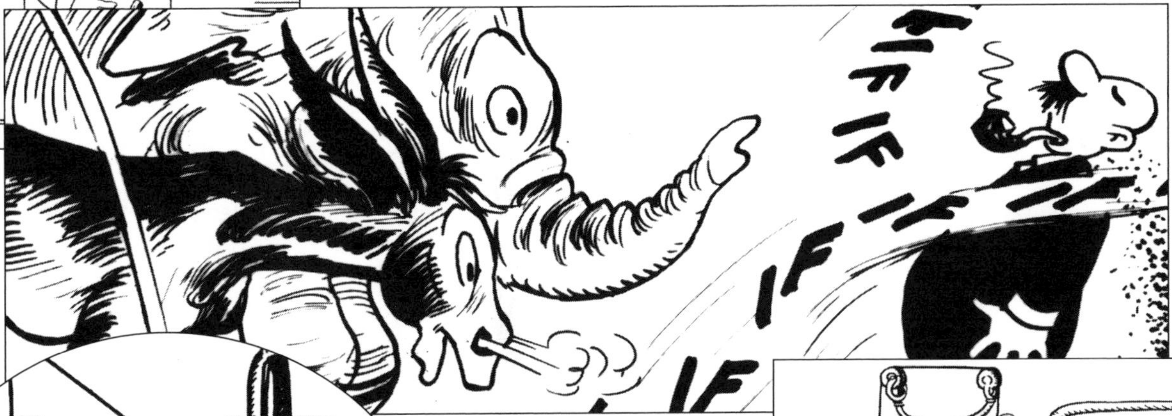

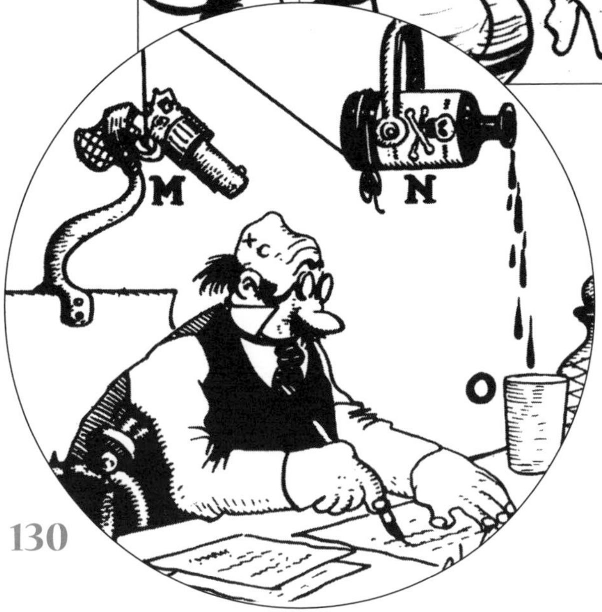
M
N
O

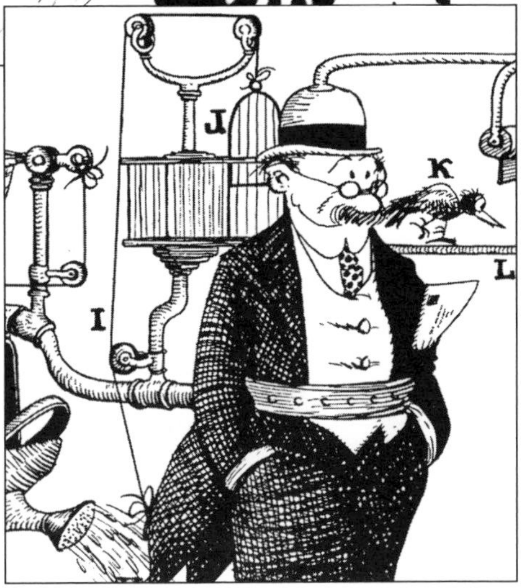
J
K
L
I

as caused by a rubefacient...

Rube Gold·berg (ro͞ob gōld′berg) *after Rube* (Reuben Lucius) *Goldberg*, US cartoonist of comically involved contrivances; designating any very complicated invention, machine, scheme, etc. laboriously contrived to perform a seemingly simple operation.

...mild infecti... ...unicable virus characterized

ru·bel·l...

Foreword

Play a free-word association game in London, or Kuala Lumpur, or Rio de Janeiro; ask a Malaysian or an Italian or a South African to list adjectives and phrases that come to mind when you say the word *American*. Assuming that the first thing said isn't "CIA-sponsored plot to destroy democracy," here's what you'll hear: "Rich. Exuberant. Slightly (or perhaps very) brassy. Optimistic. Fascinated with gadgets."

These descriptions might well be applied to that archetypal American, Reuben Lucius Goldberg, the dean of American cartoonists for most of the twentieth century. In the chain of six degrees of separation connecting Thomas Edison, "Inventor," to Gary Larson, "Cartoonist," Rube Goldberg is the most prominent of its links. For more than sixty-five years, Rube Goldberg's syndicated cartoons—he produced more than fifty different panels and strips—appeared in as many as a thousand newspapers annually. He was earning more than $100,000 a year... in 1915, or about 1.7 million in today's dollars. He was, in succession, a star in vaudeville, motion pictures, newsreels, radio, and finally television.

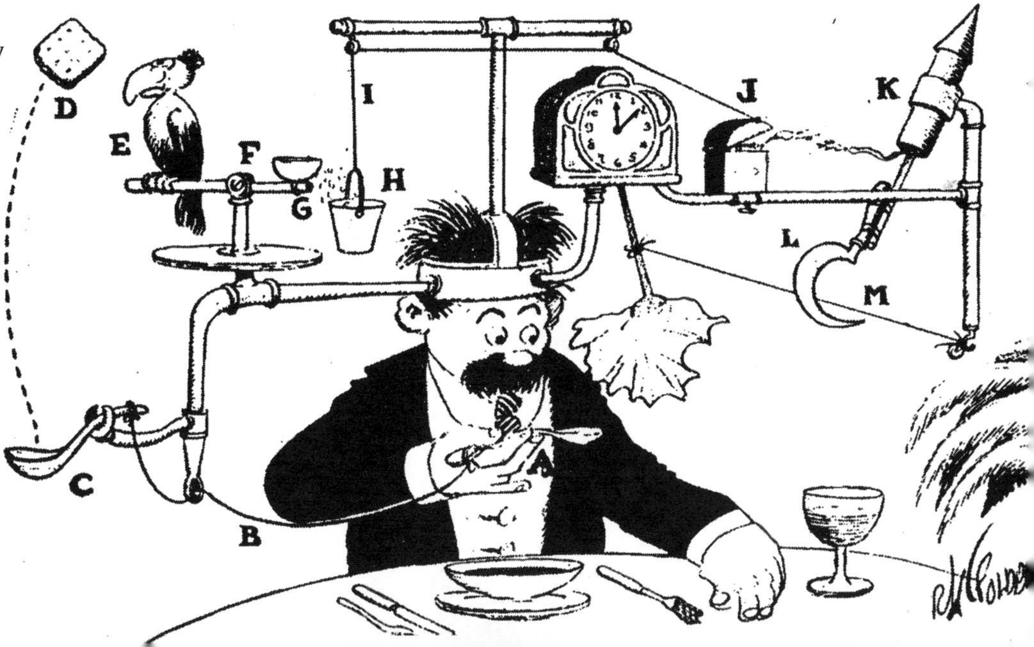
A
B
C
D
E
F
G
H
I
J
K
L
M

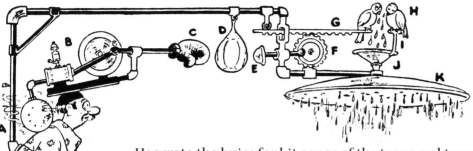

He wrote the lyrics for hit songs of the teens and twenties like "I'm The Guy."
Here's a sample:

> When they hear me talk, when they see me walk, people turn around
> to say "who's that?" All the people cry, all the ladies sigh, till they know
> exactly where I'm at. I'm the guy that gives papers all the news. I'm
> the guy who can't tell a lie, I'm always live, I'll never die. What's that?
> Who am I? Don't you know? I'm the guy, I'm the guy.

Rube won the Pulitzer Prize for his editorial cartoons, which he
started drawing in his fifties as a departure from his drawings for the
funny pages. Sure, every year *some* cartoonist wins the Pulitzer Prize, but
the National Cartoonists Society *named* their award the Reuben. Rube
began an entirely new career as a sculptor at the age of 80, and in inimitable
Goldberg fashion, was soon selling his work to galleries,
collectors, and museums all over the world.

But it was Rube's "Inventions," those drawings
of intricate and whimsical machines, that earned Rube
his very own entry in *Webster's New World Dictionary*:

> Rube Goldberg…adjective…designating
> any very complicated invention, machine,
> scheme, etc., laboriously contrived to
> perform a seemingly simple operation.

Even the earliest of Rube's invention cartoons,
dating from 1914, are still being published today.
New generations rediscover and enjoy them every
day, well after their creator cleaned his pens, put
the cap on his bottle of Higgins black India Ink,
and cleared his drawing board for the last time
almost thirty years ago.

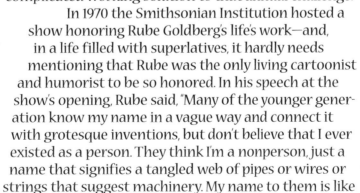

The Inventions inspired, and continue to inspire, the National Rube Goldberg Machine Contest held annually at Purdue University. Hundreds of science and engineering students from across the nation come together in a competition to build machines that perform a specified task in twenty or more steps. Past challenges include pouring a glass of water, screwing in a light bulb, setting a golf ball on a tee, and filling a time capsule with the most significant inventions of the twentieth century. Needless to say, the prize for this Olympics of Complexity is awarded to the most complicated working solution to that annual challenge.

In 1970 the Smithsonian Institution hosted a show honoring Rube Goldberg's life's work—and, in a life filled with superlatives, it hardly needs mentioning that Rube was the only living cartoonist and humorist to be so honored. In his speech at the show's opening, Rube said, "Many of the younger generation know my name in a vague way and connect it with grotesque inventions, but don't believe that I ever existed as a person. They think I'm a nonperson, just a name that signifies a tangled web of pipes or wires or strings that suggest machinery. My name to them is like a spiral staircase, veal cutlets, barber's itch—terms that give you an immediate picture of what they mean...."

Welcome to a collection of spiral staircases and veal cutlets—to the Inventions of an American original, a creative genius named Rube Goldberg.

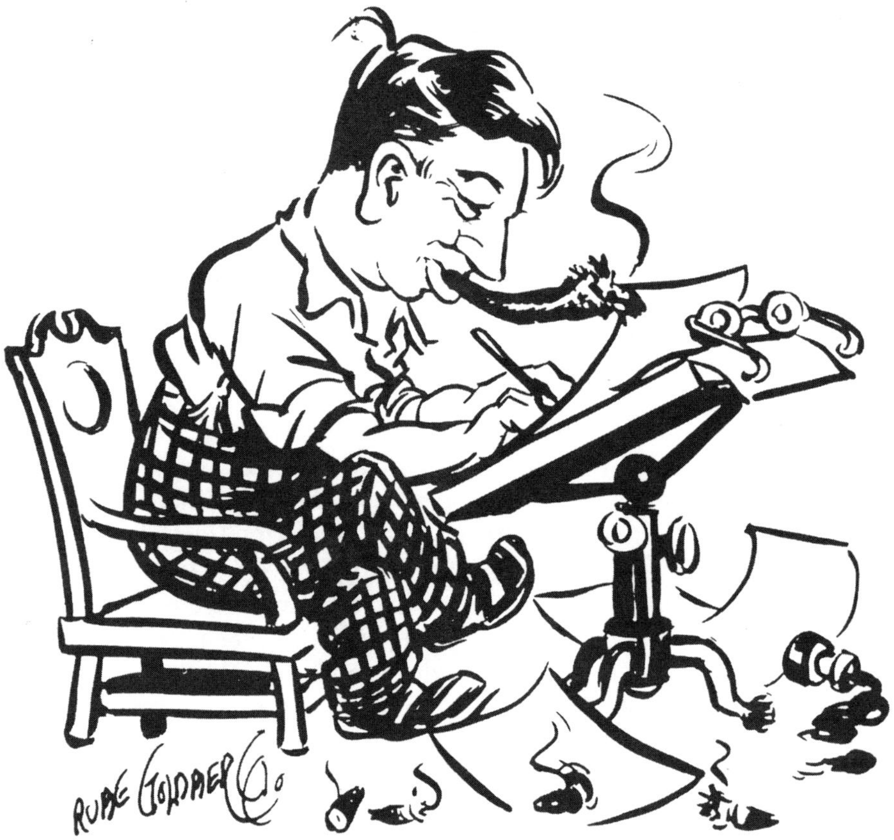
RUBE GOLDBERG ©

Biography

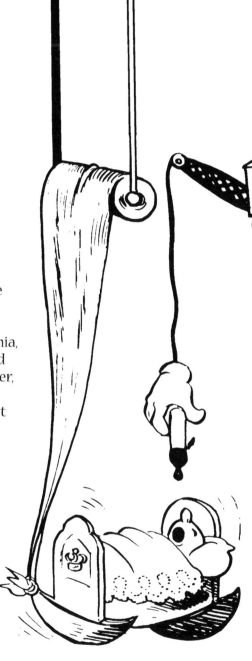

"**R**ube Goldberg": the name evokes an image of controlled chaos, wild originality, inventiveness, and good-humored laughter. The name has a familiar ring to it, but who was the guy?

The guy was an American genius whose long and fruitful career as an artist, cartoonist, and writer created and changed the way that Americans perceived the oncoming machine age that defined the start of the twentieth century.

Reuben Lucius Goldberg was born in San Francisco, California, on the Fourth of July, 1883. He was the second son of three boys and one surviving girl born to Hannah and Max Goldberg. Rube's mother, never in good health, died when Rube was in his early teens. His father had emigrated from Prussia as a very young man, living first in New York during the Civil War and then working his way west to San Francisco. Max, who never remarried after Hannah's death, maintained a comfortable upper-middle-class family home in San Francisco and raised his four children himself, forging a close family unity that lasted all through their lives.

Max Goldberg, never without his traditional Stetson hat from his days as a cattle-ranch owner in Arizona, was a well-known character in San Francisco. The city (and the state) thought of itself as young and vigorous, without the social and class restrictions of the more established East. Max Goldberg dealt in real estate, banking, and the turbulent frontier politics of San Francisco.

Rube Goldberg, 1920. In the background, Boob McNutt and other characters from his cartoons.

Rube attended the prestigious Lowell High School. His nickname "Rube" was short for Reuben, but the nickname also stuck with him because he was left-handed. In those days, a left-handed baseball pitcher was nicknamed a rube.

Rube's passion and main interest from early childhood was drawing and, at age eleven, after a great deal of persistence at wearing down his father's reservations, he began formal art lessons. The drawing and painting classes he took were given by Charles Beall every Friday night at 50 cents each. Rube said, "My parents were not very enthusiastic, either about having an artist in the family, or about permitting an eleven-year-old boy to be out late at night."

A local sign painter by day, Mr. Beall was in his heart a dedicated, although not very successful, fine artist. Rube looked forward to these Friday night art lessons all through the week. "Charles Beall was a very serious teacher," he said. "He never permitted slipshod work and there was no loafing. I studied with Mr. Beall for three years. I never missed a class. We all worked very hard. For me, it was heaven." Just before his high school graduation, Rube announced to his family (and to his father's consternation) that he wanted to go to art school and become a full-time artist.

Max was really upset. To him, art as a hobby was okay, but as a profession—unthinkable! He had to find a way to make Rube agree to go to college to study for a "real" career. Max tried everything to dissuade Rube from ruining his life, including securing a congressman's appointment for Rube to go to West Point. However, he finally recognized that neither straight parental intimidation nor the lure of a military career would have any effect. With his talent for negotiations and deal making, he began to talk to Rube about engineering, knowing that the famous mining barons of the West Coast were paying their top mining engineers annual salaries and bonuses of hundreds of thousands of dollars.

Max's most persuasive message to Rube was that the world's greatest artists, masters like Leonardo Da Vinci, were first trained as engineers before they took up their careers as artists. He was able to secure Rube a place in the School of Mining Engineering at the University of California in Berkeley, just across the San Francisco Bay. He assured Rube that with a degree from the university, and with some practical engineering experience in the business world, Rube would be able to make the important decisions about art, his career, and the future much more easily.

Rube agreed to attend the School of Mining Engineering. He lived at home, which meant, on good-weather days, a ninety-minute daily commute each way by cable car to the ferry, with a voyage across the San Francisco Bay to Oakland, and finally a train trip to the campus in Berkeley.

Rube enjoyed the university and its student life. He was popular and made many lifelong friends. He was especially active and well known on campus as a frequent contributor of drawings and cartoons to *The Pelican* (the then new and somewhat radical student humor magazine). He graduated in 1904.

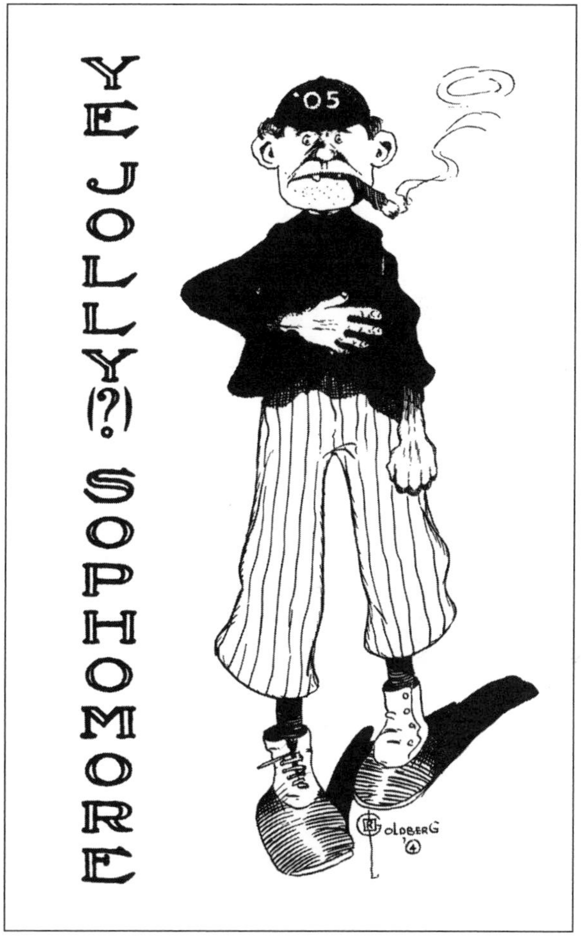
YE JOLLY (?) SOPHOMORE
'05

Drawing from the student humor magazine
The Pelican, ***University of California, Berkeley. (1903)***

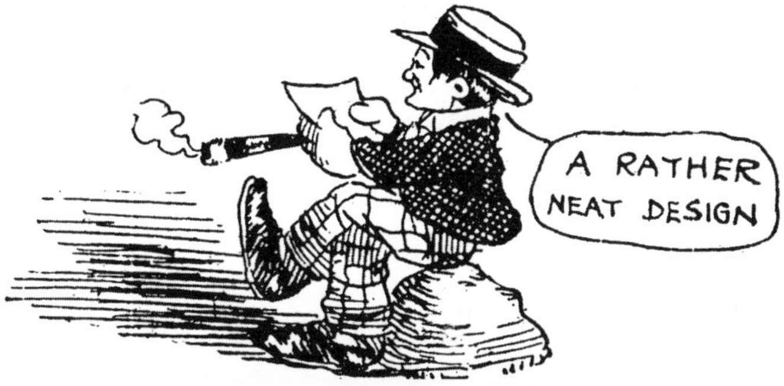
A RATHER NEAT DESIGN

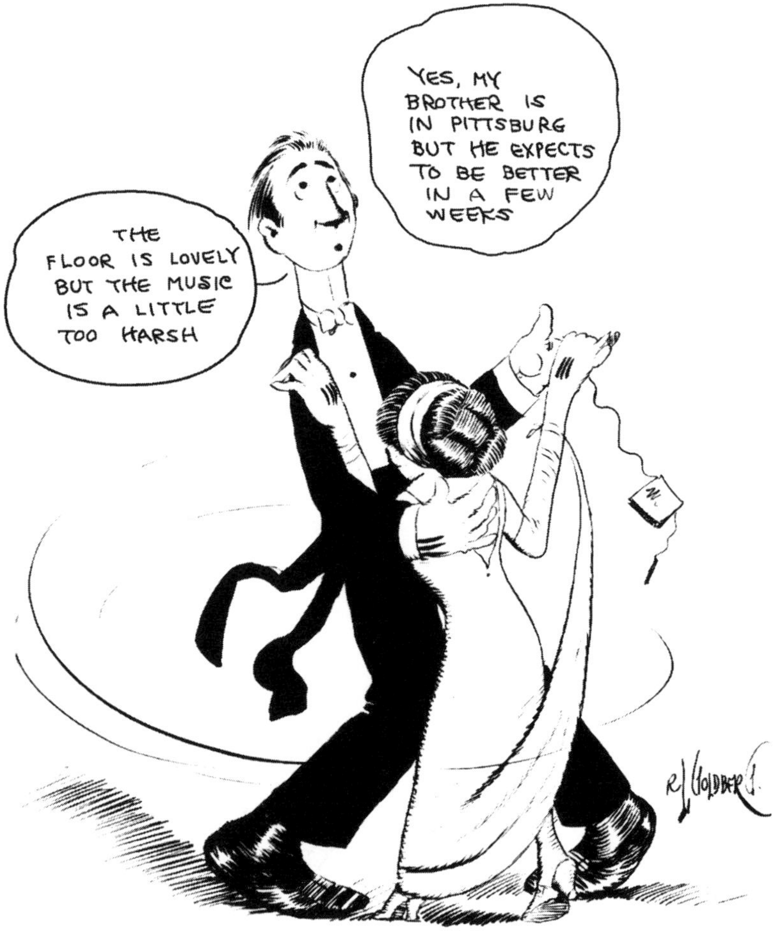
THE FLOOR IS LOVELY BUT THE MUSIC IS A LITTLE TOO HARSH
YES, MY BROTHER IS IN PITTSBURG BUT HE EXPECTS TO BE BETTER IN A FEW WEEKS
R. L. GOLDBERG

BALL ROOM CONVERSATION IS THE CLOSEST THING IN THE WORLD TO NOTHING.

Although an active alumnus and supporter of the university, Rube said that his academic work there had been a waste of his time. However, in later years (and probably because he had two sons—both college graduates, one an artist, the other a stage and screen producer-writer), he would almost grudgingly admit that the engineering training and experience really had been good for him.

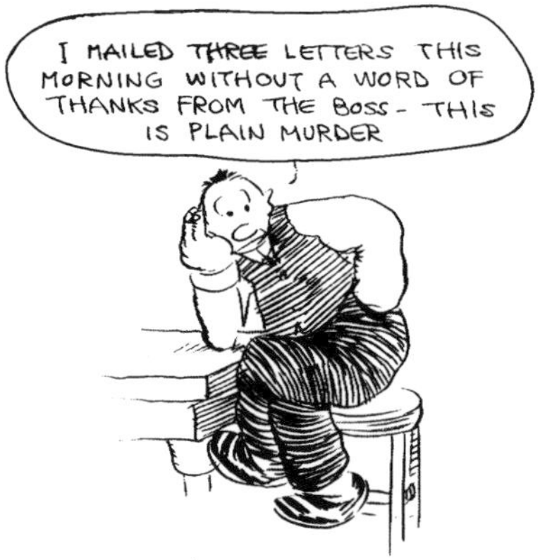
I MAILED THREE LETTERS THIS MORNING WITHOUT A WORD OF THANKS FROM THE BOSS - THIS IS PLAIN MURDER

HE'LL DOZE ALL DAY AND COMPLAIN ABOUT BEING OVERWORKED -

Rube was always being asked where he got his ideas for his Inventions. While he credited the ingenious inventor Professor Lucifer Gorgonzola Butts (the character he created), Rube would also admit that his inspiration came from two of his professors at the University of California. Samuel B. Christy, dean of the College of Mining, was Rube's stereotype for the pretentious college scientist. Christy, an evangelical convert to the then new science of time-and-motion studies, lectured long, frequently, and with great passion on training workers as to the proper angle for holding and moving a loaded wheelbarrow, so they could make more trips and save management money by working harder but more efficiently.

Professor Butts was also modeled after Rube's professor of analytic mechanics and physics, Frederick Slate. Professor Slate could have come right out of a Rube Goldberg cartoon. As Rube said, "In analytic mechanics you were introduced to the funniest-looking contrivances ever conceived by the human mind," and Professor Slate, as Rube described him, "matched his contrivances. He was a thin man with a high squeaky voice, a red beard, protruding Adam's apple and shiny gold-rimmed eyeglasses," all of which generated an ideal prototype for a caricature of a somewhat odd professor of analytical mechanics.

Professor Slate had invented and named a machine that he called the "Barodik." The origin of the name is still unknown, but its purpose, according to the professor, was to allow engineering students to calculate the weight of the earth. Rube described the Barodik as a system of tubes, retorts, hoses, and what appeared to be odds and ends salvaged from a defunct dental college. The Barodik was housed in its own basement laboratory at the university. The professor's engineering students had to use the Barodik for six months' worth of experiments to calculate the weight of the earth. Every student who completed the class got an A, because after adjusting for changing atmospheric conditions, the seasons, and so on, nobody really knew (or perhaps even cared) what the actual weight of the earth was.

Both of these men were merged by Rube to become Professor Butts, who waged his war against inefficiency by solving the problems that plagued the common man: opening a window, remembering to mail a letter, looking for one's glasses or for overshoes on a rainy day. Butts's inventions played out the dramas that people perform every day in doing things the hard way.

That Barodik laboratory with Professor Christy and his lectures on working the workers more efficiently seem to have planted seeds in Rube's mind about the consequences of hypercomplication, useless information overload, and reliance

Professor Lucifer Gorgonzola Butts, A.K., Rube's fictional character and creator of the famous Inventions. (1920)

17

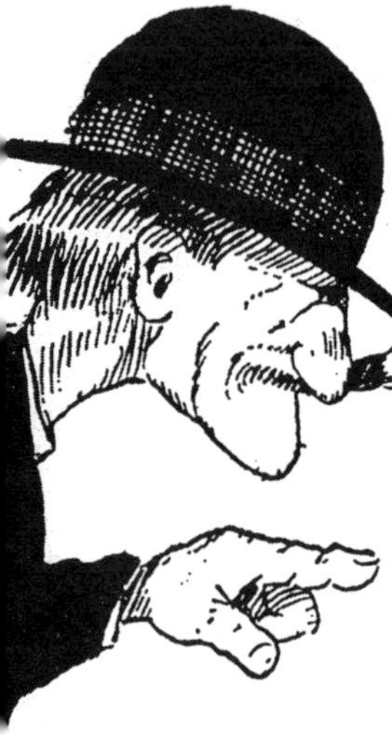

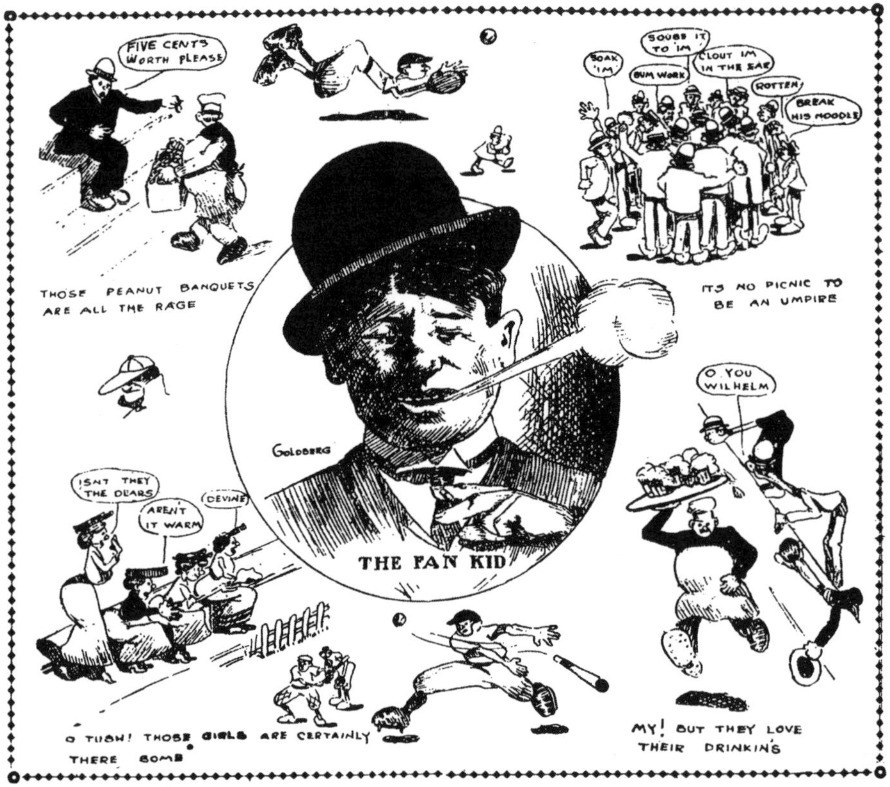
FIVE CENTS WORTH PLEASE
THOSE PEANUT BANQUETS ARE ALL THE RAGE
SOAK 'IM
BUM WORK
CLOUT IM IN THE EAR
ROTTEN
BREAK HIS NOODLE
ITS NO PICNIC TO BE AN UMPIRE
GOLDBERG
THE FAN KID
ISN'T THEY THE DEARS
AREN'T IT WARM
DEVINE
O YOU WILHELM
MY! BUT THEY LOVE THEIR DRINKIN'S

The Fan Kid, San Francisco Chronicle. *(1904)*

on technology that wasn't clearly understood, tested, or even "debugged" before being used. However, the development of that experience into Rube's "Inventions" wouldn't happen until a few years later.

While still a mining engineering student at the University of California, Rube's summer "work experience" assignments had meant working in the mine shafts and tunnels deep in the Sierra Nevada Mountains for the Oneida gold mines. After a summer of helping set dynamite charges and digging tunnels 2,000 feet below the earth's surface, followed by working in the noise, dust, and chaos of the stamping mills processing the ore, Rube knew that mining engineering was not for him.

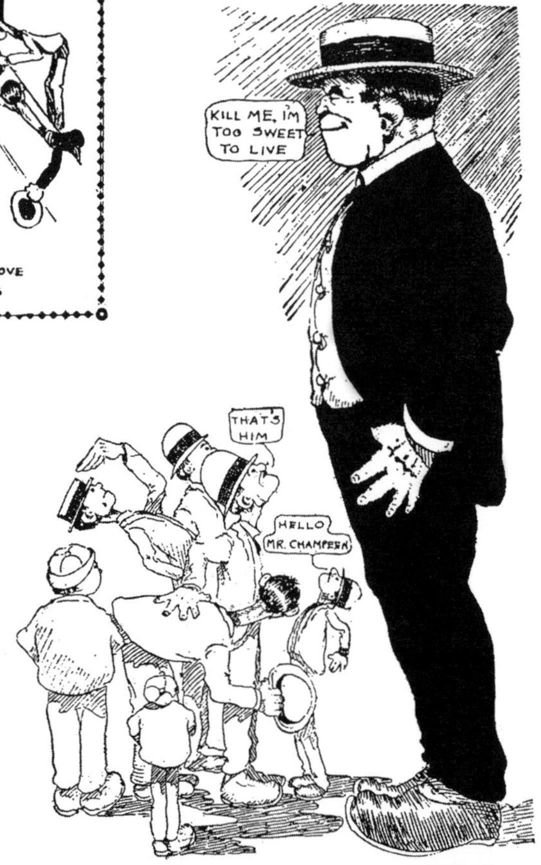
KILL ME, I'M TOO SWEET TO LIVE
THAT'S HIM
HELLO MR. CHAMPEEN

"THINGS AIN'T WHAT THEY USED TO BE"

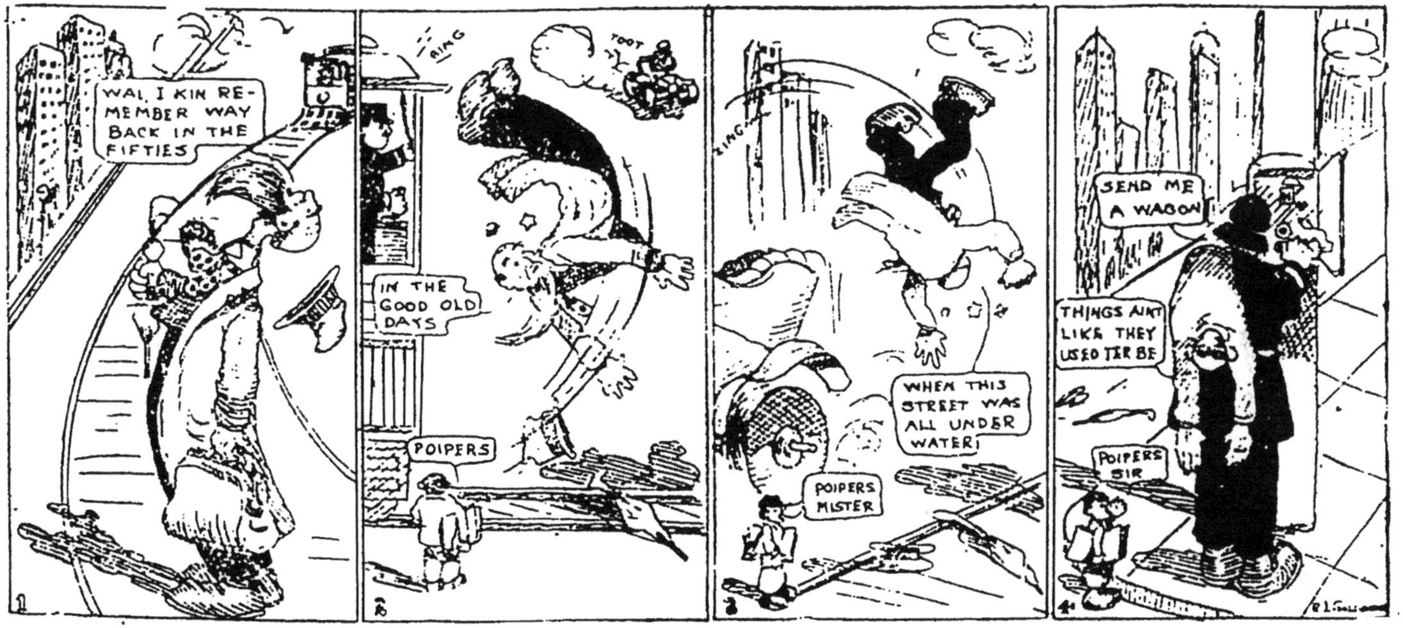
WAL, I KIN RE-MEMBER WAY BACK IN THE FIFTIES
RING
TOOT
IN THE GOOD OLD DAYS
POIPERS
ZING
WHEN THIS STREET WAS ALL UNDER WATER!
POIPERS MISTER
SEND ME A WAGON
THINGS AIN'T LIKE THEY USED TER BE
POIPERS SIR

Rube's first published strip cartoon appeared in the* San Francisco Chronicle *on October 7, 1904.

Max reminded Rube that family honor meant that a deal was a deal, but instead of insisting Rube go back down into the mines after graduation, he found Rube a job with the San Francisco City Chief Engineer's Office. Rube's salary was set at the very lucrative sum of $100 per month, a top wage for a just-out-of-college young engineer in 1904. The job was mapping and drawing water and sewer pipe plans, "a job just as exciting as it sounds," said Rube.

After working for three months for San Francisco's top sewer and water engineer, Rube decided he had to quit. "No matter what the salary was," said Rube, "I would have been willing to exchange my diploma for one clean sheet of Bristol board... to draw upon."

Facing his father's disappointment, Rube pleaded, "Pa, I can't stand it any longer, I've got to try cartooning." It took courage to stand

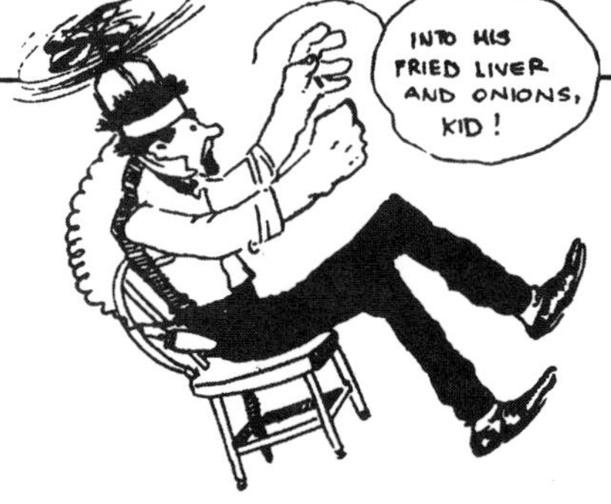
INTO HIS
FRIED LIVER
AND ONIONS,
KID!

FIGHT-GOERS SHOULD WEAR THE ELECTRIC-FAN-DRY-BATTERY-HEAD-GEAR — VERY COOLING.

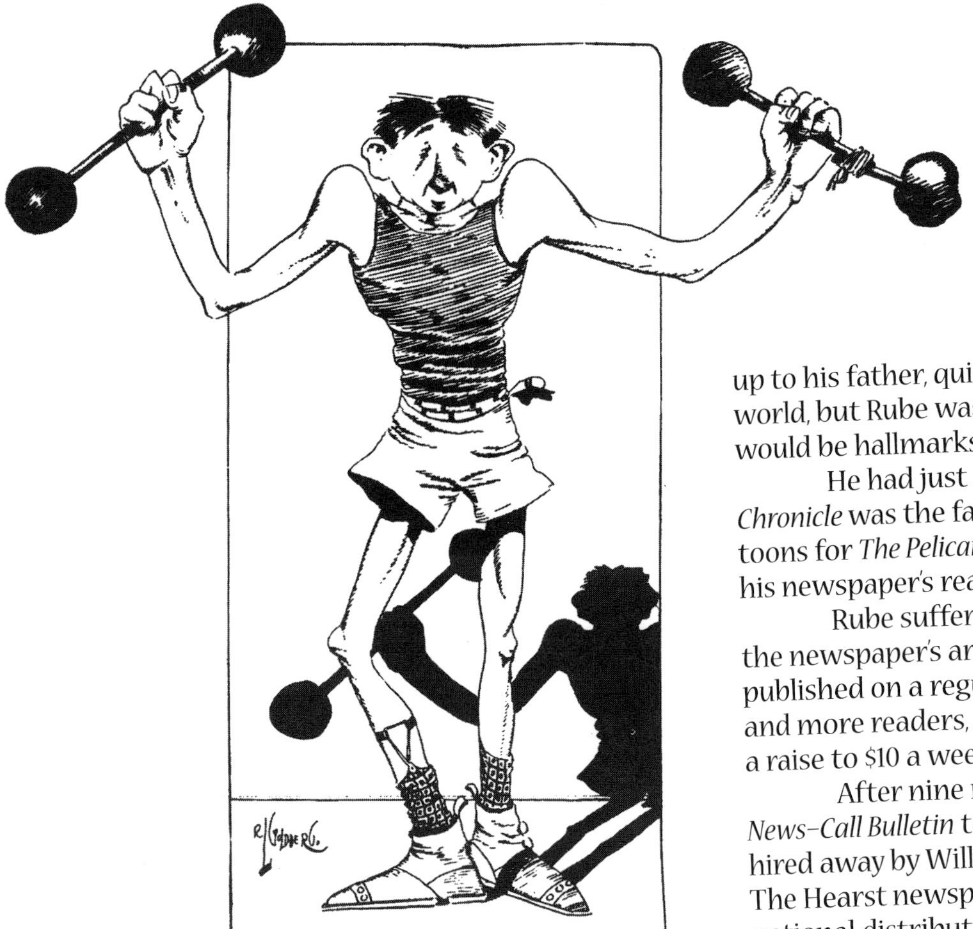

LOON VIII

THE PHYSICAL CULTURE MANIAC.

up to his father, quit his job, and attempt to enter a very competitive world, but Rube was showing the determination and perseverance that would be hallmarks of his life.

He had just one contact. The city editor of the *San Francisco Chronicle* was the father of a college classmate. He had seen Rube's cartoons for *The Pelican* and thought Rube's work just might be adapted for his newspaper's readers. He hired Rube as an art assistant at $8 a week.

Rube suffered through rejection after rejection of his work by the newspaper's art editor until his sports cartoons started to be published on a regular basis. As his humorous cartoons delighted more and more readers, he became well known in San Francisco, and gained a raise to $10 a week.

After nine months, Rube left the *Chronicle* for the *San Francisco News–Call Bulletin* to replace "TAD" (Thomas A. Dorgan), who had been hired away by William Randolph Hearst and had moved to New York. The Hearst newspapers and syndicate, based in New York City, with its national distribution, was an important force in publishing. Hearst had personally recruited a number of San Francisco's top cartoonists, and it became a point of pride in the San Francisco cartoon world to have been recruited by WRH, Himself. This was at the start of the newspaper wars. American newspapers were fiercely competitive and publishers used their cartoonists as a major circulation-building weapon.

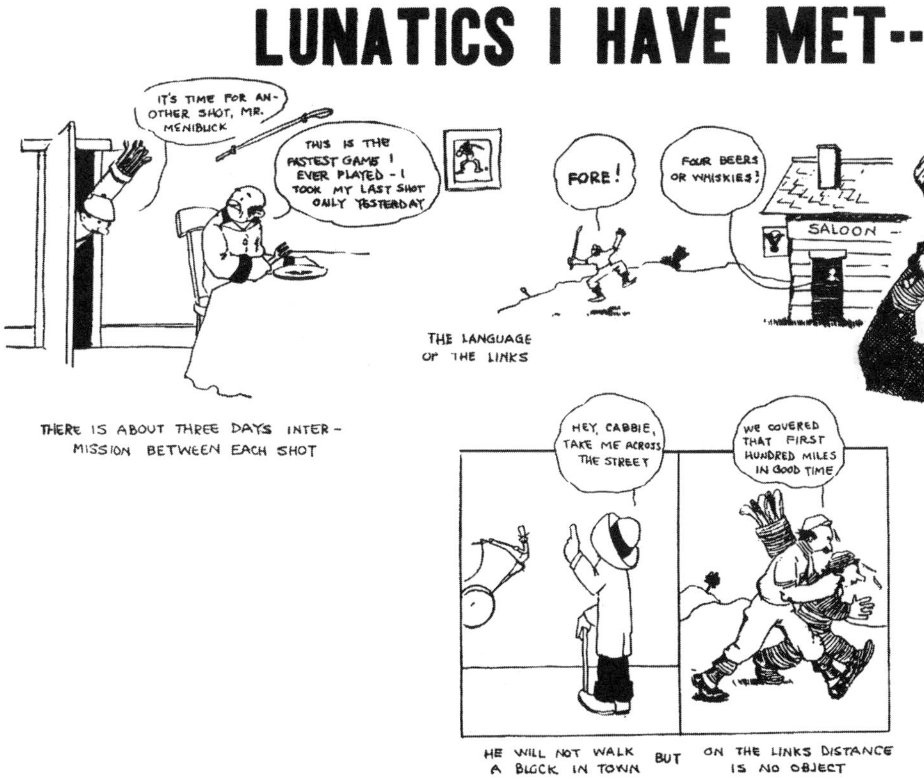
LUNATICS I HAVE MET---BY GOLDBERG.
IT'S TIME FOR ANOTHER SHOT, MR. MENIBUCK
THIS IS THE FASTEST GAME I EVER PLAYED - I TOOK MY LAST SHOT ONLY YESTERDAY
THERE IS ABOUT THREE DAYS INTERMISSION BETWEEN EACH SHOT
FORE!
FOUR BEERS OR WHISKIES!
SALOON
THE LANGUAGE OF THE LINKS
HEY, CABBIE, TAKE ME ACROSS THE STREET
WE COVERED THAT FIRST HUNDRED MILES IN GOOD TIME
HE WILL NOT WALK A BLOCK IN TOWN
BUT
ON THE LINKS DISTANCE IS NO OBJECT

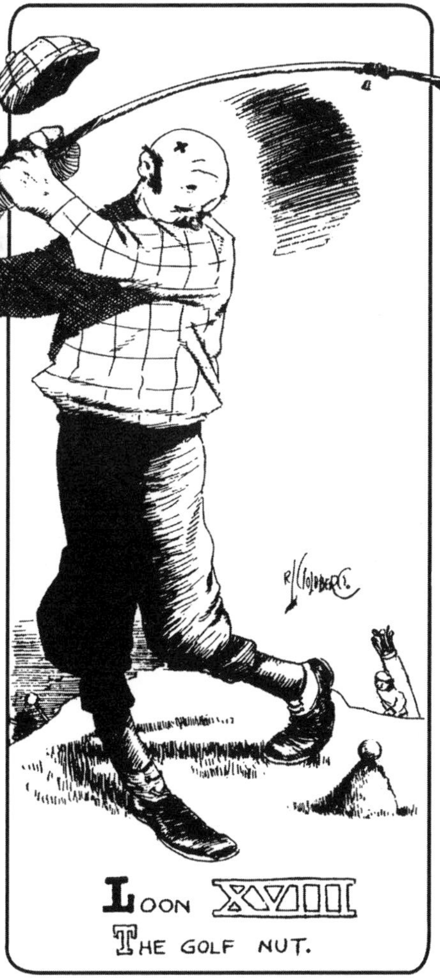
LOON XVIII
THE GOLF NUT.

Lunitics I Have Met, New York Evening Mail. *(1908)*

Surviving the San Francisco earthquake of 1906, Rube and his cartoons continued to grow in popularity, but only on the West Coast. It was now 1907 and Rube still hadn't received a call from Hearst to go to New York, the epicenter of publishing, and cartoonist heaven.

Rube, at twenty-four, decided that he had reached the limits of what he could expect to accomplish on the West Coast. Even though he didn't have an offer from Hearst (or any other New York publisher), Rube took his courage in hand, and went east to New York City.

Max Goldberg, now proud of Rube's work and reputation in San Francisco, backed his decision, although he too couldn't understand why Hearst hadn't called Rube. In Rube's words, "My security, along with my work,

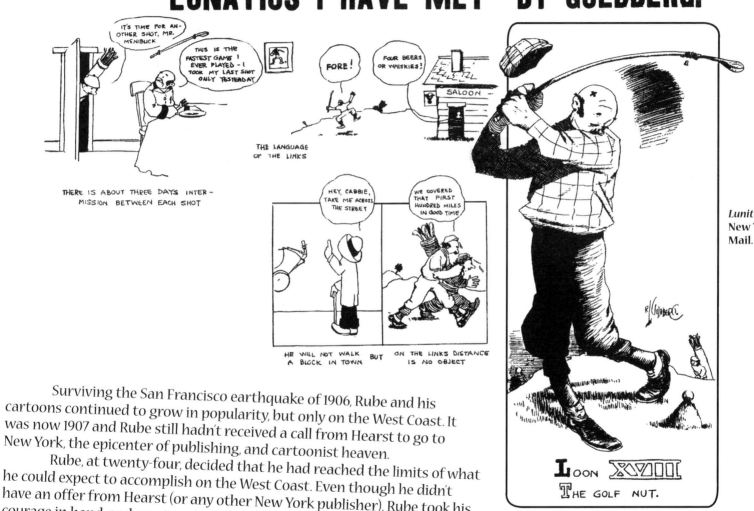

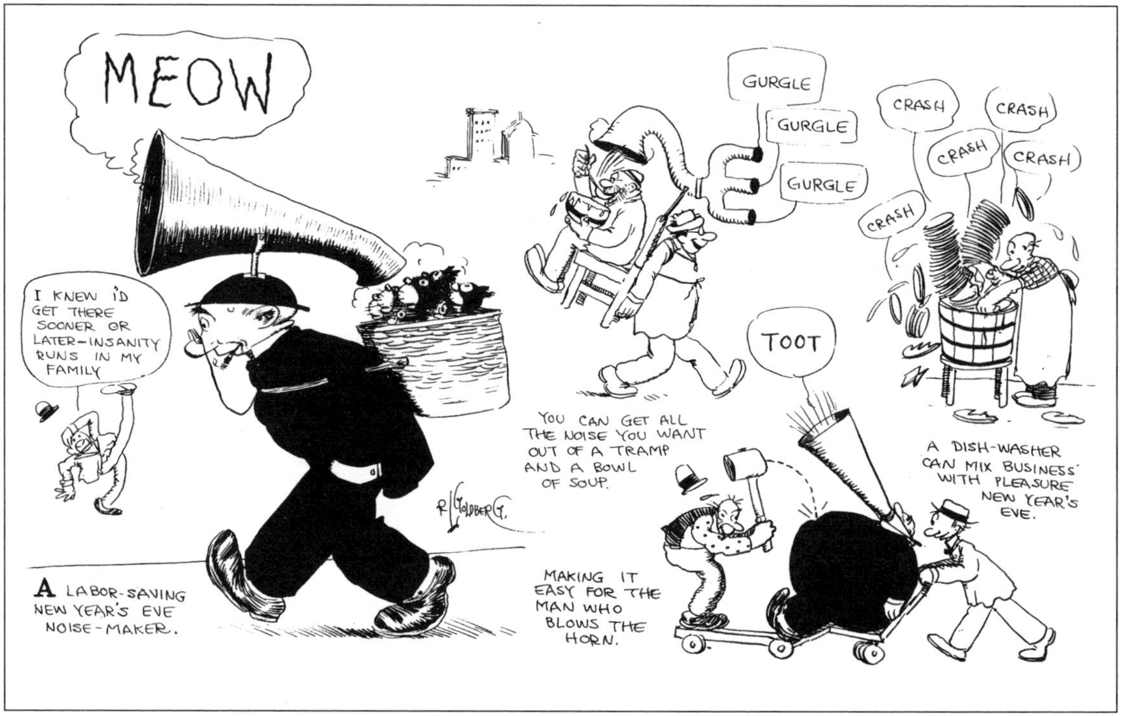
MEOW
I KNEW I'D GET THERE SOONER OR LATER—INSANITY RUNS IN MY FAMILY
A LABOR-SAVING NEW YEAR'S EVE NOISE-MAKER.
GURGLE
GURGLE
GURGLE
YOU CAN GET ALL THE NOISE YOU WANT OUT OF A TRAMP AND A BOWL OF SOUP.
CRASH
CRASH
CRASH
CRASH
CRASH
A DISH-WASHER CAN MIX BUSINESS WITH PLEASURE NEW YEAR'S EVE.
TOOT
MAKING IT EASY FOR THE MAN WHO BLOWS THE HORN.

A labor-saving New Year's Eve noisemaker. (1911)

was a diamond ring that Pa gave me. He said I could sell it for a train ticket if I needed money to come home."

At the start of his national career, Rube found New York City exciting, but not as friendly and receptive to him and his work as San Francisco had always been. After arriving in New York jobless, with only his portfolio of cartoons, Rube's first weeks there brought unsuccessful interviews with the major New York City newspapers. Aside from a few San Francisco transplants, nobody knew him or cared about his work. Just as he was thinking seriously about using his diamond ring for a ticket home, Rube was hired at the end of 1907, not as a star cartoonist as he had hoped, but as a junior sports artist-cartoonist for the *New York Evening Mail*.

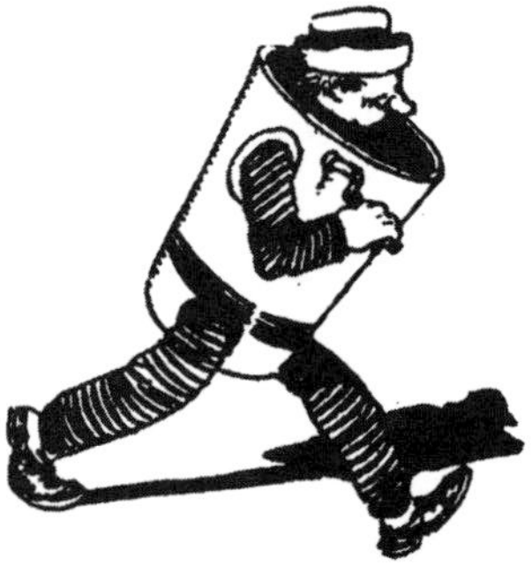
THE HUMAN ICE CREAM FREEZER IS ALWAYS REFRESHING.

He was now on his way, and it was the start of a very fast ride. 1909 saw the debut and almost instant success of his first widely acclaimed cartoon series, *Foolish Questions*. When Rube asked readers to suggest their own Foolish Questions for him to draw, as a way of showing his editors he was getting fan mail, hundreds of letters poured in. The fans' participation and the ideas they generated helped to establish Rube Goldberg as a nationally known name. By 1911, along with his regular daily sports and other cartoons, he had drawn almost four hundred cartoons in the *Foolish Questions* series alone, had published his first book with that title, and had licensed a boxed "Foolish Questions" card game that was a great success.

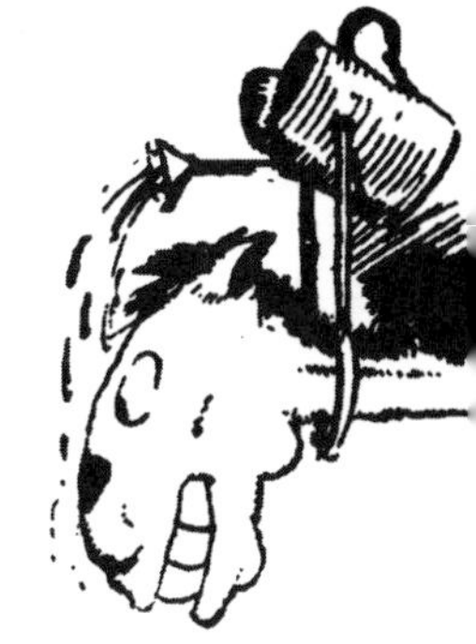

THE VIBRATORY SPRINKLING CAN FOR THOROUGHBREDS

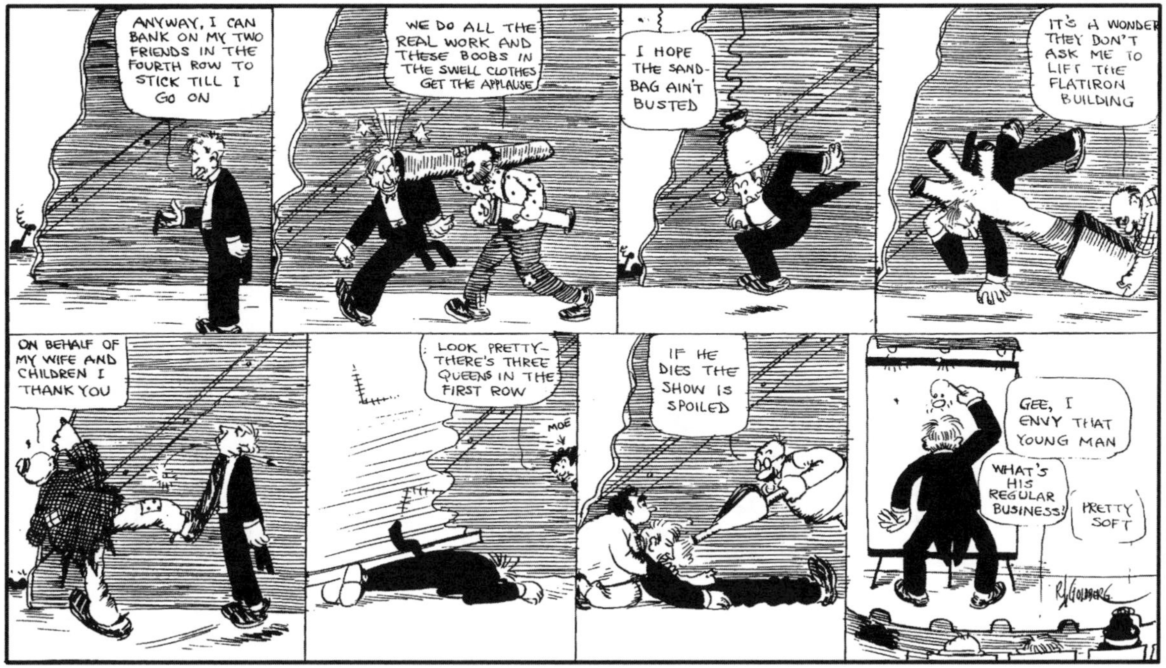
ANYWAY, I CAN BANK ON MY TWO FRIENDS IN THE FOURTH ROW TO STICK TILL I GO ON
WE DO ALL THE REAL WORK AND THESE BOOBS IN THE SWELL CLOTHES GET THE APPLAUSE
I HOPE THE SAND-BAG AIN'T BUSTED
IT'S A WONDER THEY DON'T ASK ME TO LIFT THE FLATIRON BUILDING
ON BEHALF OF MY WIFE AND CHILDREN I THANK YOU
LOOK PRETTY- THERE'S THREE QUEENS IN THE FIRST ROW
MOE
IF HE DIES THE SHOW IS SPOILED
GEE, I ENVY THAT YOUNG MAN
WHAT'S HIS REGULAR BUSINESS?
PRETTY SOFT
R.L. GOLDBERG

Rube's vaudeville experience–backstage. (circa 1912) While Rube had problems following a script all of his life, he was a great impromptu speaker, who without notes could keep an after-dinner or theater audience entertained. Onstage, he continued to captivate audiences with his improvised humor and ability to "quick draw" a cartoon on any subject while joking with an audience and telling stories.

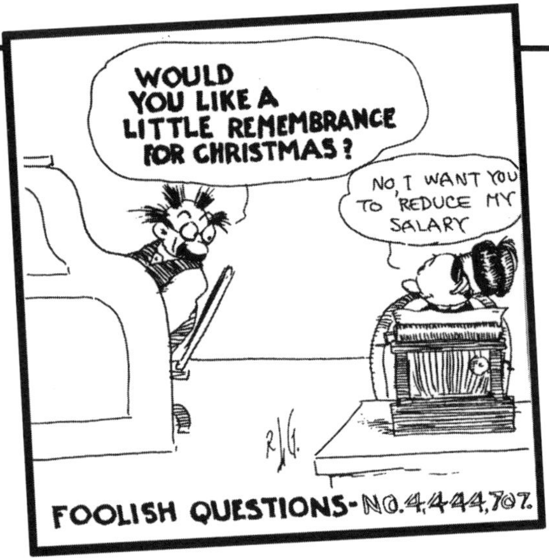
WOULD YOU LIKE A LITTLE REMEMBRANCE FOR CHRISTMAS?
NO, I WANT YOU TO REDUCE MY SALARY
R.G.
FOOLISH QUESTIONS-NO.4,444,707.

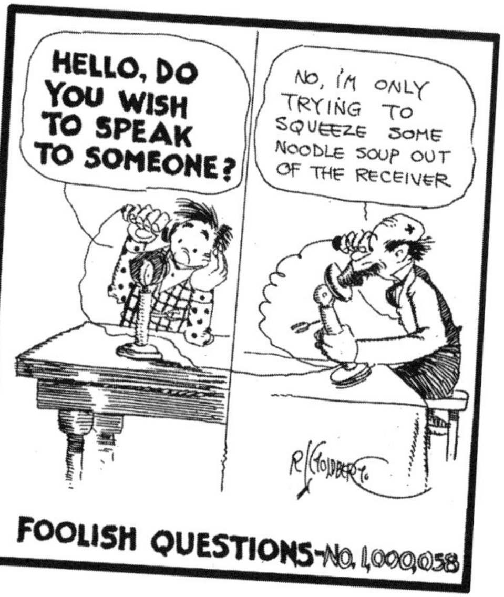
HELLO, DO YOU WISH TO SPEAK TO SOMEONE?
NO, I'M ONLY TRYING TO SQUEEZE SOME NOODLE SOUP OUT OF THE RECEIVER
R. GOLDBERG
FOOLISH QUESTIONS-NO.1,000,058

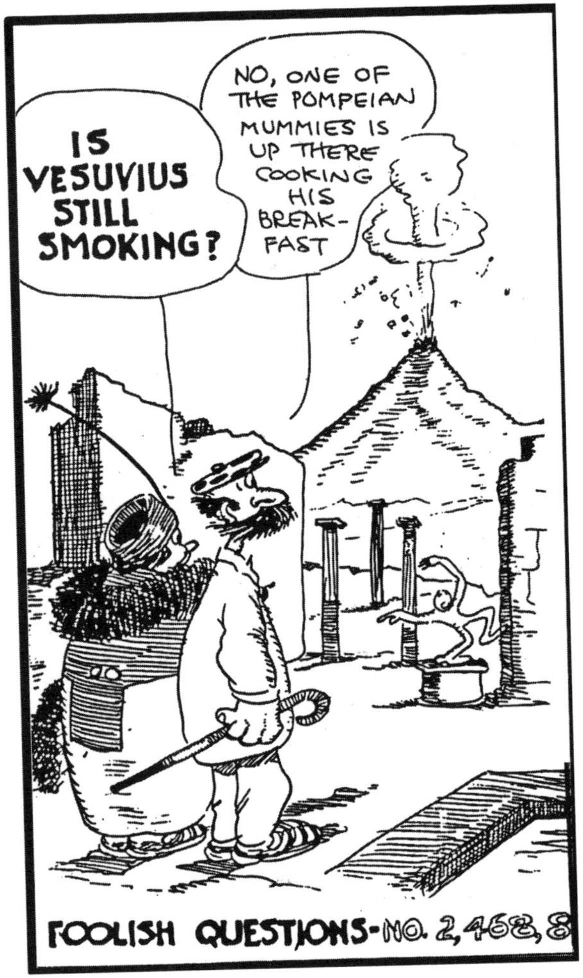
IS VESUVIUS STILL SMOKING?
NO, ONE OF THE POMPEIAN MUMMIES IS UP THERE COOKING HIS BREAK-FAST
FOOLISH QUESTIONS-NO. 2,468,8

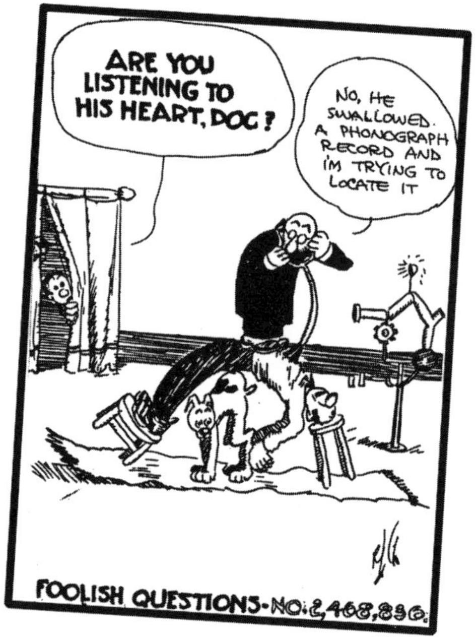
ARE YOU LISTENING TO HIS HEART, DOC?
NO, HE SWALLOWED A PHONOGRAPH RECORD AND I'M TRYING TO LOCATE IT
R.G.
FOOLISH QUESTIONS-NO.2,468,896.

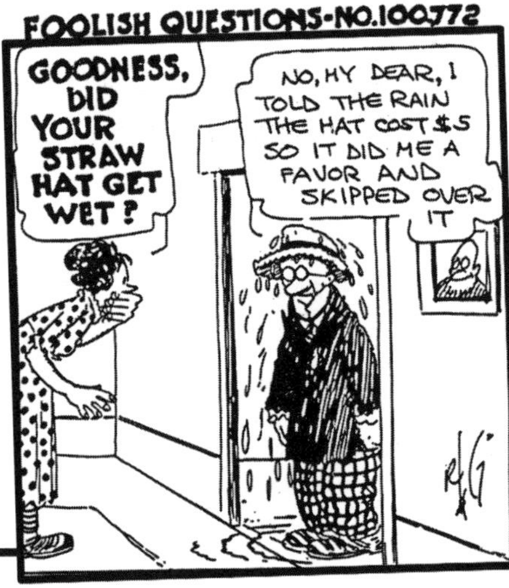
FOOLISH QUESTIONS-NO.100,772
GOODNESS, DID YOUR STRAW HAT GET WET?
NO, MY DEAR, I TOLD THE RAIN THE HAT COST $5 SO IT DID ME A FAVOR AND SKIPPED OVER IT
R.G.

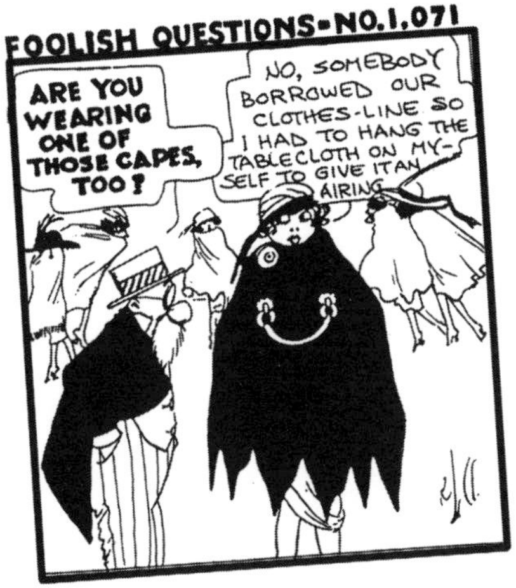
FOOLISH QUESTIONS-NO.1,071
ARE YOU WEARING ONE OF THOSE CAPES, TOO?
NO, SOMEBODY BORROWED OUR CLOTHES-LINE SO I HAD TO HANG THE TABLECLOTH ON MYSELF TO GIVE IT AN AIRING

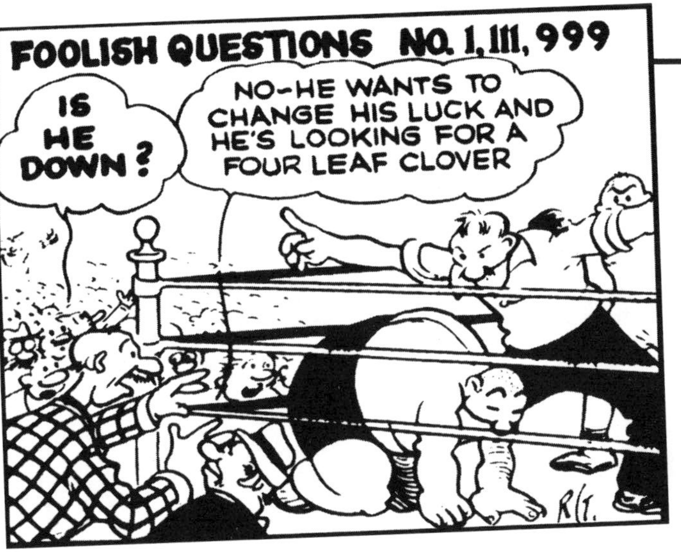
FOOLISH QUESTIONS NO. 1,111,999
IS HE DOWN?
NO-HE WANTS TO CHANGE HIS LUCK AND HE'S LOOKING FOR A FOUR LEAF CLOVER

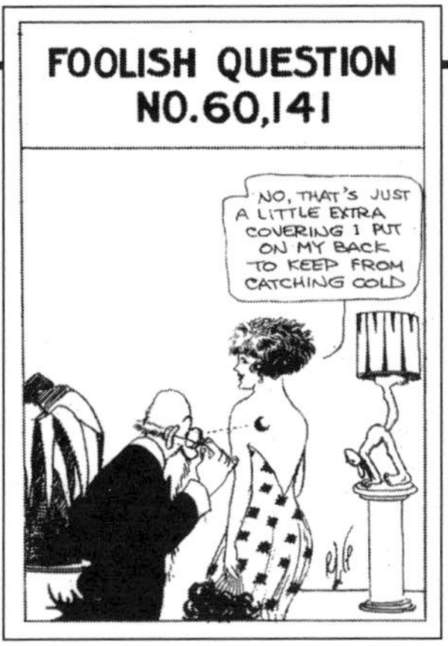
FOOLISH QUESTION NO. 60,141
NO, THAT'S JUST A LITTLE EXTRA COVERING I PUT ON MY BACK TO KEEP FROM CATCHING COLD

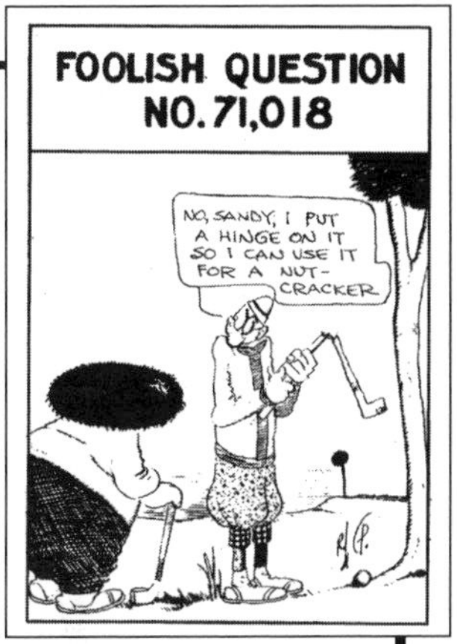
FOOLISH QUESTION NO. 71,018
NO, SANDY, I PUT A HINGE ON IT SO I CAN USE IT FOR A NUT-CRACKER

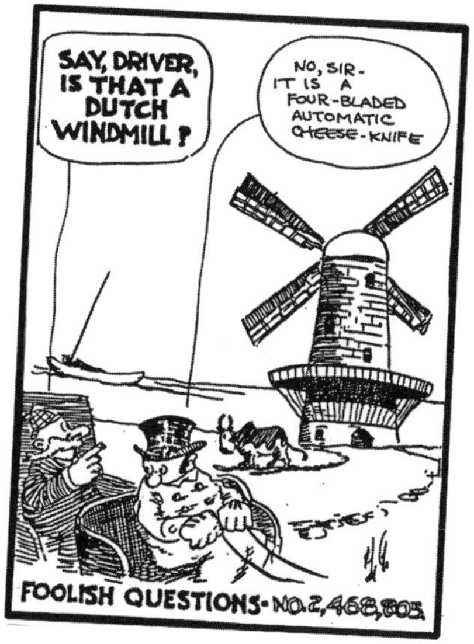
SAY, DRIVER, IS THAT A DUTCH WINDMILL?
NO, SIR-IT IS A FOUR-BLADED AUTOMATIC CHEESE-KNIFE
FOOLISH QUESTIONS-NO.2,468,805

Foolish Questions

Foolish Questions was Rube Goldberg's first major national success. The series ran from 1909 through 1934. It was one of the first direct audience-participation cartoons. When the series first appeared, hundreds of letters poured in from readers telling Rube about the foolish questions that the reader had been asked. Rube used the ones he liked, but mainly it showed his editors that the readers were not only interested in seeing his *Foolish Questions* but would take the time to write in suggestions for future *Foolish Questions*.

The popularity of *Foolish Questions* was seized upon almost immediately by a game manufacturer, who licensed the series from Rube and published the first of a long run of Foolish Questions game sets. The Foolish Question word balloon was left out, and only the response was printed on the card. The player had to guess the question. Each card was numbered and there was an answer sheet. The player who guessed the most questions won the game.

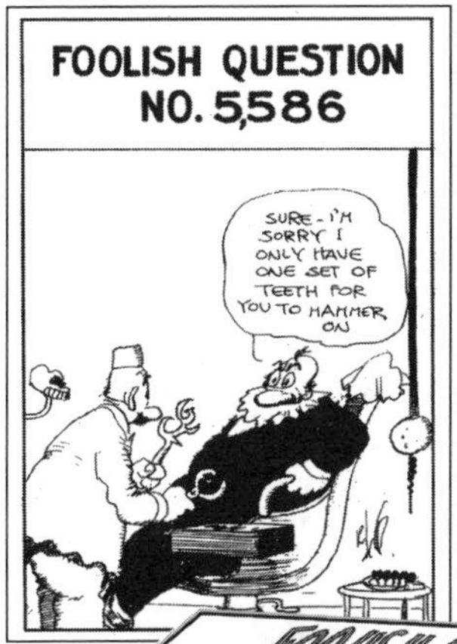
FOOLISH QUESTION NO. 5,586
SURE-I'M SORRY I ONLY HAVE ONE SET OF TEETH FOR YOU TO HAMMER ON

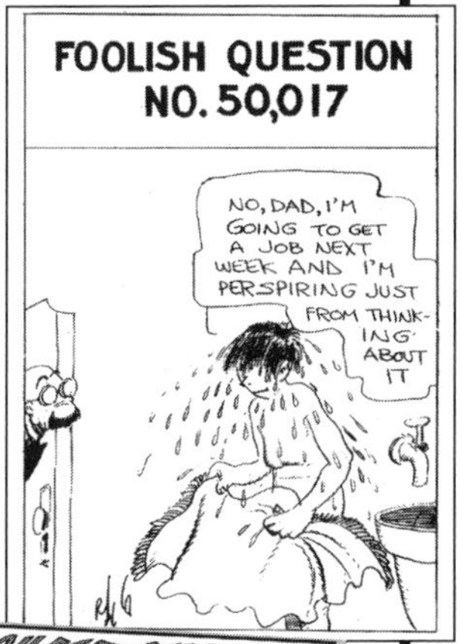
FOOLISH QUESTION NO. 50,017
NO, DAD, I'M GOING TO GET A JOB NEXT WEEK AND I'M PERSPIRING JUST FROM THINKING ABOUT IT

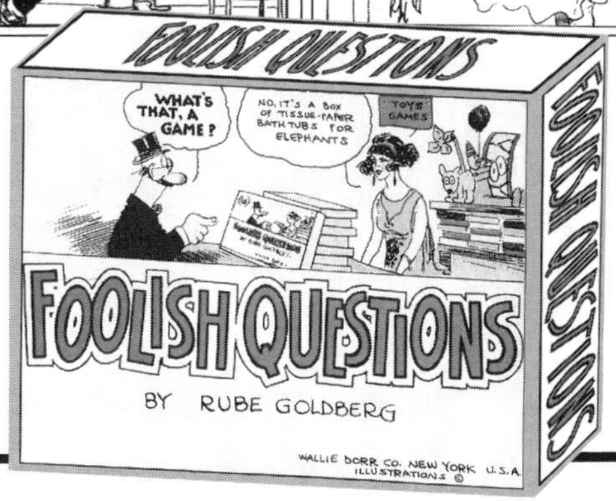
FOOLISH QUESTIONS
WHAT'S THAT, A GAME?
NO, IT'S A BOX OF TISSUE-PAPER BATH TUBS FOR ELEPHANTS
TOYS GAMES
FOOLISH QUESTIONS
BY RUBE GOLDBERG
WALLIE DORR CO. NEW YORK U.S.A
ILLUSTRATIONS ©
FOOLISH QUESTIONS

Cover from Rube's second book of cartoons. This was his first book that had a collection of humorous stories and poems along with his drawings. (1912)

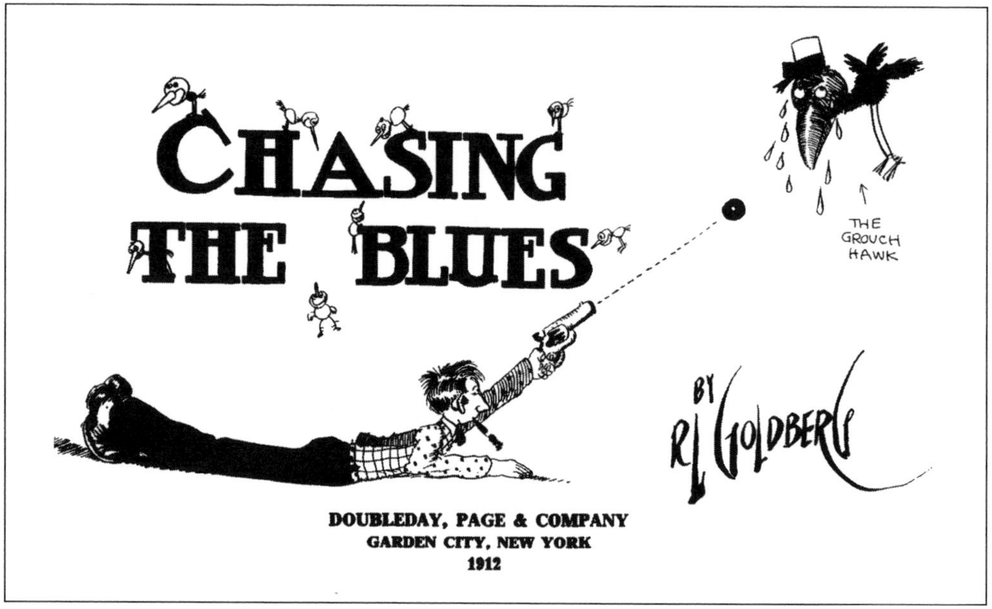
CHASING THE BLUES
THE GROUCH HAWK
BY R L GOLDBERG
DOUBLEDAY, PAGE & COMPANY
GARDEN CITY, NEW YORK
1912

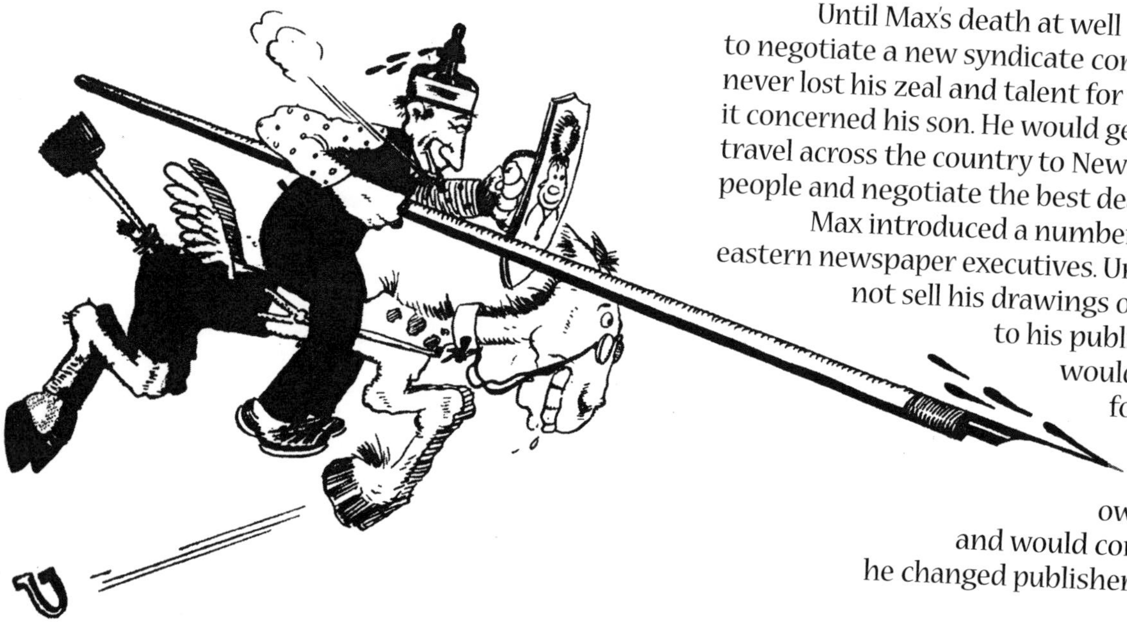

Until Max's death at well past ninety, whenever Rube wanted to negotiate a new syndicate contract, he would send for him. Max never lost his zeal and talent for "deal-making," especially when it concerned his son. He would get on a train in San Francisco and travel across the country to New York to sit down with the syndicate people and negotiate the best deal he could for Rube.

Max introduced a number of contractual innovations to the eastern newspaper executives. Unlike other cartoonists, Rube would not sell his drawings or his original characters outright to his publisher as was the custom. Rather, he would only license the use of his work for publication or syndication. Regardless of who published his work, Rube would always own the characters and properties, and would continue to receive royalties even if he changed publishers.

Advertisement to theater owners promoting Rube's animated cartoons. (1916)

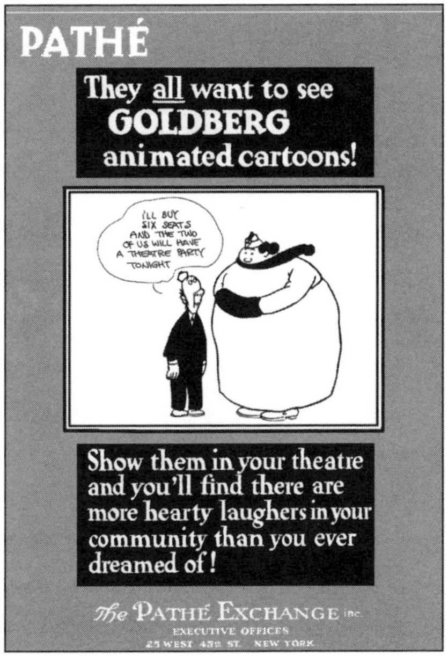
PATHÉ
They all want to see GOLDBERG animated cartoons!
I'LL BUY SIX SEATS AND THE TWO OF US WILL HAVE A THEATRE PARTY TONIGHT
Show them in your theatre and you'll find there are more hearty laughers in your community than you ever dreamed of!
The PATHÉ EXCHANGE inc.
EXECUTIVE OFFICES
25 WEST 45th ST. NEW YORK

After his successful negotiations, Max would stay on and visit with Rube and his family for a few weeks, and then, still wearing his Stetson hat, would board the train back to San Francisco, where his daughter and other two sons lived.

In an era without television and with commercial radio in its infancy, daily newspapers were the prime information source for everyone. Like the other leading cartoonists of his time, Rube was also appearing onstage in the major East Coast vaudeville theaters as a personality, drawing his funny cartoons onstage from subjects suggested by the audience.

Starting in 1915 and through 1916, Rube created and drew a series of short animated cartoons for silent motion picture release. Sixteen pictures (or frames) were needed for each foot of film, and a reel of film was about 1,000 feet, so thousands of pictures were needed for just a few minutes of on-screen entertainment. Rube was a perfectionist about his art as his drawings of that period illustrate. He was just not able to accept using other artists or assistants to draw his images, especially if he felt that these artists couldn't reach his standards. This meant that he had to draw everything himself. His personal labor and the resultant time required to make one reel of film for commercial release added up to a truly daunting commitment on Rube's part for a ten-minute show.

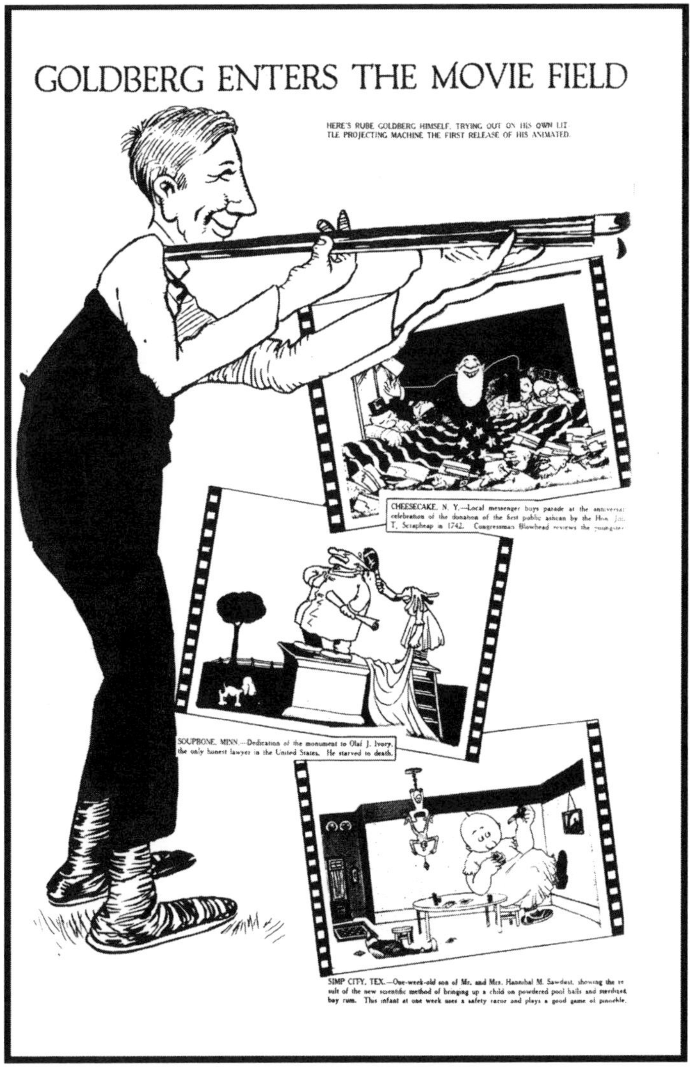
GOLDBERG ENTERS THE MOVIE FIELD
HERE'S RUBE GOLDBERG HIMSELF, TRYING OUT ON HIS OWN LITTLE PROJECTING MACHINE THE FIRST RELEASE OF HIS ANIMATED.
CHEESECAKE, N. Y.—Local messenger boys parade at the celebration of the donation of the first public ashcan by the Hon. Jas. T. Scrapheap in 1742. Congressman Blowhead reviews the
SOUPBONE, MINN.—Dedication of the monument to Olaf J. Ivory, the only honest lawyer in the United States. He starved to death.
SIMP CITY, TEX.—One-week-old son of Mr. and Mrs. Hannibal M. Sawdust, showing the result of the new scientific method of bringing up a child on powdered pool balls and sterilized bay rum. This infant at one week uses a safety razor and plays a good game of pinochle.

Poster announcing Rube's **Boob News** *animated cartoons. (1915)*

Automatic jeans machine, one of Rube's first drawings of inventions and machines. The drawing was done when Rube returned to San Francisco for an exposition held there.

IT TOOK 3 YEARS TO INSTALL THIS MACHINE AT A COST OF $ 704,329.18 — SEE COMPLETE PAIR OF OVERALLS APPEAR AT OTHER END

CIVILIZATION IS MAKING WONDERFUL PROGRESS — YOU'LL SOON HAVE TO TAKE A COURSE IN ENGINEERING TO LEARN HOW TO LACE YOUR SHOES

NOCUT SAW CO

IF WE GET THE STOCK WE'LL CONTROL FIFTY-ONE PERCENT OF THE NATIONAL FINGER BOWL COMPANY —

OFFICE OVERHEAD LAWN-MOWER TO SAVE BUSINESS MAN TROUBLE OF GOING OUT FOR HAIR CUT.

Rube would work on his daily newspaper cartoons five or six hours a day, and then dash to spend another ten hours doing his animation drawings at the studio before going back to the newspaper to do last-minute changes on his sports and editorial work. Working fifteen- to twenty-hour days, Rube had to make a choice between animated motion pictures and newspapers. His health was suffering, along with his regular newspaper and syndication work. His social life was in shambles, further complicated by his meeting and falling in love with his future wife, Irma. He chose, with some hesitation, to give up the new medium of animated films and to continue his expanding and even more lucrative syndication and newspaper work.

By 1915, Rube's cartoons were syndicated nationally and printed in newspapers all around the world. By then, even Hearst was buying his work, and Rube was earning a phenomenal $100,000 per year (1.7 million in today's dollars) just from the syndication of his drawings and his books.

The first of Rube's best-known series, "The Inventions," was published in 1914 and quickly attracted a wide readership. Other cartoonists, like Frank Crane in his "Willie Westinghouse Edison Smith" drawings (1900 to 1914), Clare Victor Dwiggins (Dwig) in his "Ophella and Her Slate" or "School Days" (1909 to 1911), and W. Heath Robinson in England, also used inventions. However, Rube's work benefited from his engineer's eye and was distinguished by his use of people, animals, flowers, and natural forces like the sun, rain, and other elements as part of the working mechanics of the invention.

Rube came of age during America's heroic Age of Invention, which lasted from the end of the Civil War until about 1920. Like the railroad, the automobile, and the telephone, Rube's inventions compressed time—the time required for a flower to grow, for a shirt to shrink, for the sun to heat water. In Rube's world, events that once

Famous cartoonists doing a World War I War Bond Show (left to right): Rube Goldberg, George McManus, Richard Outcault, Hy Mayer, Tom Powers, and Clare Briggs, 1918.

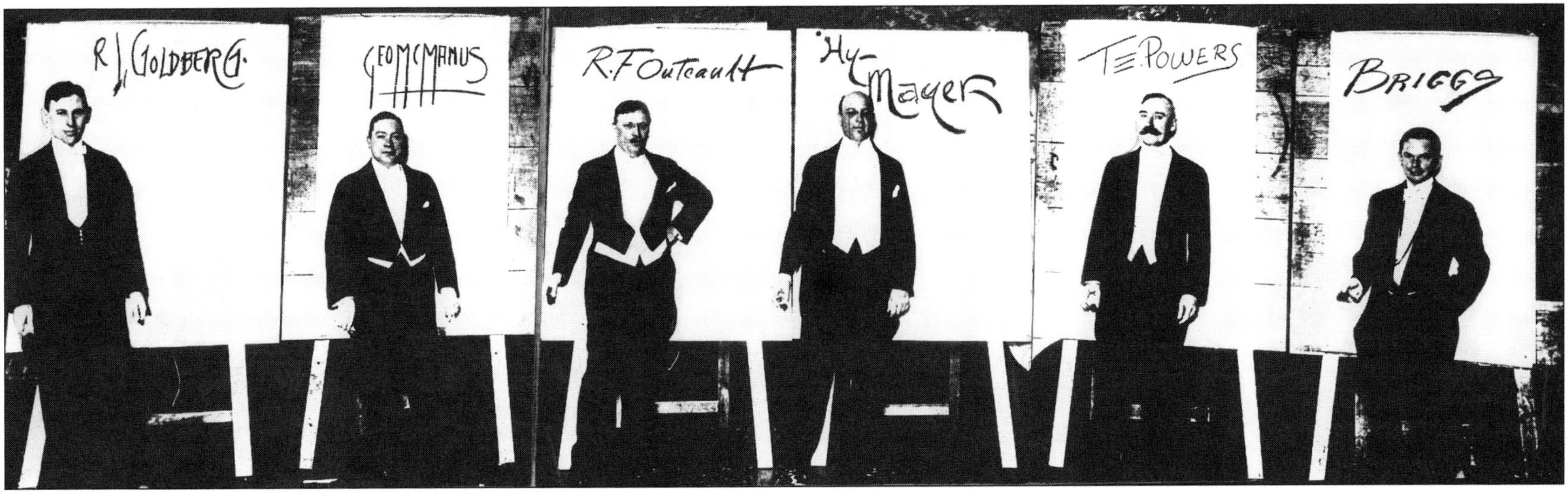
R. L. GOLDBERG.
GEO McMANUS
R.F. Outcault
Hy Mayer
T.E. POWERS
BRIGGS

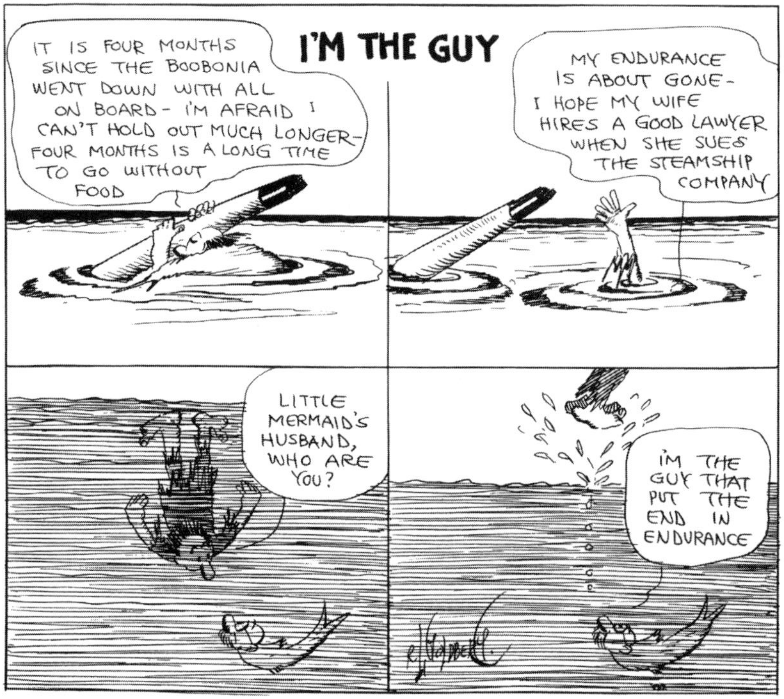
I'M THE GUY
IT IS FOUR MONTHS SINCE THE BOOBONIA WENT DOWN WITH ALL ON BOARD - I'M AFRAID I CAN'T HOLD OUT MUCH LONGER - FOUR MONTHS IS A LONG TIME TO GO WITHOUT FOOD
MY ENDURANCE IS ABOUT GONE - I HOPE MY WIFE HIRES A GOOD LAWYER WHEN SHE SUES THE STEAMSHIP COMPANY
LITTLE MERMAID'S HUSBAND, WHO ARE YOU?
I'M THE GUY THAT PUT THE END IN ENDURANCE

"I'm the Guy," daily cartoon from Rube's very popular newspaper series. Rube always liked words and made them part of his cartoon repertory. Songs, stories, and the millions of "I'm the Guy" pin-backed badges given as premiums by cigarette companies helped to popularize this slogan and its creator.

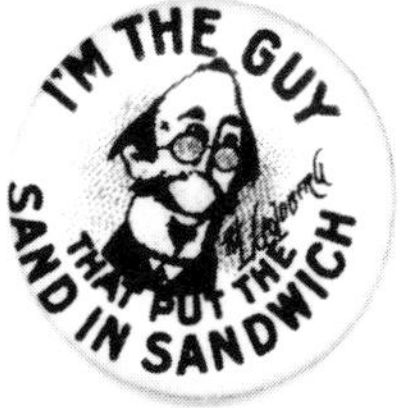
I'M THE GUY
THAT PUT THE
SAND IN SANDWICH

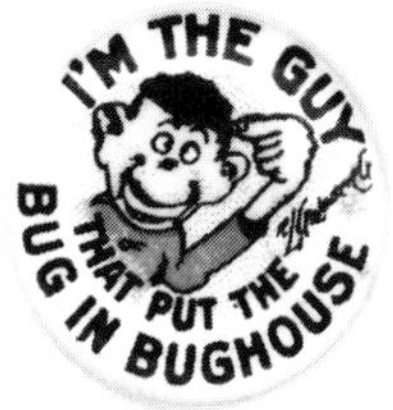
I'M THE GUY
THAT PUT THE
BUG IN BUGHOUSE

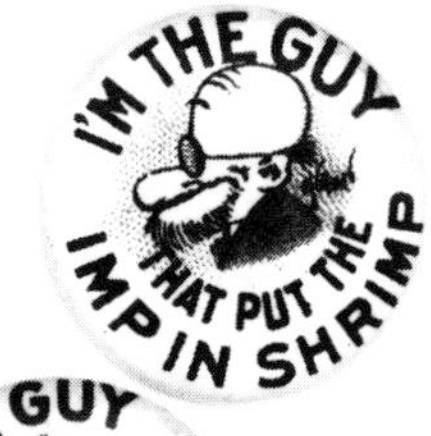
I'M THE GUY
THAT PUT THE
IMP IN SHRIMP

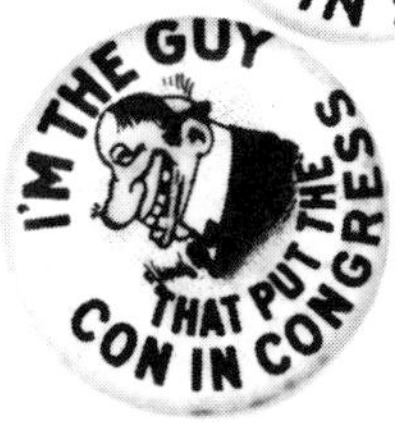
I'M THE GUY
THAT PUT THE
CON IN CONGRESS

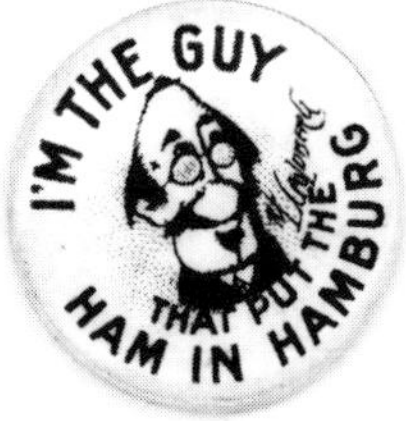
I'M THE GUY
THAT PUT THE
HAM IN HAMBURG

took minutes or hours happened virtually instantaneously... in the same amount of time, it seemed, for a new marvel to emerge from a hitherto unknown inventor's workshop. Rube's inventions echoed the Machine Age ideals of inventiveness, but, in their unnecessary complexity, mocked its zeal for efficiency.

Americans were very interested in inventions and inventing. It was the road to almost instant financial success for many an inventor who worked on inventions at night at home. Everyone was trying to invent the next electric light bulb, the telephone, or other new consumer product, and become a millionaire overnight, like Thomas Edison.

Rube's Invention cartoons were original in concept and unique in style. They had the same clarity of detail required for government patent application drawings. Rube's Inventions were interesting visually, humorous, and brilliantly satirical, while retaining an authenticity and a timeless quality. People of all ages enjoyed tracing the clever "A to B to C" of an Invention, and the improbable end result always brought surprise and amusement.

Rube's personal fascination with the emerging and quickly changing Machine Age technologies, combined with his solid training as an engineer, reinforced the impact and appeal of his invention drawings—his best-known and longest running series. He created an average of at least one of these truly inventive statements about living in the machine age every week during the next fifty years.

The Inventions inspired masterpieces in other media. Certainly, Rube's friend Charlie Chaplin must have looked at them as a key inspiration for his film *Modern Times*. Indeed, much Hollywood material—visual jokes in particular—can be traced back to Rube's Inventions.

While the Inventions series took off, Rube, now with a wife and two young sons, Tom and George, was back at his drawing board creating new strips. During his long career, Rube produced more than sixty different cartoon series (many running for more than twenty years), ranging from continuous story strips like *Boob McNutt, Bobo Baxter,* and *Lala Palooza* to theme panels like *Luke and His Uke, The Tuesday Ladies' Club, Father Was Right, Mike and Ike, Foolish Questions,* and *I'm The Guy,* as well as a full spectrum of cartoons dealing with politics, sports, and cultural events in America and the world.

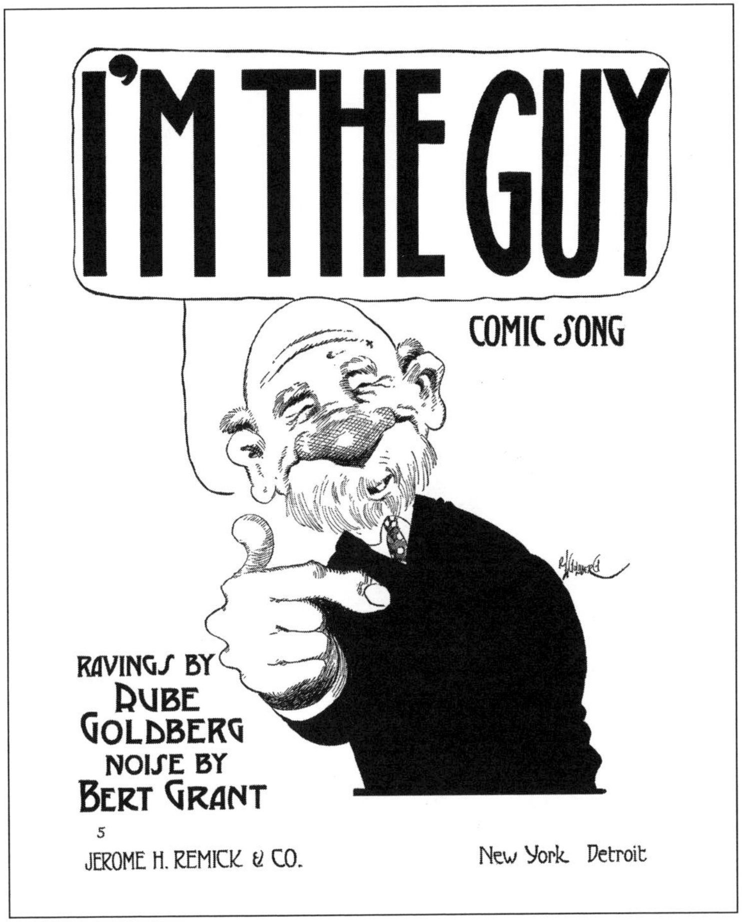
I'M THE GUY
COMIC SONG
RAVINGS BY
RUBE
GOLDBERG
NOISE BY
BERT GRANT
5
JEROME H. REMICK & CO.
New York Detroit

"I'm the Guy," sheet music for the hit song with words (and cover drawing) by Rube; music by Bert Grant. The song sparked a number of comedians who did song-and-dance routines on vaudeville stages all over the country to use it as their signature tune.

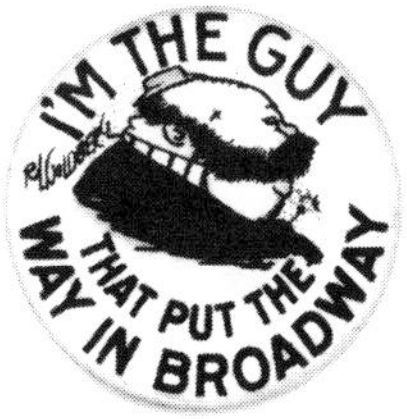
I'M THE GUY
THAT PUT THE
WAY IN BROADWAY

Boob McNutt *Sunday newspaper strip. Here, Boob is being robbed of the engagement ring he bought for Pearl, his girlfriend. The ring is found and returned, and Boob, as usual, is bewildered but happy.*

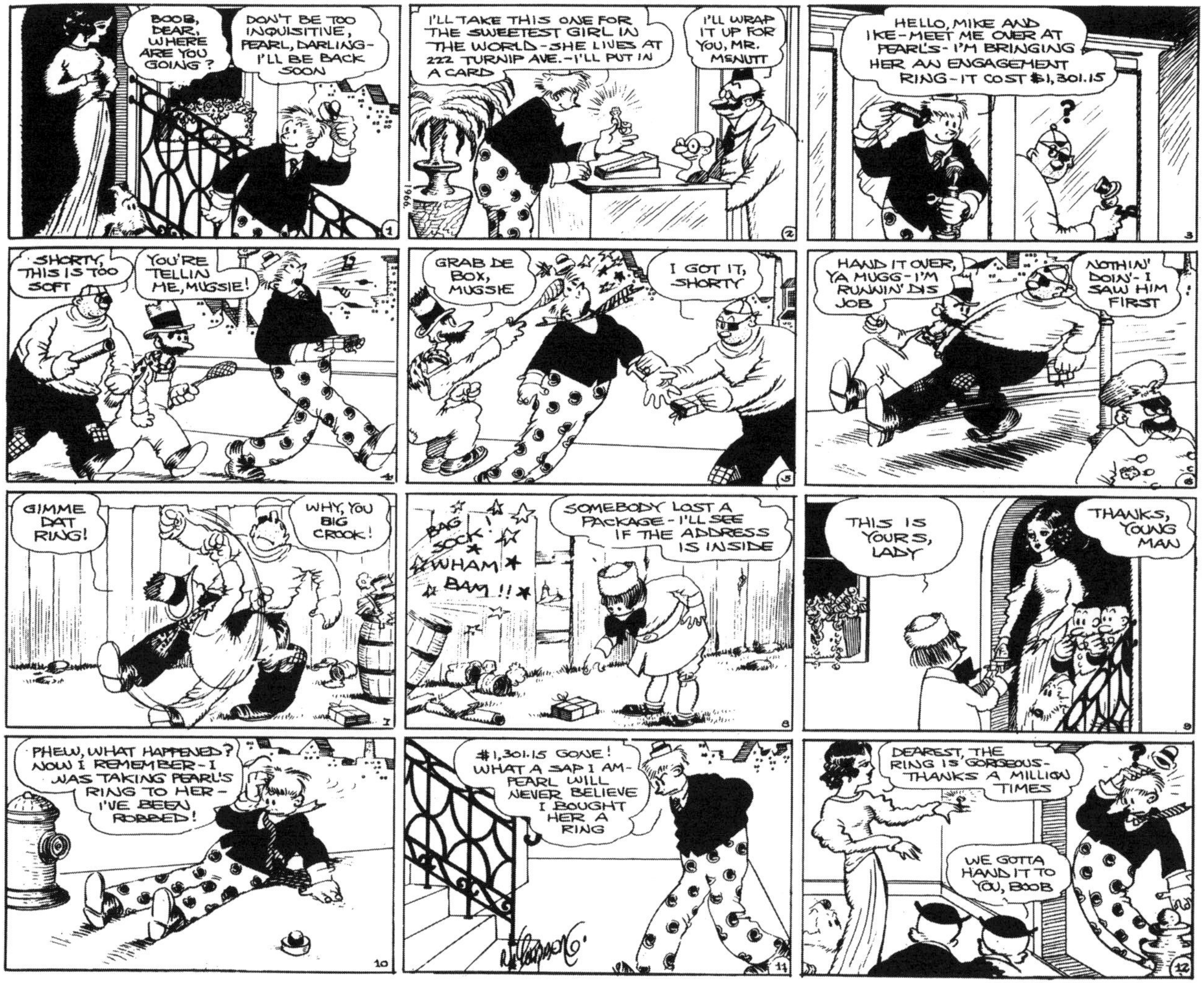
BOOB, DEAR, WHERE ARE YOU GOING?
DON'T BE TOO INQUISITIVE, PEARL, DARLING- I'LL BE BACK SOON
I'LL TAKE THIS ONE FOR THE SWEETEST GIRL IN THE WORLD-SHE LIVES AT 222 TURNIP AVE.-I'LL PUT IN A CARD
I'LL WRAP IT UP FOR YOU, MR. MCNUTT
HELLO, MIKE AND IKE-MEET ME OVER AT PEARL'S- I'M BRINGING HER AN ENGAGEMENT RING-IT COST $1,301.15
?
SHORTY, THIS IS TOO SOFT
YOU'RE TELLIN ME, MUGSIE!
GRAB DE BOX, MUGSIE
I GOT IT, SHORTY
HAND IT OVER, YA MUGG-I'M RUNNIN' DIS JOB
NOTHIN' DOIN'- I SAW HIM FIRST
GIMME DAT RING!
WHY, YOU BIG CROOK!
BAG! SOCK WHAM BAM!!
SOMEBODY LOST A PACKAGE-I'LL SEE IF THE ADDRESS IS INSIDE
THIS IS YOURS, LADY
THANKS, YOUNG MAN
PHEW, WHAT HAPPENED? NOW I REMEMBER-I WAS TAKING PEARL'S RING TO HER- I'VE BEEN ROBBED!
$1,301.15 GONE! WHAT A SAP I AM- PEARL WILL NEVER BELIEVE I BOUGHT HER A RING
DEAREST, THE RING IS GORGEOUS- THANKS A MILLION TIMES
WE GOTTA HAND IT TO YOU, BOOB

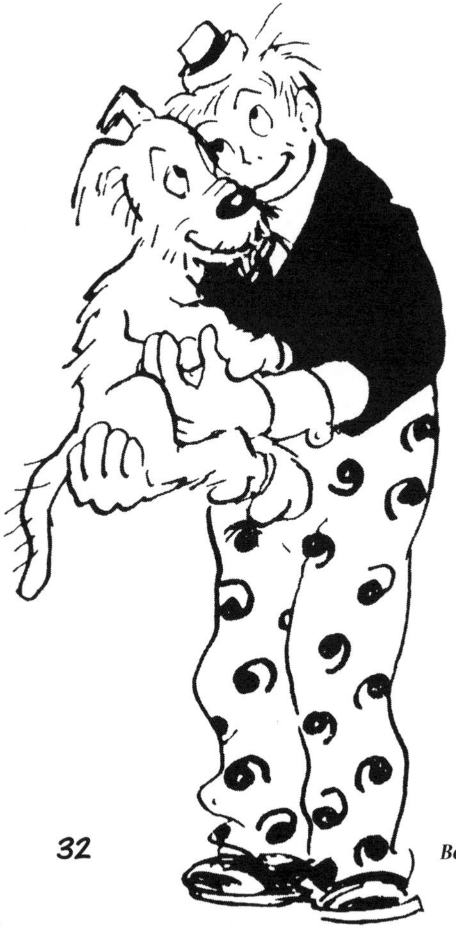

Boob McNutt, always pictured as a kindly oaf. The strip ran from 1915 to 1934.

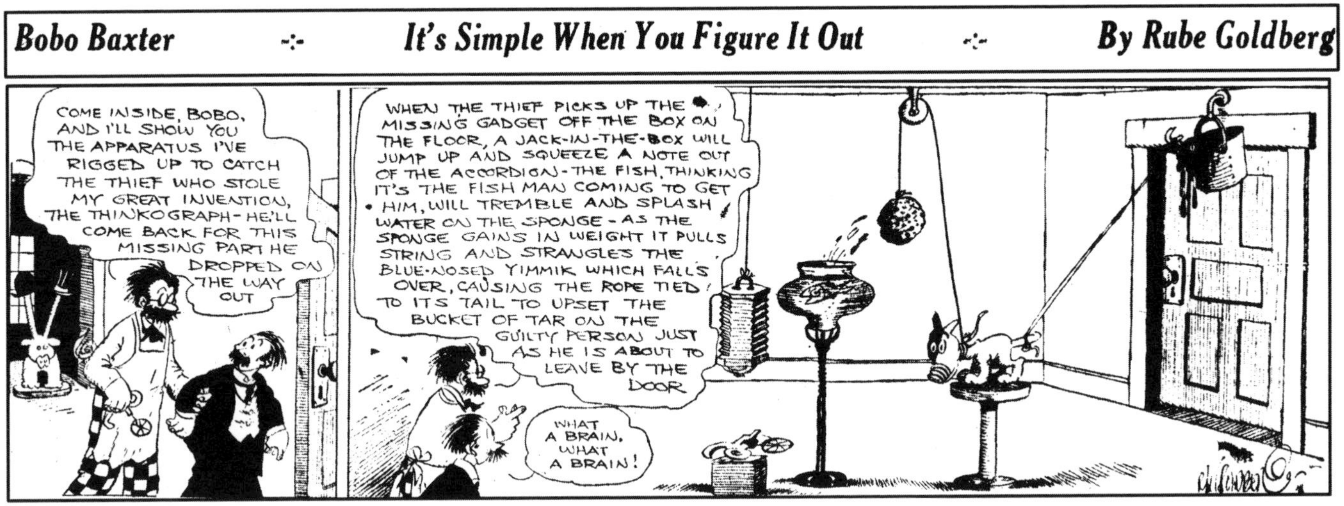
Bobo Baxter -:- It's Simple When You Figure It Out -:- By Rube Goldberg
COME INSIDE, BOBO, AND I'LL SHOW YOU THE APPARATUS I'VE RIGGED UP TO CATCH THE THIEF WHO STOLE MY GREAT INVENTION, THE THINKOGRAPH - HE'LL COME BACK FOR THIS MISSING PART HE DROPPED ON THE WAY OUT
WHEN THE THIEF PICKS UP THE MISSING GADGET OFF THE BOX ON THE FLOOR, A JACK-IN-THE-BOX WILL JUMP UP AND SQUEEZE A NOTE OUT OF THE ACCORDION - THE FISH, THINKING IT'S THE FISH MAN COMING TO GET HIM, WILL TREMBLE AND SPLASH WATER ON THE SPONGE - AS THE SPONGE GAINS IN WEIGHT IT PULLS STRING AND STRANGLES THE BLUE-NOSED YIMMIK WHICH FALLS OVER, CAUSING THE ROPE TIED TO ITS TAIL TO UPSET THE BUCKET OF TAR ON THE GUILTY PERSON JUST AS HE IS ABOUT TO LEAVE BY THE DOOR
WHAT A BRAIN, WHAT A BRAIN!

***Bobo Baxter**, 1927–28, featuring the adventures of an aviator-inventor, a character inspired by the adoration that "lone eagle" Lindbergh was receiving after his flight across the Atlantic. **Bobo Baxter** was lauded by the critics and comics historians as being on a par with **Boob McNutt**. However, after two years Rube felt that he couldn't sustain both **Bobo Baxter** and **Boob McNutt** at the same time (two multipanel strips a day, seven days a week), and so dropped **Bobo Baxter**.*

***Boob McNutt** frame (right) was exhibited (but not by Rube) at the landmark show of the Dada artists in the United States in 1921. Such Dada legends as Marcel Duchamp, Francis Picabia, and Man Ray also shared Rube's interest in technology and satire. These artists proclaimed that Rube Goldberg's art and philosophy made him "one of them." The problem was that Rube said he wasn't sure if this was flattery or not. Like many Americans of that time, he said he just couldn't understand their work.*

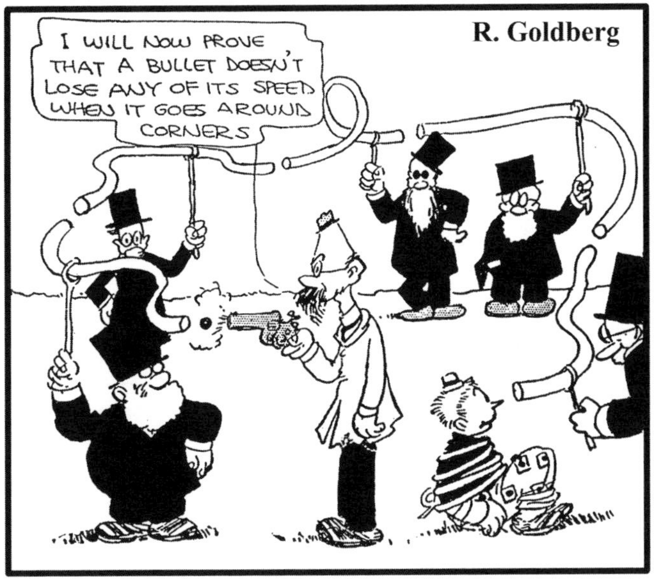
R. Goldberg
I WILL NOW PROVE THAT A BULLET DOESN'T LOSE ANY OF ITS SPEED WHEN IT GOES AROUND CORNERS

The mid-1930s saw major changes in how the public received not only Rube's work but cartoons and the funny pages in general. After almost thirty years at the top of his profession, Rube saw public taste for his panels and strip cartoons change. The public wanted continuing adventure, pathos, and drama played out by the same main characters week after week, with a lot less of the slapstick, gags, gentle satire, and instant humor of Rube's work. He tried to adapt by bringing out new continuity strips and characters, but they lacked the real Rube insight and wit of past years. Then, to compete with newsmagazines that featured photography (and especially action sports photography), newspapers started to publish more and more photographs.

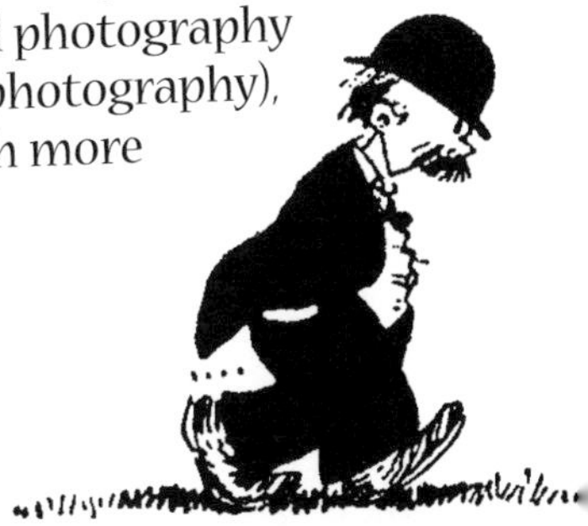

A Sunday page of Lala Palooza, *which ran between 1937 and 1938.*

LALA PALOOZA
Registered U. S. Patent Office
BY RUBE GOLDBERG
AT LAST I'VE FOUND A WAY TO HAVE FUN SELECTING CHRISTMAS PRESENTS
FOR JOE
FOR GEORGE
FOR TOM
DEAR, DEAR - THERE ISN'T NEARLY ENOUGH MONEY IN THE TREASURY OF THE "HAPPY HOLIDAY HELPERS" TO TAKE CARE OF THESE HUNDREDS OF REQUESTS FOR TOYS FROM THE LITTLE TOTS
BIG APPLE OUGHTA BE A BREEZE IN THE FOURTH RACE
SIS, IF YOU LET ME BET THE TREASURY DOUGH ON BIG APPLE AT TEN TO ONE, I'D---
I KNOW - YOU'D LOSE IT ALL - NOW YOU RUN ALONG AND GET YOUR SANTA CLAUS COSTUME - WE'LL DO THE BEST WE CAN
YOU GOTTA CHARGE THIS - MY SISTER WOULDN'T TRUST ME WITH TH' TWO BUCKS - SHE'S AFRAID I'D LAY IT ON BIG APPLE
TWO BUCKS FOR ONE APPLE? TSK TSK
LET ME STOP AN' FIGURE OUT HOW MUCH I'D WIN ON A TWO BUCK BET IF I HAD TWO BUCKS--
ULP, GRUPP, BLUPP-- WHY, WHAT-ER-BUT WHO AM I TO ASK QUESTIONS WITH ALL THAT JACK BOBBIN' UP SO SUDDEN
TO THE TRACK, BUDDIE!
WHAT'SA MATTER? IS ONE OF YOUR REINDEERS SICK AN' YOU GOTTA BUY A HORSE?
YEEE-OWW! COME ON YOU BIG APPLE!!
OH, THOSE POOR LITTLE ANGELS! WRITING ALL THOSE LETTERS TO SANTA CLAUS AND WE WON'T HAVE NEARLY ENOUGH TOYS TO GO 'ROUND - WHAT CAN WE DO? THIS IS TERRIBLE!
HEY, SIS - SANTY CLAUS IS HERE!
?
RUBE GOLDBERG
© Frank Jay Markey Syndicate, Inc.
12-12

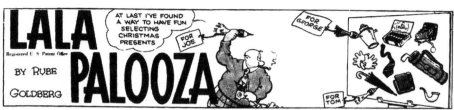

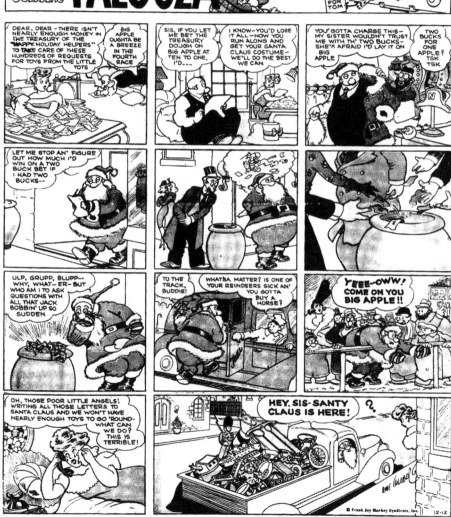

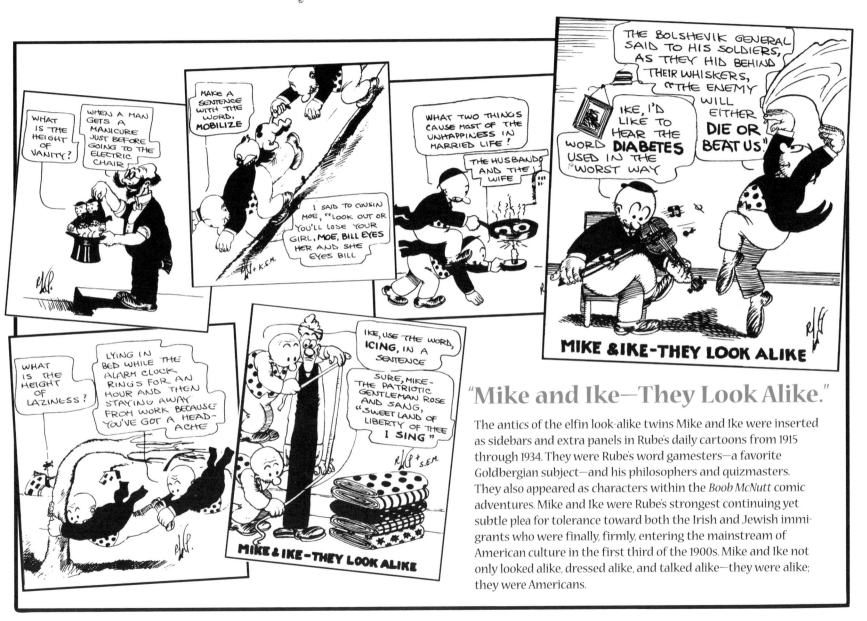

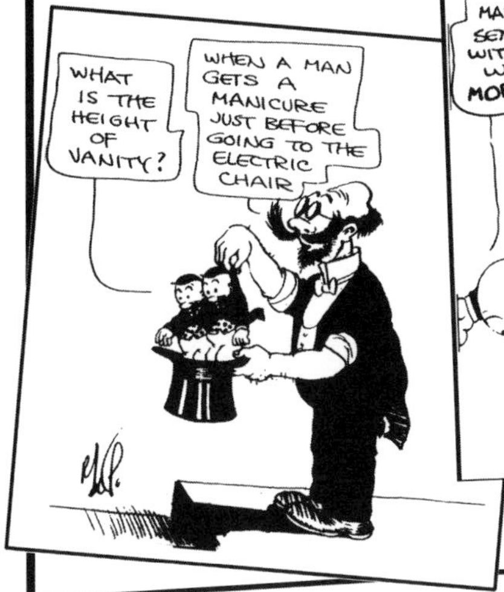
WHAT IS THE HEIGHT OF VANITY?
WHEN A MAN GETS A MANICURE JUST BEFORE GOING TO THE ELECTRIC CHAIR

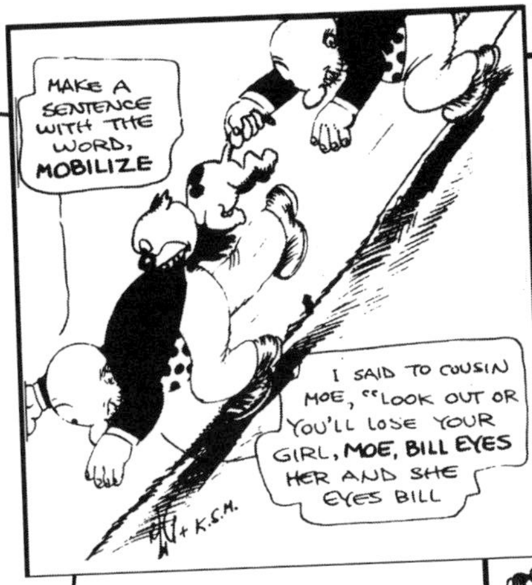
MAKE A SENTENCE WITH THE WORD, MOBILIZE
I SAID TO COUSIN MOE, "LOOK OUT OR YOU'LL LOSE YOUR GIRL, MOE, BILL EYES HER AND SHE EYES BILL

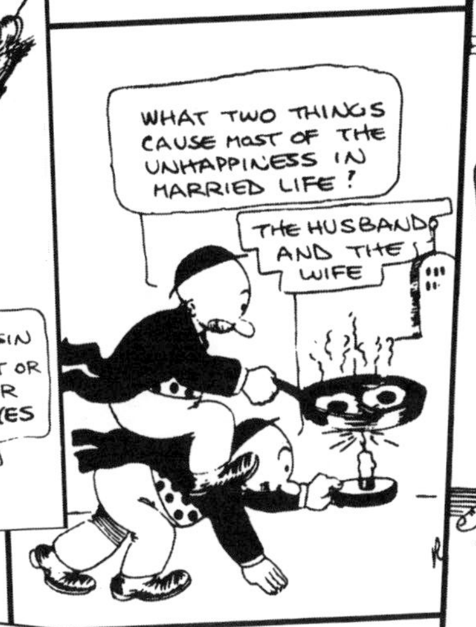
WHAT TWO THINGS CAUSE MOST OF THE UNHAPPINESS IN MARRIED LIFE?
THE HUSBAND AND THE WIFE

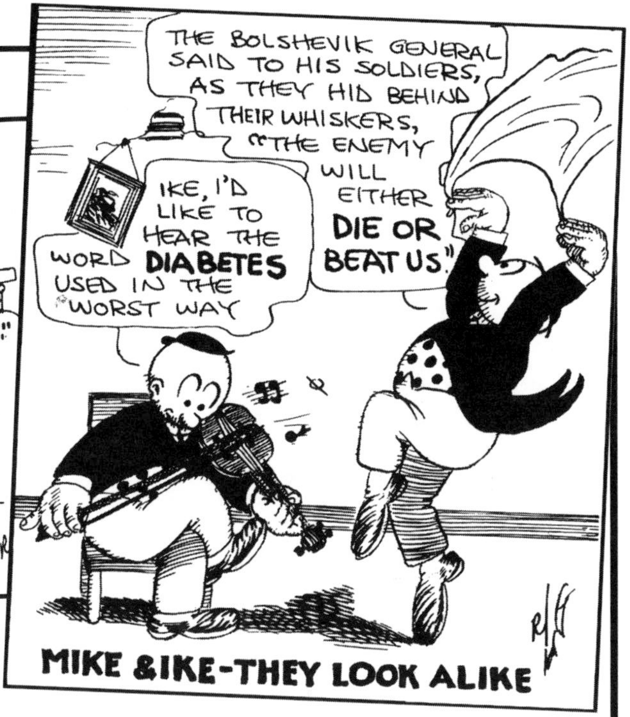
IKE, I'D LIKE TO HEAR THE WORD DIABETES USED IN THE WORST WAY
THE BOLSHEVIK GENERAL SAID TO HIS SOLDIERS, AS THEY HID BEHIND THEIR WHISKERS, "THE ENEMY WILL EITHER DIE OR BEAT US."
MIKE & IKE-THEY LOOK ALIKE

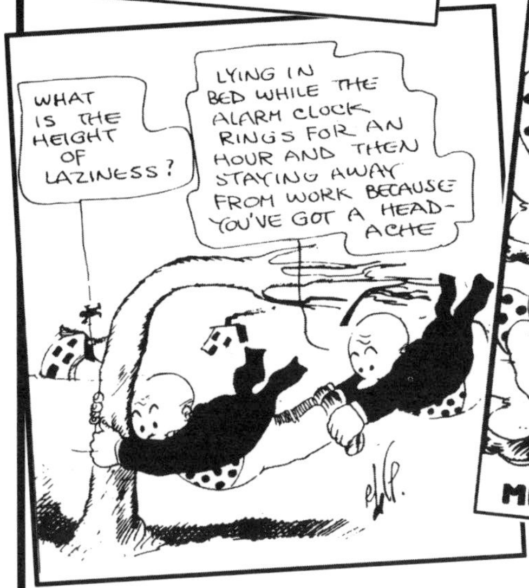
WHAT IS THE HEIGHT OF LAZINESS?
LYING IN BED WHILE THE ALARM CLOCK RINGS FOR AN HOUR AND THEN STAYING AWAY FROM WORK BECAUSE YOU'VE GOT A HEAD-ACHE

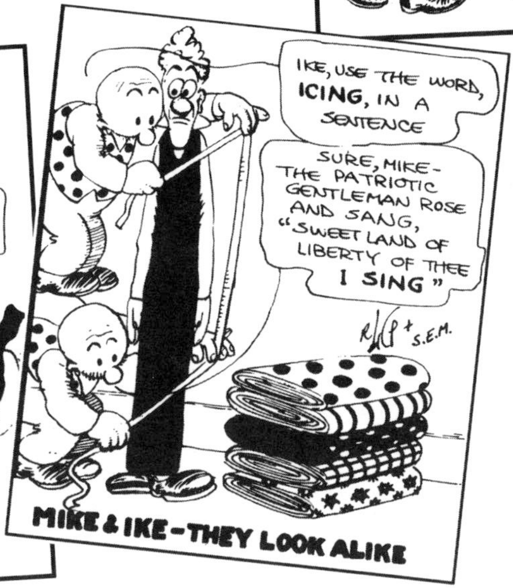
IKE, USE THE WORD, ICING, IN A SENTENCE
SURE, MIKE- THE PATRIOTIC GENTLEMAN ROSE AND SANG, "SWEET LAND OF LIBERTY OF THEE I SING"
MIKE & IKE-THEY LOOK ALIKE

"Mike and Ike—They Look Alike."

The antics of the elfin look-alike twins Mike and Ike were inserted as sidebars and extra panels in Rube's daily cartoons from 1915 through 1934. They were Rube's word gamesters—a favorite Goldbergian subject—and his philosophers and quizmasters. They also appeared as characters within the *Boob McNutt* comic adventures. Mike and Ike were Rube's strongest continuing yet subtle plea for tolerance toward both the Irish and Jewish immigrants who were finally, firmly, entering the mainstream of American culture in the first third of the 1900s. Mike and Ike not only looked alike, dressed alike, and talked alike—they were alike; they were Americans.

STUBBLE TROUBLE?
USE
Berkeley Blades
NO BETTER BLADE AT ANY PRICE!
18 for 25¢
©1944, CONSOLIDATED RAZOR BLADE CO., INC.
STUBBLE TROUBLE?
USE
Berkeley Blades
NO BETTER BLADE AT ANY PRICE!
18 for 25¢
©1944, CONSOLIDATED RAZOR BLADE CO., INC.
STUBBLE TROUBLE?
USE
Berkeley Blades
NO BETTER BLADE AT ANY PRICE!
18 for 25¢
©1944, CONSOLIDATED RAZOR BLADE CO., INC.
STUBBLE TROUBLE?
USE
Berkeley Blades
NO BETTER BLADE AT ANY PRICE!
18 for 25¢
©1944, CONSOLIDATED RAZOR BLADE CO., INC.

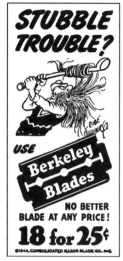

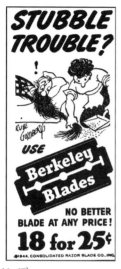

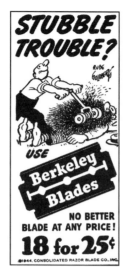

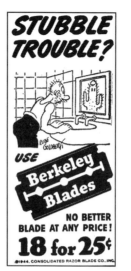

Ads for Berkeley Blades. (1946–47)

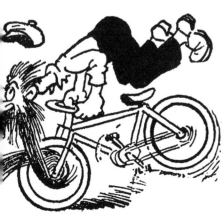

Publishers moved the daily cartoons from the popular sports pages and the other major sections of the newspaper to the specially created funny pages. They also limited the space available for each cartoon to a narrow three- or four-panel strip. Even Rube's latest Inventions were reduced in size in the dailies, and eventually in the Sunday pages as well.

Rube felt these changes were unacceptable, so in 1938, with much drama and publicity, he announced that he was giving up drawing comic strips and was going to devote himself to his writing. His short stories and feature articles had always been well received in national magazines, especially if he also did the drawings that illustrated the story. He also would continue to take on advertising assignments.

A Beacon Light
By
RUBE GOLDBERG
21
Twenty-one happy men (count 'em) hold up a beacon light to guide all other happy men to Jack & Charlie's "21".

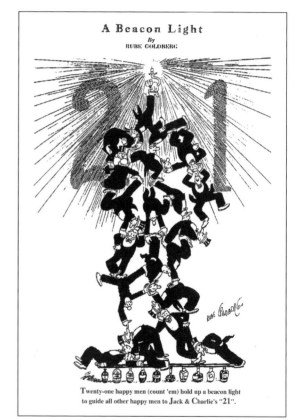

Special presentation illustration for the "21" restaurant. (1939) The "21" was a personal favorite with Rube and his friends since its opening during Prohibition.

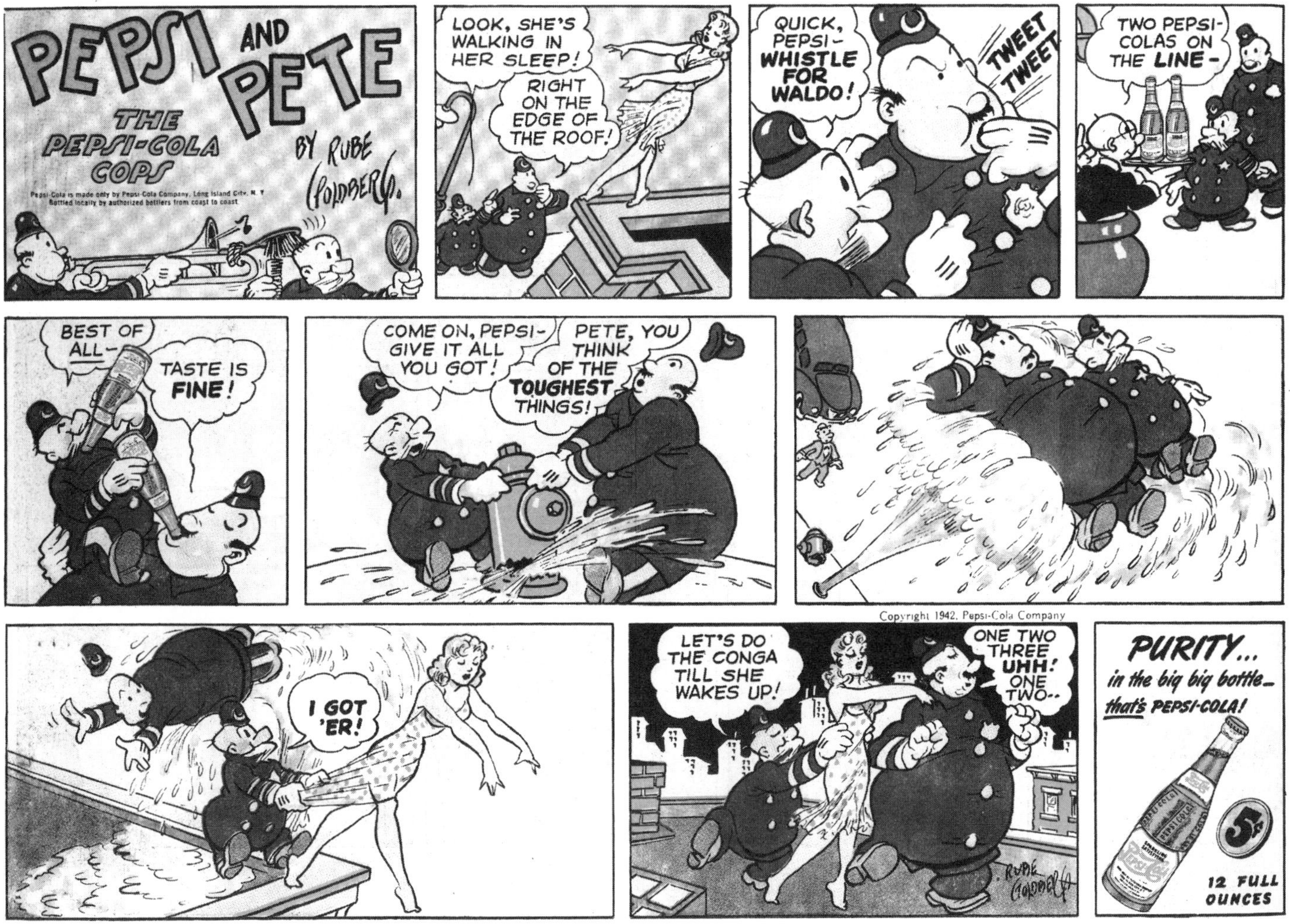
PEPSI AND PETE
THE PEPSI-COLA COPS
BY RUBE GOLDBERG
Pepsi-Cola is made only by Pepsi-Cola Company, Long Island City, N. Y. Bottled locally by authorized bottlers from coast to coast
LOOK, SHE'S WALKING IN HER SLEEP!
RIGHT ON THE EDGE OF THE ROOF!
QUICK, PEPSI– WHISTLE FOR WALDO!
TWEET TWEET
TWO PEPSI-COLAS ON THE LINE–
BEST OF ALL–
TASTE IS FINE!
COME ON, PEPSI– GIVE IT ALL YOU GOT!
PETE, YOU THINK OF THE TOUGHEST THINGS!
Copyright 1942, Pepsi-Cola Company
I GOT 'ER!
LET'S DO THE CONGA TILL SHE WAKES UP!
ONE TWO THREE UHH! ONE TWO–
RUBE GOLDBERG
PURITY...
in the big big bottle–
that's PEPSI-COLA!
5¢
12 FULL OUNCES

Rube created the Pepsi and Pete characters for Pepsi-Cola, and they ran as newspaper and magazine ads for many years. Rube stopped drawing the ads in 1942, but the series was continued, drawn by other artists.

Posture Chair, drawing for **DuPont Magazine**, 1954, typical of the commercial ads using his Invention style that Rube did for many companies.

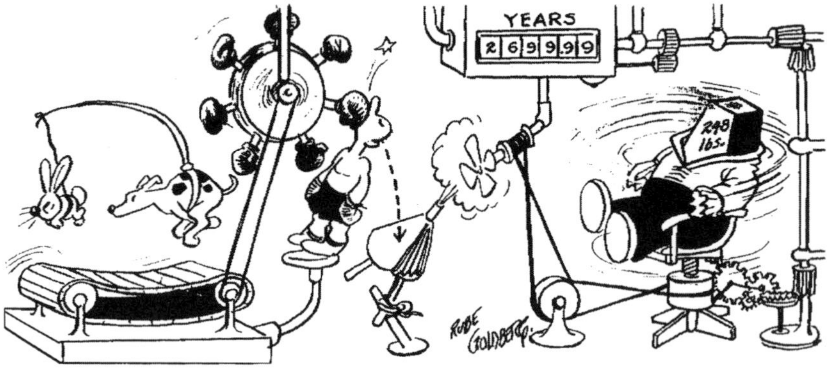
YEARS
248 lbs.
RUBE GOLDBERG

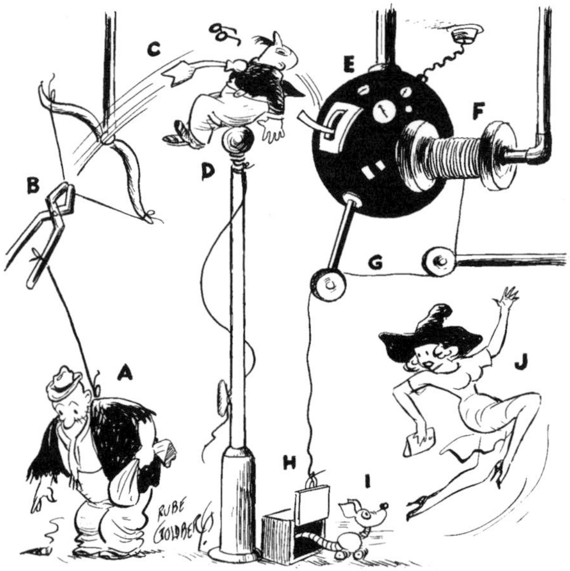
A
B
C
D
E
F
G
H
I
J
RUBE GOLDBERG

AS BUM (A) LEANS OVER TO PICK UP CIGAR BUTT, HE OPENS PLIERS (B) AND RELEASES ARROW (C) WHICH KNOCKS FLAGPOLE SITTER (D) OFF HIS PERCH, HITTING SWITCH (E) WHICH CAUSES SPOOL (F) TO START SPINNING — CORD (G) LIFTS LID FROM BOX (H), RELEASING TOY MOUSE (I)— WOMAN (J) RUNS FRANTICALLY FOR SIX BLOCKS, THUS GETTING ALL THE EXERCISE SHE NEEDS.

The Exerciser, for those who can't or won't take adequate exercise. Another in the series of medical ads. (1956) The pharmaceutical industry used Rube's Inventions to promote its medical products with mail and advertising campaigns aimed directly at doctors.

How to Get Rid of a Mouse

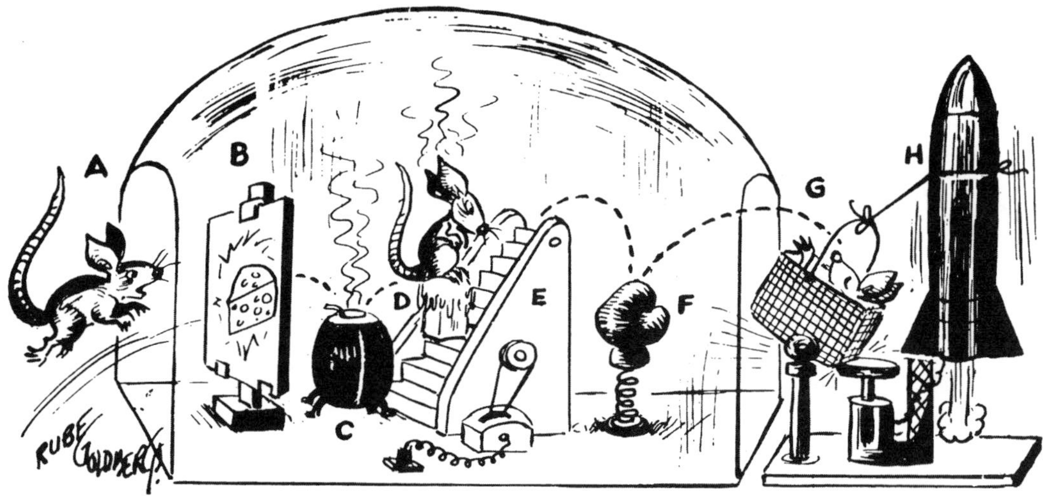
A
B
C
D
E
F
G
H
RUBE GOLDBERG

Drawn for Newsweek by Rube Goldberg

The best mousetrap by Rube Goldberg: Mouse (A) dives for painting of cheese (B), goes through canvas and lands on hot stove (C). He jumps on cake of ice (D) to cool off. Moving escalator (E) drops him on boxing glove (F) which knocks him into basket (G) setting off miniature rocket (H) which takes him to the moon.

Newsweek *magazine drawing.*

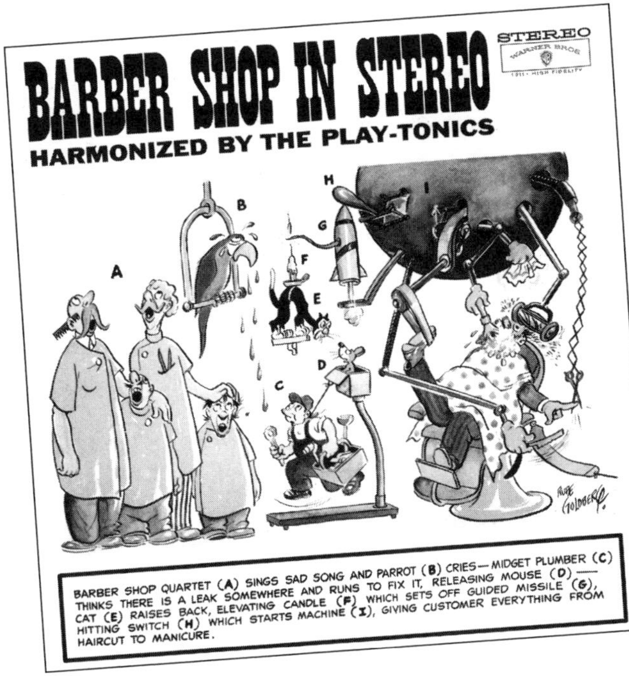
BARBER SHOP IN STEREO
STEREO
WARNER BROS.
HARMONIZED BY THE PLAY-TONICS
BARBER SHOP QUARTET (A) SINGS SAD SONG AND PARROT (B) CRIES—MIDGET PLUMBER (C) THINKS THERE IS A LEAK SOMEWHERE AND RUNS TO FIX IT, RELEASING MOUSE (D)— CAT (E) RAISES BACK, ELEVATING CANDLE (F) WHICH SETS OFF GUIDED MISSILE (G), HITTING SWITCH (H) WHICH STARTS MACHINE (I), GIVING CUSTOMER EVERYTHING FROM HAIRCUT TO MANICURE.

Barber Shop in Stereo, *Warner Bros. Music. (1959) An LP album cover illustrating another use of Rube's Inventions.*

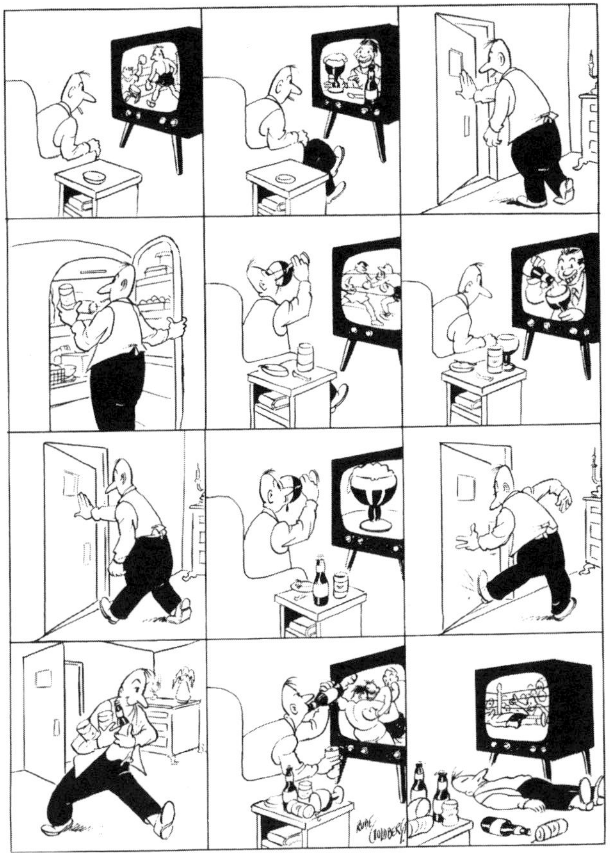

Beer commercial parody done for an advertising presentation to a client. (1959) Advertising agencies would occasionally commission drawings whose purpose was pointed humor, but not for the public. This one showed the advantages of TV advertising in the home: your customer could drink beer after beer until he passed out!

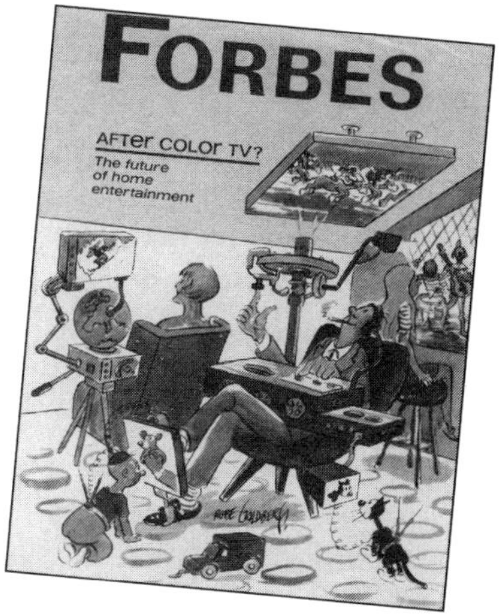
FORBES
AFTER COLOR TV?
The future of home entertainment

Forbes *magazine cover, illustrating electronic life in the future. (1967)*

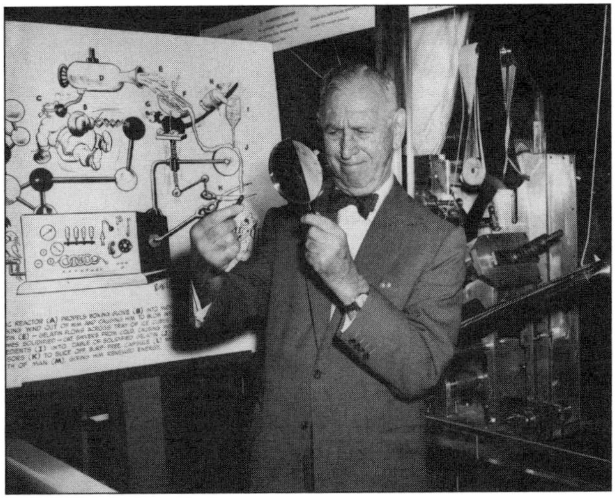

New York World's Fair, 1964. Advertising clients and their agencies always kept Rube drawing inventions for their ads and public displays.

Rube Goldberg

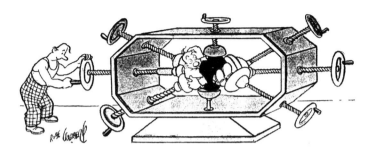

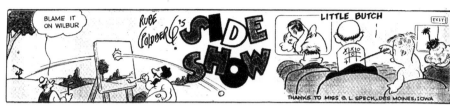

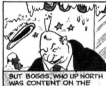

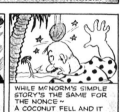

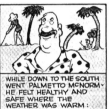

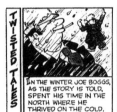

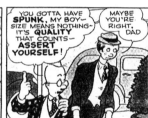

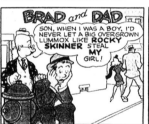

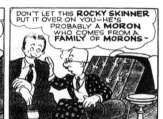

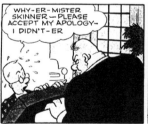

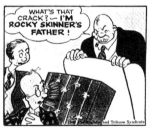

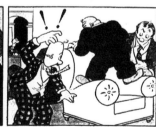

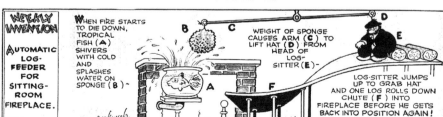

Rube could easily afford to do this in 1938. Advertisers and their agencies paid highly for his original work. Rube's drawings promoted products ranging from office equipment and pharmaceuticals to soft drinks. Furthermore, he was earning income as his past work was being reprinted, and the Inventions were finding new audiences. He also continued to draw and syndicate his Sunday page, called Rube Goldberg's *Sideshow,* a weekly collection of color cartoons, strips, quizzes, and word games. This also included Inventions that were done in a much more simplified and compressed style than his past drawings.

No longer creating daily cartoon strips, Rube wrote for popular magazines like the *Saturday Evening Post, Collier's,* and *Vanity Fair.* He played a lot of golf, his favorite sport, and wrote for golf magazines. He appeared on radio shows and in newsreels and worked on two feature films. He continued writing songs and even wrote a play. However, nothing seemed to have the same flow of creative adrenaline that a newspaper deadline gave him.

BLAME IT ON WILBUR
RUBE GOLDBERG'S SIDE SHOW
LITTLE BUTCH
EXIT
THANKS TO MISS G. L. SPECK, DES MOINES, IOWA
TWISTED TALES
IN THE WINTER JOE BOGGS, AS THE STORY IS TOLD, SPENT HIS TIME IN THE NORTH WHERE HE THRIVED ON THE COLD,
WHILE DOWN TO THE SOUTH WENT PALMETTO McNORM~ HE FELT HEALTHY AND SAFE WHERE THE WEATHER WAS WARM:
BUT BOGGS, WHO UP NORTH WAS CONTENT ON THE JOB, WAS HIT BY AN ICICLE RIGHT ON THE KNOB,
WHILE McNORM'S SIMPLE STORY'S THE SAME FOR THE NONCE~ A COCONUT FELL AND IT FRACTURED HIS SCONCE!
BRAD and DAD
SON, WHEN I WAS A BOY, I'D NEVER LET A BIG OVERGROWN LUMMOX LIKE ROCKY SKINNER STEAL MY GIRL!
YOU GOTTA HAVE SPUNK, MY BOY— SIZE MEANS NOTHING— IT'S QUALITY THAT COUNTS— ASSERT YOURSELF!
MAYBE YOU'RE RIGHT, DAD
DON'T LET THIS ROCKY SKINNER PUT IT OVER ON YOU—HE'S PROBABLY A MORON WHO COMES FROM A FAMILY OF MORONS~
WHAT'S THAT CRACK?— I'M ROCKY SKINNER'S FATHER!
WHY-ER-MISTER SKINNER— PLEASE ACCEPT MY APOLOGY— I DIDN'T-ER
! !
WEEKLY INVENTION
AUTOMATIC LOG-FEEDER FOR SITTING-ROOM FIREPLACE.
WHEN FIRE STARTS TO DIE DOWN, TROPICAL FISH (A) SHIVERS WITH COLD AND SPLASHES WATER ON SPONGE (B)~
WEIGHT OF SPONGE CAUSES ARM (C) TO LIFT HAT (D) FROM HEAD OF LOG-SITTER (E)~
LOG-SITTER JUMPS UP TO GRAB HAT AND ONE LOG ROLLS DOWN CHUTE (F) INTO FIREPLACE BEFORE HE GETS BACK INTO POSITION AGAIN!
A
B
C
D
E
F
1-14

BLAME IT ON WILBUR
VOTE FOR JOHN T. BEARD FOR STREET CLEANING COMMISSIONER
RUBE GOLDBERG'S
SIDE SHOW
LITTLE BUTCH
PICKPOCKET
TWISTED TALES
CYANIDE TURTLE TACOMA McLIME ALWAYS AMBLED ALONG AND WAS NEVER ON TIME,
WHILE A PUNCTUAL FELLOW, NAMED PHILIP DE GERM, STILL BELIEVED THAT THE EARLY BIRD CATCHES THE WORM:
TRAINS OUT
CHIEF
BUT McLIME MISSED HIS TRAIN— WHICH WAS QUITE AGGRAVATING— BUT HE MET A SWELL DAME WHILE HE STOOD AROUND WAITING
WHILE DE GERM CAUGHT THE TRAIN (NEVER TARDY, BY HECK), AND THE POOR EARLY SUCKER GOT CAUGHT IN A WRECK!
BRAD and DAD
IF WE COULD ONLY GET RID OF THESE CLOTHES, SON
I'M AFRAID THE BLOODHOUNDS WON'T WAIT.
DON'T SHOOT, BOYS—WE'LL TAKE 'EM ALIVE!
BUT, SHERIFF, THE TWO REAL CONVICTS MADE US CHANGE CLOTHES WITH 'EM AT THE POINT OF A GUN!
WE'LL CHECK UP ON THAT LATER
INSIDE, STIRBUGS!
LISSEN, CHUMS— I'M ALL SET TA BUST OUTA DIS MOUSETRAP T'NIGHT AN' YOUSE GUYS FIT RIGHT INTA ME PLANS!
BUT, BUT-
TAKE DESE AN' BLAST ANYBODY DAT GITS IN YER WAY— IF YA DON'T...
CONTINUED
WEEKLY INVENTION
NECESSARY ACCESSORIES FOR UNNECESSARY TOURING
RADIATOR-CLOCK WITH PENDULUM FOR SWEEPING NAILS AND BROKEN GLASS OUT OF THE WAY.
NON-TANGLE ROAD MAP ROLLERS.
EXTRA FRONT WHEEL FOR PARKING IN TIGHT PLACES.
RUBE GOLDBERG
8-11

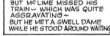

***Sideshow** (1938–40) was done in color as part of the Sunday newspaper pages that were nationally syndicated and then republished for many years in different Sunday newspapers.*

The famed sportswriter and author Grantland Rice described his friend Rube best: "Rube is a man of charm, humor, brains, imagination, the needed amount of humility, and the plain old-fashioned touch that only regular people understand."

Rube probably agreed with each adjective, for while he was never arrogant or egotistical, he hardly ducked from being the center of any crowd. When attention focussed on him (as it inevitably did), he took the center of the stage and held his audience captive.

Of average build, dignified and erect, Rube personified the sportsman-golfer. Never did he show the politician's forwardness, and was almost shy until he was approached or approached others. Then, said one acquaintance, "From the first minute, you called him 'Rube,' and you knew he was interested in what you were saying."

To quote Rice again: "There may be greater all-around guys than Rube. But I'm sorry. I never met one."

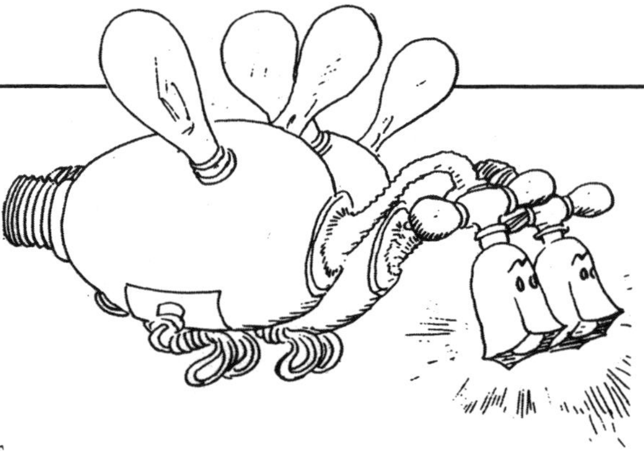

Rube was a celebrity whose close friends were other American icons of their time—personalities like Will Rogers, Grantland Rice, Jack Dempsey, Jimmy Durante, Charlie Chaplin, and his fellow members of the Friars, the Lambs, the Dutch Treat, the Society of Illustrators, and the many other clubs that were part of Rube's New York life. He was a popular after-dinner speaker and an accomplished performer. Rube did not have the day-to-day worries of earning a living for his family or himself, but like many truly creative people, he wanted to work at what he loved.

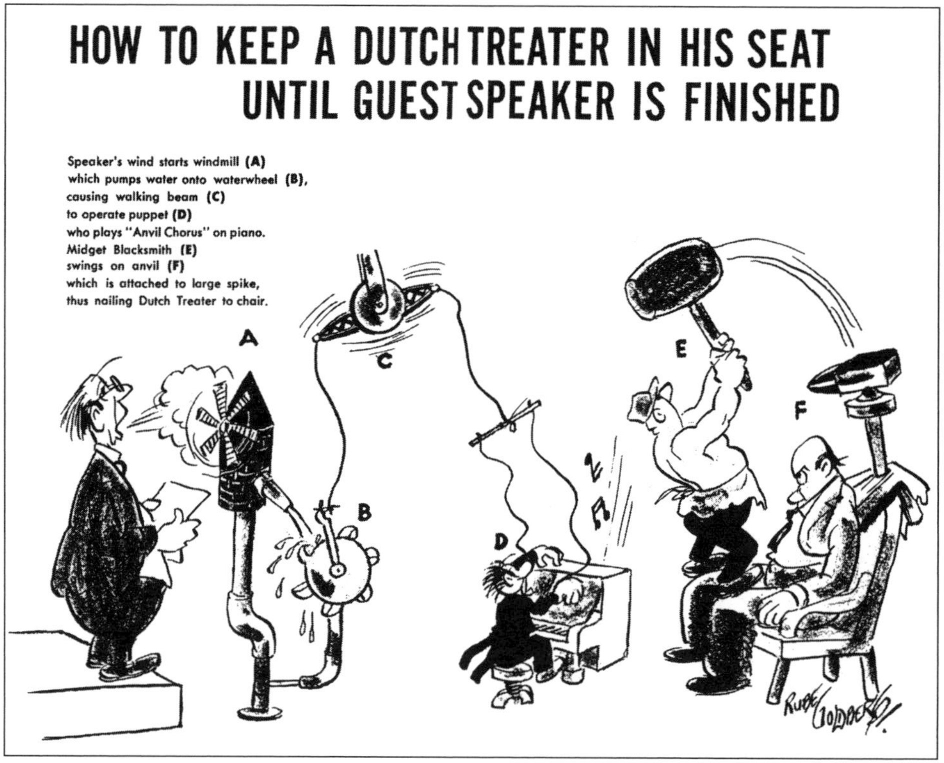
HOW TO KEEP A DUTCH TREATER IN HIS SEAT UNTIL GUEST SPEAKER IS FINISHED
Speaker's wind starts windmill (A) which pumps water onto waterwheel (B), causing walking beam (C) to operate puppet (D) who plays "Anvil Chorus" on piano. Midget Blacksmith (E) swings on anvil (F) which is attached to large spike, thus nailing Dutch Treater to chair.
A
B
C
D
E
F
RUBE GOLDBERG

The Dutch Treat is a private lunch club of politicians, writers, artists, actors, publishers, and "interesting people" that meets weekly. As a member, Rube contributed many drawings over the years to their privately printed yearbooks.

Artists and Models, Paramount Films. Rube was one of the artist-actors in this 1930s film. Rube went to Hollywood in the early thirties to write a Three Stooges screenplay titled Soup to Nuts. He never went back as a writer, but did return to films one more time, this time as an actor in Artists and Models. As Rube tells it, "I only had one line to say and after a great number of takes the director was going to cut that out of the film. My line— just my name. But in front of the cameras and lights it just wouldn't come out right."

It was soon apparent to everyone that Rube missed the pace, the applause, the action and notoriety of newspaper cartooning for a worldwide fan base. An old friend, the general manager of *The New York Sun*, called and asked if Rube would ever consider doing editorial cartoons. After thinking it over (and, according to friends, quickly deciding to accept), he waited a day to call back and indicate he might be interested in trying.

This opened a new chapter for Rube, beginning after his fifty-fifth birthday. He started doing three editorial-page drawings a week for the *Sun*, with topics of his own choosing. Rube chose a simple and more powerful drawing style, a departure from his trademark of the fine line and draftsman's approach. His editorial cartoons carried their message with directness and impact. He even used his Inventions to defend the taxpayer against the "enemy"—entrenched bureaucrats and politicians. During World War II and its aftermath, his

43

drawings were strong editorial statements against America's enemies, atomic war, poverty, and corruption. Rube was awarded the Pulitzer Prize for Editorial Cartoons in 1948 for his "Peace Today" drawing, published July 22, 1947, which commented on the insecurity the average person and his family felt living in an age of atomic bombs.

In 1950 Rube moved from *The New York Sun* to Hearst's *New York Journal* as their main editorial cartoonist. His last editorial cartoon appeared in 1964, after Rube decided not to sign a new contract with the Hearst Newspaper Group. He said he finally wanted a release from the demands of a daily deadline. But in reality Rube at eighty was about to start another new career.

Rube was awarded the Banshees Club Press Award, and this Invention commemorated the event, 1956.

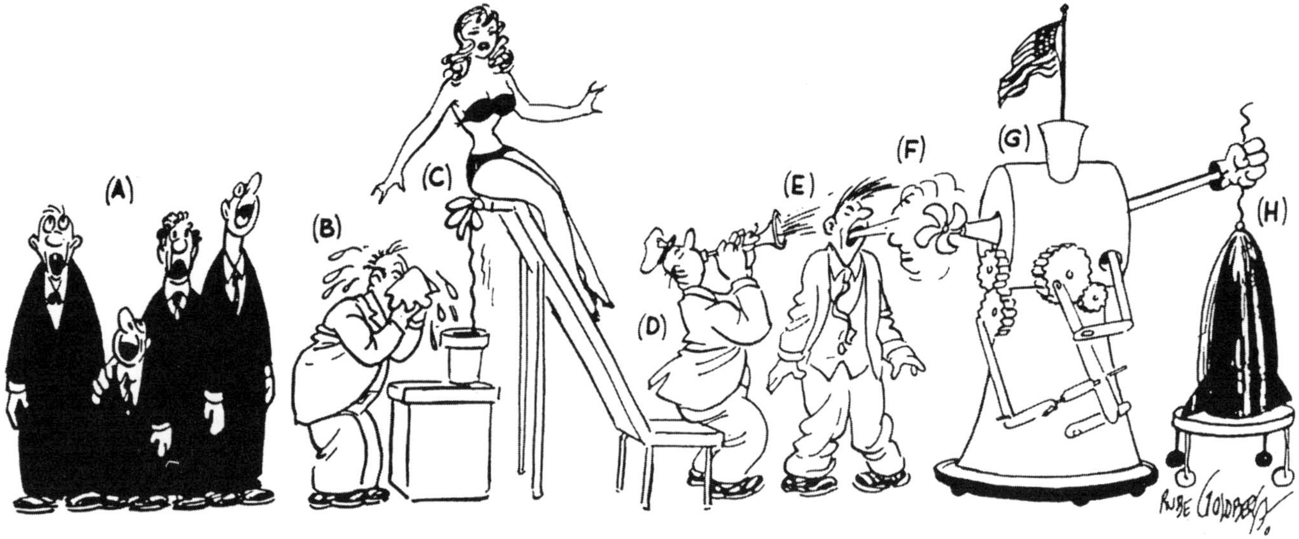
(A)
(B)
(C)
(D)
(E)
(F)
(G)
(H)
RUBE GOLDBERG

One of Rube Goldberg's "Inventions" was turned into a surprise for him. It was entitled HOW TO GET RID OF A LONG-WINDED SPEAKER with the following explanation: "Quartet (A) sings sad song that (B) causes man to weep so profusely that his tears make plant (C) shoot up and tickle (D) bathing beauty who slides down and kicks (E) trumpeter, who waking up, gives such a blast of his horn that bystander (F) catches cold and sneezes into propeller that starts machine (G) that sweeps speaker off platform. When Mr. Goldberg was to be the recipient of an award from the Banshees Club, New York, fellow artists and a famous model acted out the "Invention" with one change. The "machine" (G) was made to lift a cover (H) and reveal the award statuette.

ATOMIC BOMB
WORLD CONTROL
WORLD DESTRUCTION
RUBE GOLDBERG

PEACE TODAY

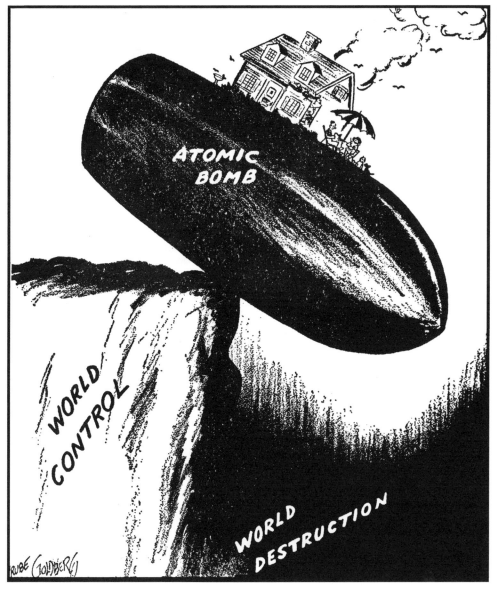

The Pulitzer Prize for Editorial Cartoons was awarded to Rube in 1948 for this drawing that reflected insecurity in the age of the atomic bomb.

The Reuben, The National Cartoonists Society Award given annually to a cartoonist by his peers. The Reuben was designed by Rube, named after him, and awarded to him, in 1967.

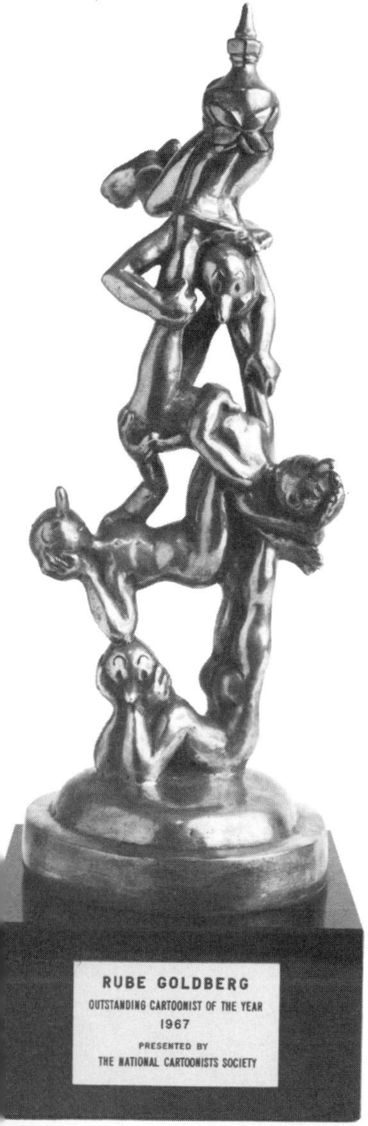
RUBE GOLDBERG
OUTSTANDING CARTOONIST OF THE YEAR
1967
PRESENTED BY
THE NATIONAL CARTOONISTS SOCIETY

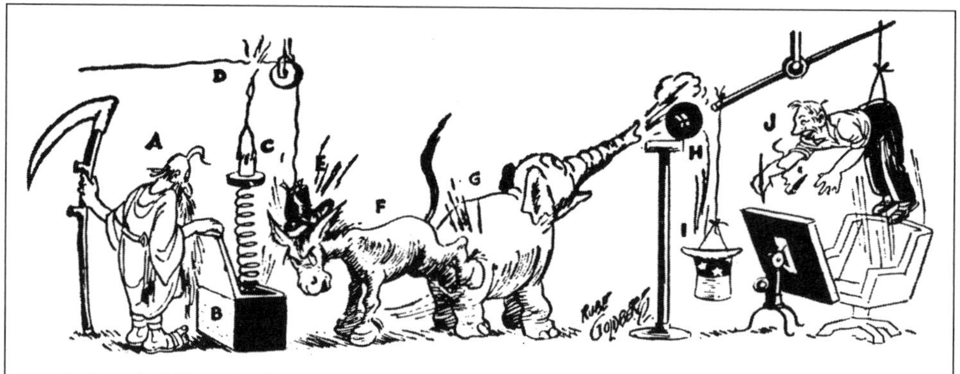
A
B
C
D
E
F
G
H
I
J

Rube Goldberg's New-Career machine
"Father Time (A) lifts lid of magic box (B), releasing spring which causes candle (C) to burn string (D) and drop iron boot (E) on Democratic donkey (F). Donkey kicks Republican elephant (G) which snorts in anger and blows cannonball (H) into Uncle Sam's hat (I), thereby lifting me (J) away from my drawing board into the 'higher art' of sculpture."

Cartoon drawn by Rube and published in Newsweek *magazine announcing that Rube was giving up editorial cartooning for a new career as a sculptor at the age of eighty. (1963)*

Sculpture had always interested him. He was an admirer of Honoré Daumier, who had evolved, over his career, from caricature drawing to sculpture. Rube liked the concept of giving his drawings a third dimension so the viewer could look in back of the figures he created. To Rube, as to other artists, this idea proved very compelling. At the age of eighty he took one lesson in sculpture from a local sculpture studio and inside of a year had his first show (a sellout), at New York's prestigious Hammer Galleries. Rube held a number of gallery shows over the next few years and sculpted an estimated three-hundred works, all sold to private collectors, galleries, and museums.

Rube continued to remain active in the cartooning world as the elder statesman and permanent honorary president of the National Cartoonists Society that he had helped found. In 1967 he was awarded the Reuben (named after and, of course, designed by him).

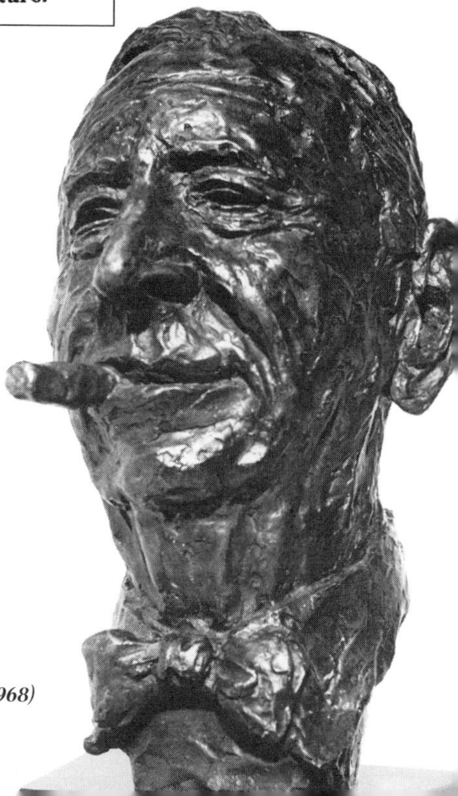

Self-portrait in bronze. (1968)

This, the highest award given to a cartoonist by the society, is still annually presented to a cartoonist voted the "best" by his peers.

In 1970 the National Museum of History and Technology of the Smithsonian Institution in Washington honored Rube Goldberg with a magnificent retrospective of his work entitled "Do It the Hard Way." This was the only one-man show ever given to a living artist-cartoonist-humorist, and it showed the vision and creative scope of Rube's work over almost seventy years. Rube died on December 7, 1970, just two weeks after the gala opening of this national celebration of his talent and dedication.

Even after his death, Rube's presence has never left the public eye. Rube's work is also shown today at various museums

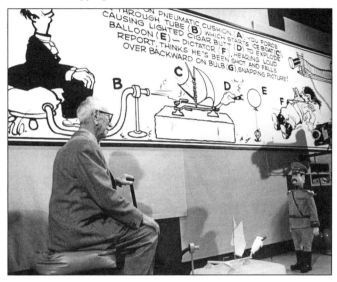

Smithsonian Museum exhibition, a retrospective of Rube's work. Rube is having his picture snapped in a full-size model of his Picture-Snapping Machine Invention shown in the cartoon. (1970)

AS YOU SIT ON PNEUMATIC CUSHION (A), YOU FORCE AIR THROUGH TUBE (B) WHICH STARTS ICE-BOAT (C), CAUSING LIGHTED CIGAR BUTT (D) TO EXPLODE BALLOON (E) — DICTATOR (F), HEARING LOUD REPORT, THINKS HE'S BEEN SHOT AND FALLS OVER BACKWARD ON BULB (G), SNAPPING PICTURE!
A
B
C
D
E
F
G
RUBE GOLDBERG

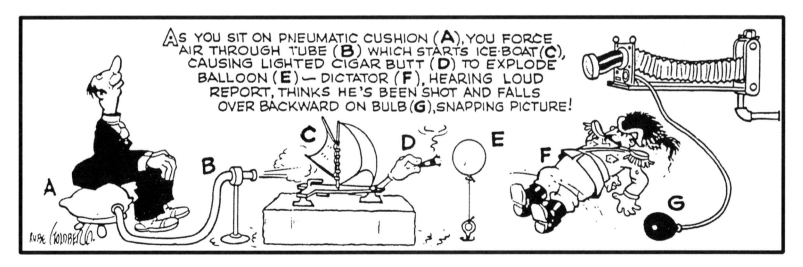

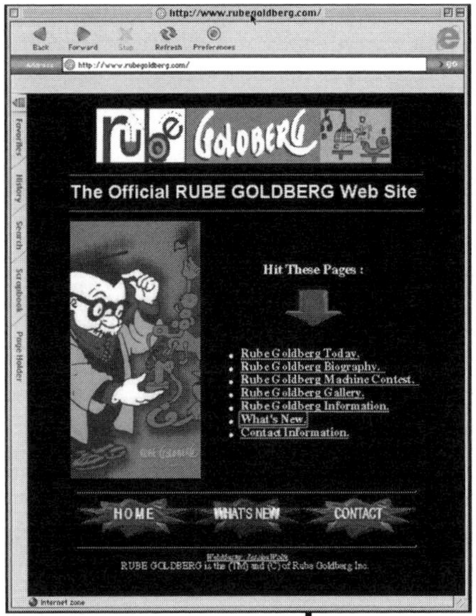
http://www.rubegoldberg.com/
Back
Forward
Stop
Refresh
Preferences
http://www.rubegoldberg.com/
The Official RUBE GOLDBERG Web Site
Hit These Pages :
Rube Goldberg Today.
Rube Goldberg Biography.
Rube Goldberg Machine Contest.
Rube Goldberg Gallery.
Rube Goldberg Information.
What's New.
Contact Information.
HOME
WHAT'S NEW
CONTACT
RUBE GOLDBERG is the (TM) and (C) of Rube Goldberg Inc.
Internet zone

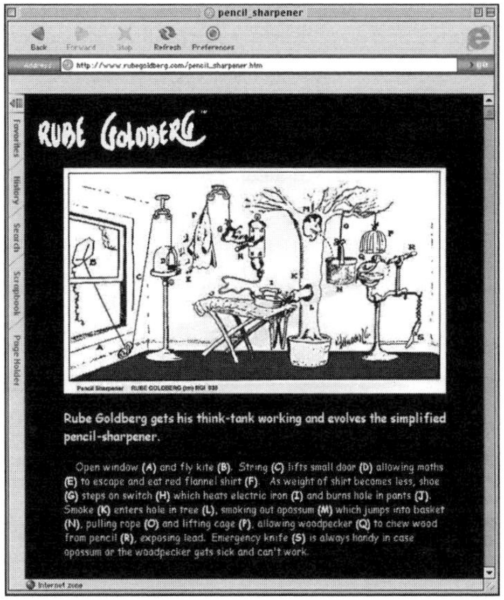
pencil_sharpener
Back
Forward
Stop
Refresh
Preferences
RUBE GOLDBERG
Rube Goldberg gets his think-tank working and evolves the simplified pencil-sharpener.
Open window (A) and fly kite (B). String (C) lifts small door (D) allowing moths (E) to escape and eat red flannel shirt (F). As weight of shirt becomes less, shoe (G) steps on switch (H) which heats electric iron (I) and burns hole in pants (J). Smoke (K) enters hole in tree (L), smoking out opossum (M) which jumps into basket (N), pulling rope (O) and lifting cage (P), allowing woodpecker (Q) to chew wood from pencil (R), exposing lead. Emergency knife (S) is always handy in case opossum or the woodpecker gets sick and can't work.
Internet zone

The Official Rube Goldberg Web Site is one of the thousands of references to Rube Goldberg and his work on the Worldwide Web.

and science centers throughout the country. There have been memorial exhibitions at the University of California, where his archives are held, and an exhibition at Williams College Art Museum, which also has a collection of Rube's work. In 1995 an outstanding show was held at the Salander-O'Reilly Galleries in New York City on the twenty-fifth anniversary of his death. Throughout his working life (almost seventy years), Rube authored ten books as well as a great number of short stories and feature articles for magazines. His cartoons are still being reprinted. A documentary and a feature film about Rube are both in development now.

Rube was also honored by having a U.S. postage stamp issued commemorating the Inventions as part of the Classic Comic Series. Of course, the stamp commemorating Rube had his name blazoned across it. He was the only cartoonist so honored; the others carried the name of their character on the front of the stamp, but not the name of its creator.

The Official Rube Goldberg Web site on the Internet at www.rubegoldberg.com is constantly being accessed, not only by interested adults but, most often, by boys and girls from elementary, middle, and high schools who are given simple machine projects by their teachers as classroom assignments that translate into their designing Rube Goldberg Invention Machines.

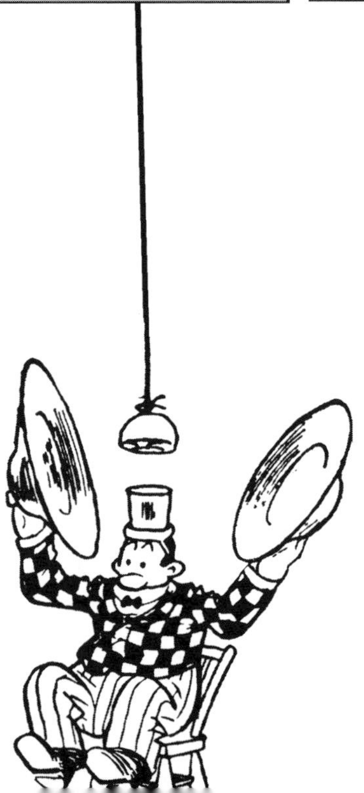

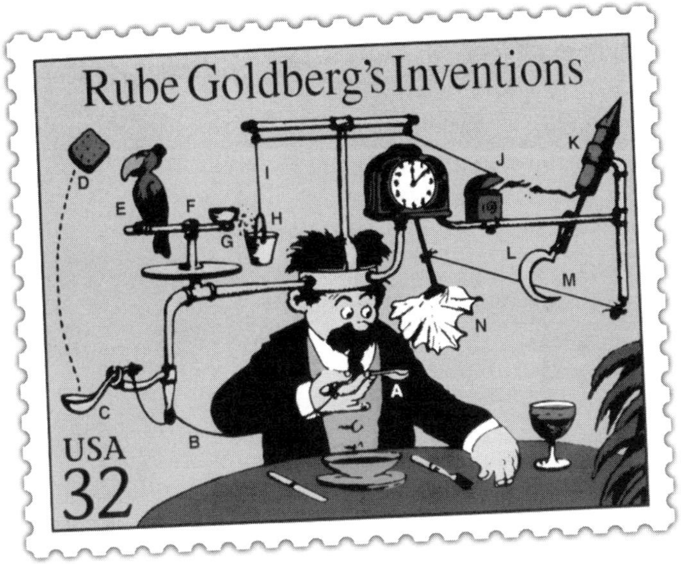
Rube Goldberg's Inventions
D
E
F
G
H
I
J
K
L
M
N
A
C
B
USA
32

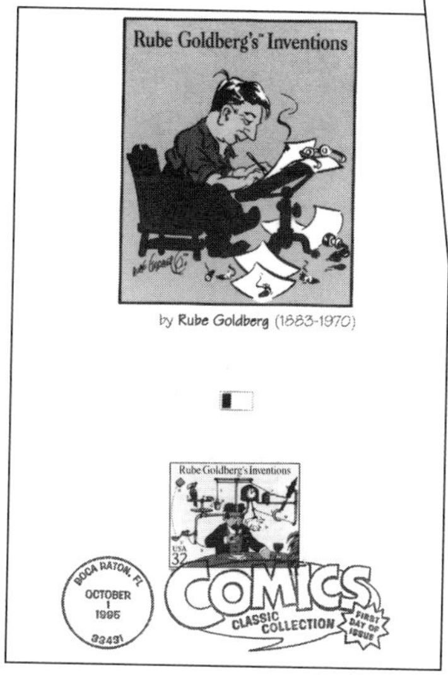
Rube Goldberg's' Inventions
by Rube Goldberg (1883-1970)
Rube Goldberg's Inventions
BOCA RATON, FL
OCTOBER
1
1995
33431
COMICS
CLASSIC COLLECTION
FIRST DAY OF ISSUE

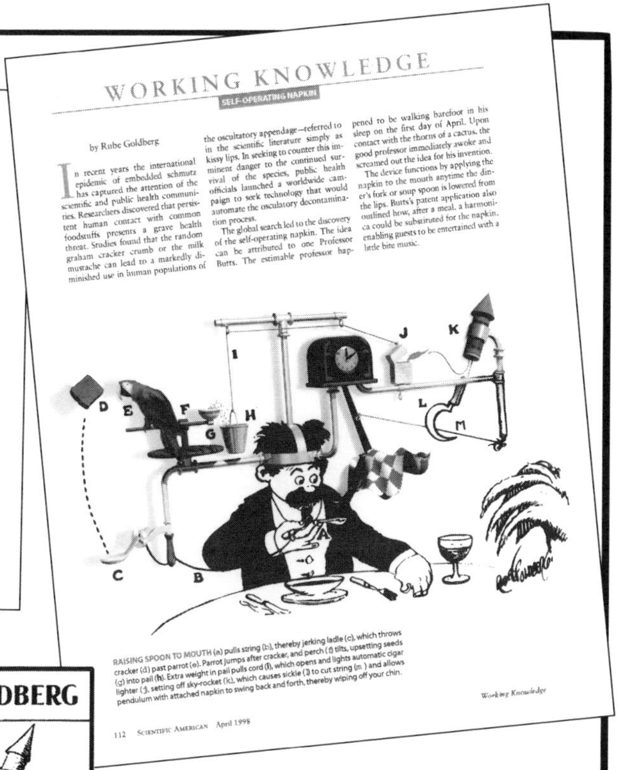

WORKING KNOWLEDGE

SELF-OPERATING NAPKIN

by Rube Goldberg

In recent years the international epidemic of embedded schmutz has captured the attention of the scientific and public health communities. Researchers discovered that persistent human contact with common foodstuffs presents a grave health threat. Studies found that the random graham cracker crumb or the milk mustache can lead to a markedly diminished use in human populations of the osculatory appendage—referred to in the scientific literature simply as kissy lips. In seeking to counter this imminent danger to the continued survival of the species, public health officials launched a worldwide campaign to seek technology that would automate the osculatory decontamination process.

The global search led to the discovery of the self-operating napkin. The idea can be attributed to one Professor Butts. The estimable professor happened to be walking barefoot in his sleep on the first day of April. Upon contact with the thorns of a cactus, the good professor immediately awoke and screamed out the idea for his invention.

The device functions by applying the napkin to the mouth anytime the diner's fork or soup spoon is lowered from the lips. Butts's patent application also outlined how, after a meal, a harmonica could be substituted for the napkin, enabling guests to be entertained with a little bite music.

I
J
K
D
E
F
G
H
L
M
C
B

RAISING SPOON TO MOUTH (a) pulls string (b), thereby jerking ladle (c), which throws cracker (d) past parrot (e). Parrot jumps after cracker, and perch (f) tilts, upsetting seeds (g) into pail (h). Extra weight in pail pulls cord (i), which opens and lights automatic cigar lighter (j), setting off sky-rocket (k), which causes sickle (l) to cut string (m) and allows pendulum with attached napkin to swing back and forth, thereby wiping off your chin.

Working Knowledge

112 Scientific American April 1998

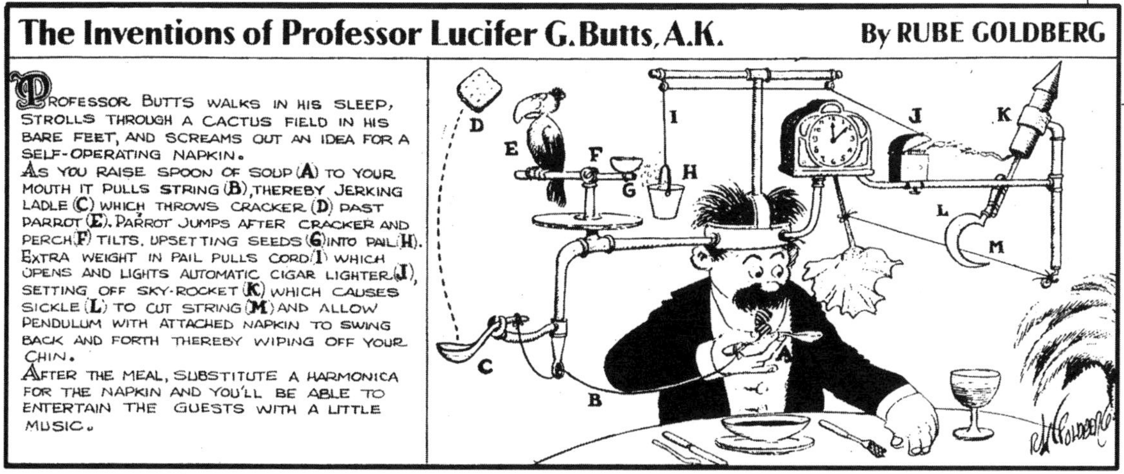
The Inventions of Professor Lucifer G. Butts, A.K.
By RUBE GOLDBERG
PROFESSOR BUTTS WALKS IN HIS SLEEP, STROLLS THROUGH A CACTUS FIELD IN HIS BARE FEET, AND SCREAMS OUT AN IDEA FOR A SELF-OPERATING NAPKIN.
AS YOU RAISE SPOON OF SOUP (A) TO YOUR MOUTH IT PULLS STRING (B), THEREBY JERKING LADLE (C) WHICH THROWS CRACKER (D) PAST PARROT (E). PARROT JUMPS AFTER CRACKER AND PERCH (F) TILTS, UPSETTING SEEDS (G) INTO PAIL (H). EXTRA WEIGHT IN PAIL PULLS CORD (I) WHICH OPENS AND LIGHTS AUTOMATIC CIGAR LIGHTER (J), SETTING OFF SKY-ROCKET (K) WHICH CAUSES SICKLE (L) TO CUT STRING (M) AND ALLOW PENDULUM WITH ATTACHED NAPKIN TO SWING BACK AND FORTH THEREBY WIPING OFF YOUR CHIN.
AFTER THE MEAL, SUBSTITUTE A HARMONICA FOR THE NAPKIN AND YOU'LL BE ABLE TO ENTERTAIN THE GUESTS WITH A LITTLE MUSIC.
D
E
F
G
H
I
J
K
L
M
A
C
B

Self-Operating Napkin

The Self-Operating Napkin was Rube Goldberg's most famous Invention. It has been reproduced in a number of different media, from Animated Animations' electronic tableau to Scientific American's 3-D combination of art and photography to the U.S. postage stamp that was part of the 1995 Classic Comics Commemorative series.

A Purdue University student cheers after a successful run of his team's machine at the annual Rube Goldberg Machine Contest held at the university. Teams were challenged to fill and seal a time capsule with significant inventions of the twentieth century.

Rube Goldberg's Inventions continue to inspire regional Rube Goldberg Machine Contests. Young engineering students from universities and colleges all over North America work to complete and run these inventive machines to meet the national challenge in the most complicated way possible. At the university level these local contest-winners meet at the annual national contest held at Purdue University. High schools are also now competing in rapidly expanding statewide contests that will lead to a high school national competition in the future.

Rube's name is quoted on a daily basis by the media in newspapers, magazines, radio, and television as an adjective to describe over-complicated, red-taped, complex rules, and other bureaucratic blunders, such as our "Rube Goldberg tax system" (*Congressional Record*).

Argonne National Labs Rube Goldberg Machine Contest for high schools.

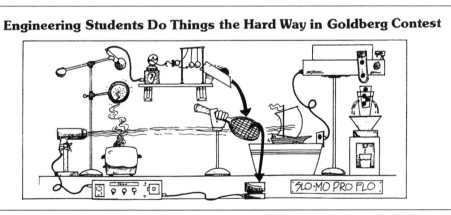

Engineering Students Do Things the Hard Way in Goldberg Contest

SLO-MO PRO FLO

This is the instructional drawing that illustrates the concept of the Rube Goldberg Machine Contest. The challenge is to build a machine that will fill a glass of water in twenty or more steps. Here, the task is accomplished in true Rube Goldberg style by burning a waffle in a toaster, which sets off a smoke alarm, which activates a microphone, which then starts a small electric motor that winds up a string attached to a magnet that pulls a ball back ... well, you get the idea. The glass of water is shown being filled at the lower right of the picture.

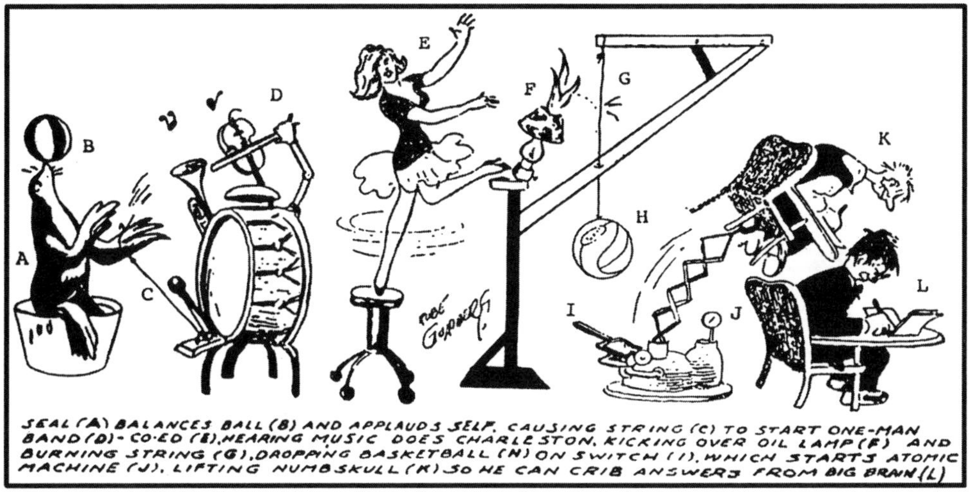
A
B
C
D
E
F
G
H
I
J
K
L
SEAL (A) BALANCES BALL (B) AND APPLAUDS SELF, CAUSING STRING (C) TO START ONE-MAN BAND (D) - CO-ED (E), HEARING MUSIC DOES CHARLESTON, KICKING OVER OIL LAMP (F) AND BURNING STRING (G), DROPPING BASKETBALL (H) ON SWITCH (I), WHICH STARTS ATOMIC MACHINE (J), LIFTING NUMBSKULL (K) SO HE CAN CRIB ANSWERS FROM BIG BRAIN (L)

Rube Goldberg drew this Invention drawing for the Phi chapter of the national engineering fraternity Theta Tau, which started the Rube Goldberg Machine Contest at Purdue University more than forty years ago.

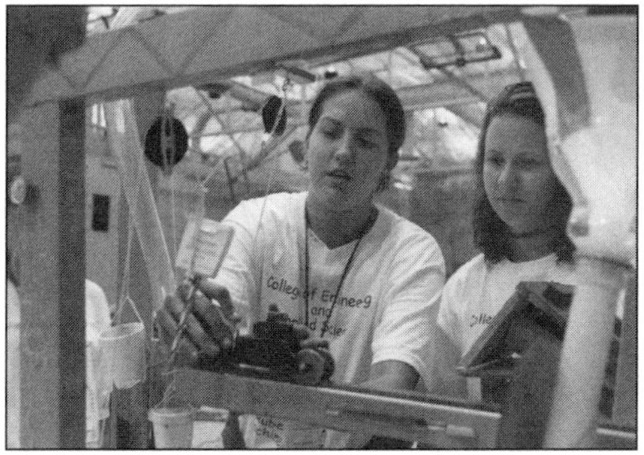

Wisconsin State High School Rube Goldberg Machine Contest, held at the University of Wisconsin's Milwaukee campus.

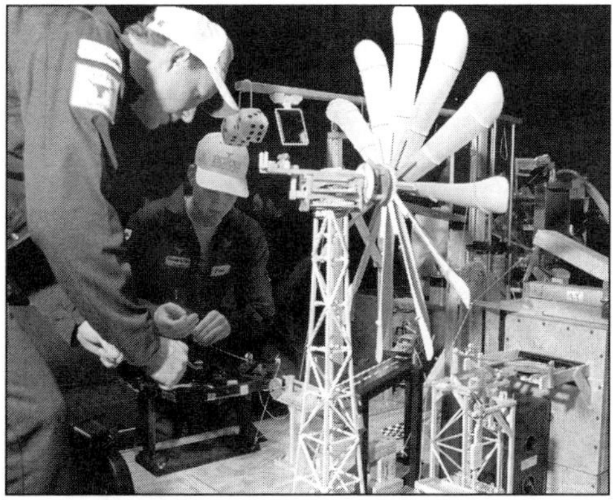

Rube Goldberg Machine Contest at Purdue University. Winning University of Texas team with a golf cart that set and teed up a golf ball.

Here are a few more recent Rube Goldberg mentions:

The New York Times: "Rube Goldberg Meets Government Planners: Overhauling the Federal Milk-Pricing System."

Newsweek: "Rube Goldberg in Silicon Valley: Could This Contraption One Day Be in Wide Use to Clean Air?"

Time: "Federal officials examined the aircraft and decided it owed more to Rube Goldberg than Orville Wright."

On a more positive note, Rube's name was used by NASA engineers to describe their very successful Mars *Sojourner* vehicle as a "Rube Goldberg contraption" put together on a very tight budget and with a lot of hope. Rube would have been enormously proud to have been part of America's first trip to Mars.

In his own way, Rube resembled quantum physicists who turn classical notions of time and space topsy-turvy. Physicists do it with digits. Rube did it with dogs, birds, people, plants, levers, wheels, gears, and pulleys. By disobeying Mother Nature, Rube Goldberg took his readers on wonderful journeys to his own delightful universe.

Inventions

Rube Goldberg's Inventions were, in his own words, "symbols of man's capacity for exerting maximum effort to accomplish minimum results."

The Inventions use their unique Goldbergian logic to solve the stresses that occur when technology meets daily life…stresses that are as pertinent today as they were when Rube created them.

Rube used his talent for storytelling as well as his drawing skills (aided not only by his sense of humor but also by an engineering degree) to make sure that his Inventions worked. They might need time, lots of time with very patient and dedicated people, animals, and growing plants to accomplish their inventors' goal, but they worked.

Today, the phrase "Rube Goldberg Inventions" has become such a familiar part of the English language that its mention brings almost instant recognition, a laugh, and an image of how the simplest task can be done in the most convoluted and complicated way.

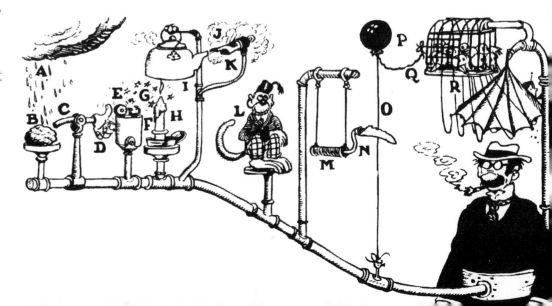

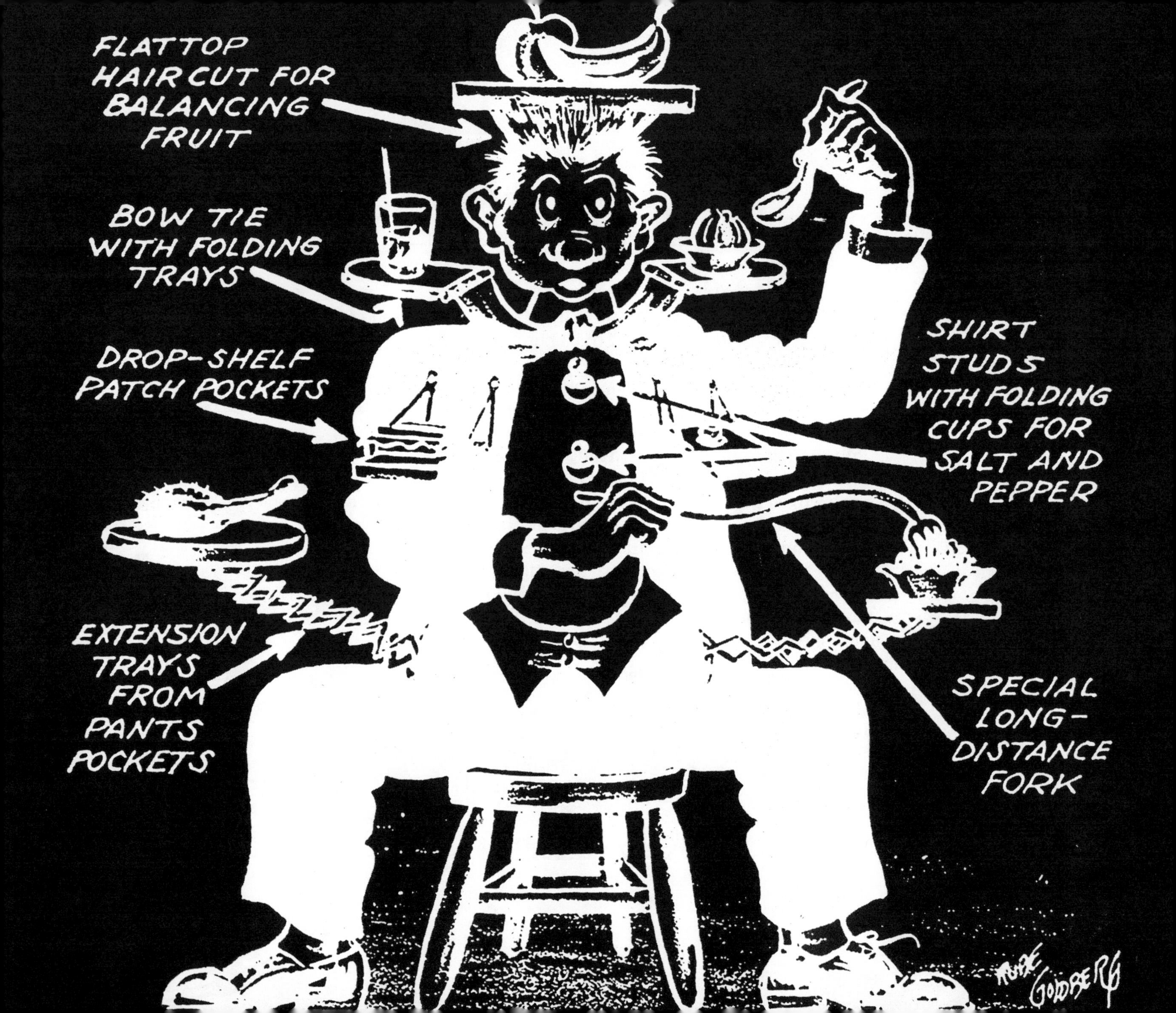
FLATTOP HAIRCUT FOR BALANCING FRUIT
BOW TIE WITH FOLDING TRAYS
DROP-SHELF PATCH POCKETS
SHIRT STUDS WITH FOLDING CUPS FOR SALT AND PEPPER
EXTENSION TRAYS FROM PANTS POCKETS
SPECIAL LONG-DISTANCE FORK
RUBE GOLDBERG

Eating & Drinking

Whether one frequents restaurants, attends the theater or movies, or stays home, a good part of the good life—or even the not-so-good life—is taken up with eating and drinking. Entertaining at home, especially, requires attention and dedication to all the details, from making small talk to opening the bottles of your guests' favorite drinks.

Rube Goldberg wanted to make sure that modern technology was there to help, from the time you get up in the morning for breakfast to bedtime, from your first glass of orange juice to washing the supper dishes. Rube Goldberg's Inventions are there to make life much easier ... often by the most complicated means.

You can solve almost any problem, and prevent the potential disasters that can happen to people who want to celebrate life and entertain without worrying about it, by using "Goldbergian logic," as illustrated on the following pages.

Automatic Liquor Tester

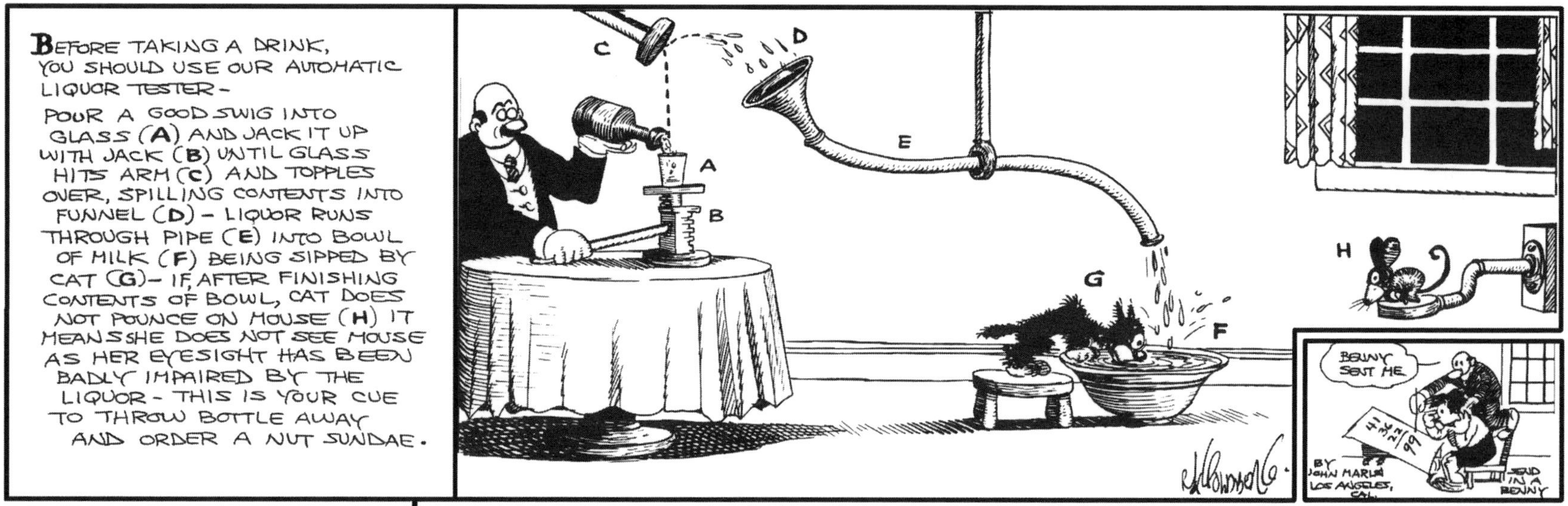
BEFORE TAKING A DRINK, YOU SHOULD USE OUR AUTOMATIC LIQUOR TESTER-
POUR A GOOD SWIG INTO GLASS (A) AND JACK IT UP WITH JACK (B) UNTIL GLASS HITS ARM (C) AND TOPPLES OVER, SPILLING CONTENTS INTO FUNNEL (D) - LIQUOR RUNS THROUGH PIPE (E) INTO BOWL OF MILK (F) BEING SIPPED BY CAT (G)- IF, AFTER FINISHING CONTENTS OF BOWL, CAT DOES NOT POUNCE ON MOUSE (H) IT MEANS SHE DOES NOT SEE MOUSE AS HER EYESIGHT HAS BEEN BADLY IMPAIRED BY THE LIQUOR - THIS IS YOUR CUE TO THROW BOTTLE AWAY AND ORDER A NUT SUNDAE.
C
D
A
B
E
G
F
H
BENNY SENT ME
BY JOHN MARLIN LOS ANGELES, CAL.
SEND IN A BENNY

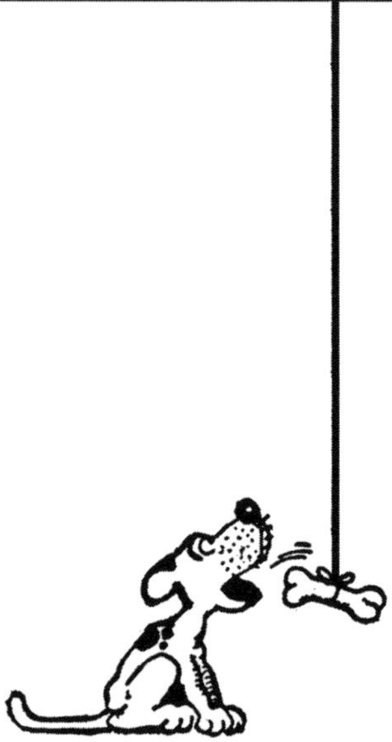

Simple Idea for Cooling a Plate of Soup

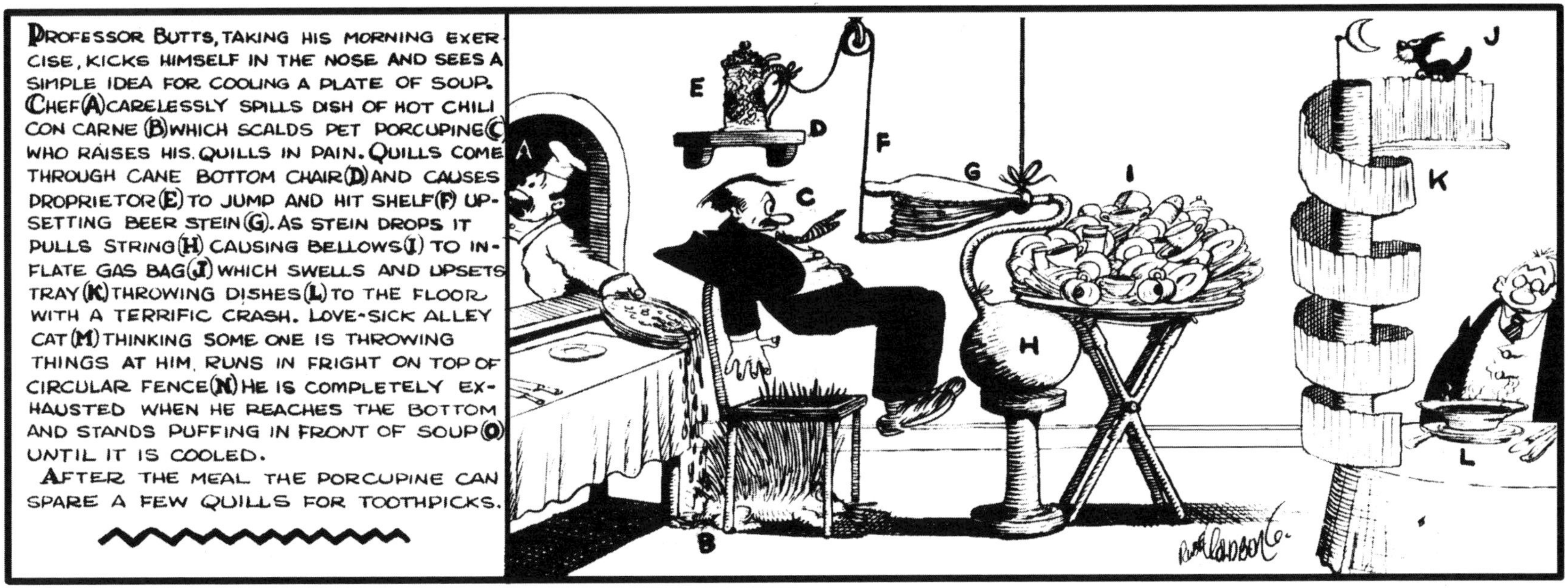
PROFESSOR BUTTS, TAKING HIS MORNING EXERCISE, KICKS HIMSELF IN THE NOSE AND SEES A SIMPLE IDEA FOR COOLING A PLATE OF SOUP. CHEF(A) CARELESSLY SPILLS DISH OF HOT CHILI CON CARNE (B) WHICH SCALDS PET PORCUPINE (C) WHO RAISES HIS QUILLS IN PAIN. QUILLS COME THROUGH CANE BOTTOM CHAIR (D) AND CAUSES PROPRIETOR (E) TO JUMP AND HIT SHELF (F) UPSETTING BEER STEIN (G). AS STEIN DROPS IT PULLS STRING (H) CAUSING BELLOWS (I) TO INFLATE GAS BAG (J) WHICH SWELLS AND UPSETS TRAY (K) THROWING DISHES (L) TO THE FLOOR WITH A TERRIFIC CRASH. LOVE-SICK ALLEY CAT (M) THINKING SOME ONE IS THROWING THINGS AT HIM, RUNS IN FRIGHT ON TOP OF CIRCULAR FENCE (N) HE IS COMPLETELY EXHAUSTED WHEN HE REACHES THE BOTTOM AND STANDS PUFFING IN FRONT OF SOUP (O) UNTIL IT IS COOLED.
AFTER THE MEAL THE PORCUPINE CAN SPARE A FEW QUILLS FOR TOOTHPICKS.
A
B
C
D
E
F
G
H
I
J
K
L

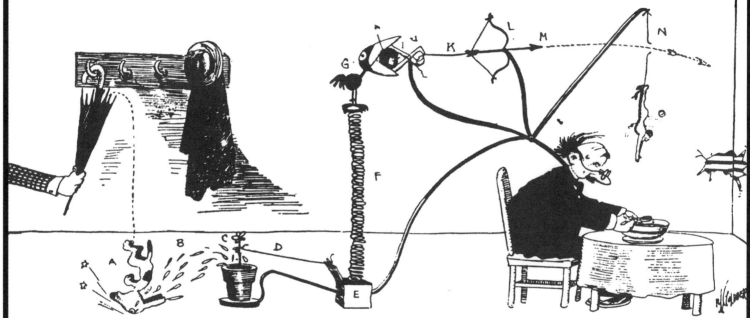

WEAR ONE OF OUR UMBRELLA-ALARMS AND NO ONE CAN STEAL YOUR UMBRELLA—By Goldberg

ALWAYS CARRY A PRUNE-HOUND IN YOUR UMBRELLA - WHEN THIEF'S HAND GRABS UMBRELLA, PRUNE-HOUND (A) WAKES UP AND JUMPS OUT FROM FRIGHT-HE HITS HEAD TERRIBLE BUMP ON FLOOR AND STARTS CRYING - TEARS (B) WATER PLANT (C) WHICH GROWS AND PULLS STRING (D), OPENING BOX (E) AND RELEASING SPRING (F). BOOB-BIRD (G) IS RAISED TO APPLE (H), HELD BETWEEN TWEEZERS (I) - BIRD BITES APPLE, OPENING GRIP (J), LETTING CORD (K) LOOSE. CONSEQUENTLY, BOW (L) SHOOTS ARROW (M) INTO THREAD (N), CUTTING IT IN HALF AND DROPPING IMAGE OF ANNETTE KELLERMAN (O) INTO THE SOUP, GIVING THE OWNER OF THE UMBRELLA INSTANT WARNING OF FOUL PLAY.

Simple Way to Open an Egg Without Dropping It in Your Lap

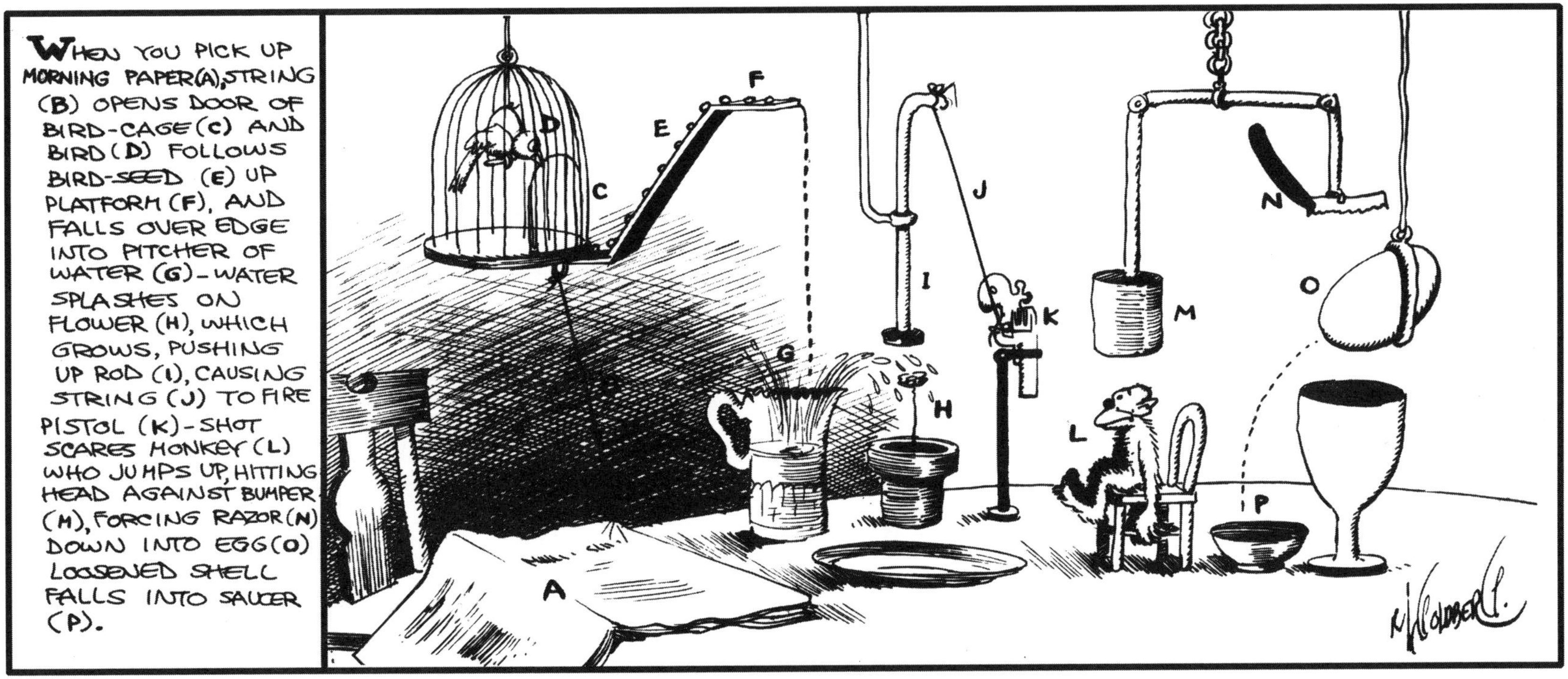
WHEN YOU PICK UP MORNING PAPER (A), STRING (B) OPENS DOOR OF BIRD-CAGE (C) AND BIRD (D) FOLLOWS BIRD-SEED (E) UP PLATFORM (F), AND FALLS OVER EDGE INTO PITCHER OF WATER (G) - WATER SPLASHES ON FLOWER (H), WHICH GROWS, PUSHING UP ROD (I), CAUSING STRING (J) TO FIRE PISTOL (K) - SHOT SCARES MONKEY (L) WHO JUMPS UP, HITTING HEAD AGAINST BUMPER (M), FORCING RAZOR (N) DOWN INTO EGG (O) LOOSENED SHELL FALLS INTO SAUCER (P).
A
C
D
E
F
G
H
I
J
K
L
M
N
O
P

Simple Way to Fish an Olive Out of One of Those Long-Necked Bottles

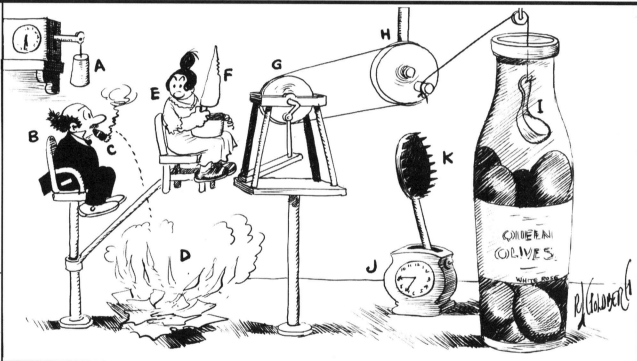

AT 6:30 WEIGHT (A) AUTOMATICALLY DROPS ON HEAD OF DWARF (B), CAUSING HIM TO YELL AND DROP CIGAR (C), WHICH SETS FIRE TO PAPER (D)-HEAT FROM FIRE ANGERS DWARF'S WIFE (E)-SHE SHARPEN'S POTATO KNIFE (F) ON GRINDSTONE (G) WHICH TURNS WHEEL (H) CAUSING OLIVE SPOON (I) TO DIP REPEATEDLY INTO OLIVES-IF SPOON DOES NOT LIFT AN OLIVE IN 15 MINUTES, CLOCK (J) AUTOMATICALLY PUSHES GLASS-CUTTER (K) AGAINST BOTTLE AND TAKES OUT CHUNK OF GLASS BIG ENOUGH FOR YOU TO STICK YOUR FINGER IN AND PULL OUT AN OLIVE.
A
B
C
D
E
F
G
H
I
J
K
QUEEN OLIVES
WHITE ROSE

A Self-Working Corkscrew

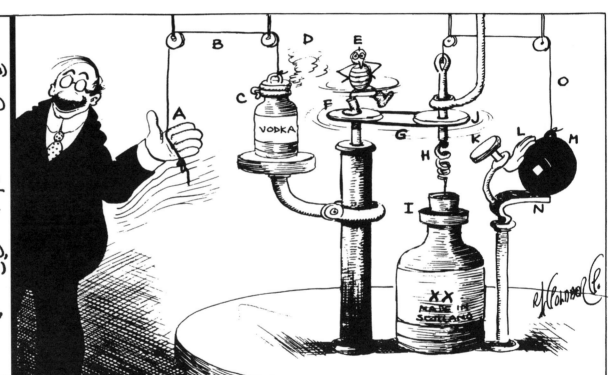

WHEN YOU SAY "HAVE A DRINK", NATURAL MOTION OF HAND (A) PULLS STRING (B) AND LIFTS LID (C), RE-LEASING VODKA FUMES (D) WHICH MAKE RUSSIAN DANCING-BUG (E) FEEL GIDDY - HE STARTS DANCING NATIONL DANCE OF RUSSIA AND REVOLVES PLATFORM (F)- PULLEY (G) TURNS CORK-SCREW (H) AND IT SINKS INTO CORK (I) BRINGING DOWN DISC (J), WHICH HITS SURFACE (K) AND CAUSES WOODEN HAND TO PUSH IRON BALL (M) OFF SUPPORT (N), CAUSING CORD (O) TO PULL CORKSCREW WITH CORK FROM BOTTLE.
VODKA
XX
MADE IN SCOTLAND

Simple Way to Carve a Turkey

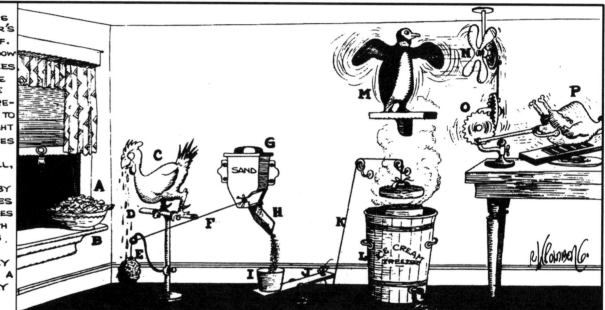

SIMPLE WAY TO CARVE A TURKEY. THIS INVENTION FELL OFF THE PROFESSOR'S HEAD WITH THE REST OF THE DANDRUFF.

PUT BOWL OF CHICKEN SALAD (A) ON WINDOW SILL (B) TO COOL. ROOSTER (C) RECOGNIZES HIS WIFE IN SALAD AND IS OVERCOME WITH GRIEF. HIS TEARS (D) SATURATE SPONGE (E), PULLING STRING (F) WHICH RELEASES TRAP DOOR (G) AND ALLOWS SAND TO RUN DOWN TROUGH (H) INTO PAIL (I). WEIGHT RAISES END OF SEE-SAW (J) WHICH MAKES CORD (K) LIFT COVER OF ICE CREAM FREEZER (L). PENGUIN (M) FEELING CHILL, THINKS HE IS AT THE NORTH POLE AND FLAPS WINGS FOR JOY, THEREBY FANNING PROPELLER (N) WHICH REVOLVES AND TURNS COGS (O) WHICH IN TURN CAUSES TURKEY (P) TO SLIDE BACK AND FORTH OVER CABBAGE-CUTTER UNTIL IT IS SLICED TO A FRAZZLE —

DON'T GET DISCOURAGED IF THE TURKEY GETS PRETTY WELL MESSED UP. IT'S A CINCH IT WOULD HAVE EVENTUALLY BECOME TURKEY HASH ANYWAY.

A
B
C
D
E
F
G
SAND
H
I
J
K
L
ICE CREAM FREEZER
M
N
O
P

Sending a Late Stayer Home

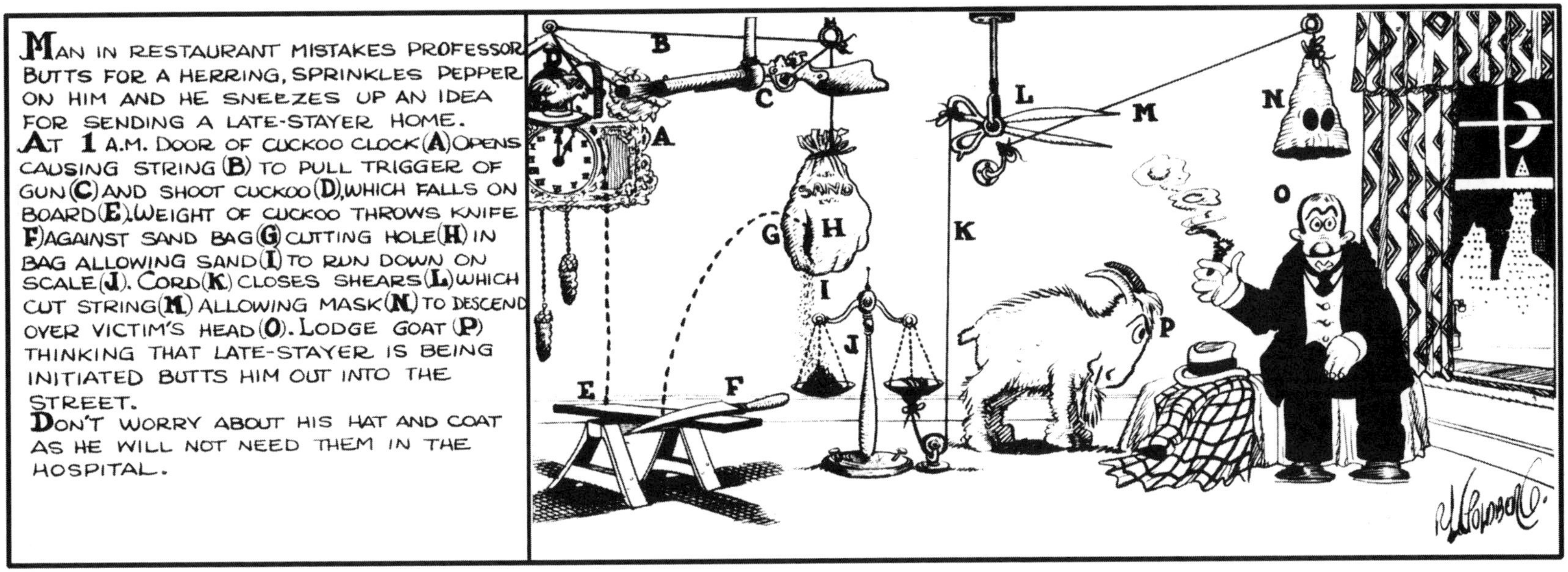
MAN IN RESTAURANT MISTAKES PROFESSOR BUTTS FOR A HERRING, SPRINKLES PEPPER ON HIM AND HE SNEEZES UP AN IDEA FOR SENDING A LATE-STAYER HOME.
AT 1 A.M. DOOR OF CUCKOO CLOCK (A) OPENS CAUSING STRING (B) TO PULL TRIGGER OF GUN (C) AND SHOOT CUCKOO (D), WHICH FALLS ON BOARD (E). WEIGHT OF CUCKOO THROWS KNIFE (F) AGAINST SAND BAG (G) CUTTING HOLE (H) IN BAG ALLOWING SAND (I) TO RUN DOWN ON SCALE (J). CORD (K) CLOSES SHEARS (L) WHICH CUT STRING (M) ALLOWING MASK (N) TO DESCEND OVER VICTIM'S HEAD (O). LODGE GOAT (P) THINKING THAT LATE-STAYER IS BEING INITIATED BUTTS HIM OUT INTO THE STREET.
DON'T WORRY ABOUT HIS HAT AND COAT AS HE WILL NOT NEED THEM IN THE HOSPITAL.
SAND
A
B
C
D
E
F
G
H
I
J
K
L
M
N
O
P

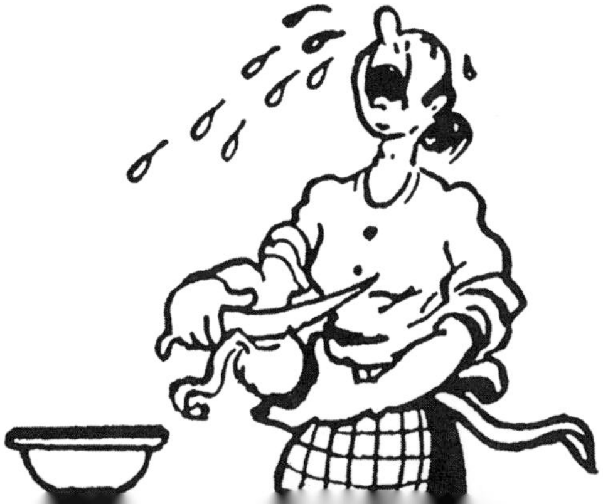

Invention for Putting Sardine in a Can

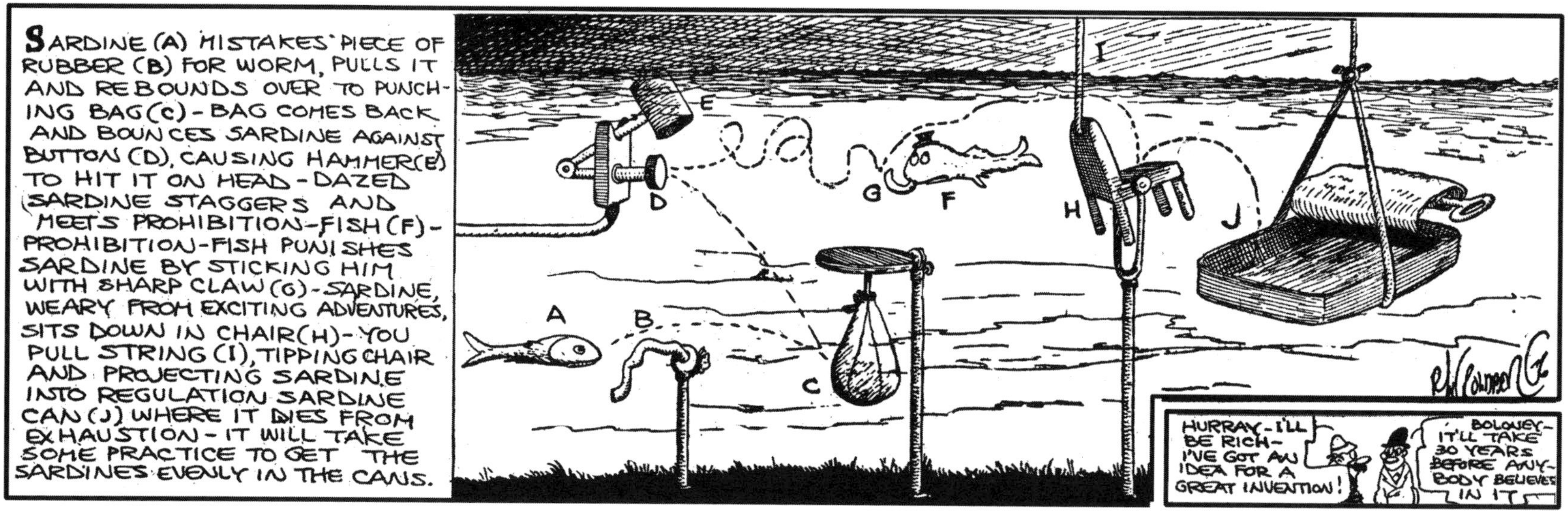
SARDINE (A) MISTAKES PIECE OF RUBBER (B) FOR WORM, PULLS IT AND REBOUNDS OVER TO PUNCHING BAG (C) - BAG COMES BACK AND BOUNCES SARDINE AGAINST BUTTON (D), CAUSING HAMMER (E) TO HIT IT ON HEAD - DAZED SARDINE STAGGERS AND MEETS PROHIBITION-FISH (F) - PROHIBITION-FISH PUNISHES SARDINE BY STICKING HIM WITH SHARP CLAW (G) - SARDINE, WEARY FROM EXCITING ADVENTURES, SITS DOWN IN CHAIR (H) - YOU PULL STRING (I), TIPPING CHAIR AND PROJECTING SARDINE INTO REGULATION SARDINE CAN (J) WHERE IT DIES FROM EXHAUSTION - IT WILL TAKE SOME PRACTICE TO GET THE SARDINES EVENLY IN THE CANS.
E
D
G
F
I
H
J
A
B
C
HURRAY - I'LL BE RICH - I'VE GOT AN IDEA FOR A GREAT INVENTION!
BOLONEY - IT'LL TAKE 30 YEARS BEFORE ANYBODY BELIEVES IN IT

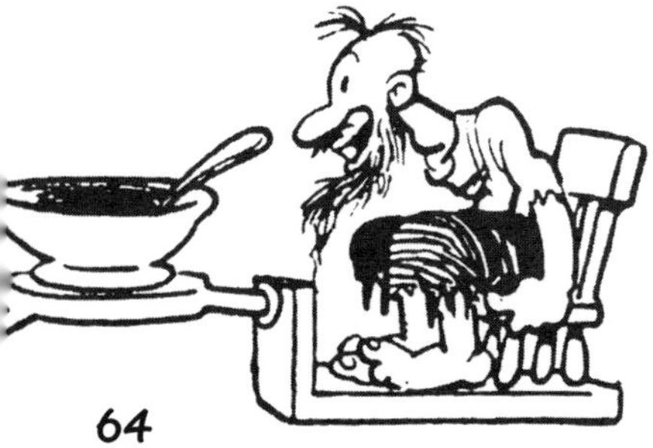

Automatic Dishwasher

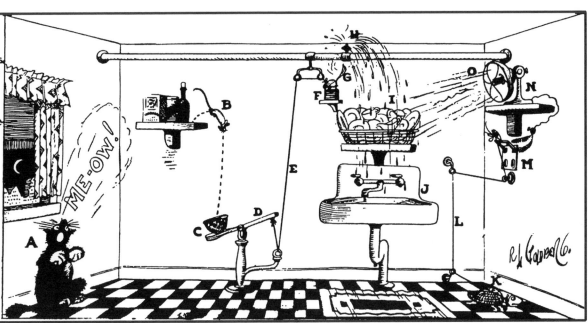

THE PROFESSOR TURNS ON HIS THINK-FAUCET AND DOPES OUT A MACHINE FOR WASHING DISHES WHILE YOU ARE AT THE MOVIES.
WHEN SPOILED TOMCAT (A) DISCOVERS HE IS ALONE HE LETS OUT A YELL WHICH SCARES MOUSE (B) INTO JUMPING INTO BASKET (C), CAUSING LEVER END (D) TO RISE AND PULL STRING (E) WHICH SNAPS AUTOMATIC CIGAR LIGHTER (F). FLAME (G) STARTS FIRE SPRINKLER (H). WATER RUNS ON DISHES (I) AND DRIPS INTO SINK (J). TURTLE (K), THINKING HE HEARS BABBLING BROOK BABBLING, AND HAVING NO SENSE OF DIRECTION, STARTS WRONG WAY AND PULLS STRING (L), WHICH TURNS ON SWITCH (M) THAT STARTS ELECTRIC GLOW HEATER (N). HEAT RAY (O) DRIES THE DISHES.
IF THE CAT AND THE TURTLE GET ON TO YOUR SCHEME AND REFUSE TO COOPERATE, SIMPLY PUT THE DISHES ON THE FRONT PORCH AND PRAY FOR RAIN.
ME-OW!
A
B
C
D
E
F
G
H
I
J
K
L
M
N
O
R. Goldberg

Simple Orange-Squeezing Machine

PROFESSOR BUTTS STEPS INTO AN OPEN ELEVATOR SHAFT AND WHEN HE LANDS AT THE BOTTOM HE FINDS A SIMPLE ORANGE SQUEEZING MACHINE. MILK MAN TAKES EMPTY MILK BOTTLE (A) PULLING STRING (B) WHICH CAUSES SWORD (C) TO SEVER CORD (D) AND ALLOW GUILLOTINE BLADE (E) TO DROP AND CUT ROPE (F) WHICH RELEASES BATTERING RAM (G). RAM BUMPS AGAINST OPEN DOOR (H) CAUSING IT TO CLOSE. GRASS SICKLE (I) CUTS A SLICE OFF END OF ORANGE (J) AT THE SAME TIME SPIKE (K) STABS "PRUNE HAWK" (L) HE OPENS HIS MOUTH TO YELL IN AGONY, THEREBY RELEASING PRUNE AND ALLOWING DIVER'S BOOT (M) TO DROP AND STEP ON SLEEPING OCTOPUS (N). OCTOPUS AWAKENS IN A RAGE AND SEEING DIVER'S FACE WHICH IS PAINTED ON ORANGE, ATTACKS IT AND CRUSHES IT WITH TENTACLES, THEREBY CAUSING ALL THE JUICE IN THE ORANGE TO RUN INTO GLASS (O).

LATER ON YOU CAN USE THE LOG TO BUILD A LOG CABIN WHERE YOU CAN RAISE YOUR SON TO BE PRESIDENT LIKE ABRAHAM LINCOLN.

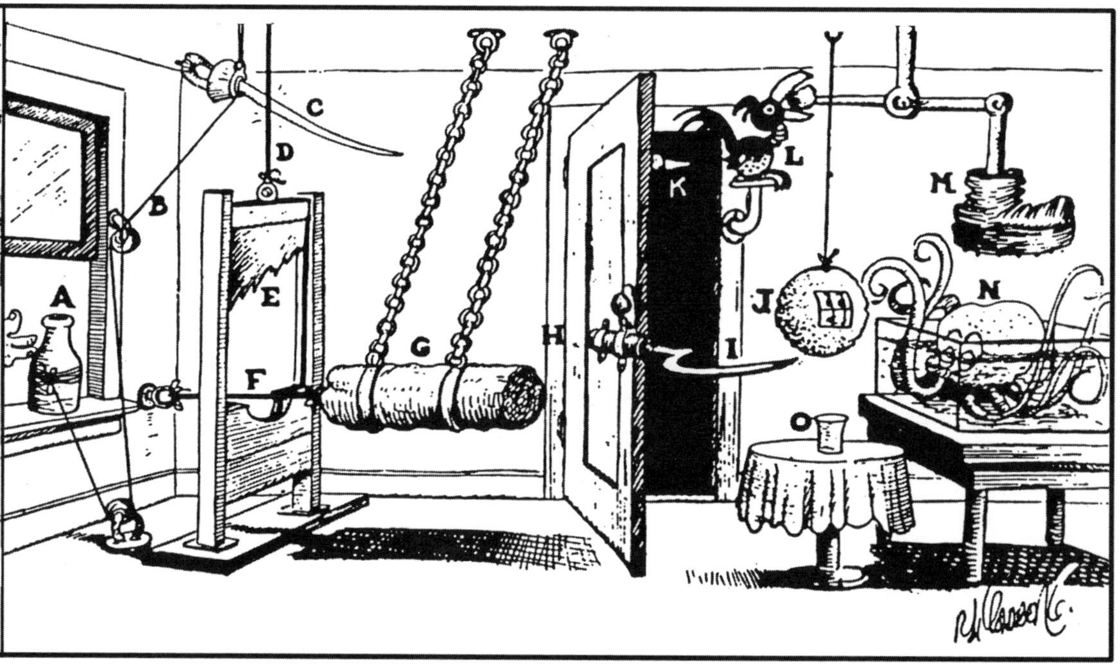
A
B
C
D
E
F
G
H
I
J
K
L
M
N
O

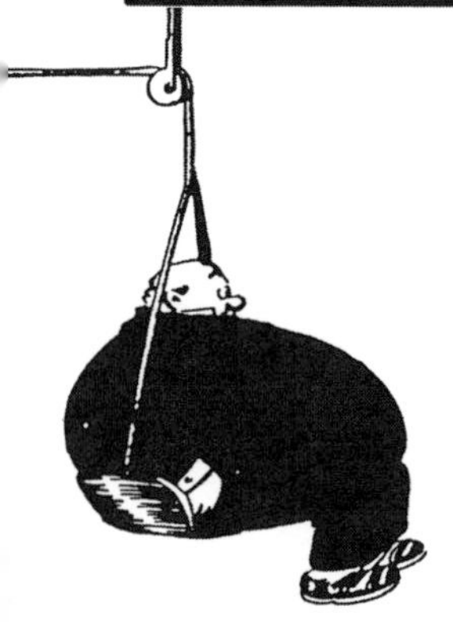

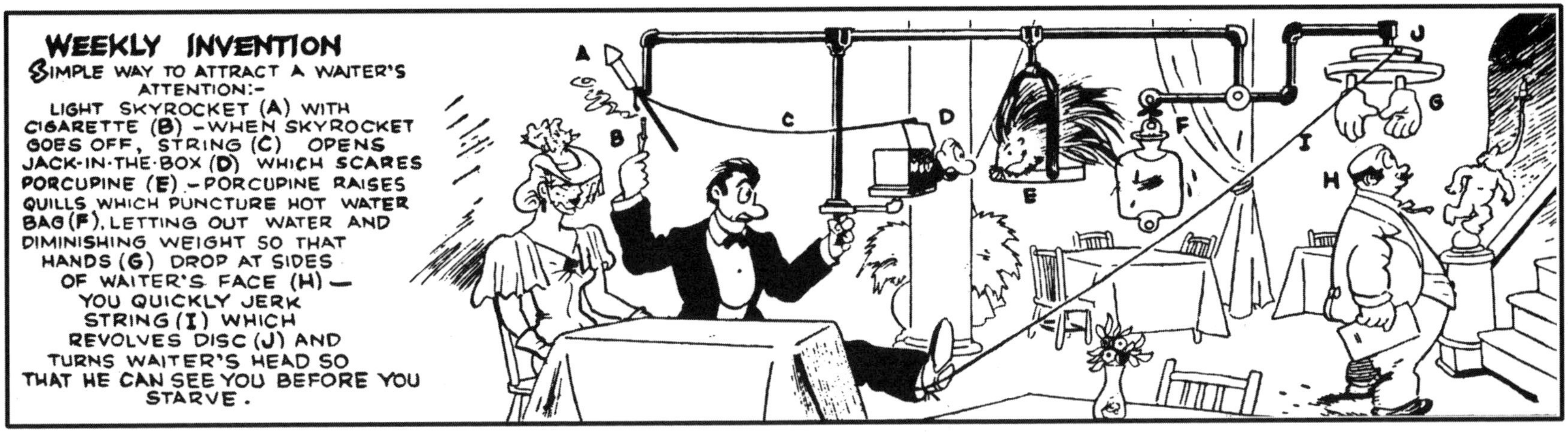
WEEKLY INVENTION
SIMPLE WAY TO ATTRACT A WAITER'S ATTENTION:- LIGHT SKYROCKET (A) WITH CIGARETTE (B) - WHEN SKYROCKET GOES OFF, STRING (C) OPENS JACK-IN-THE-BOX (D) WHICH SCARES PORCUPINE (E) - PORCUPINE RAISES QUILLS WHICH PUNCTURE HOT WATER BAG (F), LETTING OUT WATER AND DIMINISHING WEIGHT SO THAT HANDS (G) DROP AT SIDES OF WAITER'S FACE (H) — YOU QUICKLY JERK STRING (I) WHICH REVOLVES DISC (J) AND TURNS WAITER'S HEAD SO THAT HE CAN SEE YOU BEFORE YOU STARVE.
A
B
C
D
E
F
G
H
I
J

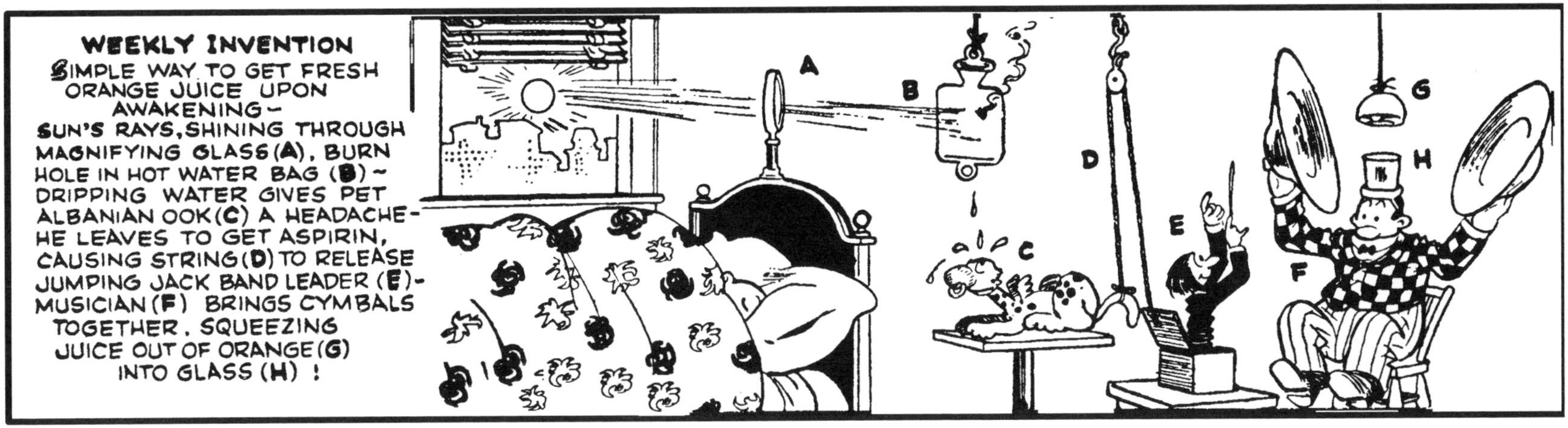
WEEKLY INVENTION
SIMPLE WAY TO GET FRESH ORANGE JUICE UPON AWAKENING - SUN'S RAYS, SHINING THROUGH MAGNIFYING GLASS (A), BURN HOLE IN HOT WATER BAG (B) - DRIPPING WATER GIVES PET ALBANIAN OOK (C) A HEADACHE - HE LEAVES TO GET ASPIRIN, CAUSING STRING (D) TO RELEASE JUMPING JACK BAND LEADER (E) - MUSICIAN (F) BRINGS CYMBALS TOGETHER, SQUEEZING JUICE OUT OF ORANGE (G) INTO GLASS (H) !
A
B
C
D
E
F
G
H

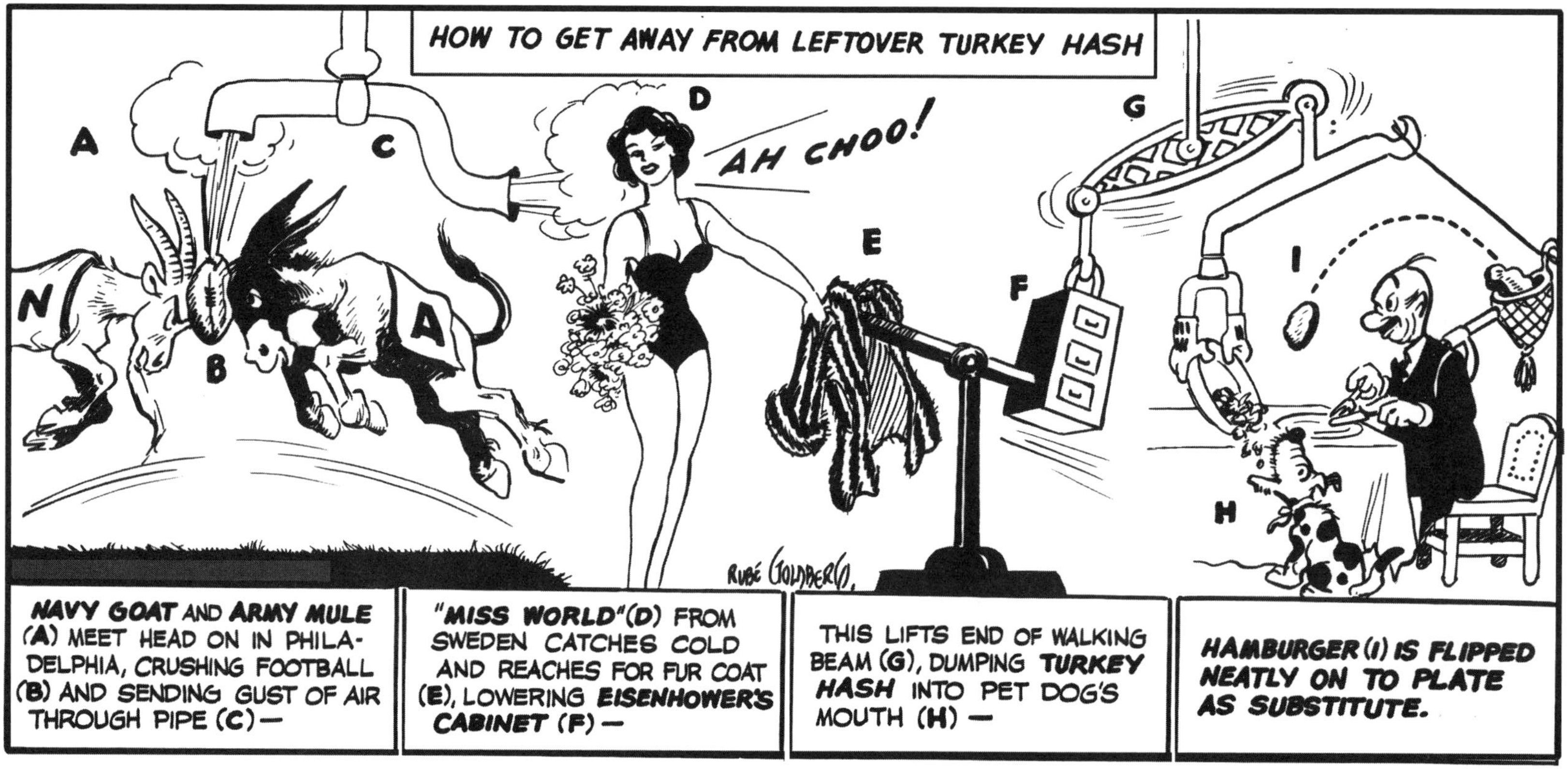
HOW TO GET AWAY FROM LEFTOVER TURKEY HASH
A
C
D
AH CHOO!
G
N
B
A
E
F
I
H
NAVY GOAT AND ARMY MULE (A) MEET HEAD ON IN PHILA-DELPHIA, CRUSHING FOOTBALL (B) AND SENDING GUST OF AIR THROUGH PIPE (C)—
"MISS WORLD" (D) FROM SWEDEN CATCHES COLD AND REACHES FOR FUR COAT (E), LOWERING EISENHOWER'S CABINET (F)—
THIS LIFTS END OF WALKING BEAM (G), DUMPING TURKEY HASH INTO PET DOG'S MOUTH (H)—
HAMBURGER (I) IS FLIPPED NEATLY ON TO PLATE AS SUBSTITUTE.

HOW TO ENJOY HOLIDAYS
SNOW FALLS INTO BUCKET, CAUSING THUMB TO OPEN BOTTLE OF CHAMPAGNE- CORK HITS LEVER, LIFTING HEAVY LOAD OFF YOUR NECK SO YOU CAN SIT UP AND SEE BEAUTIFUL GIRL THROUGH SPARKLING CHAMPAGNE BUBBLES!
BILLS
PRICES
TAXES
TENSION
RUBE GOLDBERG

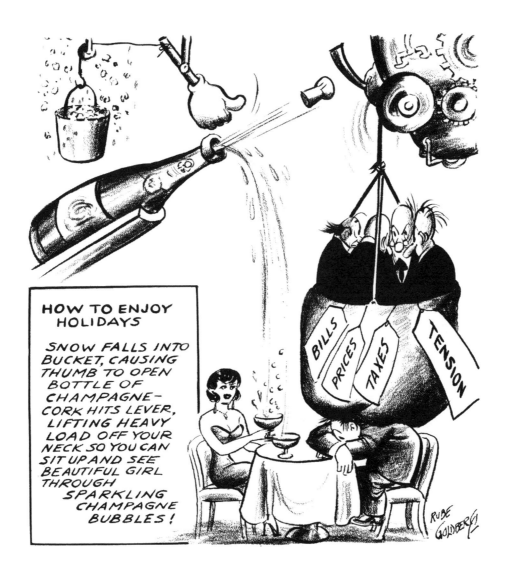

Every Woman Can Have a Perfect Figure

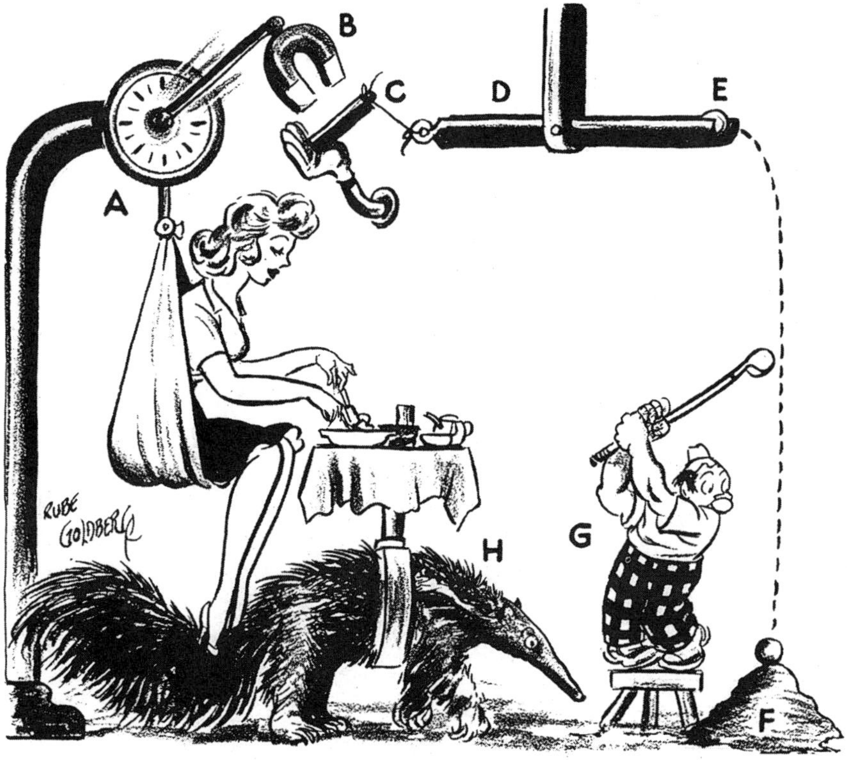
A
B
C
D
E
F
G
H
RUBE GOLDBERG

EVERY WOMAN TO HAVE A PERFECT FIGURE–
SHE SITS DOWN TO EAT IN SCALE (A) – AS WEIGHT INCREASES, MAGNET (B) MOVES TOWARDS SMALL STEEL BAR (C), PICKING IT UP AND TILTING GROOVE (D)– GOLF BALL (E) DROPS ON ANT-HILL (F) – MIDGET BEGINNER (G) TAKES SWING AT BALL, MISSES IT AND KNOCKS CHUNK OUT OF ANT-HILL, SCATTERING ANTS– ANTEATER (H) GOES AFTER ANTS, MOVING TABLE AWAY FROM HUNGRY YOUNG LADY, ALLOWING HER TO PRESERVE HER BEAUTIFUL FIGURE.

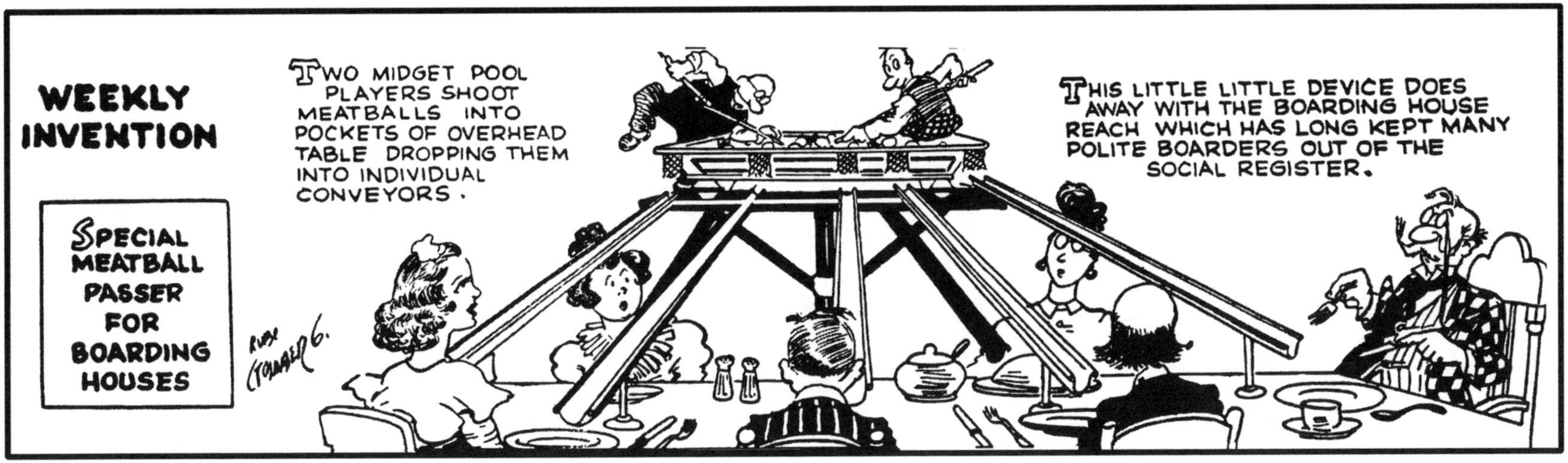
WEEKLY INVENTION
SPECIAL MEATBALL PASSER FOR BOARDING HOUSES
TWO MIDGET POOL PLAYERS SHOOT MEATBALLS INTO POCKETS OF OVERHEAD TABLE DROPPING THEM INTO INDIVIDUAL CONVEYORS.
THIS LITTLE LITTLE DEVICE DOES AWAY WITH THE BOARDING HOUSE REACH WHICH HAS LONG KEPT MANY POLITE BOARDERS OUT OF THE SOCIAL REGISTER.

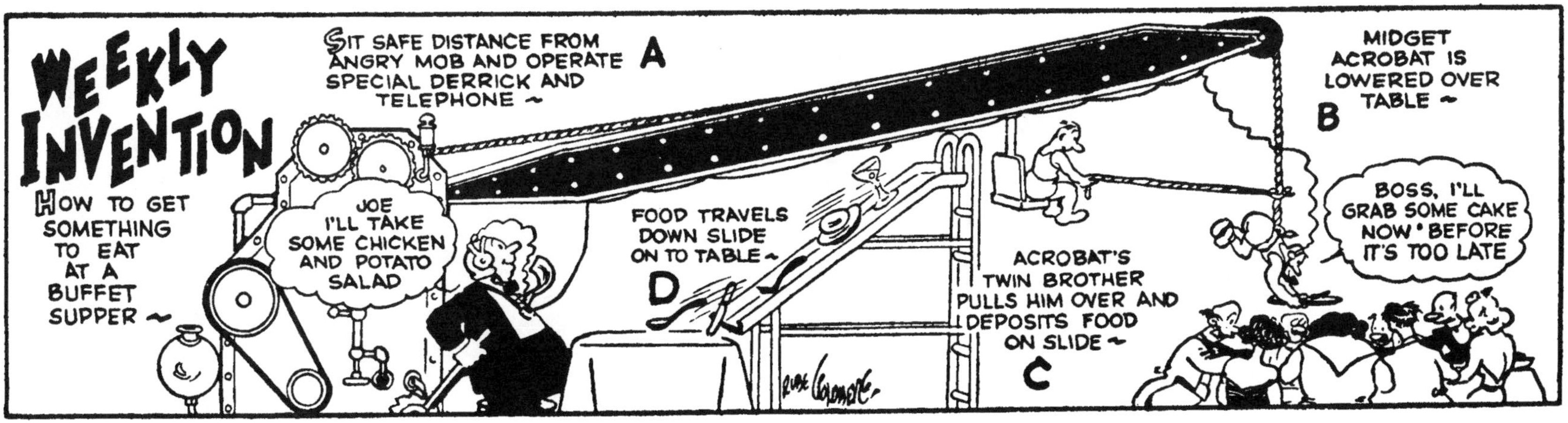
WEEKLY INVENTION
HOW TO GET SOMETHING TO EAT AT A BUFFET SUPPER ~
SIT SAFE DISTANCE FROM ANGRY MOB AND OPERATE SPECIAL DERRICK AND TELEPHONE ~ A
JOE I'LL TAKE SOME CHICKEN AND POTATO SALAD
MIDGET ACROBAT IS LOWERED OVER TABLE ~ B
BOSS, I'LL GRAB SOME CAKE NOW BEFORE IT'S TOO LATE
ACROBAT'S TWIN BROTHER PULLS HIM OVER AND DEPOSITS FOOD ON SLIDE ~ C
FOOD TRAVELS DOWN SLIDE ON TO TABLE ~ D

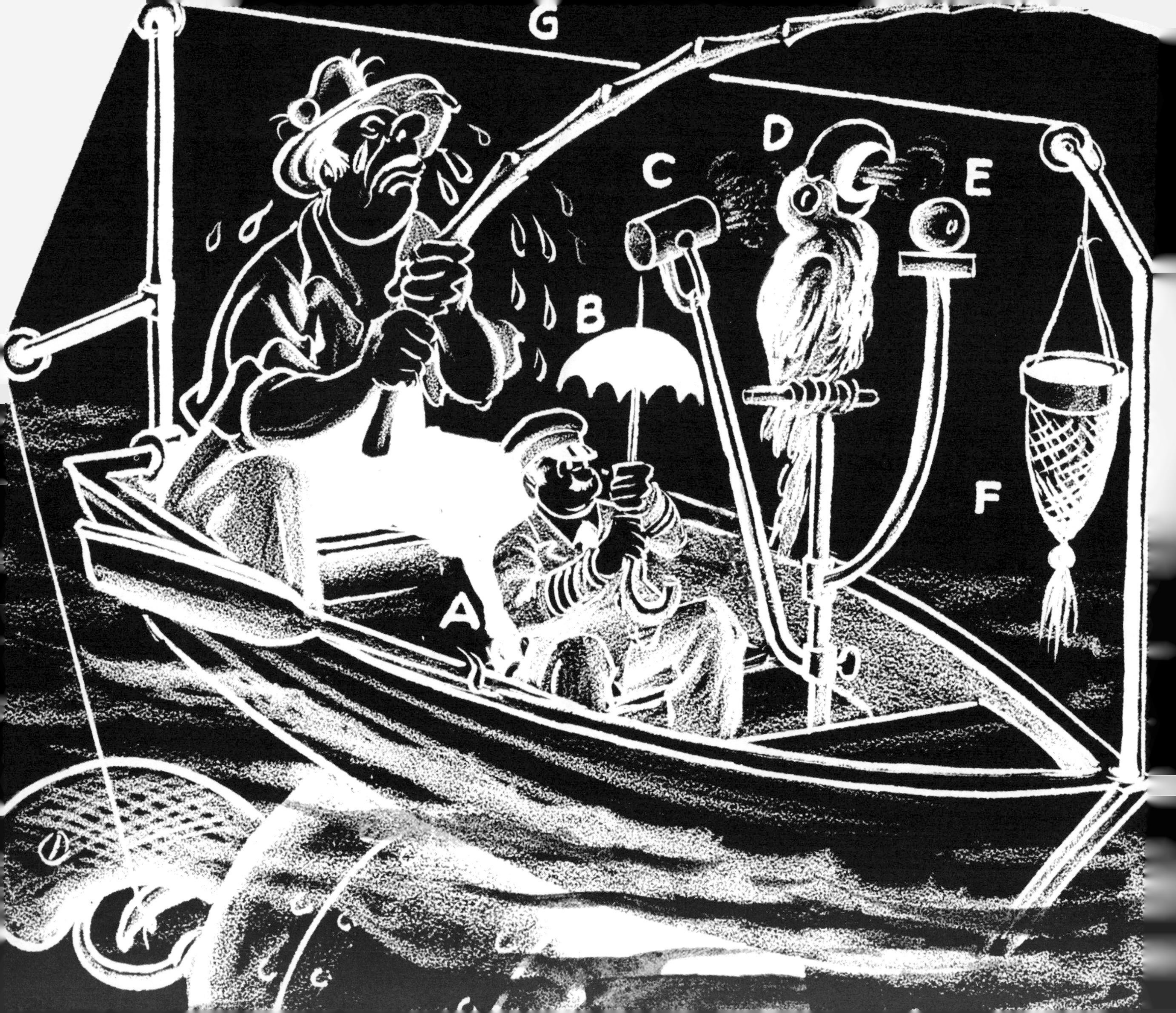
G
D
C
E
B
F
A

Sports & Games

Rube Goldberg started his career as a sports cartoonist, drawing boxers and baseball players, but golf was always his personal passion. A left-handed golfer, he said, "I have left-hand clubs, right-hand clubs, and if they flavored the handle with vanilla or chocolate I would hold the club with my teeth." Rube always admired "the definite finality of sports that meant you either win, or you lose."

Rube's Inventions reflected a no-holds-barred, win-at-any-cost school of sports. His Inventions show that technology didn't have to be denied to competitive sports. Whether reinventing baseball bats and golf tees, or offering a new perspective on wrestling and boxing, sports with a Rube Goldberg Invention were no longer just routine games. Every knowledgeable player soon realized that one of Rube's Inventions could give that player and his team that very special advantage over their opponents … and would do so in the most complicated—and funny—way imaginable.

A Sure Way to Keep Your Head Down During a Golf Shot

PROFESSOR BUTTS' LANDLADY HITS HIM OVER THE HEAD WITH A PITCHER FOR NONPAYMENT OF RENT AND HE DISCOVERS A SURE WAY TO KEEP THE HEAD DOWN DURING A GOLF SHOT. GOLFER (A) SWINGS CLUB (B) AND HITS BRANCH OF TREE (C) SHAKING APPLES DOWN ON KETTLE-DRUM (D). CADDIE (E) HEARING NOISE THINKS A THUNDER STORM IS APPROACHING AND RUNS FOR CLUB HOUSE, STUMBLING OVER GOLF BAG AND PUSHING FLAG POLE (G) AGAINST BAG OF PEANUTS (H) WHICH BREAKS AND THROWS PEANUTS IN BASKET (I). AS SQUIRREL (J) JUMPS INTO BASKET TO GET THE PEANUTS, HIS WEIGHT RAISES END OF PADDLE (K) AND DRAWS FISH (L) OUT OF WATER HAZARD. HUNGRY SEAL (M) SEEING FISH FLAPS HIS FLIPPERS (N) FOR JOY AND CAUSES BREEZE TO ENTER FUNNEL (O) THEREBY BLOWING MARDI-GRAS TICKLER (P) WHICH STRAIGHTENS OUT AND DEPOSITS DOLLAR BILL (Q) NEXT TO GOLF BALL, FOCUSSING EYES OF PLAYER ON THIS SPOT DURING SWING.

IF YOU MISS THE BALL AND SWING INTO APPLE TREE OFTEN ENOUGH YOU CAN HAVE APPLE SAUCE FOR DINNER.

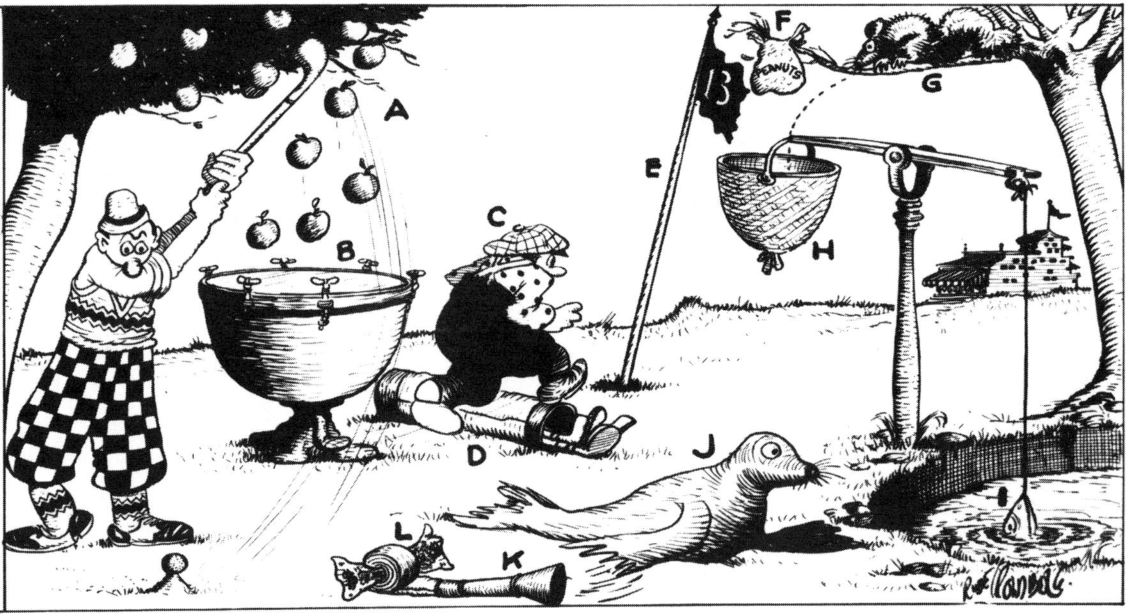
A
B
C
D
E
F
G
H
I
J
K
L
13
PEANUTS

Simple Way to Tee Up Your Ball

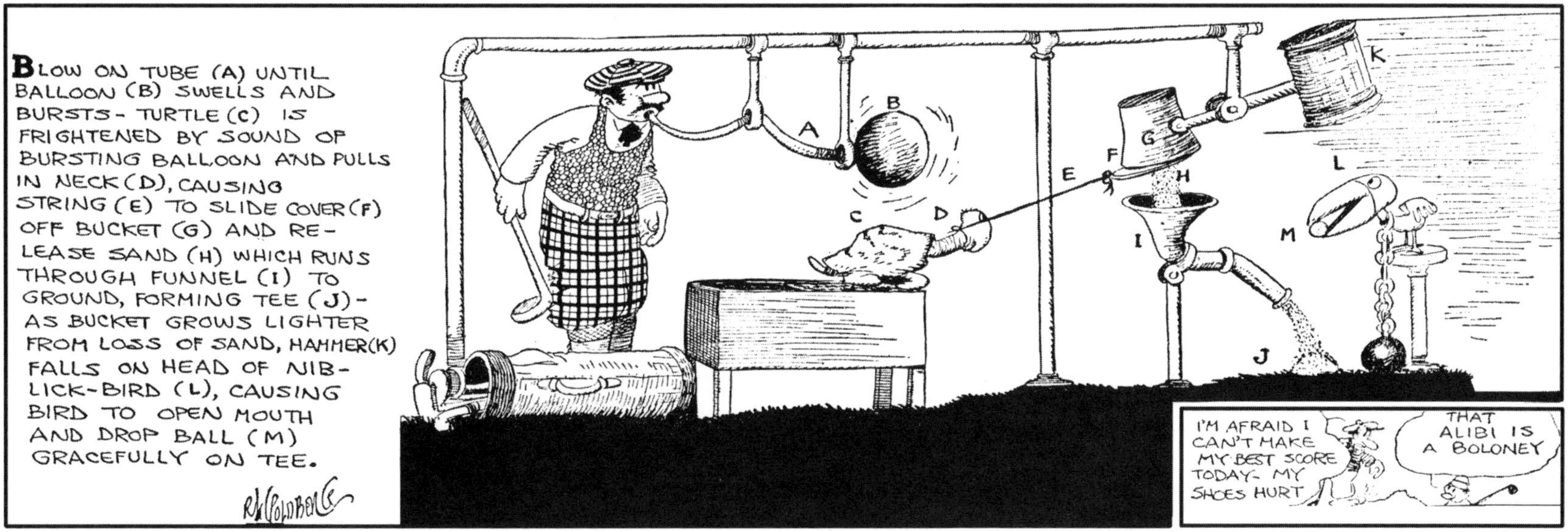
BLOW ON TUBE (A) UNTIL BALLOON (B) SWELLS AND BURSTS - TURTLE (C) IS FRIGHTENED BY SOUND OF BURSTING BALLOON AND PULLS IN NECK (D), CAUSING STRING (E) TO SLIDE COVER (F) OFF BUCKET (G) AND RE-LEASE SAND (H) WHICH RUNS THROUGH FUNNEL (I) TO GROUND, FORMING TEE (J) - AS BUCKET GROWS LIGHTER FROM LOSS OF SAND, HAMMER (K) FALLS ON HEAD OF NIB-LICK-BIRD (L), CAUSING BIRD TO OPEN MOUTH AND DROP BALL (M) GRACEFULLY ON TEE.
A
B
C
D
E
F
G
H
I
J
K
L
M
I'M AFRAID I CAN'T MAKE MY BEST SCORE TODAY - MY SHOES HURT
THAT ALIBI IS A BOLONEY

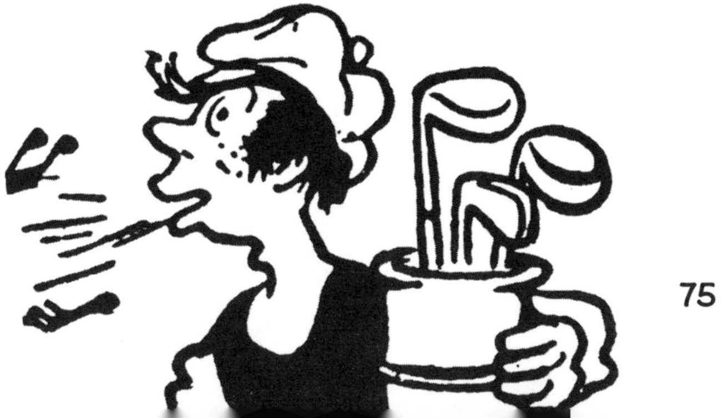

How to Get a Slow Foursome off the Green

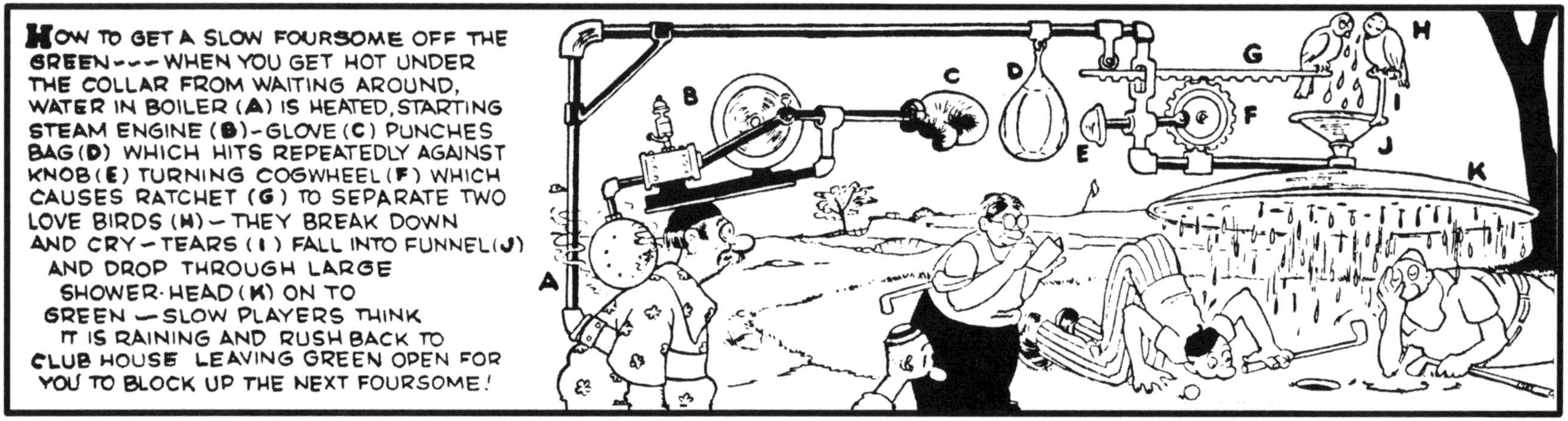
HOW TO GET A SLOW FOURSOME OFF THE GREEN---WHEN YOU GET HOT UNDER THE COLLAR FROM WAITING AROUND, WATER IN BOILER (A) IS HEATED, STARTING STEAM ENGINE (B)-GLOVE (C) PUNCHES BAG (D) WHICH HITS REPEATEDLY AGAINST KNOB (E) TURNING COGWHEEL (F) WHICH CAUSES RATCHET (G) TO SEPARATE TWO LOVE BIRDS (H)—THEY BREAK DOWN AND CRY—TEARS (I) FALL INTO FUNNEL (J) AND DROP THROUGH LARGE SHOWER-HEAD (K) ON TO GREEN—SLOW PLAYERS THINK IT IS RAINING AND RUSH BACK TO CLUB HOUSE LEAVING GREEN OPEN FOR YOU TO BLOCK UP THE NEXT FOURSOME!
A
B
C
D
E
F
G
H
I
J
K

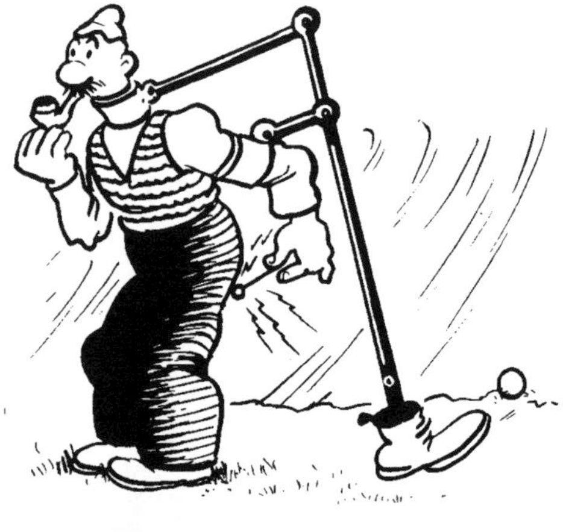

An Idea for Keeping Your Golf Opponent from Cheating

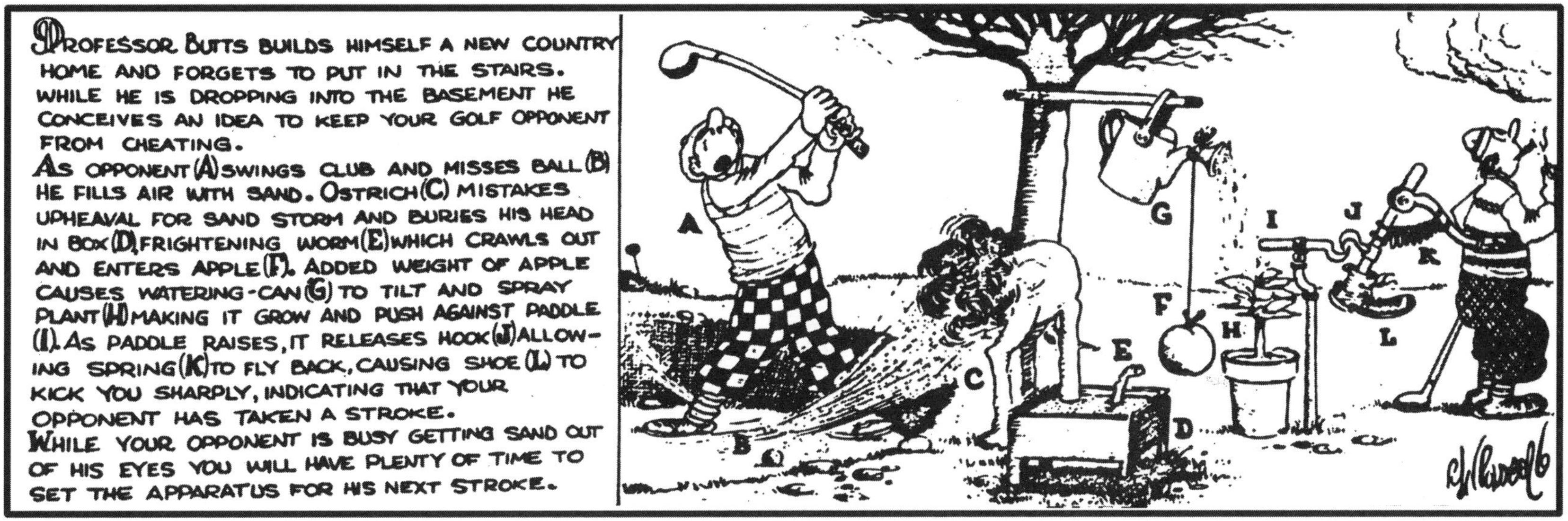
Professor Butts builds himself a new country home and forgets to put in the stairs. While he is dropping into the basement he conceives an idea to keep your golf opponent from cheating.
As opponent (A) swings club and misses ball (B) he fills air with sand. Ostrich (C) mistakes upheaval for sand storm and buries his head in box (D), frightening worm (E) which crawls out and enters apple (F). Added weight of apple causes watering-can (G) to tilt and spray plant (H) making it grow and push against paddle (I). As paddle raises, it releases hook (J) allowing spring (K) to fly back, causing shoe (L) to kick you sharply, indicating that your opponent has taken a stroke.
While your opponent is busy getting sand out of his eyes you will have plenty of time to set the apparatus for his next stroke.
A
B
C
D
E
F
G
H
I
J
K
L

How to Practice Keeping Your Head Down While Golfing Indoors

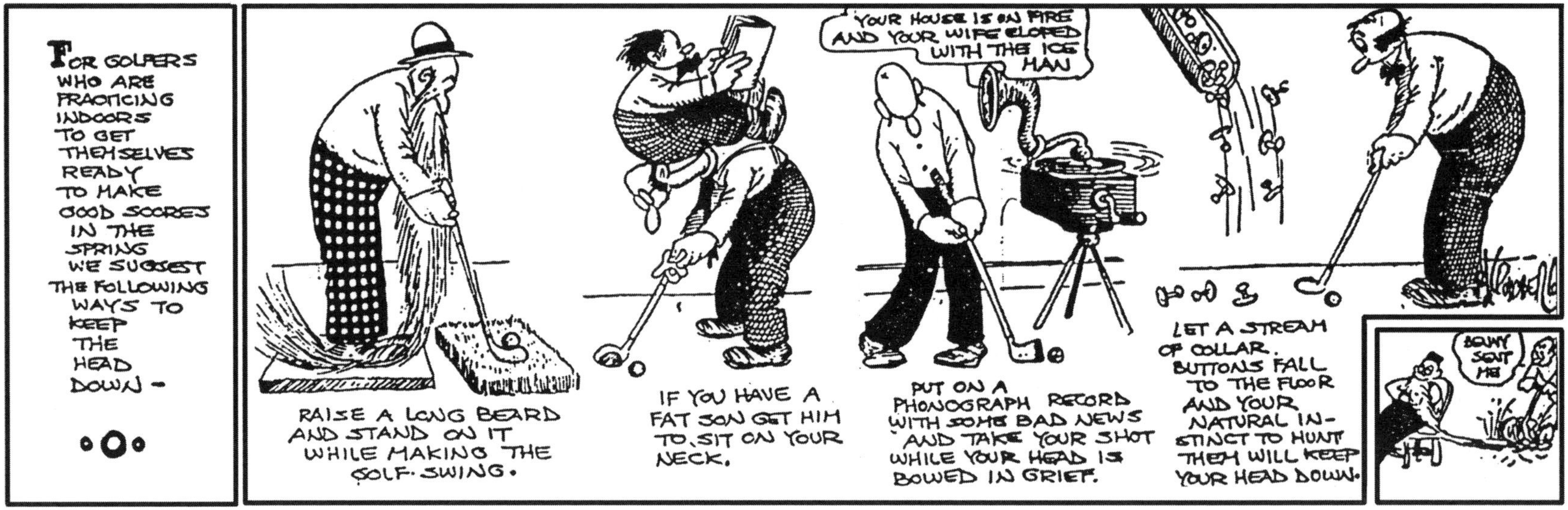
FOR GOLFERS WHO ARE PRACTICING INDOORS TO GET THEMSELVES READY TO MAKE GOOD SCORES IN THE SPRING WE SUGGEST THE FOLLOWING WAYS TO KEEP THE HEAD DOWN -
RAISE A LONG BEARD AND STAND ON IT WHILE MAKING THE GOLF SWING.
IF YOU HAVE A FAT SON GET HIM TO SIT ON YOUR NECK.
YOUR HOUSE IS ON FIRE AND YOUR WIFE ELOPED WITH THE ICE MAN
PUT ON A PHONOGRAPH RECORD WITH SOME BAD NEWS AND TAKE YOUR SHOT WHILE YOUR HEAD IS BOWED IN GRIEF.
LET A STREAM OF COLLAR BUTTONS FALL TO THE FLOOR AND YOUR NATURAL INSTINCT TO HUNT THEM WILL KEEP YOUR HEAD DOWN.
BENNY SENT ME

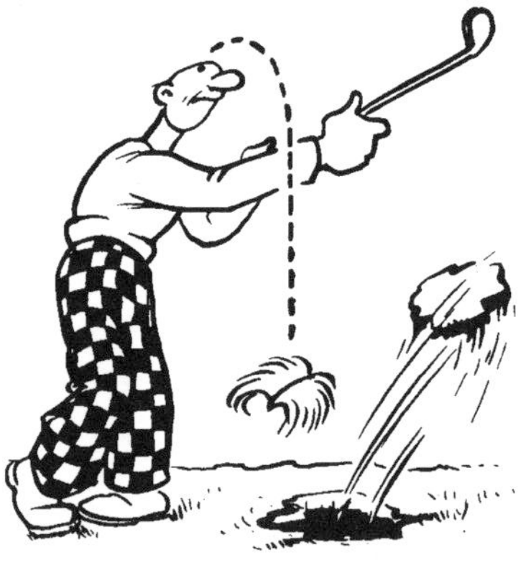

Moving a Slow Player off the Tee

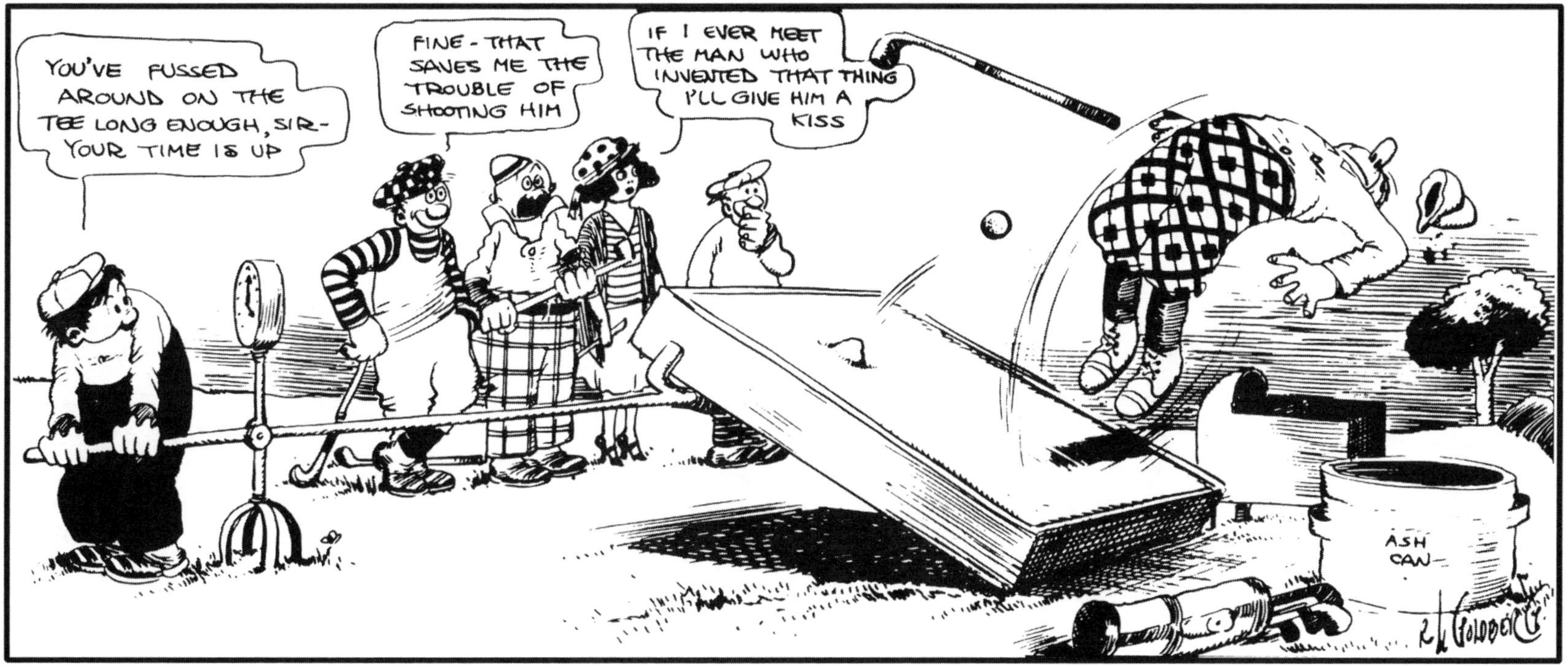
YOU'VE FUSSED AROUND ON THE TEE LONG ENOUGH, SIR- YOUR TIME IS UP
FINE - THAT SAVES ME THE TROUBLE OF SHOOTING HIM
IF I EVER MEET THE MAN WHO INVENTED THAT THING I'LL GIVE HIM A KISS
ASH CAN
R L GOLDBERG

The New "Pusher-Uppa" for Goat-Hill Golf Courses

It is our pleasure to announce the new golf club, "THE PUSHER-UPPA", invented to make the game a real pleasure on Goat-Hill golf courses.

Simple Way for the Winter Golfer to Keep Warm

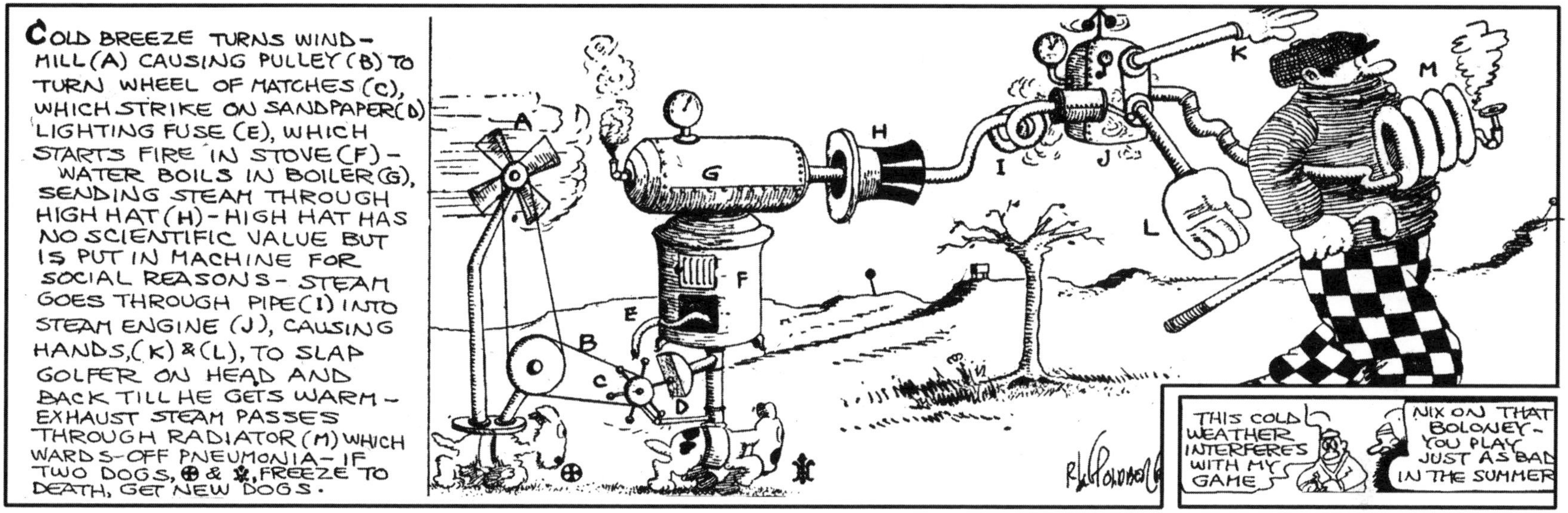
COLD BREEZE TURNS WIND-MILL (A) CAUSING PULLEY (B) TO TURN WHEEL OF MATCHES (C), WHICH STRIKE ON SANDPAPER (D) LIGHTING FUSE (E), WHICH STARTS FIRE IN STOVE (F) - WATER BOILS IN BOILER (G), SENDING STEAM THROUGH HIGH HAT (H) - HIGH HAT HAS NO SCIENTIFIC VALUE BUT IS PUT IN MACHINE FOR SOCIAL REASONS - STEAM GOES THROUGH PIPE (I) INTO STEAM ENGINE (J), CAUSING HANDS, (K) & (L), TO SLAP GOLFER ON HEAD AND BACK TILL HE GETS WARM - EXHAUST STEAM PASSES THROUGH RADIATOR (M) WHICH WARDS-OFF PNEUMONIA - IF TWO DOGS, ⊕ & ✲, FREEZE TO DEATH, GET NEW DOGS.
A
B
C
D
E
F
G
H
I
J
K
L
M
THIS COLD WEATHER INTERFERES WITH MY GAME
NIX ON THAT BOLONEY - YOU PLAY JUST AS BAD IN THE SUMMER

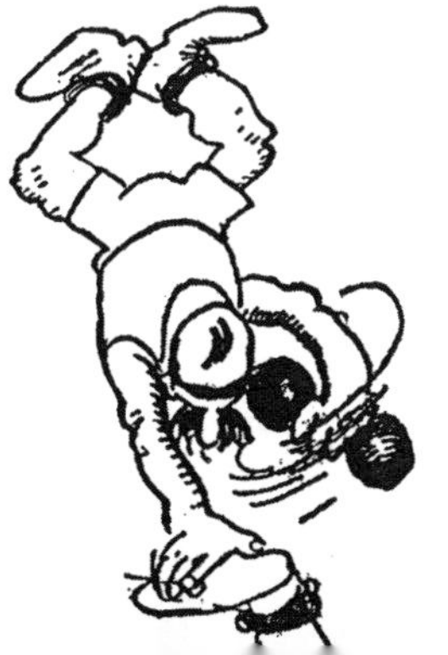

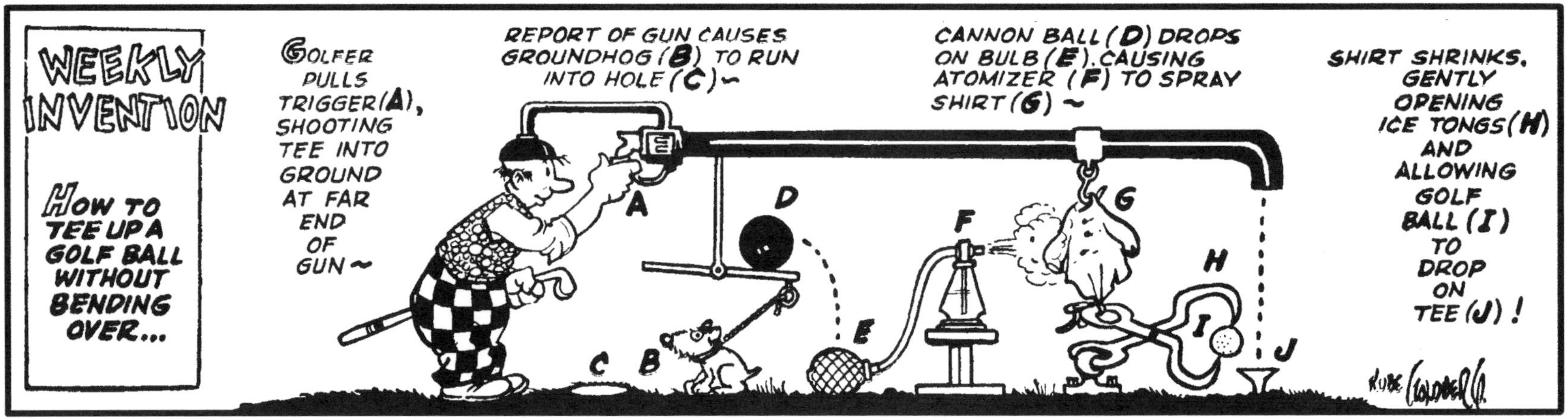
WEEKLY INVENTION
HOW TO TEE UP A GOLF BALL WITHOUT BENDING OVER...
GOLFER PULLS TRIGGER (A), SHOOTING TEE INTO GROUND AT FAR END OF GUN ~
REPORT OF GUN CAUSES GROUNDHOG (B) TO RUN INTO HOLE (C) ~
CANNON BALL (D) DROPS ON BULB (E), CAUSING ATOMIZER (F) TO SPRAY SHIRT (G) ~
SHIRT SHRINKS, GENTLY OPENING ICE TONGS (H) AND ALLOWING GOLF BALL (I) TO DROP ON TEE (J) !
A
B
C
D
E
F
G
H
I
J

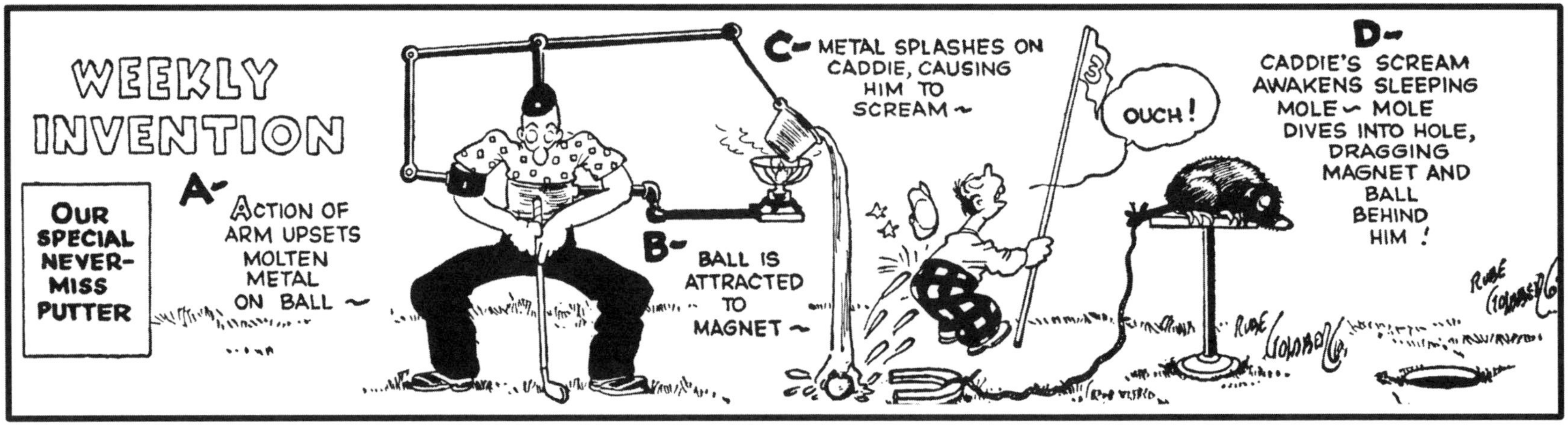
WEEKLY INVENTION
OUR SPECIAL NEVER-MISS PUTTER
A- ACTION OF ARM UPSETS MOLTEN METAL ON BALL ~
B- BALL IS ATTRACTED TO MAGNET ~
C- METAL SPLASHES ON CADDIE, CAUSING HIM TO SCREAM ~
OUCH !
D- CADDIE'S SCREAM AWAKENS SLEEPING MOLE ~ MOLE DIVES INTO HOLE, DRAGGING MAGNET AND BALL BEHIND HIM !
3

Neglected Wives Take Action Against Golfing Husbands

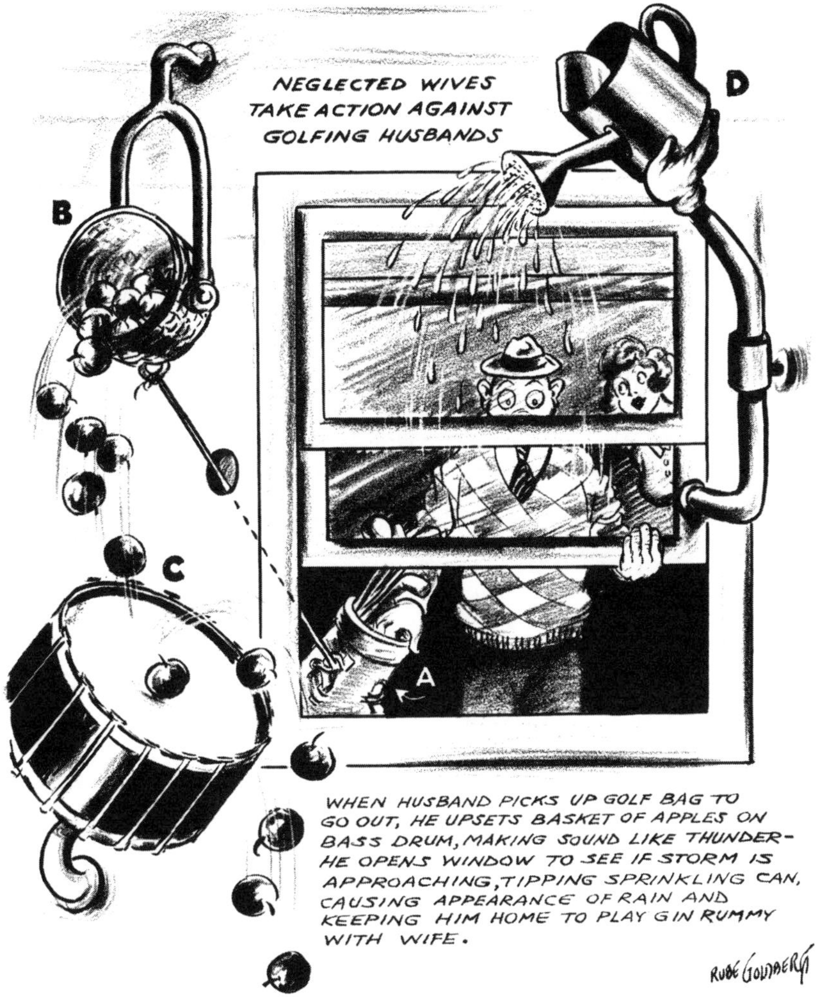
NEGLECTED WIVES
TAKE ACTION AGAINST
GOLFING HUSBANDS
B
D
C
A
WHEN HUSBAND PICKS UP GOLF BAG TO GO OUT, HE UPSETS BASKET OF APPLES ON BASS DRUM, MAKING SOUND LIKE THUNDER- HE OPENS WINDOW TO SEE IF STORM IS APPROACHING, TIPPING SPRINKLING CAN, CAUSING APPEARANCE OF RAIN AND KEEPING HIM HOME TO PLAY GIN RUMMY WITH WIFE.
RUBE GOLDBERG

Apparatus for Making the Football Game More Realistic over the Radio

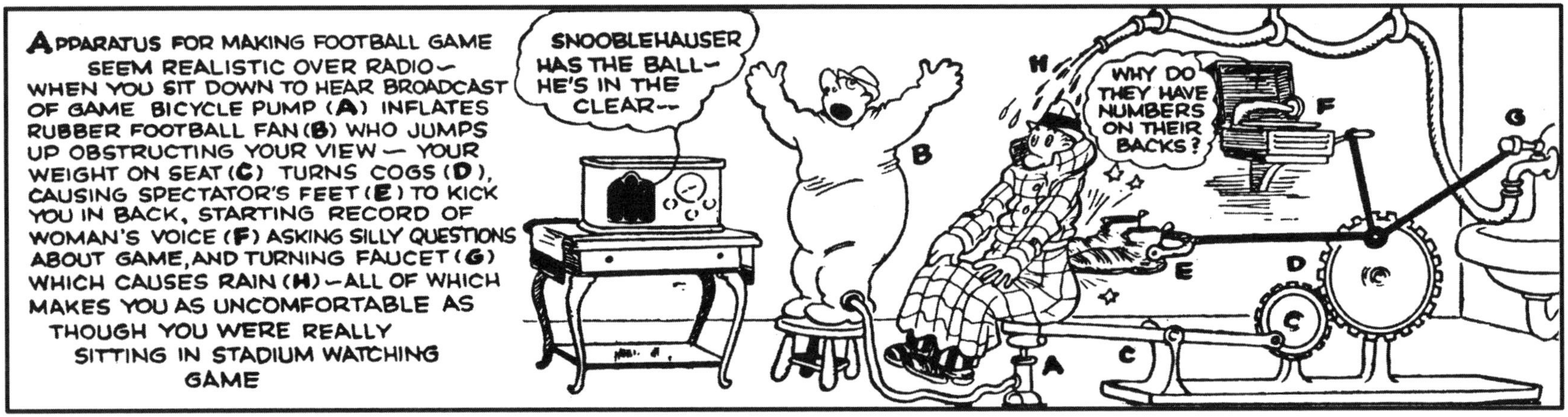
APPARATUS FOR MAKING FOOTBALL GAME SEEM REALISTIC OVER RADIO— WHEN YOU SIT DOWN TO HEAR BROADCAST OF GAME BICYCLE PUMP (A) INFLATES RUBBER FOOTBALL FAN (B) WHO JUMPS UP OBSTRUCTING YOUR VIEW — YOUR WEIGHT ON SEAT (C) TURNS COGS (D), CAUSING SPECTATOR'S FEET (E) TO KICK YOU IN BACK, STARTING RECORD OF WOMAN'S VOICE (F) ASKING SILLY QUESTIONS ABOUT GAME, AND TURNING FAUCET (G) WHICH CAUSES RAIN (H)—ALL OF WHICH MAKES YOU AS UNCOMFORTABLE AS THOUGH YOU WERE REALLY SITTING IN STADIUM WATCHING GAME
SNOOBLEHAUSER HAS THE BALL— HE'S IN THE CLEAR—
B
H
WHY DO THEY HAVE NUMBERS ON THEIR BACKS?
F
G
E
D
C
A
C

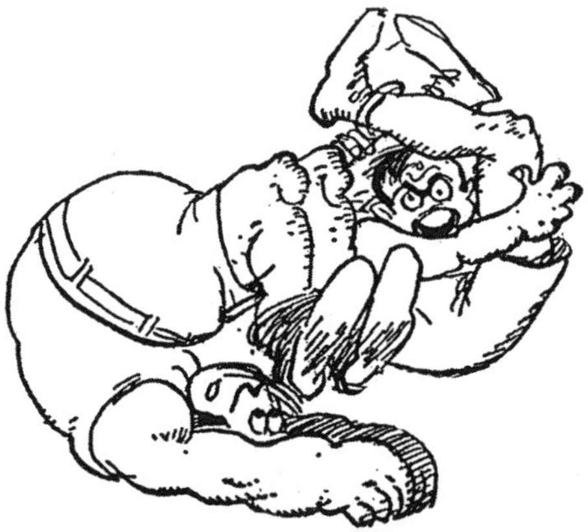

Keeping a Wrestler's Shoulders off the Mat

TO SHOW HOW YOUNG HE FEELS, PROFESSOR BUTTS JUMPS OVER A FENCE WITHOUT REALIZING THAT THE GRAND CANYON IS ON THE OTHER SIDE. WHEN HE HITS BOTTOM HE FINDS AN IDEA FOR KEEPING A WRESTLER'S SHOULDERS OFF THE MAT.

AS WRESTLER (A) PUSHES OPPONENT TOWARDS MAT. HE UPSETS GLASS OF WATER (B) ON SPONGE (C). WEIGHT OF WATER CAUSES SPONGE TO PULL TRIGGER OF GUN (D) WHICH SHOOTS BULLET THROUGH COCOANUT (E). COCOANUT MILK RUNS INTO CUP (F). WEIGHT IN CUP CAUSES STRING (G) TO PULL CORK OUT OF BOTTLE (H) LETTING FUMES OF AMMONIA ESCAPE. GERMAN DACHSHUND (I) IS OVERCOME AND FALLS OVER UNCONSCIOUS. FRENCH POODLE (J), STILL CARRYING GRUDGE FROM WAR, IS OVERJOYED AT FATE OF DACHSHUND AND JUMPS UP AND DOWN FOR JOY THEREBY JACKING FALLEN WRESTLER'S SHOULDERS UP OFF THE MAT.

OF COURSE, A WRESTLER CAN AVOID ALL THIS TROUBLE BY FIXING THE MATCH BEFOREHAND AND SPLITTING THE PURSE WITH THE WINNER.

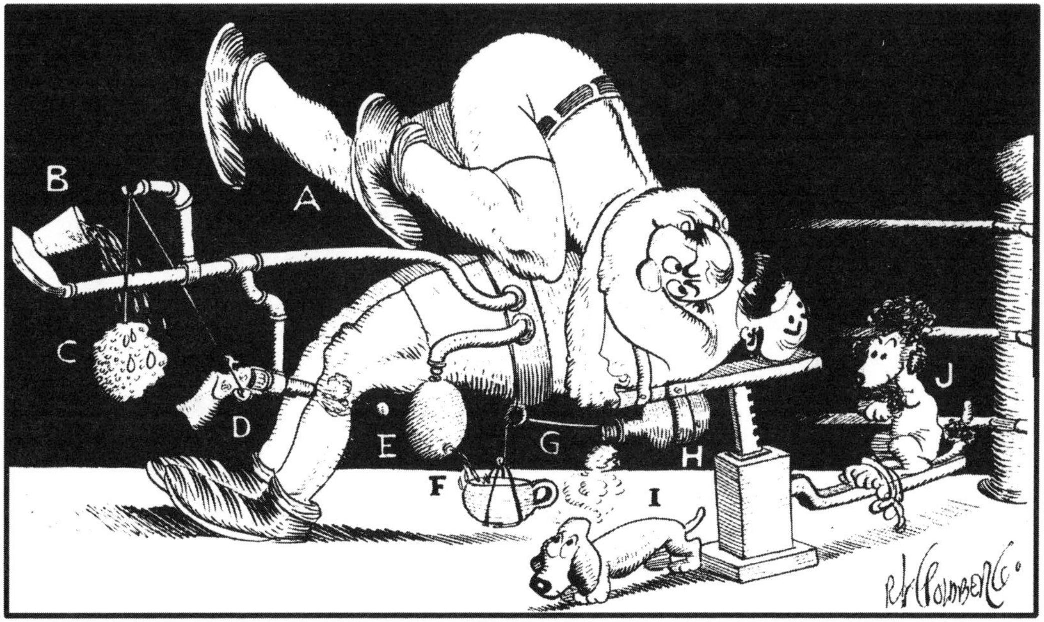
B
A
C
D
E
F
G
H
I
J
R.L. Goldberg

Self-Teaching Diving Machine

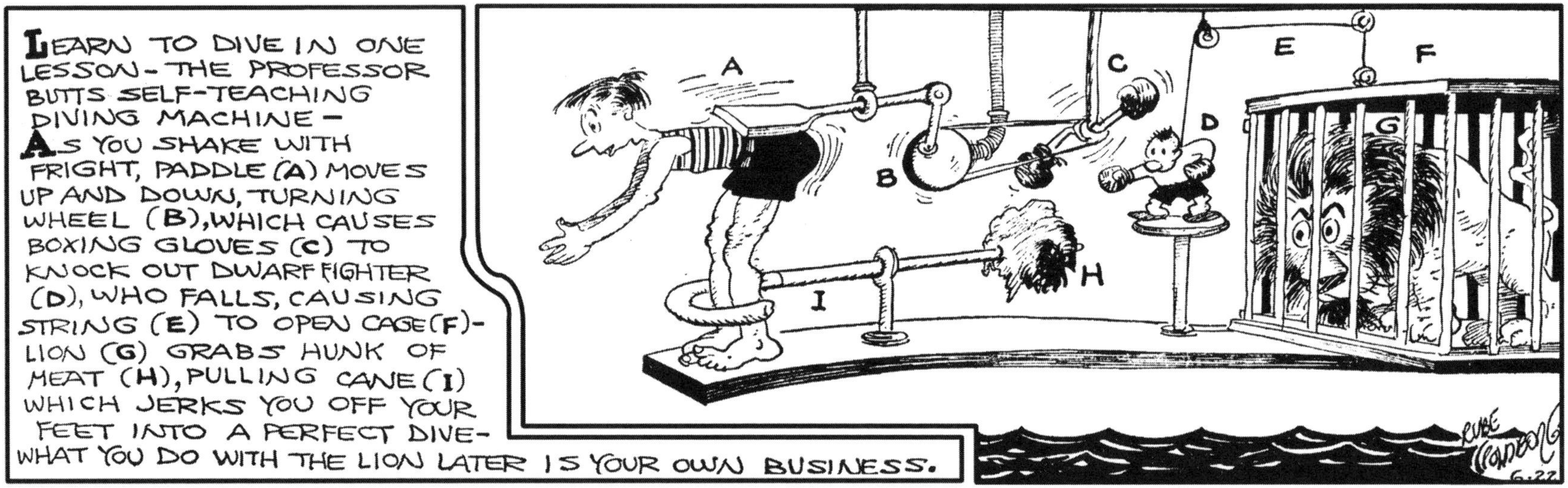
LEARN TO DIVE IN ONE LESSON - THE PROFESSOR BUTTS SELF-TEACHING DIVING MACHINE -
AS YOU SHAKE WITH FRIGHT, PADDLE (A) MOVES UP AND DOWN, TURNING WHEEL (B), WHICH CAUSES BOXING GLOVES (C) TO KNOCK OUT DWARF FIGHTER (D), WHO FALLS, CAUSING STRING (E) TO OPEN CAGE (F) - LION (G) GRABS HUNK OF MEAT (H), PULLING CANE (I) WHICH JERKS YOU OFF YOUR FEET INTO A PERFECT DIVE - WHAT YOU DO WITH THE LION LATER IS YOUR OWN BUSINESS.
A
B
C
D
E
F
G
H
I

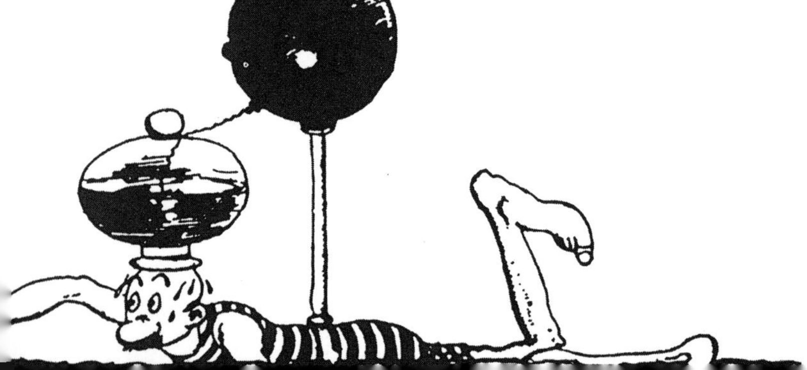

Simple System for Blowing Up Water Wings

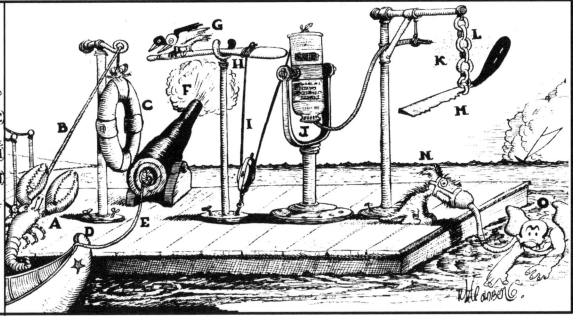

SOME ONE SENDS PROFESSOR BUTTS A BOMB THROUGH THE MAIL AND WHEN HE COLLECTS ALL THE PIECES HE FINDS AN IDEA FOR BLOWING UP WATER WINGS.

LOBSTER (A) CRAWLS UP ON FLOAT AND BITES ROPE (B) IN TWO CAUSING LIFE PRESERVER (C) TO DROP AND ROLL AGAINST CANOE (D) FORCING IT TO DRIFT AWAY FROM FLOAT AND PULL ROPE (E) WHICH FIRES SALUTE (F). SEA GULLS (G) MISTAKE REPORT FOR THE SIGNAL OF SUNSET AND COME HOME TO ROOST. WEIGHT OF BIRDS ON OAR (H) CAUSES IT TO TIP AND PULLS CORD (I) WHICH REVERSES POSITION OF FIRE EXTINGUISHER (J) (ACCORDING TO DIRECTIONS) FORCING ACID (K) TO SPRAY ON CHAIN (L). LINKS RUST AND EVENTUALLY BREAK, DROPPING RAZOR (M) WHICH CUTS HAIR OFF BRAZILIAN SPANIEL (N). SPANIEL CATCHES COLD, SNEEZES AND BLOWS UP WATER WINGS (O).

IF RAZOR KILLS SPANIEL, THEN YOU WILL SINK AND NEVER KNOW THAT PROFESSOR BUTTS HAS FAILED FOR THE FIRST TIME IN HIS LIFE.

No More Unlucky Fisherman

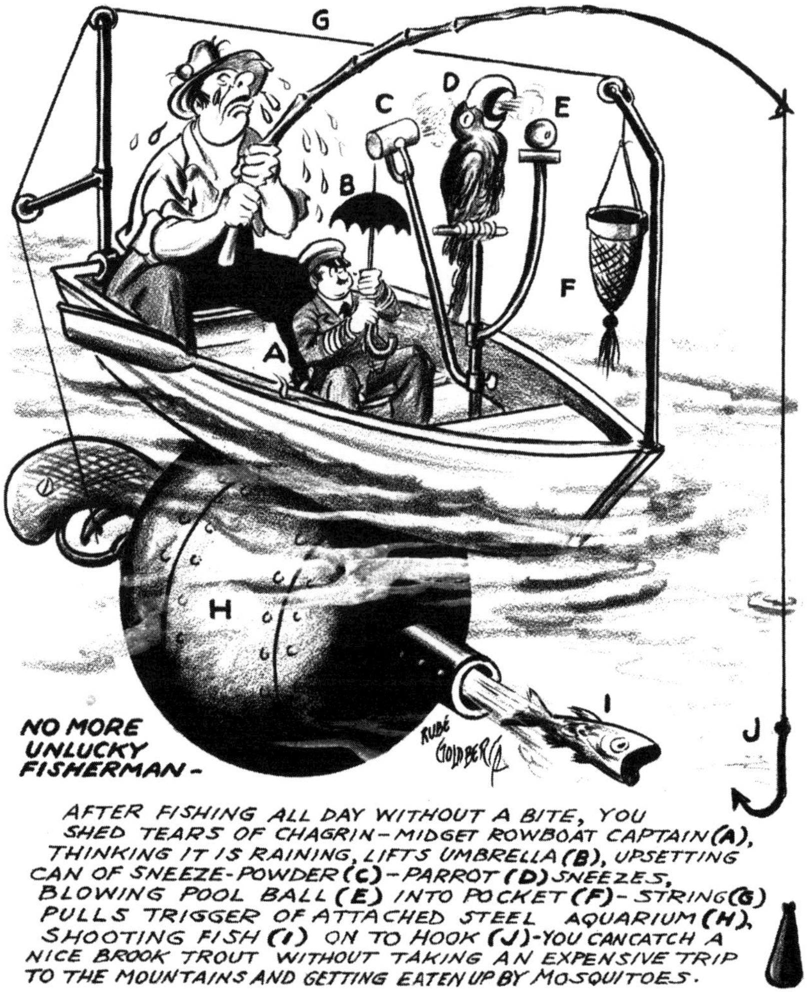
G
D
C
E
B
F
A
H
I
J
NO MORE UNLUCKY FISHERMAN -
RUBE GOLDBERG
AFTER FISHING ALL DAY WITHOUT A BITE, YOU SHED TEARS OF CHAGRIN - MIDGET ROWBOAT CAPTAIN (A), THINKING IT IS RAINING, LIFTS UMBRELLA (B), UPSETTING CAN OF SNEEZE-POWDER (C) - PARROT (D) SNEEZES, BLOWING POOL BALL (E) INTO POCKET (F) - STRING (G) PULLS TRIGGER OF ATTACHED STEEL AQUARIUM (H), SHOOTING FISH (I) ON TO HOOK (J) - YOU CAN CATCH A NICE BROOK TROUT WITHOUT TAKING AN EXPENSIVE TRIP TO THE MOUNTAINS AND GETTING EATEN UP BY MOSQUITOES.

Invention for Digging Up Bait for Fishing

A BARBER PUTS A SCALDING TOWEL ON PROFESSOR BUTTS'S FACE AND WHILE HE IS SCREAMING WITH PAIN HE THINKS UP AN INVENTION FOR DIGGING UP BAIT FOR FISHING. THE MAID(A)PEELS AN ONION AND CRIES INTO FUNNEL(B). TEARS(C)RUN THROUGH PIPE(D) AND DRIP INTO PAN(E) OF JEWELER'S SCALE(F), CAUSING END OF BAR(G)TO PRESS AGAINST SMALL BELLOWS(H), WHICH BLOWS INSECT POWDER(I) ON SHELF AND KNOCKS OFF ROACHES(J). ROACHES FALL ON EDGE OF ANTIQUE FAN(K), CAUSING IT TO CLOSE AND EXPOSE SURFACE OF MIRROR(L). SELFISH PALOOKA HOUND(M)SEES HIS REFLECTION IN MIRROR AND, THINKING IT IS ANOTHER DOG, HASTENS TO BURY BONE(N). AS HE DIGS, HE UNCOVERS WORM(O) WHICH IS SEEN IMMEDIATELY BY EARLY BIRD(P)WHO DIVES FOR IT OFF PERCH. WEIGHT(Q) DROPS ON HEAD OF BIRD AND KNOCKS HIM COLD JUST AS HE PULLS WORM FAR ENOUGH OUT OF GROUND FOR FISHERMAN TO GRAB IT EASILY.

WHEN THE EARLY BIRD WAKES UP YOU CAN LET HIM EAT THE ONION JUST SO HE WILL NOT BE GETTING TOO RAW A DEAL.

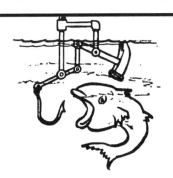

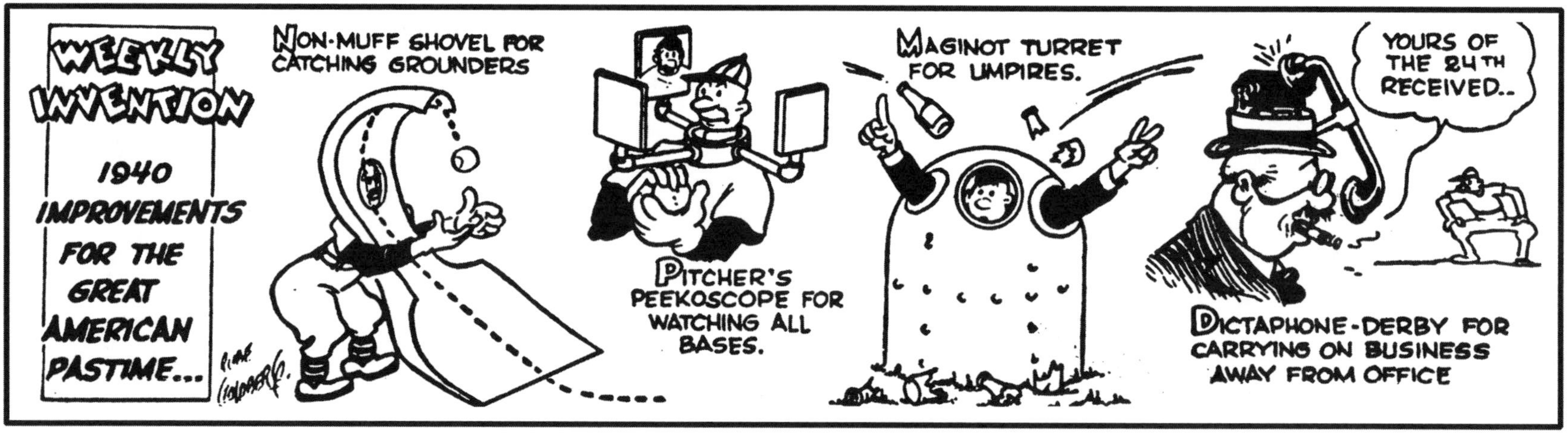
WEEKLY INVENTION
1940 IMPROVEMENTS FOR THE GREAT AMERICAN PASTIME...
NON-MUFF SHOVEL FOR CATCHING GROUNDERS
PITCHER'S PEEKOSCOPE FOR WATCHING ALL BASES.
MAGINOT TURRET FOR UMPIRES.
YOURS OF THE 24TH RECEIVED..
DICTAPHONE-DERBY FOR CARRYING ON BUSINESS AWAY FROM OFFICE

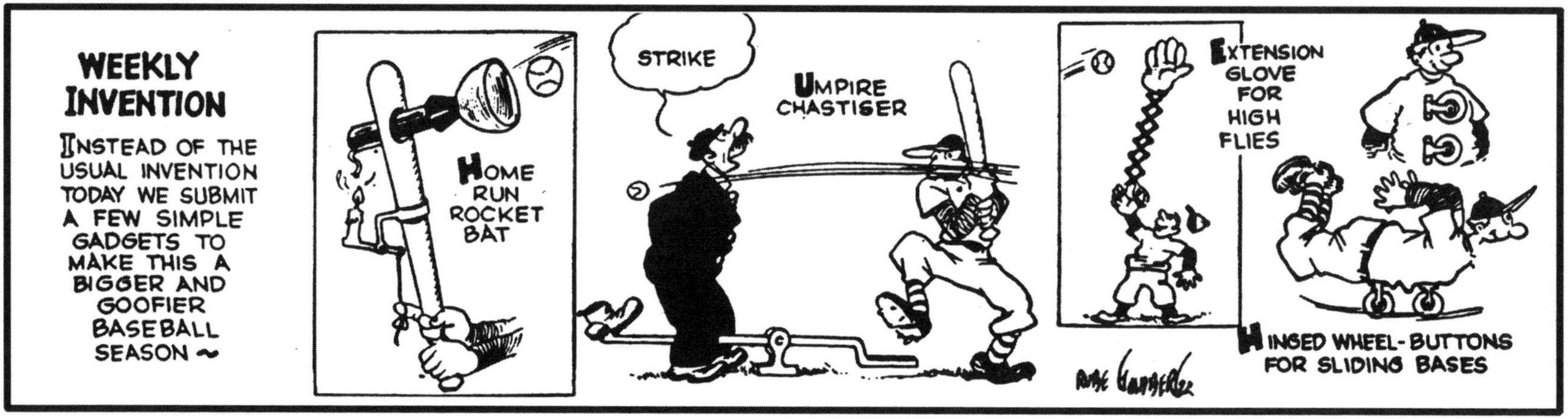
WEEKLY INVENTION
INSTEAD OF THE USUAL INVENTION TODAY WE SUBMIT A FEW SIMPLE GADGETS TO MAKE THIS A BIGGER AND GOOFIER BASEBALL SEASON ~
HOME RUN ROCKET BAT
STRIKE
UMPIRE CHASTISER
EXTENSION GLOVE FOR HIGH FLIES
HINGED WHEEL-BUTTONS FOR SLIDING BASES

Some New Ideas for Baseball Bats

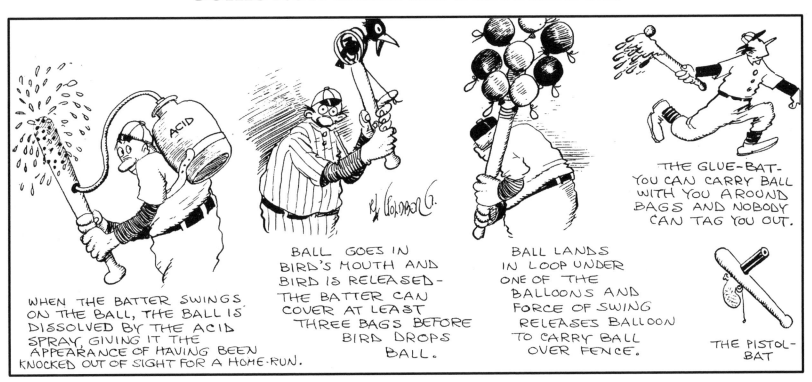

WHEN THE BATTER SWINGS ON THE BALL, THE BALL IS DISSOLVED BY THE ACID SPRAY, GIVING IT THE APPEARANCE OF HAVING BEEN KNOCKED OUT OF SIGHT FOR A HOME-RUN.

BALL GOES IN BIRD'S MOUTH AND BIRD IS RELEASED- THE BATTER CAN COVER AT LEAST THREE BAGS BEFORE BIRD DROPS BALL.

BALL LANDS IN LOOP UNDER ONE OF THE BALLOONS AND FORCE OF SWING RELEASES BALLOON TO CARRY BALL OVER FENCE.

THE GLUE-BAT- YOU CAN CARRY BALL WITH YOU AROUND BAGS AND NOBODY CAN TAG YOU OUT.

THE PISTOL-BAT

A Simple Way to Sharpen Ice Skates

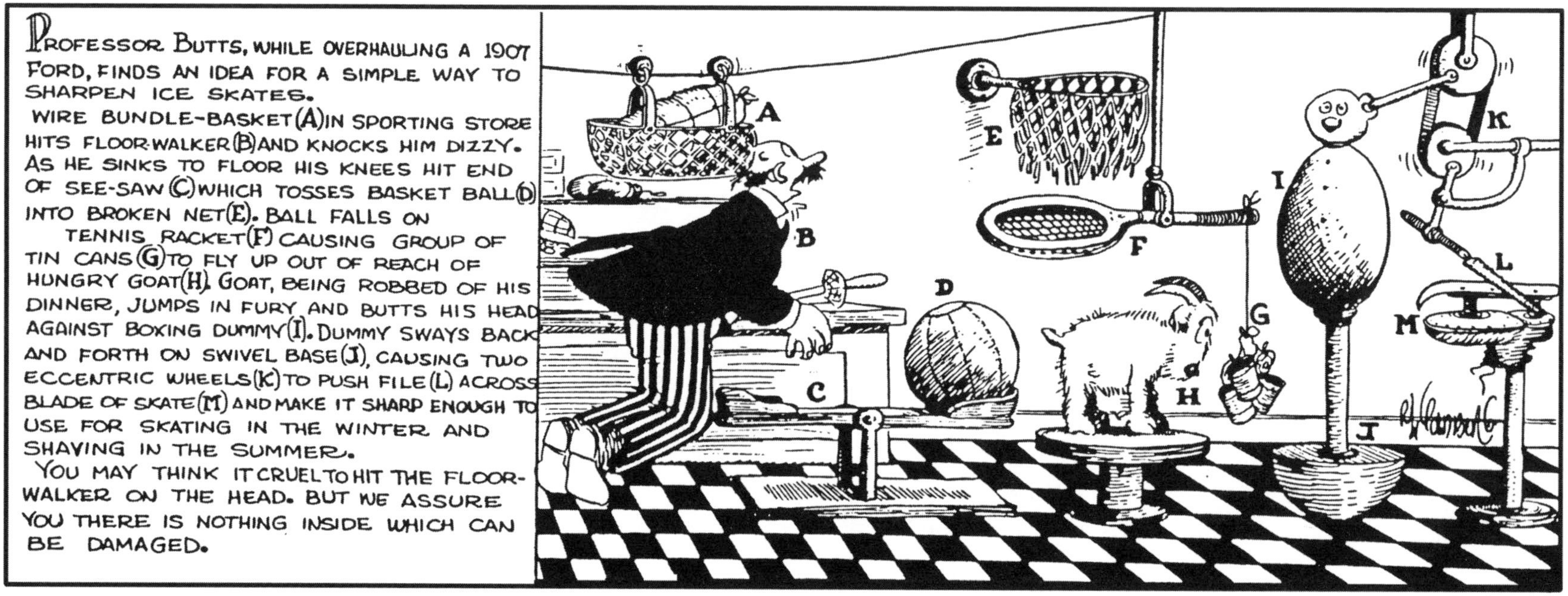
PROFESSOR BUTTS, WHILE OVERHAULING A 1907 FORD, FINDS AN IDEA FOR A SIMPLE WAY TO SHARPEN ICE SKATES.
WIRE BUNDLE-BASKET (A) IN SPORTING STORE HITS FLOOR-WALKER (B) AND KNOCKS HIM DIZZY. AS HE SINKS TO FLOOR HIS KNEES HIT END OF SEE-SAW (C) WHICH TOSSES BASKET BALL (D) INTO BROKEN NET (E). BALL FALLS ON TENNIS RACKET (F) CAUSING GROUP OF TIN CANS (G) TO FLY UP OUT OF REACH OF HUNGRY GOAT (H). GOAT, BEING ROBBED OF HIS DINNER, JUMPS IN FURY AND BUTTS HIS HEAD AGAINST BOXING DUMMY (I). DUMMY SWAYS BACK AND FORTH ON SWIVEL BASE (J), CAUSING TWO ECCENTRIC WHEELS (K) TO PUSH FILE (L) ACROSS BLADE OF SKATE (M) AND MAKE IT SHARP ENOUGH TO USE FOR SKATING IN THE WINTER AND SHAVING IN THE SUMMER.
YOU MAY THINK IT CRUEL TO HIT THE FLOOR-WALKER ON THE HEAD. BUT WE ASSURE YOU THERE IS NOTHING INSIDE WHICH CAN BE DAMAGED.
A
B
C
D
E
F
G
H
I
J
K
L
M

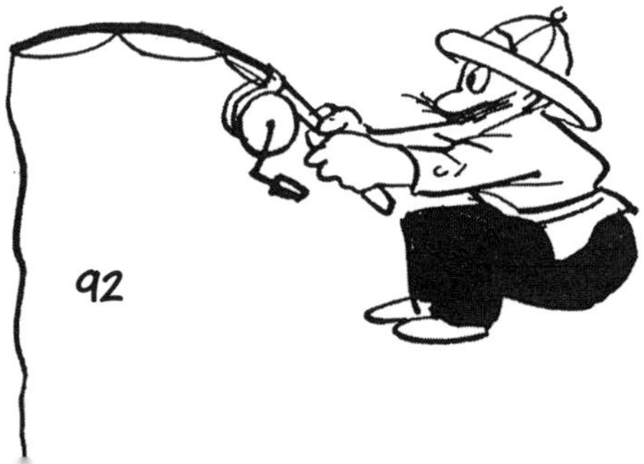

How to Signal Your Bridge Partner

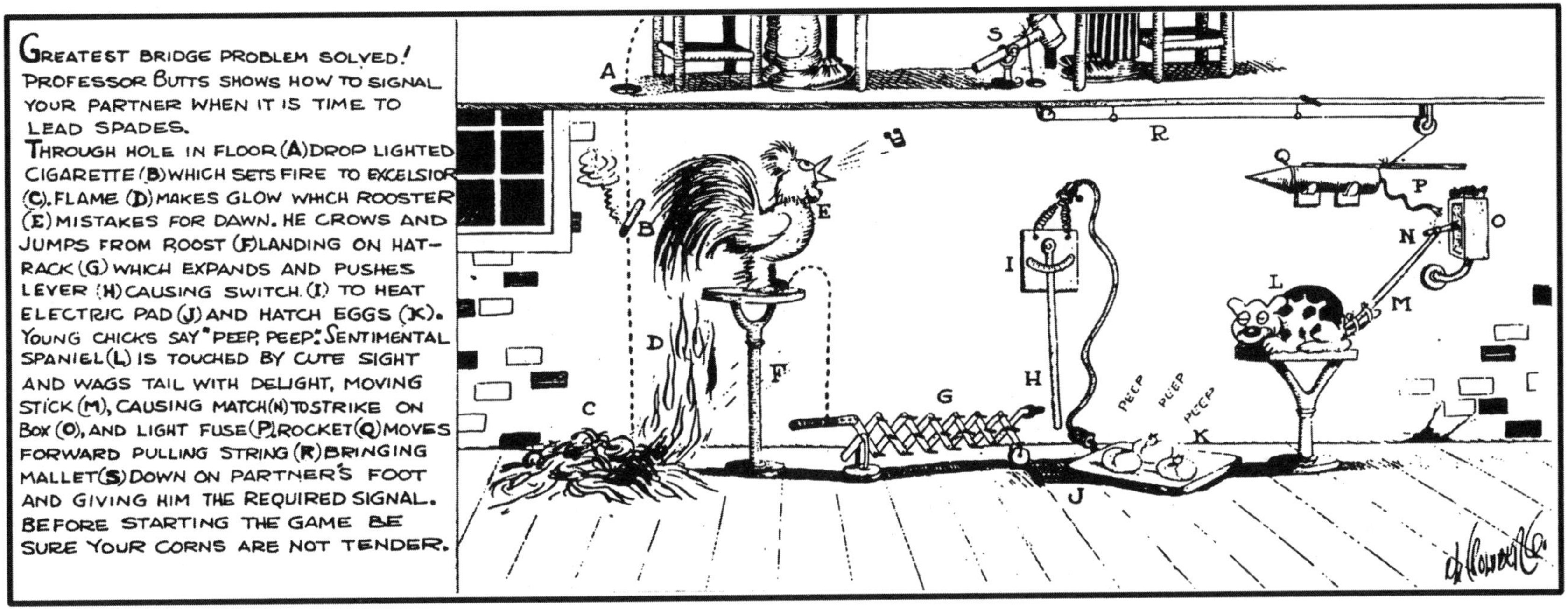
GREATEST BRIDGE PROBLEM SOLVED! PROFESSOR BUTTS SHOWS HOW TO SIGNAL YOUR PARTNER WHEN IT IS TIME TO LEAD SPADES.
THROUGH HOLE IN FLOOR (A) DROP LIGHTED CIGARETTE (B) WHICH SETS FIRE TO EXCELSIOR (C). FLAME (D) MAKES GLOW WHICH ROOSTER (E) MISTAKES FOR DAWN. HE CROWS AND JUMPS FROM ROOST (F) LANDING ON HAT-RACK (G) WHICH EXPANDS AND PUSHES LEVER (H) CAUSING SWITCH (I) TO HEAT ELECTRIC PAD (J) AND HATCH EGGS (K). YOUNG CHICKS SAY "PEEP, PEEP." SENTIMENTAL SPANIEL (L) IS TOUCHED BY CUTE SIGHT AND WAGS TAIL WITH DELIGHT, MOVING STICK (M), CAUSING MATCH (N) TO STRIKE ON BOX (O), AND LIGHT FUSE (P). ROCKET (Q) MOVES FORWARD PULLING STRING (R) BRINGING MALLET (S) DOWN ON PARTNER'S FOOT AND GIVING HIM THE REQUIRED SIGNAL. BEFORE STARTING THE GAME BE SURE YOUR CORNS ARE NOT TENDER.
PEEP
PEEP
PEEP

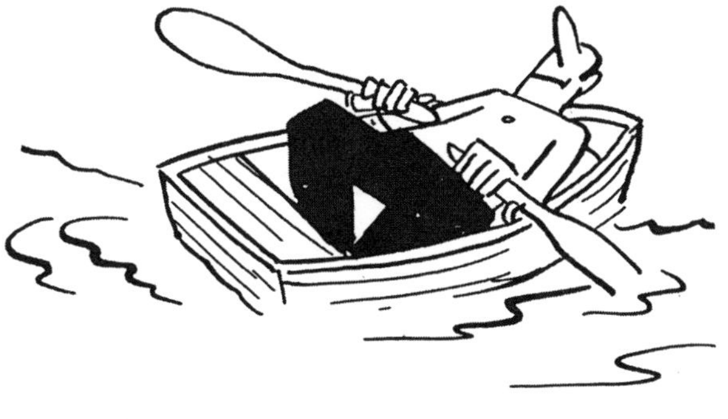

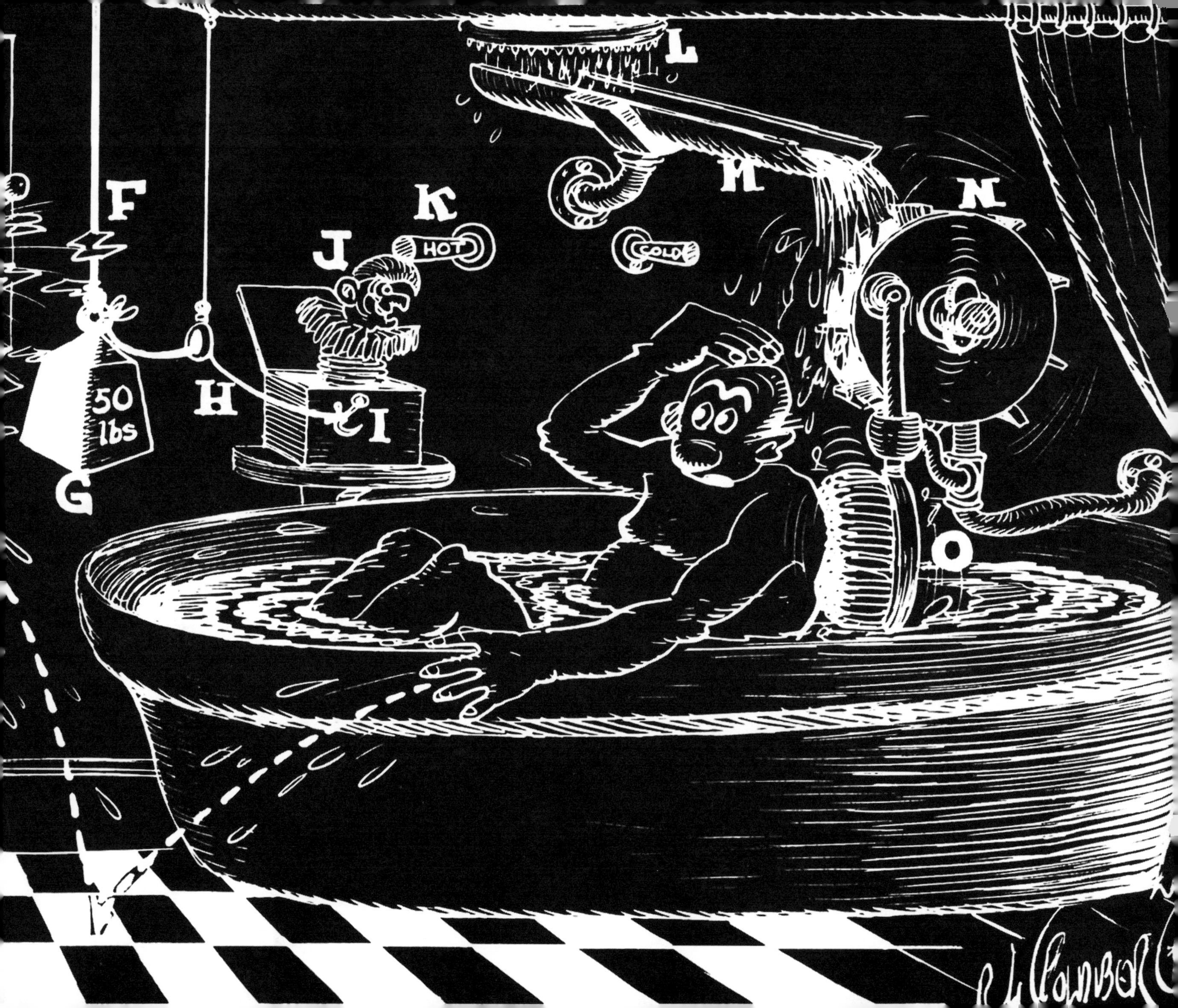
L
M
N
F
K
J
HOT
COLD
50 lbs
H
I
G
O

Good Grooming

We are all burdened by the time it takes to perform those common tasks that we have to complete every day, those necessary personal jobs like scrubbing your own back in the bath, putting toothpaste on a toothbrush, or finding your overshoes on a rainy day. Where, you might well ask, can one find those indispensable inventions that the research centers at the world's major corporations have sadly ignored?

Rube Goldberg was far from the stereotype of the absent-minded artist-inventor; he prided himself on being always well brushed and well dressed. Ever vigilant in his quest to improve the quality of life for the human race as well as for cats, dogs, and other beings, Rube invented products that included eliminating expensive dry-cleaning bills and a nonchemical way to grow hair.

The latest cutting-edge technology can't hold a candle to these tried-and-true Rube Goldberg solutions necessary to keeping up appearances with the added reward of personal convenience.

Solution for Growing Hair on Balding Men

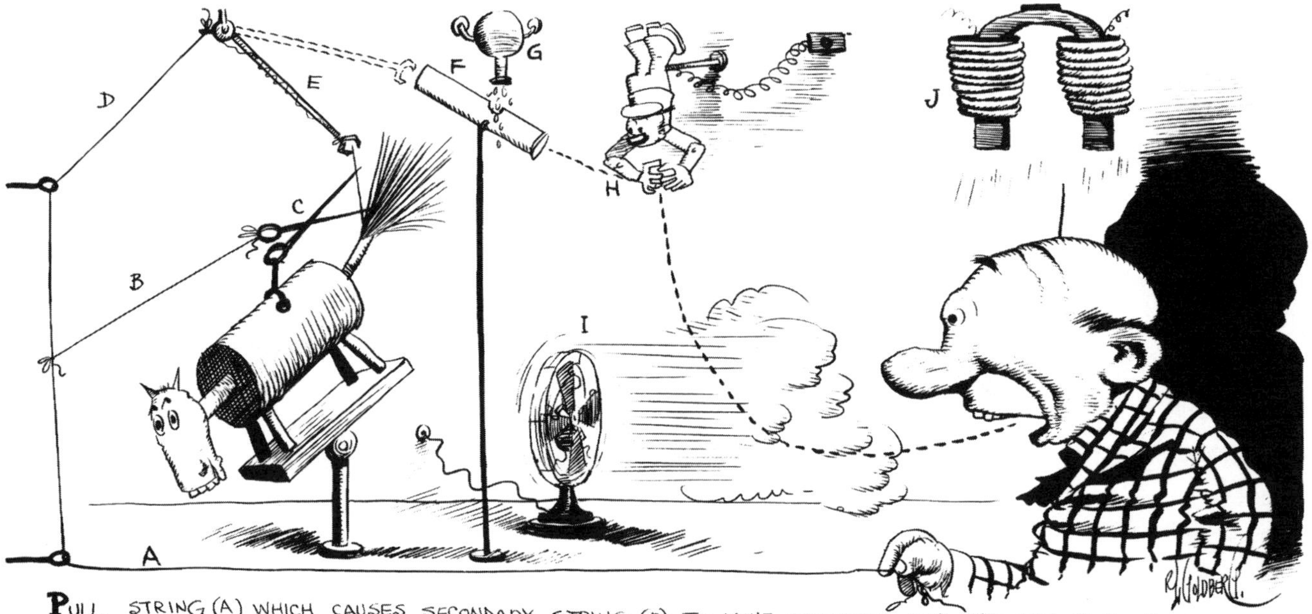
D
E
F
G
C
B
A
H
I
J

PULL STRING (A) WHICH CAUSES SECONDARY STRING (B) TO MOVE SCISSORS AND CUT ONE HAIR FROM WOODEN HORSE'S TAIL - CLUTCH (E) GRABS HAIR, LIFTS IT AT PULL OF STRING (D) AND DROPS IT IN TUBE (F) - TINCTURE OF IRON DROPS ON HAIR FROM BEAKER (G) - HAIR FALLS INTO HANDS OF TOY-SAILOR (H) WHO TIES A SAILOR'S KNOT ON THE END OF IT - WHEN IT LEAVES SAILOR'S HANDS, FAN (I) BLOWS IT INTO MOUTH OF BALD-HEADED MAN - STRONG ELECTRIC MAGNET (J) PULLS IRON-SOAKED HAIR THROUGH THE TOP OF HIS HEAD - SAILOR'S KNOT PREVENTS IT FROM LEAVING HEAD - OPERATION IS REPEATED UNTIL THERE IS ENOUGH HAIR ON TOP OF HEAD TO COMB.

Keep from Losing Your Hat on a Windy Day

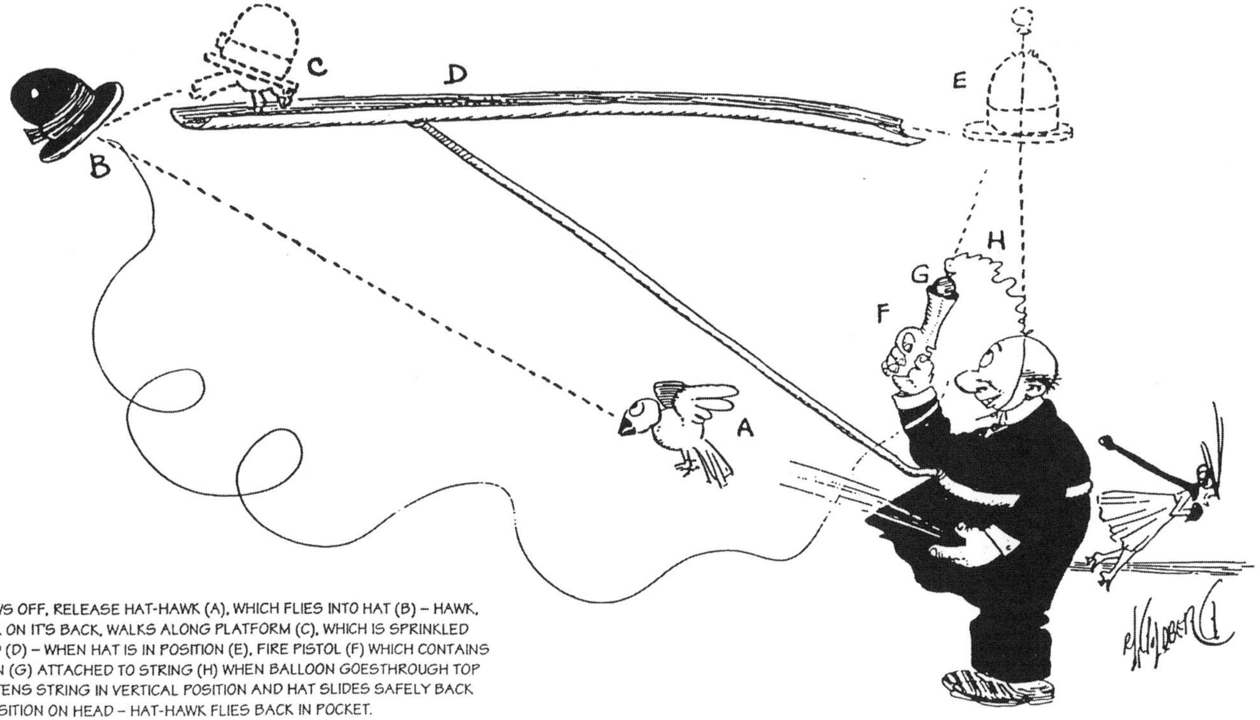
C
D
E
B
H
G
F
A

WHEN HAT BLOWS OFF, RELEASE HAT-HAWK (A), WHICH FLIES INTO HAT (B) – HAWK, WITH HAT STUCK ON IT'S BACK, WALKS ALONG PLATFORM (C), WHICH IS SPRINKLED WITH BIRD-SEED (D) – WHEN HAT IS IN POSITION (E), FIRE PISTOL (F) WHICH CONTAINS SMALL BALLOON (G) ATTACHED TO STRING (H) WHEN BALLOON GOESTHROUGH TOP OF HAT, IT TIGHTENS STRING IN VERTICAL POSITION AND HAT SLIDES SAFELY BACK TO ORIGINAL POSITION ON HEAD – HAT-HAWK FLIES BACK IN POCKET.

Read This and Learn How to Button Your Collar in a Hurry

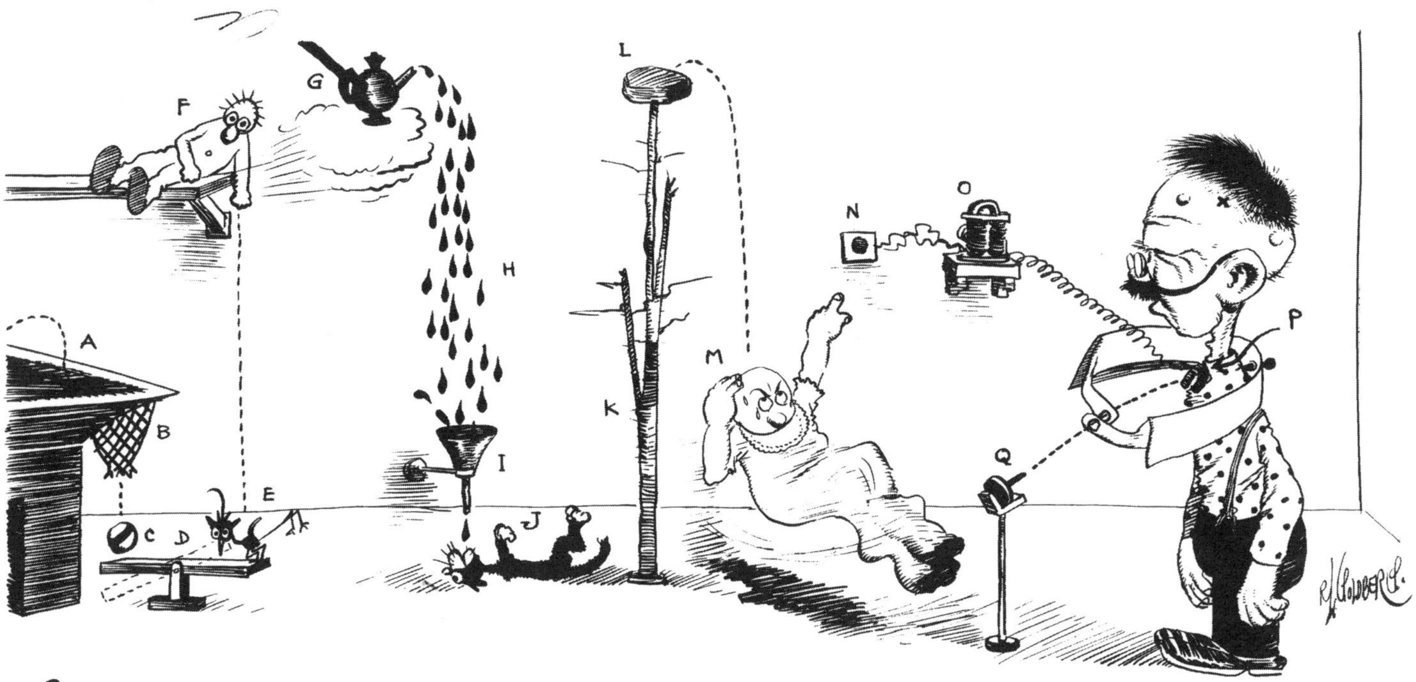
A
B
C
D
E
F
G
H
I
J
K
L
M
N
O
P
Q

STAND NEAR POOL TABLE (A) - BALL (C) FALLS THROUGH POCKET (B) STARTING SEE-SAW (D) AND BOUNCING MEASLES-GERM (E) INTO THE AIR - GERM HITS DOLL (F) WHICH IMMEDIATELY CATCHES MEASLES AND DEVELOPS A HIGH FEVER - FEVER HEATS COFFEE POT (G) AND COFFEE BOILS OVER, DROPPING THROUGH FUNNEL (I) INTO CAT'S MOUTH, GIVING CAT (J) INSOMNIA - CAT CLIMBS TREE (K) FOR DIVERSION AND KNOCKS OFF BRICK (L) - BRICK HITS CHILD (M) IN HEAD - CHILD PRESSES BUTTON (N) THINKING IT WILL SUMMON HELP - BUTTON SETS UP CURRENT IN COIL (O) WHICH CHARGES MAGNET (P) WHICH ATTRACTS TACK (Q) THROUGH BUTTON-HOLES IN COLLAR, HOLDING COLLAR SECURELY IN POSITION.

A Modest Mosquito-Bite Scratcher

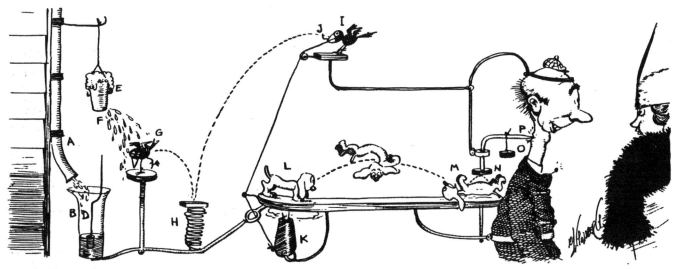

WATER FROM DRAIN-PIPE (A) DROPS INTO FLASK (B) - CORK (C) RISES WITH WATER CARRYING NEEDLE (D) WITH IT - NEEDLE PUNCTURES PAPER TUMBLER (E) CONTAINING BEER (F) - BEER SPRINKLES OVER BLUEBIRD (G) AND HE BECOMES INTOXICATED AND FALLS ON SPRING (H), WHICH BOUNCES HIM TO PLATFORM (I) - HE PULLS STRING (J) THINKING IT IS A WORM - STRING FIRES OFF CANNON (K) WHICH FRIGHTENS PEACE-HOUND (L), CAUSING HIM TO JUMP IN AIR, LANDING ON BACK IN POSITION (M) - HIS HEAVY BREATHING RAISES DISC (N), WHICH IS BROUGHT BACK INTO ITS ORIGINAL POSITION BY WEIGHT (O),- THE CONTINUAL BREATHING OF THE DOG MOVES SCRATCHER (P) UP AND DOWN OVER MOSQUITO BITE, CAUSING NO EMBARRASSMENT WHILE TALKING TO A LADY.

Simple Way of Hiding a Gravy Spot on Your Vest

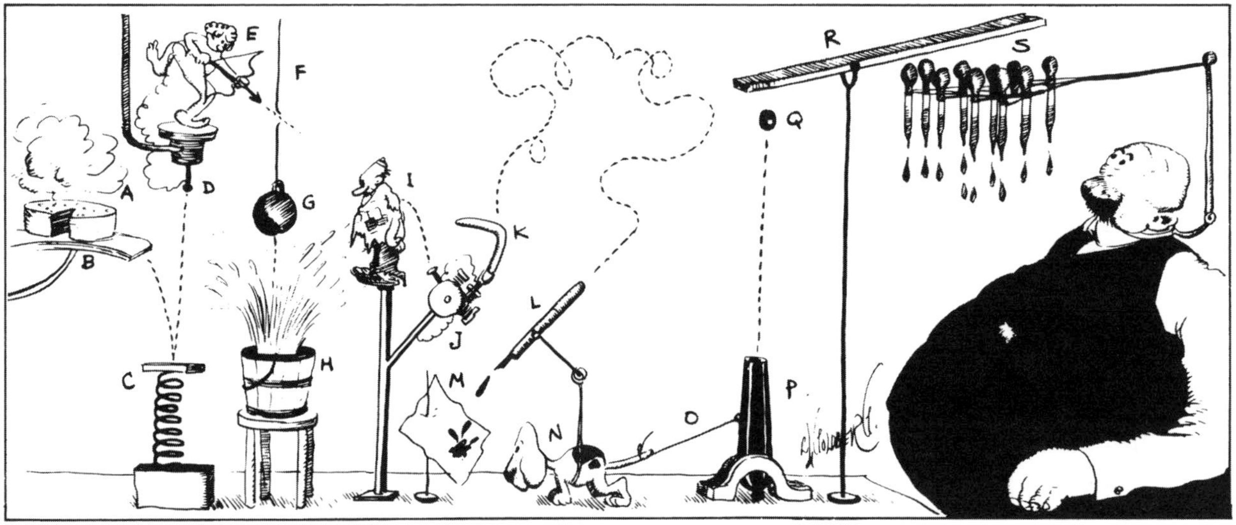
A
B
C
D
E
F
G
H
I
J
K
L
M
N
O
P
Q
R
S

CHEESE (A), AFTER STANDING AROUND FOR SEVERAL WEEKS, GROWS RESTLESS AND FALLS OF PLATFORM (B), HITTING SPRING (C) AND BOUNCING AGAINST ELECTRIC BUTTON (D) WHICH RELEASES ARROW HELD BY MECHANICAL CUPID (E) - ARROW CUTS STRING (F) DROPPING WEIGHT (G) INTO BUCKET OF WATER (H) - WATER SPLASHES ON TRAMP (I) WHO FAINTS FROM THE SHOCK AND DROPS AGAINST BOOMERANG-THROWING MACHINE (J) - BOOMERANG (K) SHOOTS ALL OVER THE PLACE AND FINALLY STRIKES END OF FOUNTAIN PEN (L) KNOCKING INK-BLOT ON PAPER (M) - ERASER-HOUND (N) JUMPS AT PAPER TO RUB OUT INK-BLOT WITH HIS NOSE - STRING (O) SETS OFF AEROPLANE GUN (P) - BULLET (Q) HITS BOARD (R) WHICH SQUEEZES BULBS ON END OF DROPPERS (S) - DROPPERS CONTAIN INK THE SAME COLOR AS THE GRAVY SPOT - THE INK DROPS FALL ALL OVER VEST MAKING IT IMPOSSIBLE TO TELL WHICH ONE OF THE SPOTS IS GRAVY - AND YOU HAVE A FANCY VEST IN THE BARGAIN.

A Self-Scrubbing Bath Brush

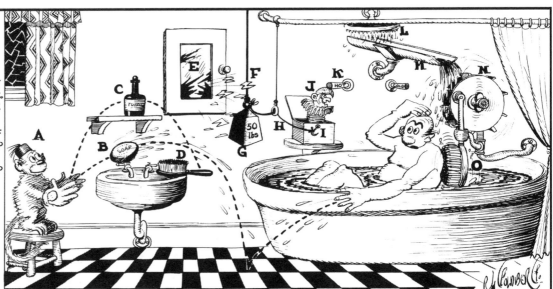

PROFESSOR BUTTS JUMPS FROM A PLANE IN A MOTH-EATEN PARACHUTE, LANDS ON HIS HEAD AND LIVES TO INVENT A SELF-SCRUBBING BATH BRUSH.
SOAP SLIPS FROM BATHER'S HANDS. MONKEY OUTFIELDER (A) TRIES TO CATCH IT AND FUMBLES. SOAP (B) HITS BOTTLE (C) WHICH FALLS ON HANDLE OF HAIR BRUSH (D) CAUSING BRUSH TO FLY UP AND SMASH MIRROR (E). FLYING FRAGMENTS OF GLASS CUT CORD (F) ALLOWING WEIGHT (G) TO DROP AND PULL STRING (H) WHICH OPENS HOOK (I) RELEASING JACK-IN-THE-BOX (J), WHICH JUMPS UP AND HITS HANDLE (K) TURNING ON WATER IN SHOWER (L). AS WATER RUNS DOWN TROUGH (M) IT FALLS ON MILL-WHEEL (N) CAUSING IT TO REVOLVE AND WORK BRUSH (O) UP AND DOWN ON BATHER'S BACK.
YOU CAN RENT AN ORGAN AND KEEP THE MONKEY BUSY WHEN YOU ARE NOT TAKING A BATH.
A
B
SOAP
C
D
E
F
G
50 lbs
H
I
J
K
HOT
COLD
L
M
N
O

Now You Know How to Cut Your Own Hair

LAUGHING HYENA (A) LAUGHS - BLIND MOUSE (B) THINKS HYENA IS LAUGHING AT HIM, GETS INSULTED, WALKS OFF AND BUMPS INTO DISC (C) MOTION OF DISC IS TRANSFERRED THROUGH SERIES OF RODS AND DISCS (D-E) TO STUFFED GLOVE (F), WHICH PUSHES WEAK, STARVING LILLIPUTIAN GOAT (G) AGAINST HEAD (H) - GOAT MOVES FORWARD AND EATS OFF HAIR UNTIL HE FALLS OVER INTO GOAT CRADLE (I) ON OTHER SIDE WHEN HE IS FULL.

N.B. ONE ORDINARY HEAD OF HAIR IS JUST ENOUGH TO FILL A REGULATION LILLIPUTIAN GOAT.

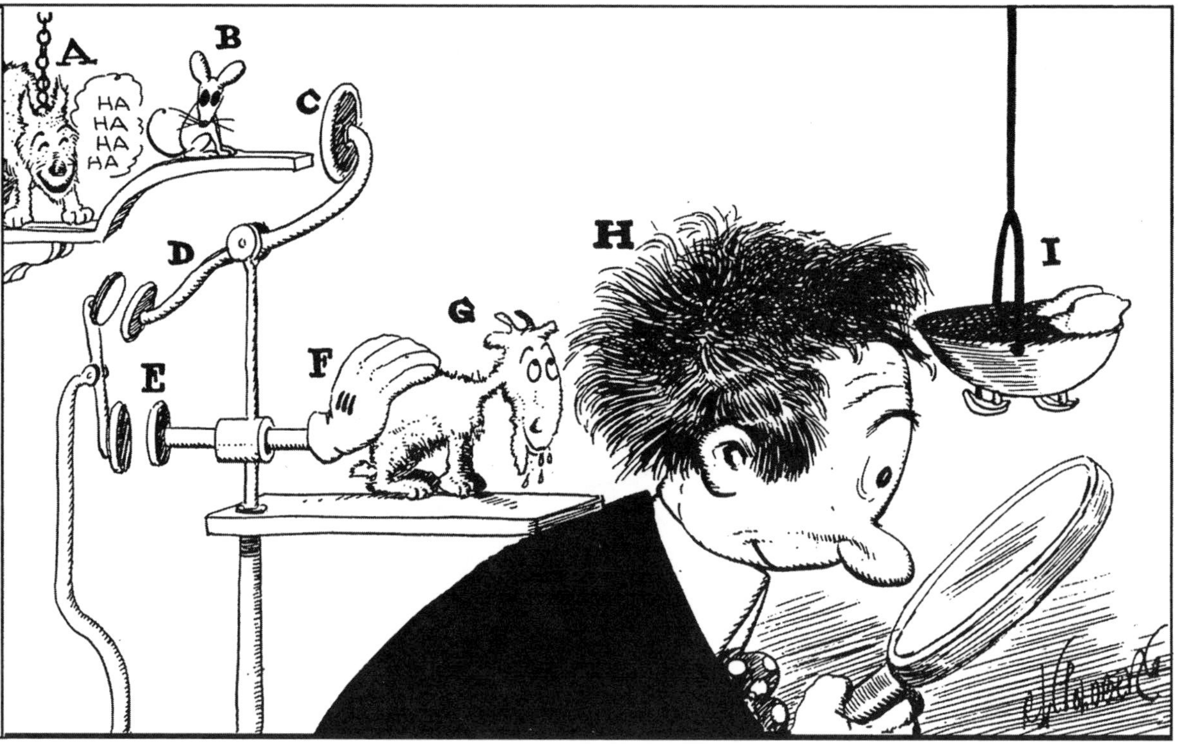
A
B
HA
HA
HA
HA
C
D
E
F
G
H
I

Try the New Patent Clothes Brush

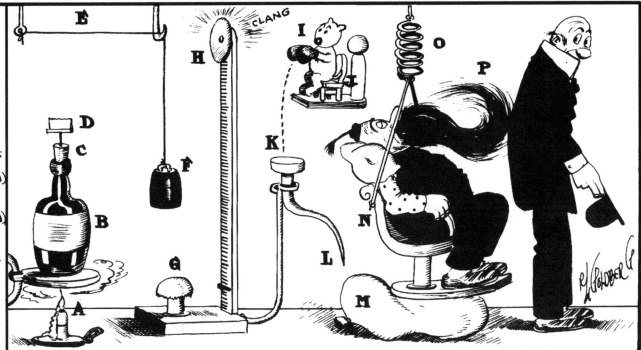

HEAT FROM FLAME (A) EXPANDS HOME BREW IN BOTTLE (B) AND CORK (C) FLIES OUT WITH ATTACHED SAFETY RAZOR BLADE (D), WHICH CUTS STRING (E) – WEIGHT (F) DROPS ON STRENGTH-TESTING MACHINE (G) RINGING BELL (H) – BOXING DOG (I) THINKS ROUND IS STARTING AND JUMPS OFF CHAIR (J) FALLING ON HEAD OF SPIKE (K) – POINT (L) PUNCTURES BALLOON (M) DROPPING CHAIR (N), WHICH BOBS UP AND DOWN ON SPRING (O), CAUSING WHISKERS (P) TO BRUSH OFF CLOTHES WITH NEATNESS AND CARE.

Keeping a Buttonhole Flower Fresh

PROFESSOR BUTTS STROLLS BETWEEN TWO SETS OF GANGSTERS HAVING A MACHINE-GUN BATTLE AND IS STRUCK BY AN IDEA FOR KEEPING A BUTTON-HOLE FLOWER FRESH.

BREEZE (A) REVOLVES PINWHEEL (B) AND WINDS CORD (C) WHICH PULLS TRIGGER (D), RELEASING STRING (E) AND SHOOTING ARROW (F) AGAINST BUTTON (G) OF CIGAR-LIGHTER (H). HEAT FROM FLAME (I), RISING THROUGH FLUE (J), CAUSES ICE (K) TO MELT INTO PAN (L) AND DRIP INTO SMALL DERBY HAT (M). EXTRA WEIGHT PULLS CORD (N) WHICH MOVES ARROW (O), DIRECTING ATTENTION OF BABY SEAL (P) TO BASIN OF WATER (Q). SEAL DIVES IN, SPLASHING WATER INTO TROUGH (R). IT RUNS ON FLOWER (S) KEEPING IT FRESH.

IF THERE IS NO BREEZE TO START THE PINWHEEL, SNEAK UP BEHIND A BRIDE AND STEAL A FRESH FLOWER.

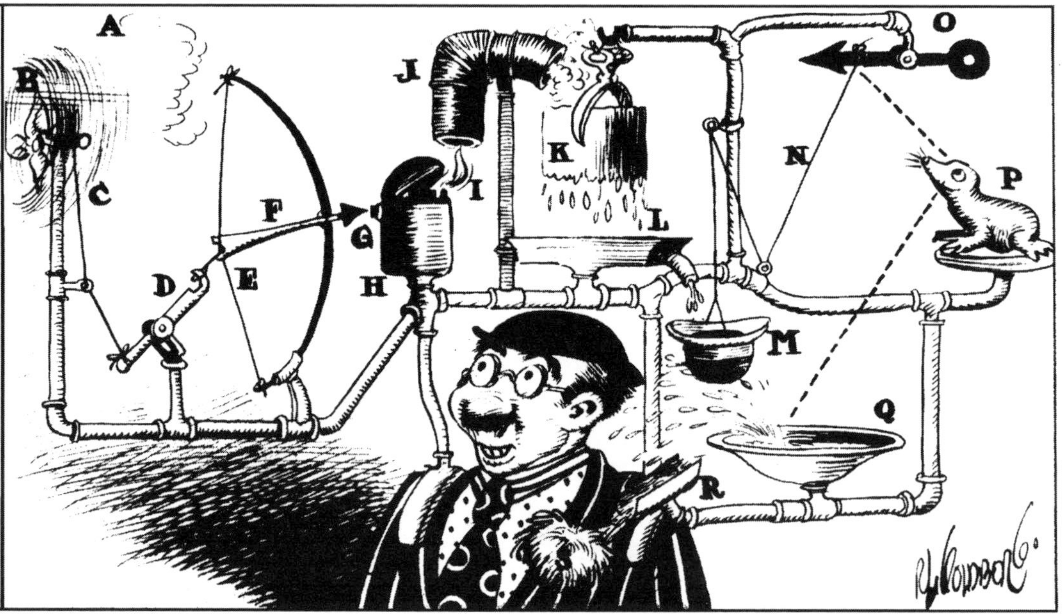
A
B
C
D
E
F
G
H
I
J
K
L
M
N
O
P
Q
R

A Simple Way to Locate Your Rubbers on a Rainy Day

PROFESSOR BUTTS LIES DOWN ON A FUR RUG WHICH TURNS OUT TO BE A SLEEPING LION AND DISCOVERS A SIMPLE WAY TO LOCATE YOUR RUBBERS ON A RAINY DAY.

AS RAIN (A) STARTS YOU WONDER WHERE YOU PUT YOUR RUBBERS. WHEN YOU PUT YOUR HAND (B) TO YOUR HEAD TO THINK, ELBOW (C) UPSETS BAG OF FLOWER SEEDS (D) INTO JARDINIERE (E) CAUSING PLANT TO GROW AND BLOSSOM, ATTRACTING BEES (F) WHICH FLY FROM THEIR HIVE (G). HIVE NATURALLY BECOMES LIGHTER IN WEIGHT AND ALLOWS END OF BOARD (H) TO DIP AND PULL CORD (I) TIPPING SALT SHAKER (J). AS SALT SPILLS ON SQUIRREL'S TAIL (K) HE THINKS SOME ONE IS TRYING TO CATCH HIM AND STARTS TO RUN THEREBY TURNING WHEEL (L) CAUSING WALKING-BEAM (M) TO MOVE SHOE (N) WHICH STAMPS FIRMLY ON BULBS OF AUTO HORNS (O) WHICH CONTINUE TO HONK UNTIL YOU HAVE PICKED UP YOUR RUBBERS. OF COURSE, AFTER YOU FIND YOUR RUBBERS YOU'LL HAVE TO BUY TWO AUTOMOBILES IF YOU DO NOT WANT HORNS TO GO TO WASTE.

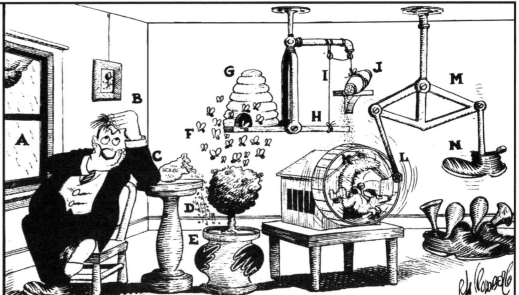

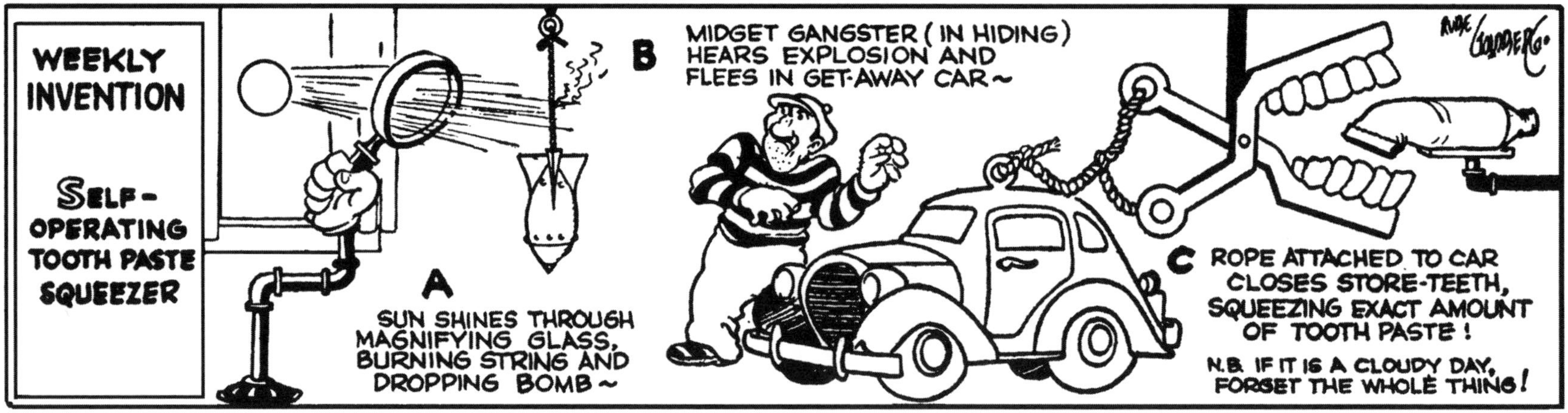
WEEKLY INVENTION
SELF-OPERATING TOOTH PASTE SQUEEZER
A
SUN SHINES THROUGH MAGNIFYING GLASS, BURNING STRING AND DROPPING BOMB ~
B
MIDGET GANGSTER (IN HIDING) HEARS EXPLOSION AND FLEES IN GET-AWAY CAR ~
C
ROPE ATTACHED TO CAR CLOSES STORE-TEETH, SQUEEZING EXACT AMOUNT OF TOOTH PASTE !
N.B. IF IT IS A CLOUDY DAY, FORGET THE WHOLE THING !
RUBE GOLDBERG

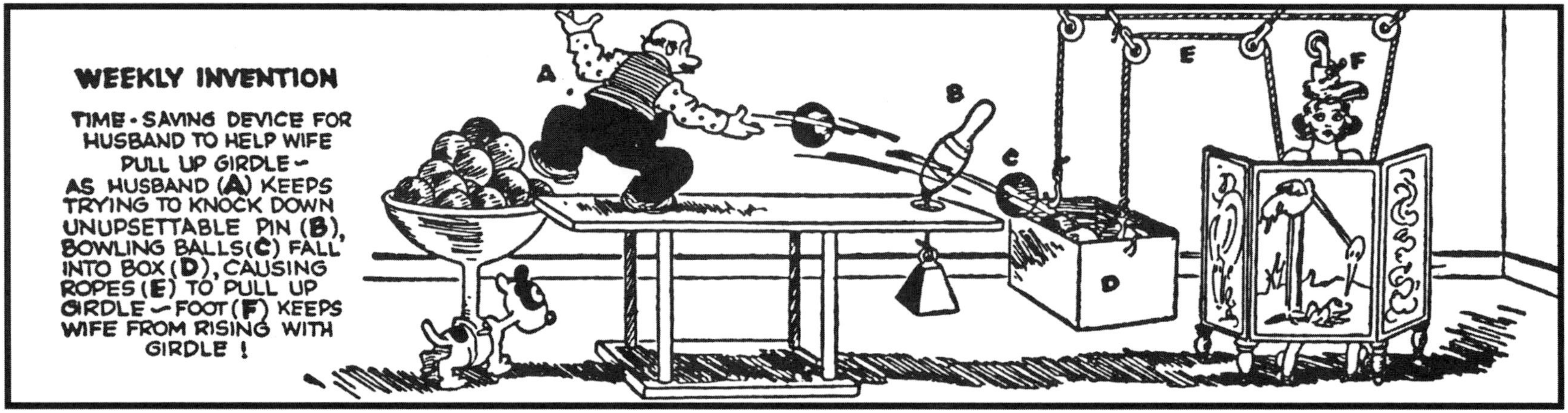
WEEKLY INVENTION
TIME-SAVING DEVICE FOR HUSBAND TO HELP WIFE PULL UP GIRDLE - AS HUSBAND (A) KEEPS TRYING TO KNOCK DOWN UNUPSETTABLE PIN (B), BOWLING BALLS (C) FALL INTO BOX (D), CAUSING ROPES (E) TO PULL UP GIRDLE - FOOT (F) KEEPS WIFE FROM RISING WITH GIRDLE !
A
B
C
D
E
F

Finding Your Lost Collar Button

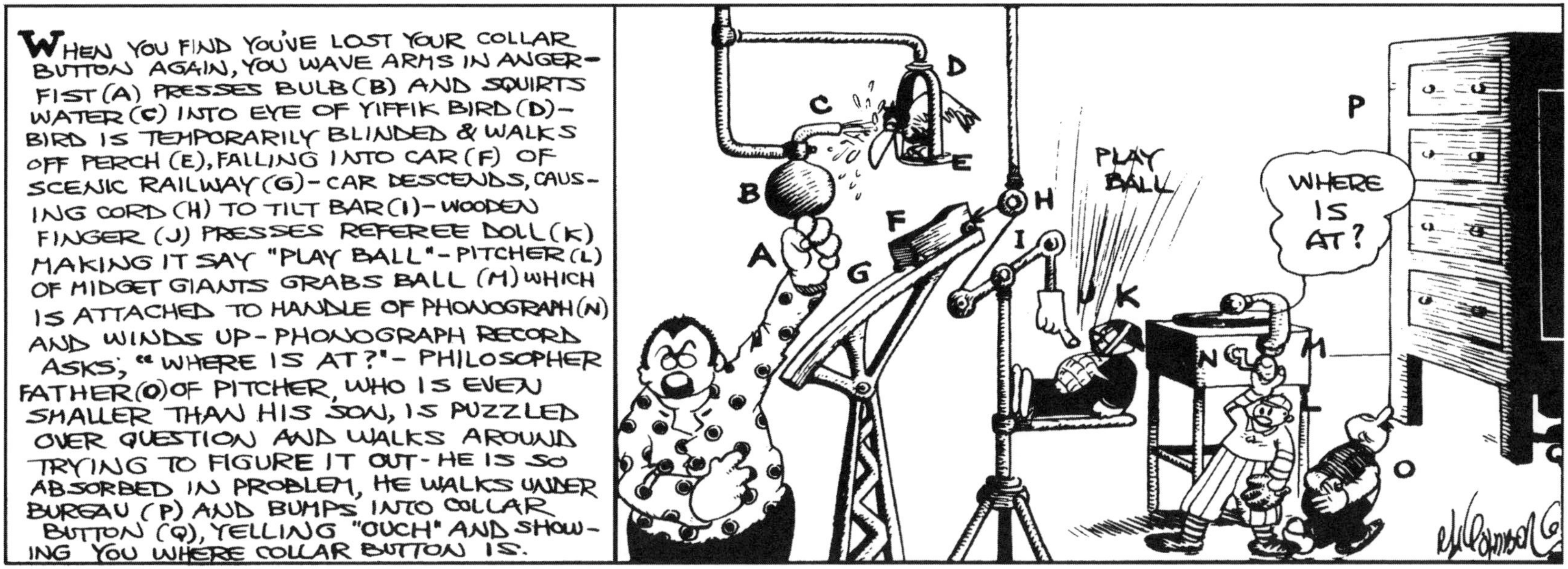
WHEN YOU FIND YOU'VE LOST YOUR COLLAR BUTTON AGAIN, YOU WAVE ARMS IN ANGER-FIST (A) PRESSES BULB (B) AND SQUIRTS WATER (C) INTO EYE OF YIFFIK BIRD (D)- BIRD IS TEMPORARILY BLINDED & WALKS OFF PERCH (E), FALLING INTO CAR (F) OF SCENIC RAILWAY (G) - CAR DESCENDS, CAUSING CORD (H) TO TILT BAR (I) - WOODEN FINGER (J) PRESSES REFEREE DOLL (K) MAKING IT SAY "PLAY BALL" - PITCHER (L) OF MIDGET GIANTS GRABS BALL (M) WHICH IS ATTACHED TO HANDLE OF PHONOGRAPH (N) AND WINDS UP - PHONOGRAPH RECORD ASKS; "WHERE IS AT?" - PHILOSOPHER FATHER (O) OF PITCHER, WHO IS EVEN SMALLER THAN HIS SON, IS PUZZLED OVER QUESTION AND WALKS AROUND TRYING TO FIGURE IT OUT - HE IS SO ABSORBED IN PROBLEM, HE WALKS UNDER BUREAU (P) AND BUMPS INTO COLLAR BUTTON (Q), YELLING "OUCH" AND SHOWING YOU WHERE COLLAR BUTTON IS.
PLAY BALL
WHERE IS AT?

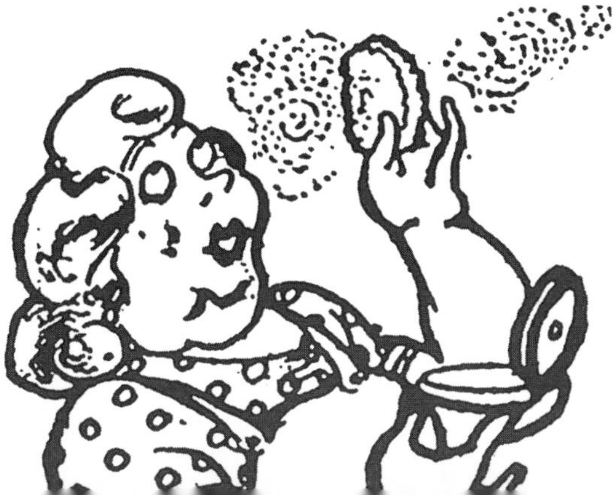

No More Laundry Delays

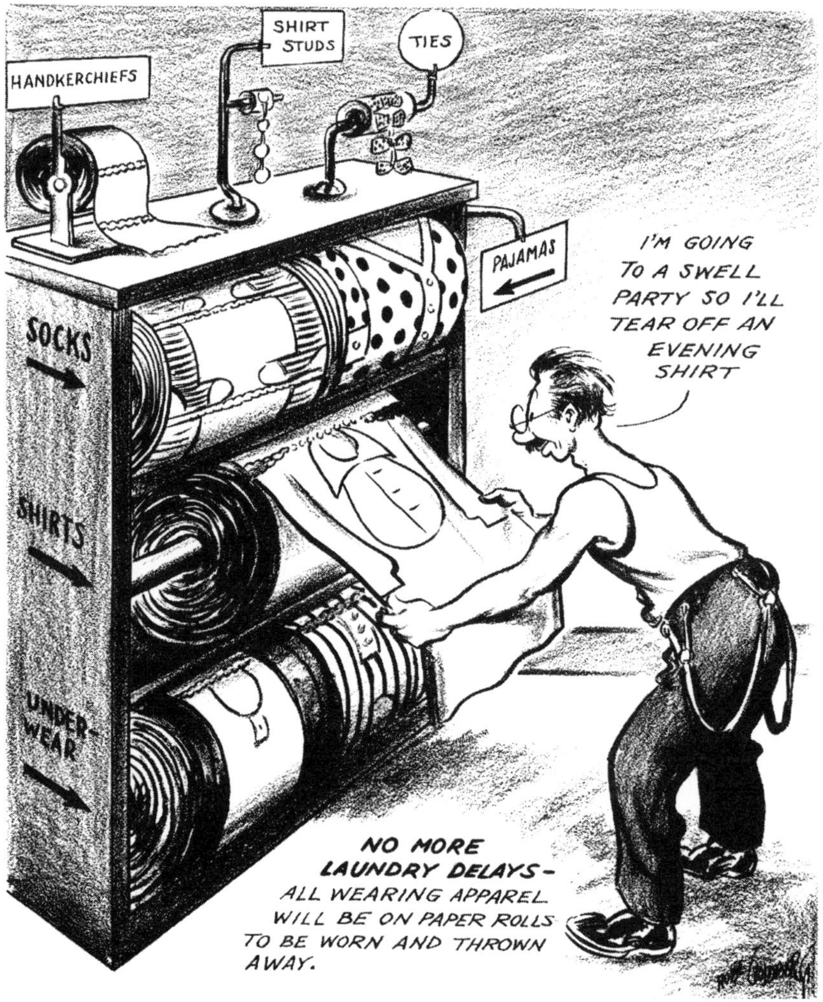
SHIRT STUDS
TIES
HANDKERCHIEFS
PAJAMAS
SOCKS
SHIRTS
UNDER-WEAR
I'M GOING TO A SWELL PARTY SO I'LL TEAR OFF AN EVENING SHIRT
NO MORE LAUNDRY DELAYS - ALL WEARING APPAREL WILL BE ON PAPER ROLLS TO BE WORN AND THROWN AWAY.

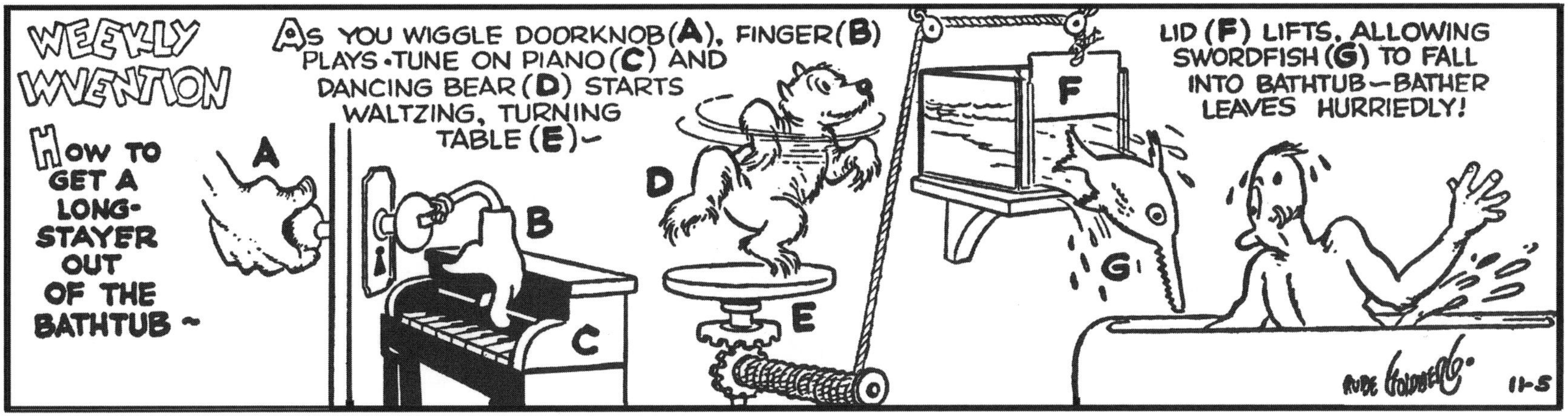
WEEKLY INVENTION
HOW TO GET A LONG-STAYER OUT OF THE BATHTUB ~
AS YOU WIGGLE DOORKNOB (A), FINGER (B) PLAYS • TUNE ON PIANO (C) AND DANCING BEAR (D) STARTS WALTZING, TURNING TABLE (E) -
LID (F) LIFTS, ALLOWING SWORDFISH (G) TO FALL INTO BATHTUB—BATHER LEAVES HURRIEDLY!
RUBE GOLDBERG
11-5

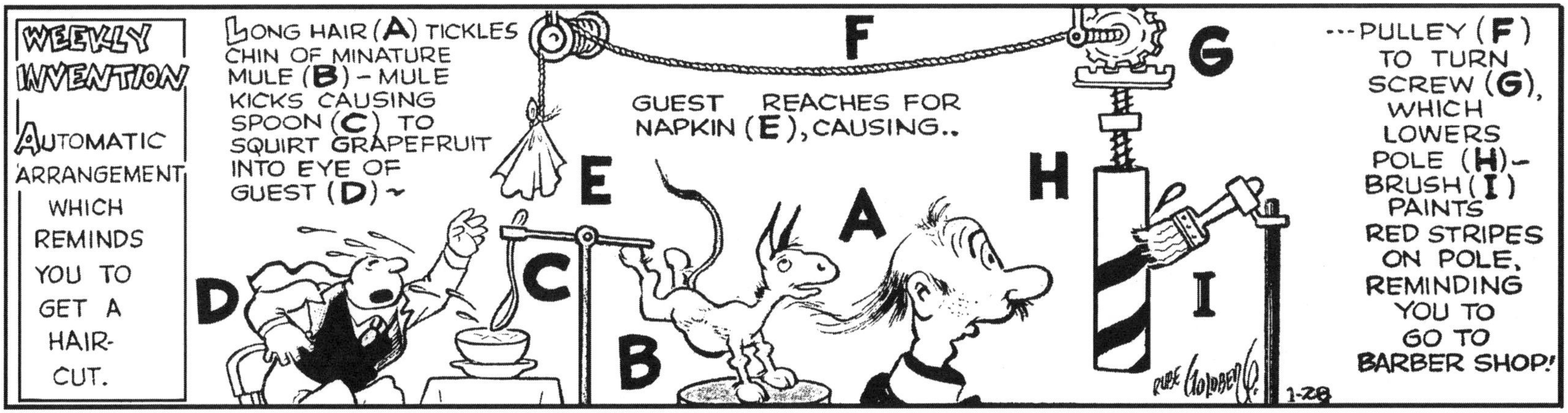
WEEKLY INVENTION
AUTOMATIC ARRANGEMENT WHICH REMINDS YOU TO GET A HAIR-CUT.
LONG HAIR (A) TICKLES CHIN OF MINATURE MULE (B) - MULE KICKS CAUSING SPOON (C) TO SQUIRT GRAPEFRUIT INTO EYE OF GUEST (D) ~
GUEST REACHES FOR NAPKIN (E), CAUSING..
---PULLEY (F) TO TURN SCREW (G), WHICH LOWERS POLE (H)- BRUSH (I) PAINTS RED STRIPES ON POLE, REMINDING YOU TO GO TO BARBER SHOP!
RUBE GOLDBERG
1-28

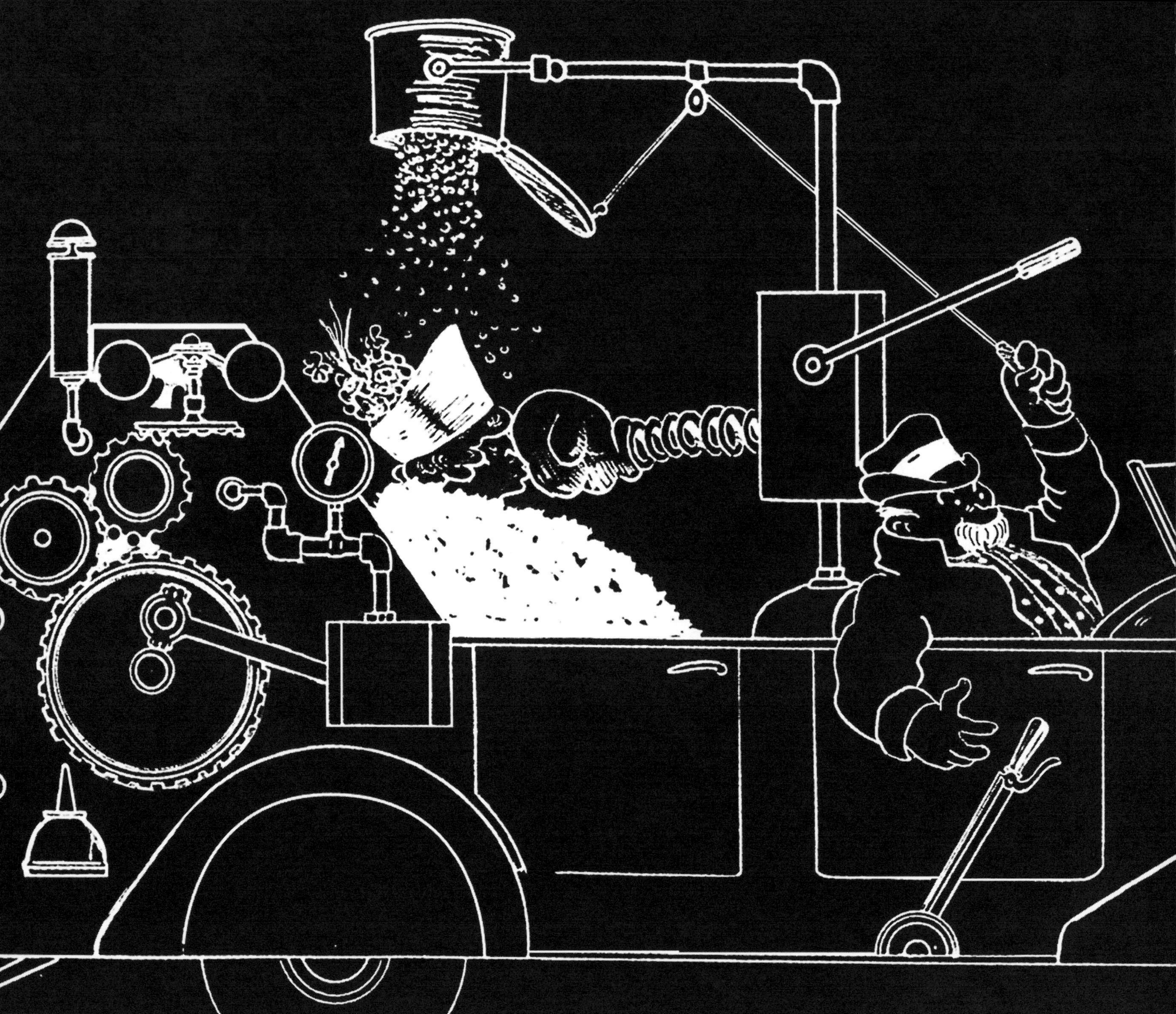

Traveling

Nothing defines the twentieth century better than the phrase *Machine Age*. Within the space of a relatively few years, the passenger ship and the train were joined by the automobile and then the airplane to make travel accessible and practical for everyone.

Rube Goldberg's Inventions helped to bring those Machine Age travelers to their destinations on foot, in the air, or in boats of all sizes. But nothing captured Rube's imagination like the family automobile.

Rube's automobile inventions eliminated fossil fuels, combated road rage, and helped drivers to escape traffic tickets, all in the comfort of their own automobiles. On the street, Rube's Inventions protected pedestrians from hot weather, street violence, and muggings, as well as hit-and-run drivers. Traveling on the road for business or on vacation, Rube's Inventions made sure that you got there and back home with a laugh, no matter how tough the trip was.

Get One of Our Patent Fans and Keep Cool

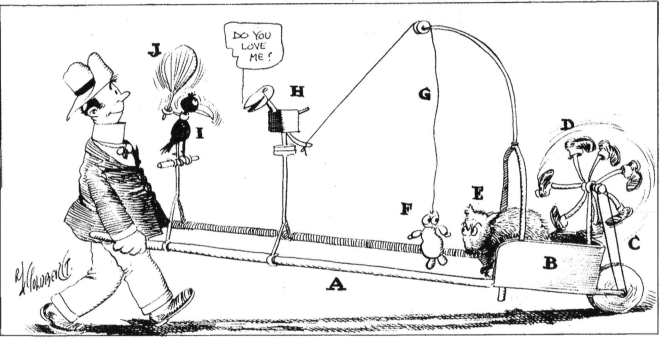

TAKE HOLD OF HANDLES (A) OF WHEELBARROW (B) AND START WALKING—PULLEY (C) TURNS KICKING ARRANGEMENT (D) WHICH ANNOYS BEAR (E)—BEAR SUSPECTS DOLL (F) AND EATS IT, PULLING STRING (G) WHICH STARTS MECHANICAL BIRD (H) SAYING, "DO YOU LOVE ME?"—LOVE-BIRD (I) KEEPS SHAKING HEAD "YES", CAUSING FAN (J) TO MOVE BACK AND FORTH MAKING NICE BREEZE BLOW RIGHT IN YOUR FACE.

DO YOU LOVE ME?

Simple Way to Light a Cigar in an Automobile Traveling Fifty Miles an Hour

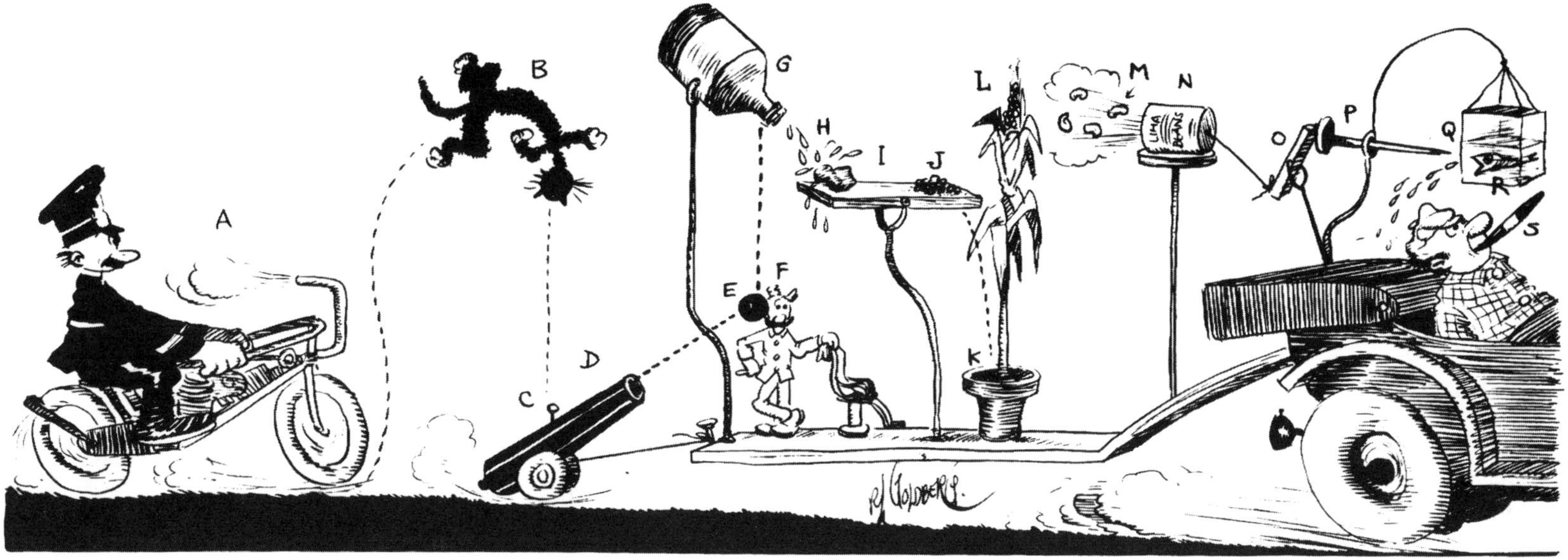
A
B
C
D
E
F
G
H
I
J
K
L
M
N
LIMA BEANS
O
P
Q
R
S

WHEN AUTOMOBILE SPEEDS AT FIFTY MILES AN HOUR MOTORCYCLE COP (A) STARTS IN PERSUIT - MOTORCYCLE HITS CAT (B) CAUSING IT TO FALL ON BUTTON (C) WHICH SETS OFF CANNON (D) - CANNON BALL (E) HITS IVORY DOME OF BARBER (F), BOUNCING OFF AND KNOCKING NECK OFF BOTTLE OF STRONG ACID (G) - ACID DROPS ON GOLD NUGGET (H) DISOLVING IT - WEIGHT OF KERNELS OF CORN (J) LOWER BOARD (I) AND FALL INTO FLOWER POT (K) - CORN GROWS TILL IT REACHES HEIGHT (L) - CAN(N) OF LIMA BEANS (M) JUMPS AT CORN ON ACCOUNT OF THE NATURAL AFFINITY FOR SUCCOTASH - STRING ON END OF CAN PULLS LEVER (O) WHICH PUSHES POINTER (P) INTO PAPER TANK (Q) HALF FILLED WITH WATER IN WHICH SARDINE (R) IS SWIMMING - POINTER PUNCTURES PAPER TANK, WATER RUNS OUT AND SARDINE CATCHES SEVERE COLD FROM EXPOSURE - SARDINE CONTRACTS A VERY HIGH FEVER THAT FINALLY SETS FIRE TO PAPER TANK AND LIGHTS CIGAR (S).

Simple Idea to Ensure Safety at Railroad Crossings

PROFESSOR BUTTS STEALS A RIDE ON TOP OF A TRAIN, FORGETS TO DUCK AT THE ENTRANCE OF A TUNNEL, AND BLURTS OUT AN IDEA TO INSURE SAFETY AT RAILROAD CROSSINGS. AS COMMUTER (A) HEARS TRAIN WHISTLE HE THINKS HE IS LATE AND RUNS ACROSS FIELD TO MAKE SHORT-CUT, SCARING OUT JACK-RABBIT (B) WHO ATTRACTS ATTENTION OF GIFFIK HOUND (C). HOUND JUMPS, PULLING STRING (D) WHICH RAISES END OF BOARD (E) AND PUSHES HANDLE OF SQUIRT GUN (F) WHICH WETS BACK OF DUCK (G). AS WATER ROLLS OFF DUCK'S BACK IT RUNS DOWN TROUGH (H) ON TO SPONGE (I). AS SPONGE BECOMES HEAVY, EXTRA WEIGHT PULLS HOOK (J) CAUSING IT TO RELEASE SPRING (K) CAUSING BASEBALL BAT (L) TO HIT BASEBALL (M) INTO CATCHER'S GLOVE (N) AND PUSH BOX OF TACKS (O) FROM SHELF. AS TACKS SPILL ON ROAD THEY PUNCTURE TIRES AND FORCE DUMB DRIVER TO STOP EVEN THOUGH HE WANTS TO BEAT SPEEDING TRAIN AT CROSSING. THE TIRE EXPENSE IS QUITE AN ITEM BUT TIRE BILLS ARE GENERALLY SMALLER THAN UNDERTAKERS' BILLS.

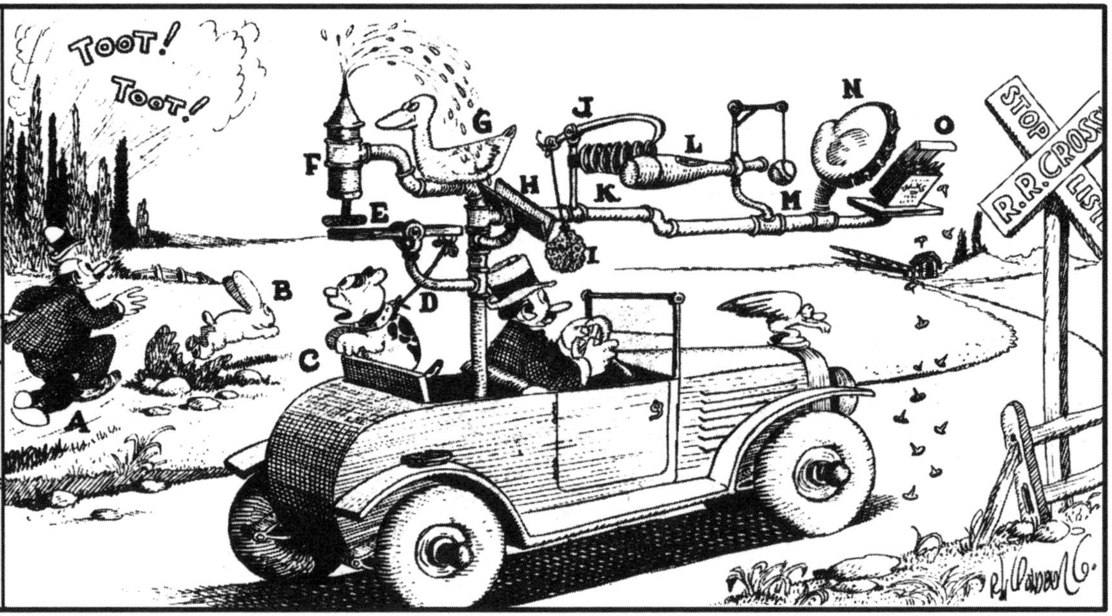
TOOT!
TOOT!
A
B
C
D
E
F
G
H
I
J
K
L
M
N
O
STOP

Now You Can Cross the Street Without Worrying

HERE IS A SIMPLE WAY TO PROTECT YOURSELF AGAINST RECKLESS DRIVERS— AS YOU FLY THROUGH THE AIR, THE LITTLE FANS ON THE CAMERAS REVOLVE AND SNAP A PICTURE OF THE LICENSE NUMBER OF THE CAR THAT KNOCKS YOU DOWN— THIS MAKES IT EASY TO LOCATE THE OWNER SO YOU CAN SUE HIM WHEN YOU GET OUT OF THE HOSPITAL— THE CAMERAS ARE ARRANGED SO THE PHOTOGRAPH CAN BE TAKEN FROM ANY POSITION.

JUDGE, I WAS ONLY GOING 10 MILES AN HOUR AND HE WALKED RIGHT INTO MY CAR

THAT'S THE OLD BOLONEY! THIRTY DAYS!

Drivers–Simple Way to Stop Shouting at Other Drivers

PROFESSOR LUCIFER GORGONZOLA BUTTS A.K. HAS INVENTED A CHANGEABLE ELECTRIC SIGN TO SAVE AUTOMOBILISTS THE TROUBLE OF SHOUTING THEIR SENTIMENTS AT OTHER AUTOMOBILISTS.

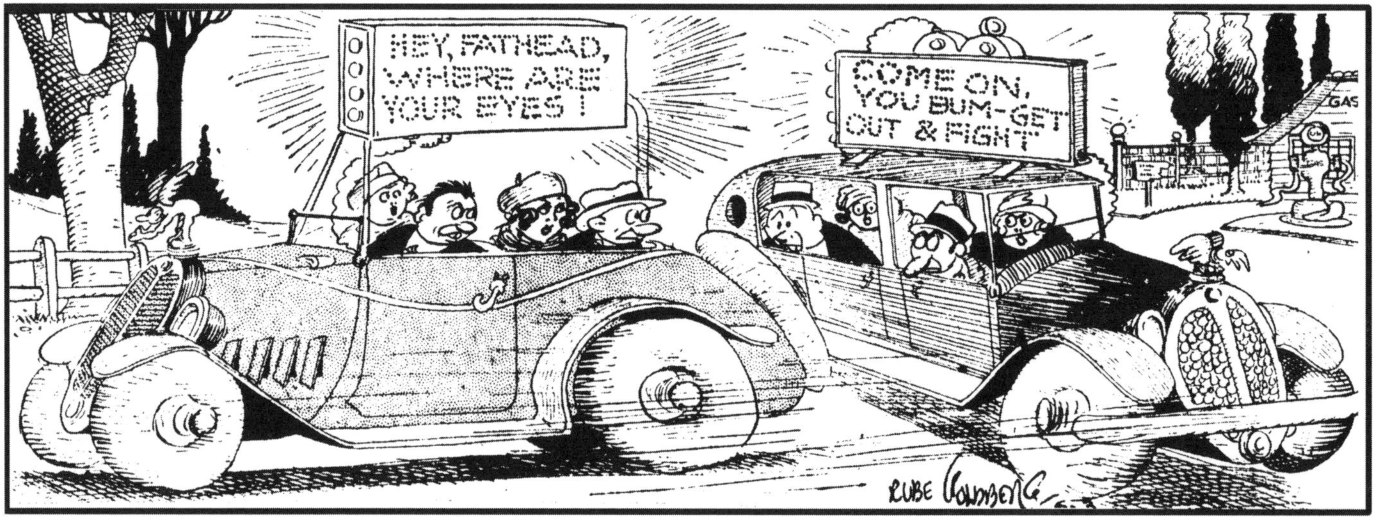
HEY, FATHEAD, WHERE ARE YOUR EYES!
COME ON, YOU BUM–GET OUT & FIGHT
GAS
RUBE GOLDBERG

Self-Working Tire Pump

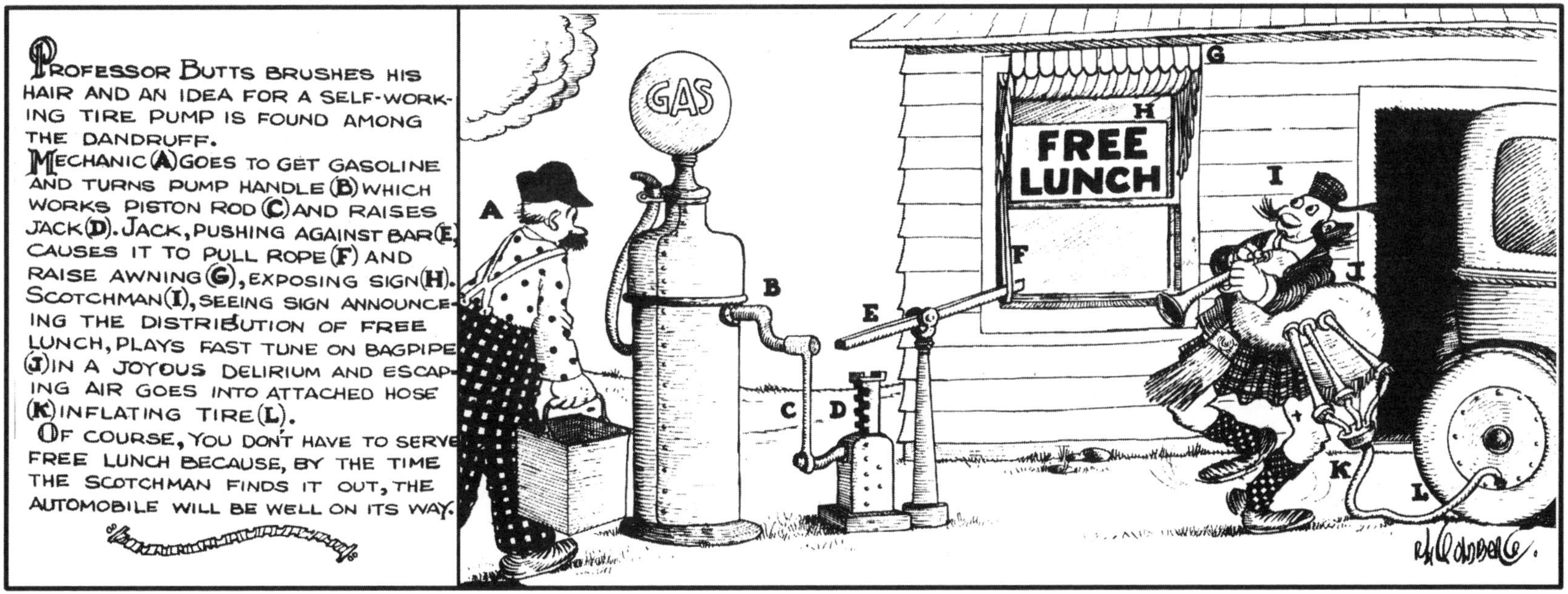
PROFESSOR BUTTS BRUSHES HIS HAIR AND AN IDEA FOR A SELF-WORKING TIRE PUMP IS FOUND AMONG THE DANDRUFF.
MECHANIC (A) GOES TO GET GASOLINE AND TURNS PUMP HANDLE (B) WHICH WORKS PISTON ROD (C) AND RAISES JACK (D). JACK, PUSHING AGAINST BAR (E), CAUSES IT TO PULL ROPE (F) AND RAISE AWNING (G), EXPOSING SIGN (H). SCOTCHMAN (I), SEEING SIGN ANNOUNCING THE DISTRIBUTION OF FREE LUNCH, PLAYS FAST TUNE ON BAGPIPE (J) IN A JOYOUS DELIRIUM AND ESCAPING AIR GOES INTO ATTACHED HOSE (K) INFLATING TIRE (L).
OF COURSE, YOU DON'T HAVE TO SERVE FREE LUNCH BECAUSE, BY THE TIME THE SCOTCHMAN FINDS IT OUT, THE AUTOMOBILE WILL BE WELL ON ITS WAY.
GAS
FREE LUNCH
A
B
C
D
E
F
G
H
I
J
K
L

Sure Cure for Nagging Wife (or Husband) Who Criticizes Your Driving

SURE CURE FOR NAGGING WIFE (OR HUSBAND) WHO CONTINUALLY CRITICIZES YOUR DRIVING

Simple Way to Escape a Motorcycle Cop

PROFESSOR LUCIFER GORGONZOLA BUTTS A.K. DOPES OUT SIMPLE WAY TO ESCAPE MOTORCYCLE COP - WIFE (A) SEES PURSUING COP IN MIRROR (B) AND SCREAMS, SCARING DOG (C) - DOG JUMPS AND LANDS ON STOMACH OF FAT DWARF (D) - DWARF GRUNTS AND AIR (E) REVOLVES WHEEL (F) COMPOSED OF ORDINARY MATCHES - MATCHES RUB ON SAND-PAPER (G), IGNITING FUSE (H) AND SETTING OFF SMOKE BOMB (I) - SMOKE BOMB LEAVES CAR AT RIGHT ANGLES AND COP FOLLOWS TRAIL OF SMOKE DOWN SIDE ROAD THINKING IT IS YOUR CAR - IF THE BOMB IS OFF LINE AND HITS THE COP THAT WILL BE ALL RIGHT, TOO.

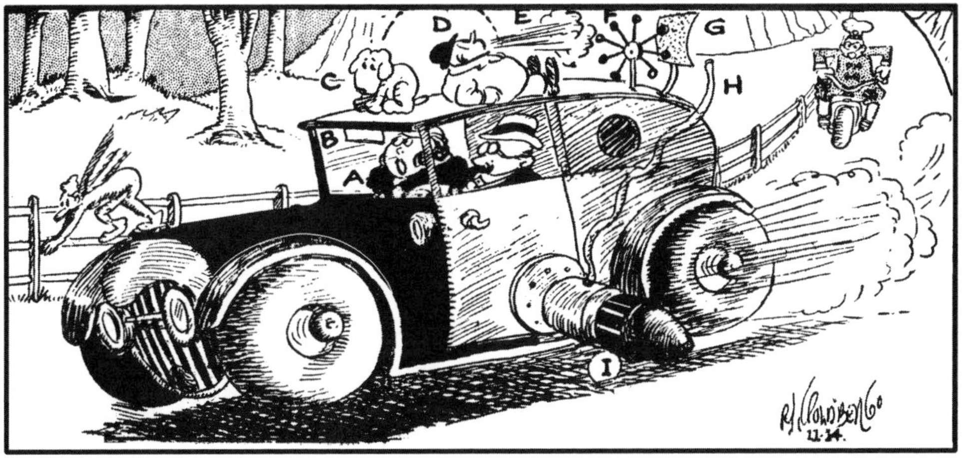
D
E
F
G
C
H
B
A
I

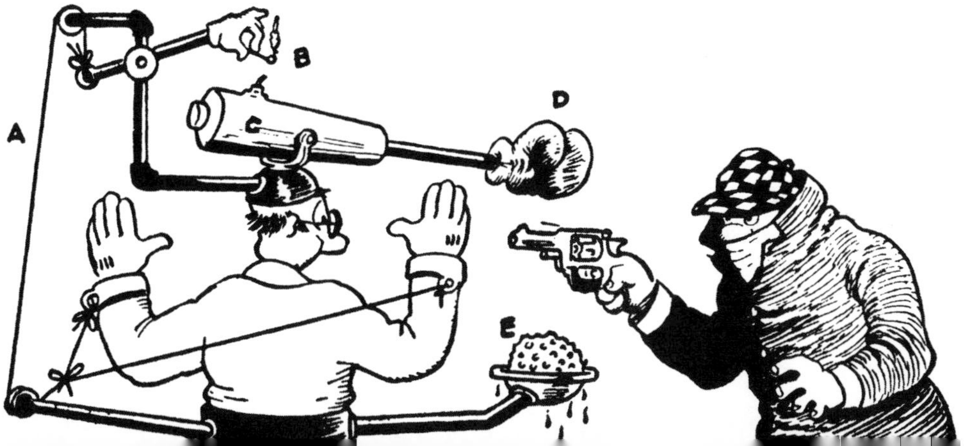
A
B
C
D
E

No More Gasoline Problems

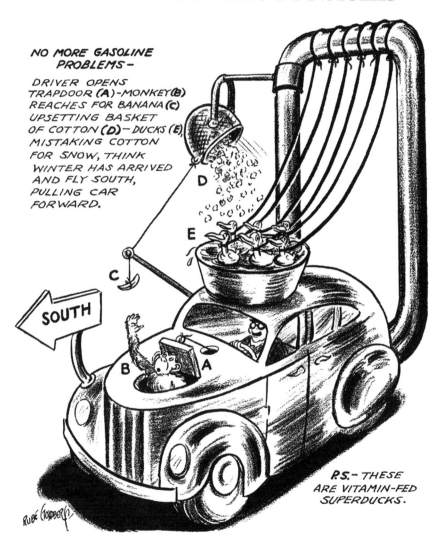

NO MORE GASOLINE
PROBLEMS—

DRIVER OPENS
TRAPDOOR (A)—MONKEY (B)
REACHES FOR BANANA (C)
UPSETTING BASKET
OF COTTON (D)—DUCKS (E),
MISTAKING COTTON
FOR SNOW, THINK
WINTER HAS ARRIVED
AND FLY SOUTH,
PULLING CAR
FORWARD.

SOUTH

P.S.— THESE
ARE VITAMIN-FED
SUPERDUCKS.

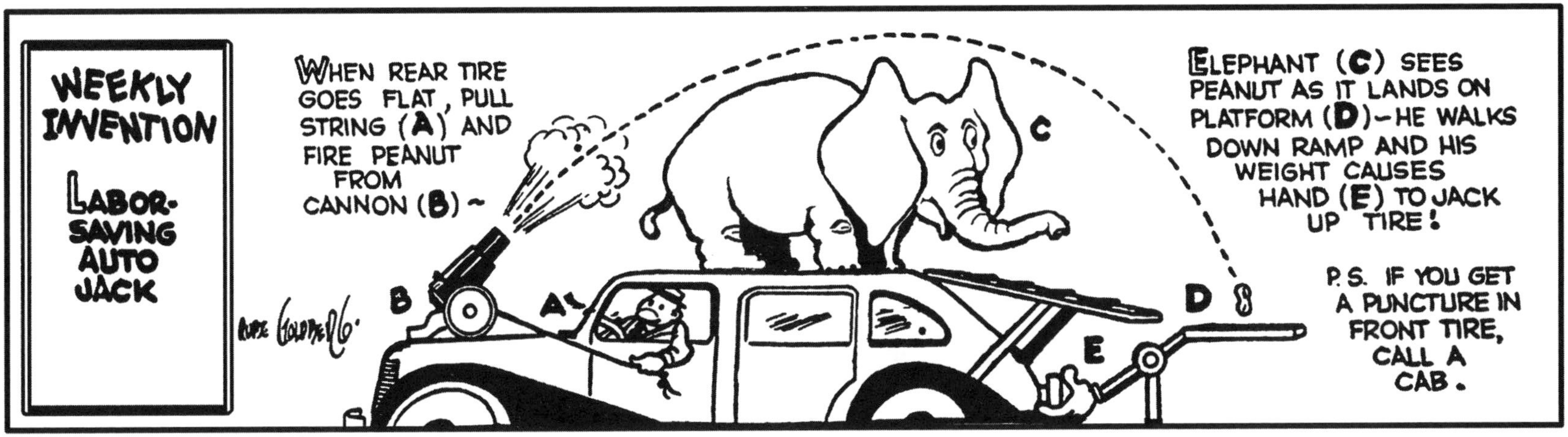
WEEKLY INVENTION
LABOR-SAVING AUTO JACK
WHEN REAR TIRE GOES FLAT, PULL STRING (A) AND FIRE PEANUT FROM CANNON (B) ~
ELEPHANT (C) SEES PEANUT AS IT LANDS ON PLATFORM (D) - HE WALKS DOWN RAMP AND HIS WEIGHT CAUSES HAND (E) TO JACK UP TIRE!
P.S. IF YOU GET A PUNCTURE IN FRONT TIRE, CALL A CAB.
A
B
C
D
E
RUBE GOLDBERG

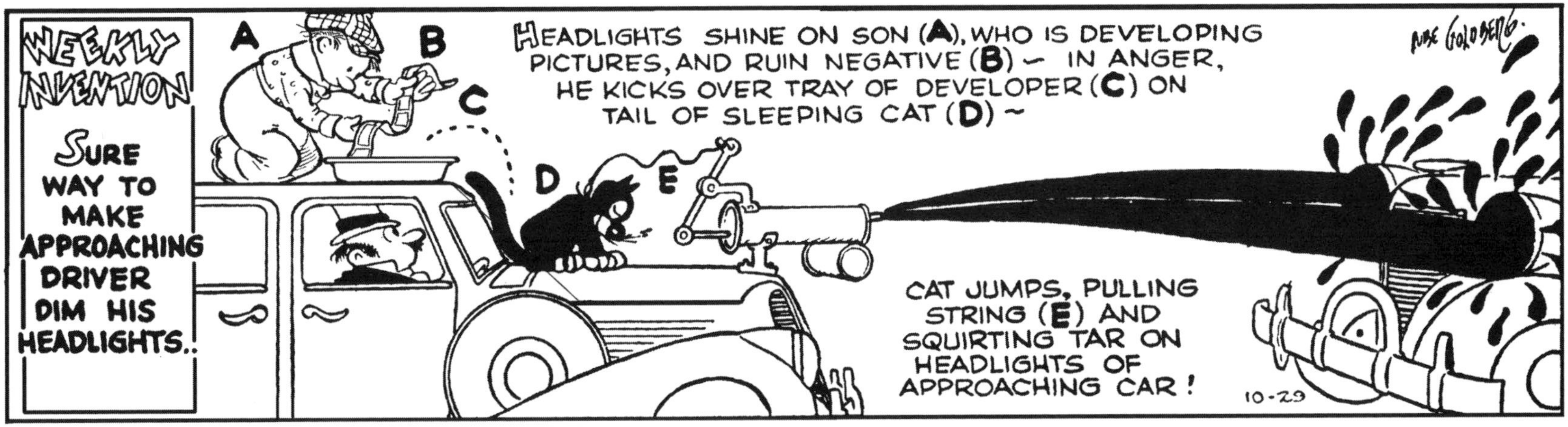
WEEKLY INVENTION
SURE WAY TO MAKE APPROACHING DRIVER DIM HIS HEADLIGHTS..
HEADLIGHTS SHINE ON SON (A), WHO IS DEVELOPING PICTURES, AND RUIN NEGATIVE (B) ~ IN ANGER, HE KICKS OVER TRAY OF DEVELOPER (C) ON TAIL OF SLEEPING CAT (D) ~
CAT JUMPS, PULLING STRING (E) AND SQUIRTING TAR ON HEADLIGHTS OF APPROACHING CAR!
A
B
C
D
E
RUBE GOLDBERG
10-29

Automatic Garage Door Opener

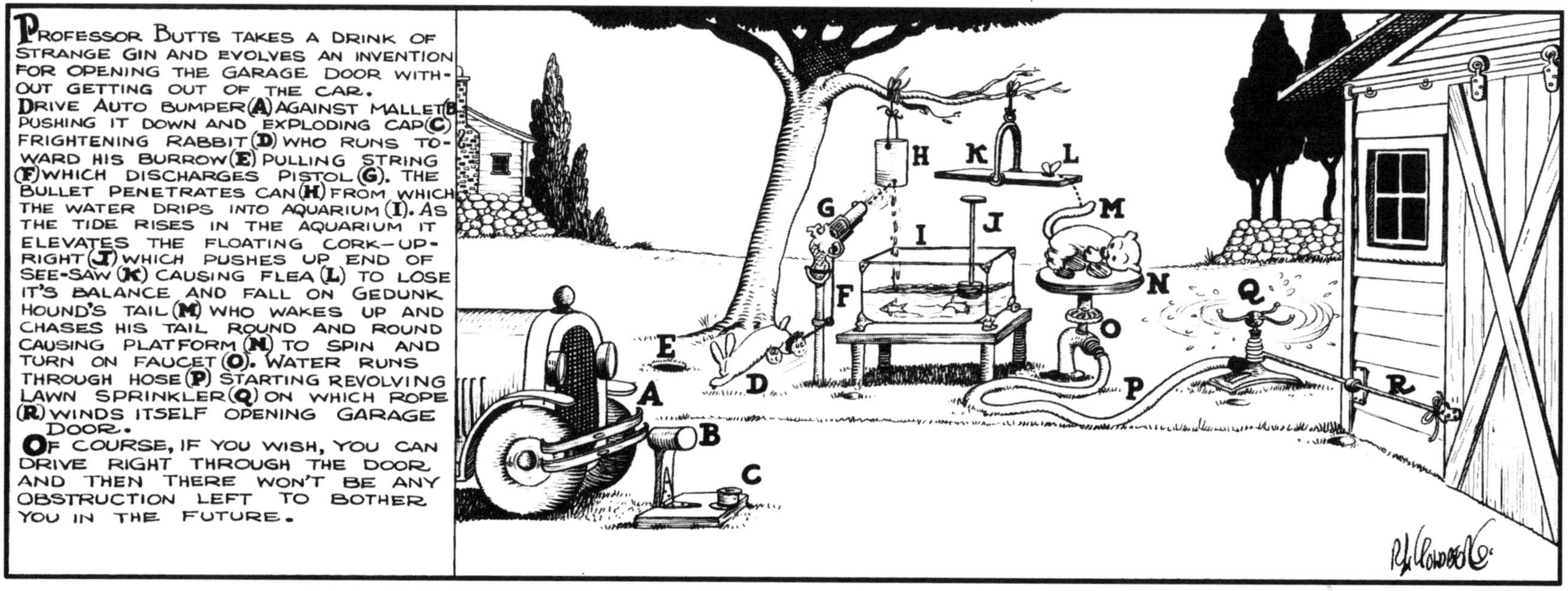
PROFESSOR BUTTS TAKES A DRINK OF STRANGE GIN AND EVOLVES AN INVENTION FOR OPENING THE GARAGE DOOR WITHOUT GETTING OUT OF THE CAR.
DRIVE AUTO BUMPER (A) AGAINST MALLET (B) PUSHING IT DOWN AND EXPLODING CAP (C) FRIGHTENING RABBIT (D) WHO RUNS TOWARD HIS BURROW (E) PULLING STRING (F) WHICH DISCHARGES PISTOL (G). THE BULLET PENETRATES CAN (H) FROM WHICH THE WATER DRIPS INTO AQUARIUM (I). AS THE TIDE RISES IN THE AQUARIUM IT ELEVATES THE FLOATING CORK-UPRIGHT (J) WHICH PUSHES UP END OF SEE-SAW (K) CAUSING FLEA (L) TO LOSE IT'S BALANCE AND FALL ON GEDUNK HOUND'S TAIL (M) WHO WAKES UP AND CHASES HIS TAIL ROUND AND ROUND CAUSING PLATFORM (N) TO SPIN AND TURN ON FAUCET (O). WATER RUNS THROUGH HOSE (P) STARTING REVOLVING LAWN SPRINKLER (Q) ON WHICH ROPE (R) WINDS ITSELF OPENING GARAGE DOOR.
OF COURSE, IF YOU WISH, YOU CAN DRIVE RIGHT THROUGH THE DOOR AND THEN THERE WON'T BE ANY OBSTRUCTION LEFT TO BOTHER YOU IN THE FUTURE.
A
B
C
D
E
F
G
H
I
J
K
L
M
N
O
P
Q
R

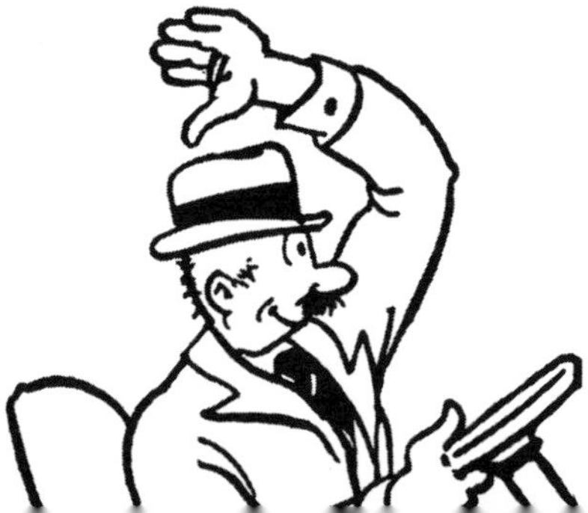

Life-Saving Apparatus for People Who Ride in Taxicabs

HEAVY SPRING UNDER **HIGH HAT** TO KEEP YOU FROM KNOCKING YOUR BRAINS OUT WHEN YOUR HEAD BUMPS AGAINST TOP OF TAXI.

GLASS-CUTTER ON THE END OF NOSE, TO CLEAR THE WAY WHEN YOU FLY THROUGH THE FRONT OF TAXI, AFTER COLLISION.

PNEUMATIC TROUSERS TO TAKE UP GENERAL SHOCK OF TAXI-RIDING.

SHADE ON DERBY, TO PULL DOWN SO YOU WON'T SEE TELL-TALE TAXI-METER.

ANCHOR FOR GENERAL USE IN KEEPING YOU FROM TRAVELING AROUND TOO MUCH INSIDE OF TAXI.

Outboard Motor That Requires No Fuel

PROFESSOR BUTTS TRIES TO FIX A LEAK IN THE BOILER AND WHEN HE IS RESCUED FROM DROWNING HE COUGHS UP AN IDEA FOR AN OUTBOARD MOTOR THAT REQUIRES NO FUEL.

AS YOU REACH FOR ANCHOR, BUTTON (A) SNAPS LOOSE AND HITS SPIGOT (B) CAUSING BEER TO RUN INTO PAIL (C). WEIGHT PULLS CORD (D) FIRING SHOT GUN (E). REPORT FRIGHTENS SEA GULL (F) WHICH FLIES AWAY AND CAUSES ICE (G) TO LOWER IN FRONT OF FALSE TEETH (H). AS TEETH CHATTER FROM COLD THEY BITE CORD (I) IN HALF ALLOWING POINTED TOOL (J) TO DROP AND RIP BAG OF CORN (K). CORN FALLS INTO NET (L). WEIGHT CAUSES IT TO SNAP LATCH OPENING FLOOR OF CAGE (M) AND DROPPING DUCK INTO SHAFTS (N). AS DUCK (O) TRIES TO REACH CORN IT SWIMS AND CAUSES CANOE TO MOVE AHEAD.

IF THE FALSE TEETH KEEP ON CHATTERING YOU CAN LET THEM CHEW YOUR GUM TO GIVE YOUR OWN JAWS A REST.

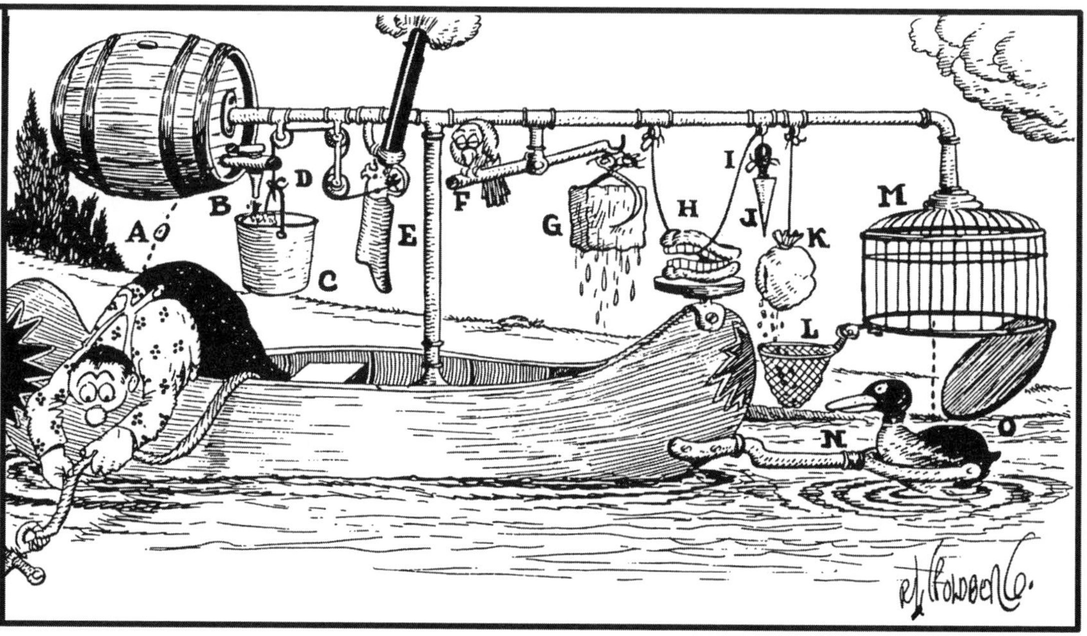
A
B
C
D
E
F
G
H
I
J
K
L
M
N
O

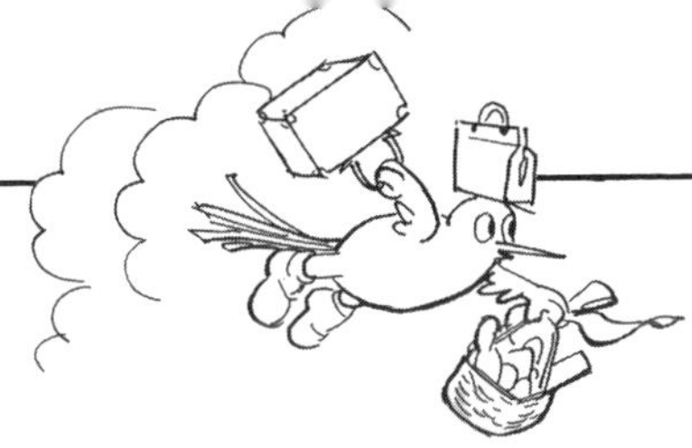

Simple Parachute for Aviators

PROFESSOR BUTTS GETS HIS WHISKERS CAUGHT IN A LAUNDRY WRINGER AND AS HE COMES OUT THE OTHER END HE THINKS OF AN IDEA FOR A SIMPLE PARACHUTE.

AS AVIATOR JUMPS FROM PLANE FORCE OF WIND OPENS UMBRELLA (A) WHICH PULLS CORD (B) AND CLOSES SHEARS (C), CUTTING OFF CORNER OF FEATHER PILLOW (D). AS WHITE FEATHERS (E) FLY FROM PILLOW, PENGUIN (F) MISTAKES THEM FOR SNOW FLAKES AND FLAPS HIS WINGS FOR JOY WHICH DRAWS BUCK-SAW (G) BACK AND FORTH CUTTING LOG OF WOOD (H). AS PIECE OF WOOD FALLS INTO BASKET (I) ITS WEIGHT CAUSES ROPE (J) TO PULL TRIGGER OF GUN (K) WHICH EXPLODES AND SHOOTS LOCK FROM CAGE (L) RELEASING GIANT UMPHA BIRD (M) WHICH FLIES AND KEEPS AVIATOR AFLOAT WITH ROPE (N). AVIATOR BREAKS PAPER BAG OF CORN (O) CAUSING CORN TO FALL TO GROUND. WHEN BIRD SWOOPS DOWN TO EAT CORN, FLIER UNHOOKS APPARATUS AND WALKS HOME.

THE BIGGEST PROBLEM IS WHERE TO GET THE UMPHA BIRD. WRITE YOUR CONGRESSMAN.

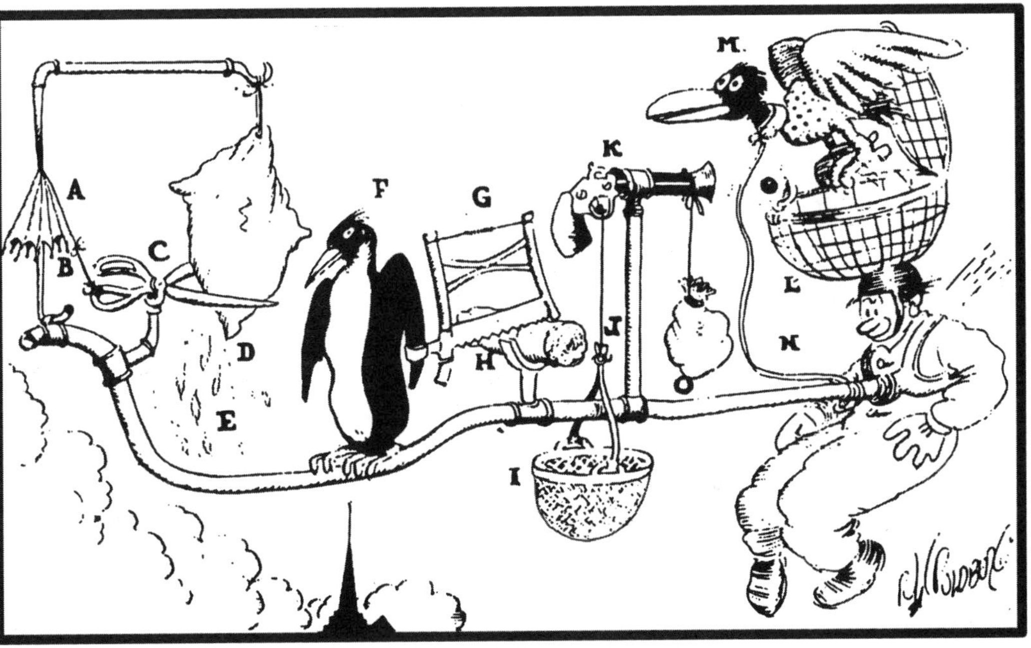
A
B
C
D
E
F
G
H
I
J
K
L
M.
N
O

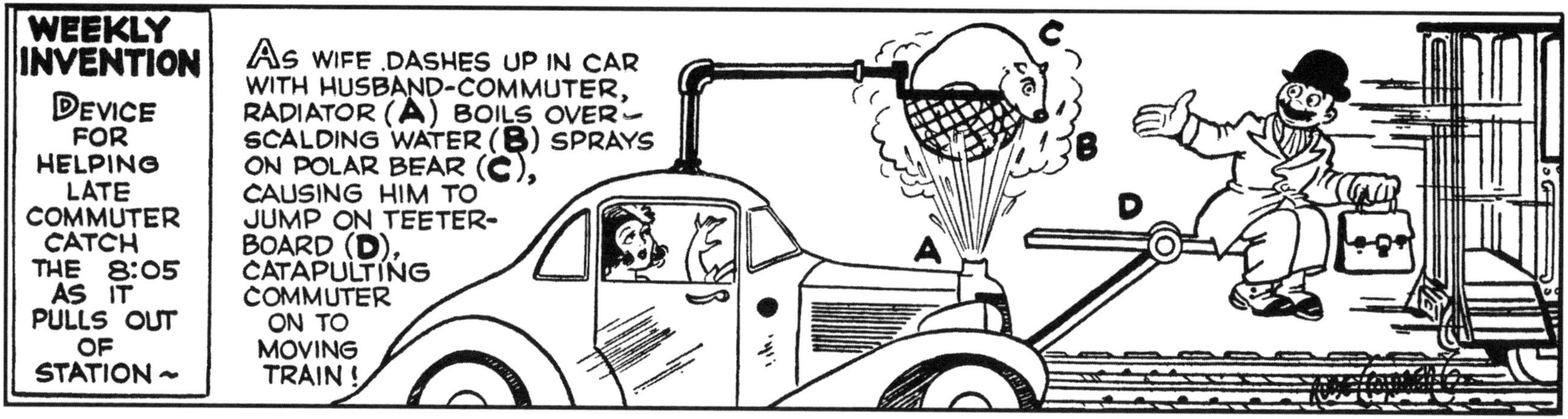
WEEKLY INVENTION
DEVICE FOR HELPING LATE COMMUTER CATCH THE 8:05 AS IT PULLS OUT OF STATION ~
AS WIFE DASHES UP IN CAR WITH HUSBAND-COMMUTER, RADIATOR (A) BOILS OVER – SCALDING WATER (B) SPRAYS ON POLAR BEAR (C), CAUSING HIM TO JUMP ON TEETER-BOARD (D), CATAPULTING COMMUTER ON TO MOVING TRAIN!
C
B
D
A

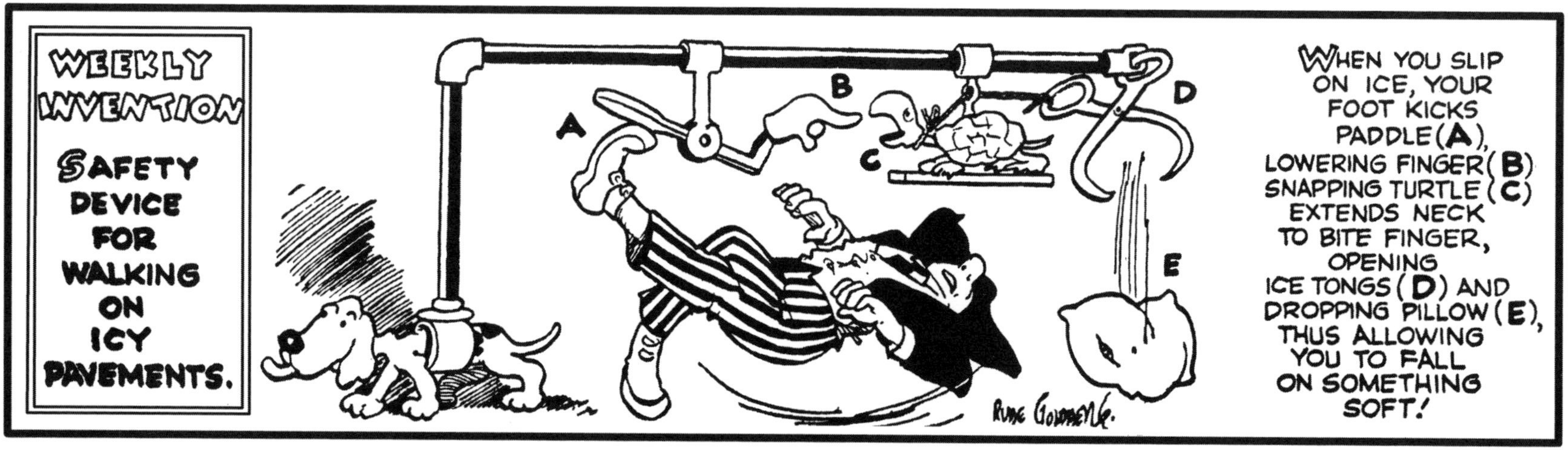
WEEKLY INVENTION
SAFETY DEVICE FOR WALKING ON ICY PAVEMENTS.
A
B
C
D
E
WHEN YOU SLIP ON ICE, YOUR FOOT KICKS PADDLE (A), LOWERING FINGER (B) SNAPPING TURTLE (C) EXTENDS NECK TO BITE FINGER, OPENING ICE TONGS (D) AND DROPPING PILLOW (E), THUS ALLOWING YOU TO FALL ON SOMETHING SOFT!

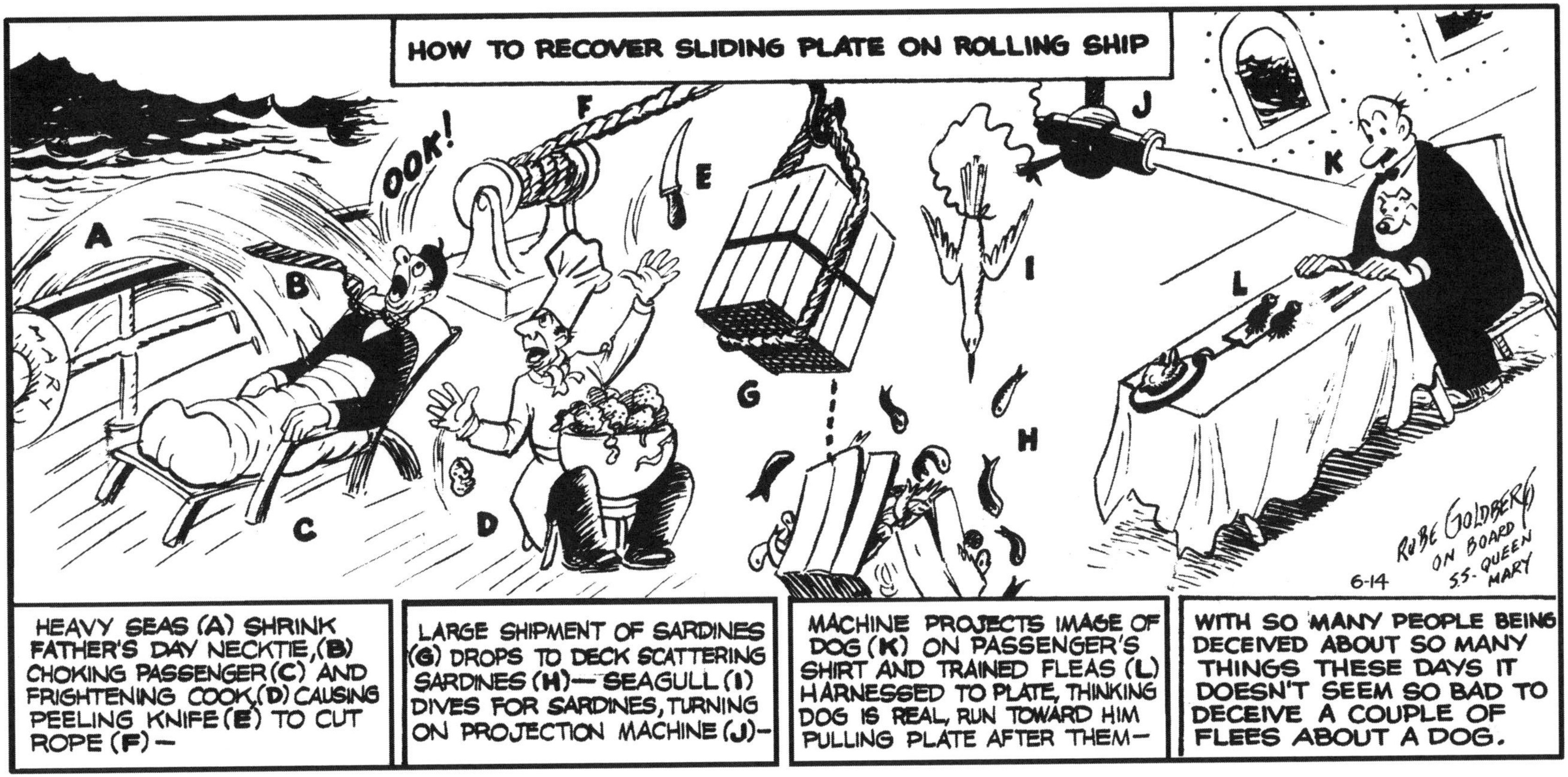
HOW TO RECOVER SLIDING PLATE ON ROLLING SHIP
OOK!
A
B
C
D
E
F
G
H
I
J
K
L
MARY
RUBE GOLDBERG ON BOARD S.S. QUEEN MARY
6-14
HEAVY SEAS (A) SHRINK FATHER'S DAY NECKTIE, (B) CHOKING PASSENGER (C) AND FRIGHTENING COOK, (D) CAUSING PEELING KNIFE (E) TO CUT ROPE (F) —
LARGE SHIPMENT OF SARDINES (G) DROPS TO DECK SCATTERING SARDINES (H) — SEAGULL (I) DIVES FOR SARDINES, TURNING ON PROJECTION MACHINE (J) —
MACHINE PROJECTS IMAGE OF DOG (K) ON PASSENGER'S SHIRT AND TRAINED FLEAS (L) HARNESSED TO PLATE, THINKING DOG IS REAL, RUN TOWARD HIM PULLING PLATE AFTER THEM —
WITH SO MANY PEOPLE BEING DECEIVED ABOUT SO MANY THINGS THESE DAYS IT DOESN'T SEEM SO BAD TO DECEIVE A COUPLE OF FLEES ABOUT A DOG.

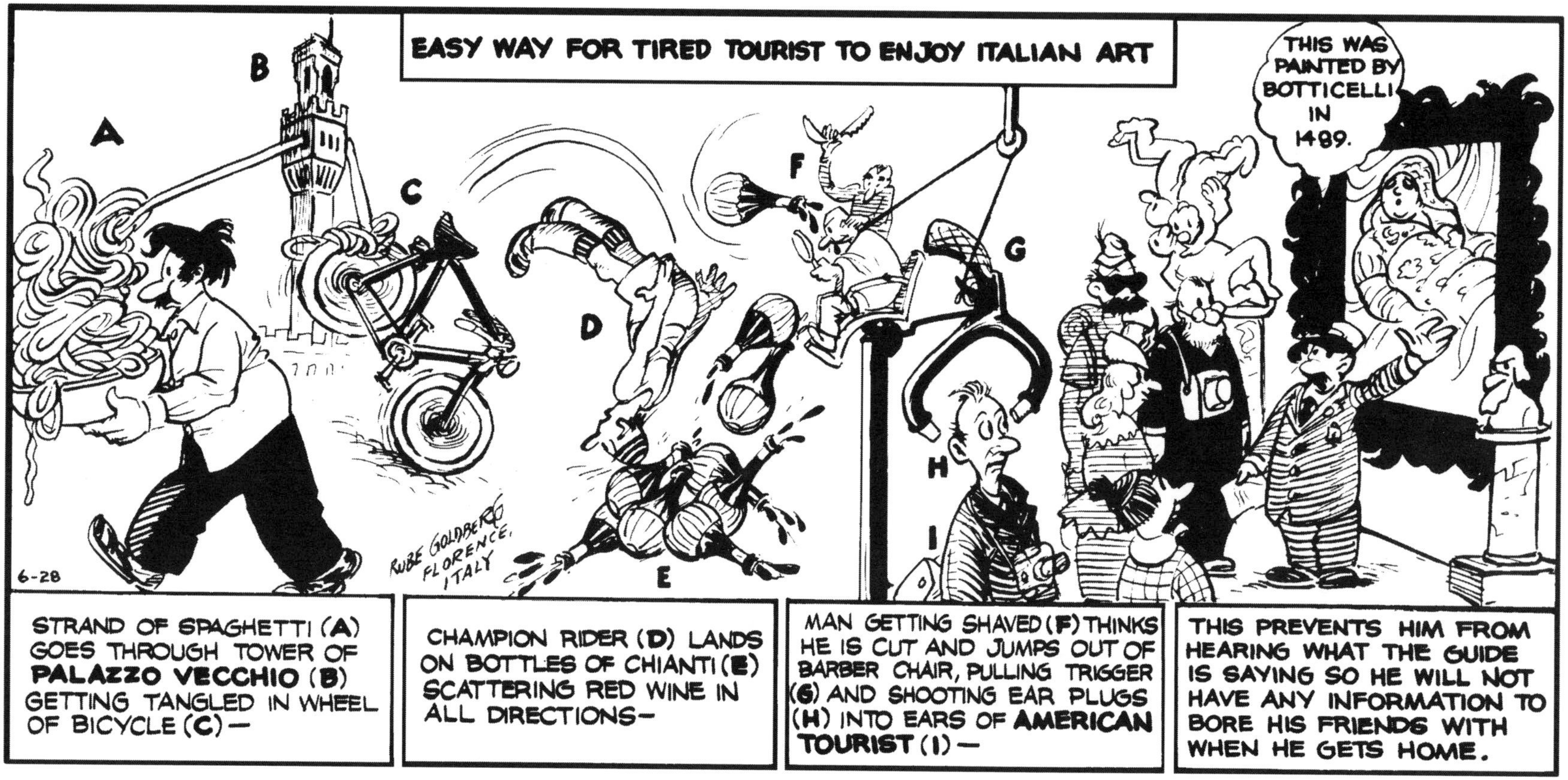
EASY WAY FOR TIRED TOURIST TO ENJOY ITALIAN ART
A
B
C
D
E
F
G
H
I
THIS WAS PAINTED BY BOTTICELLI IN 1489.
6-28
RUBE GOLDBERG FLORENCE, ITALY
STRAND OF SPAGHETTI (A) GOES THROUGH TOWER OF PALAZZO VECCHIO (B) GETTING TANGLED IN WHEEL OF BICYCLE (C)—
CHAMPION RIDER (D) LANDS ON BOTTLES OF CHIANTI (E) SCATTERING RED WINE IN ALL DIRECTIONS—
MAN GETTING SHAVED (F) THINKS HE IS CUT AND JUMPS OUT OF BARBER CHAIR, PULLING TRIGGER (G) AND SHOOTING EAR PLUGS (H) INTO EARS OF AMERICAN TOURIST (I)—
THIS PREVENTS HIM FROM HEARING WHAT THE GUIDE IS SAYING SO HE WILL NOT HAVE ANY INFORMATION TO BORE HIS FRIENDS WITH WHEN HE GETS HOME.

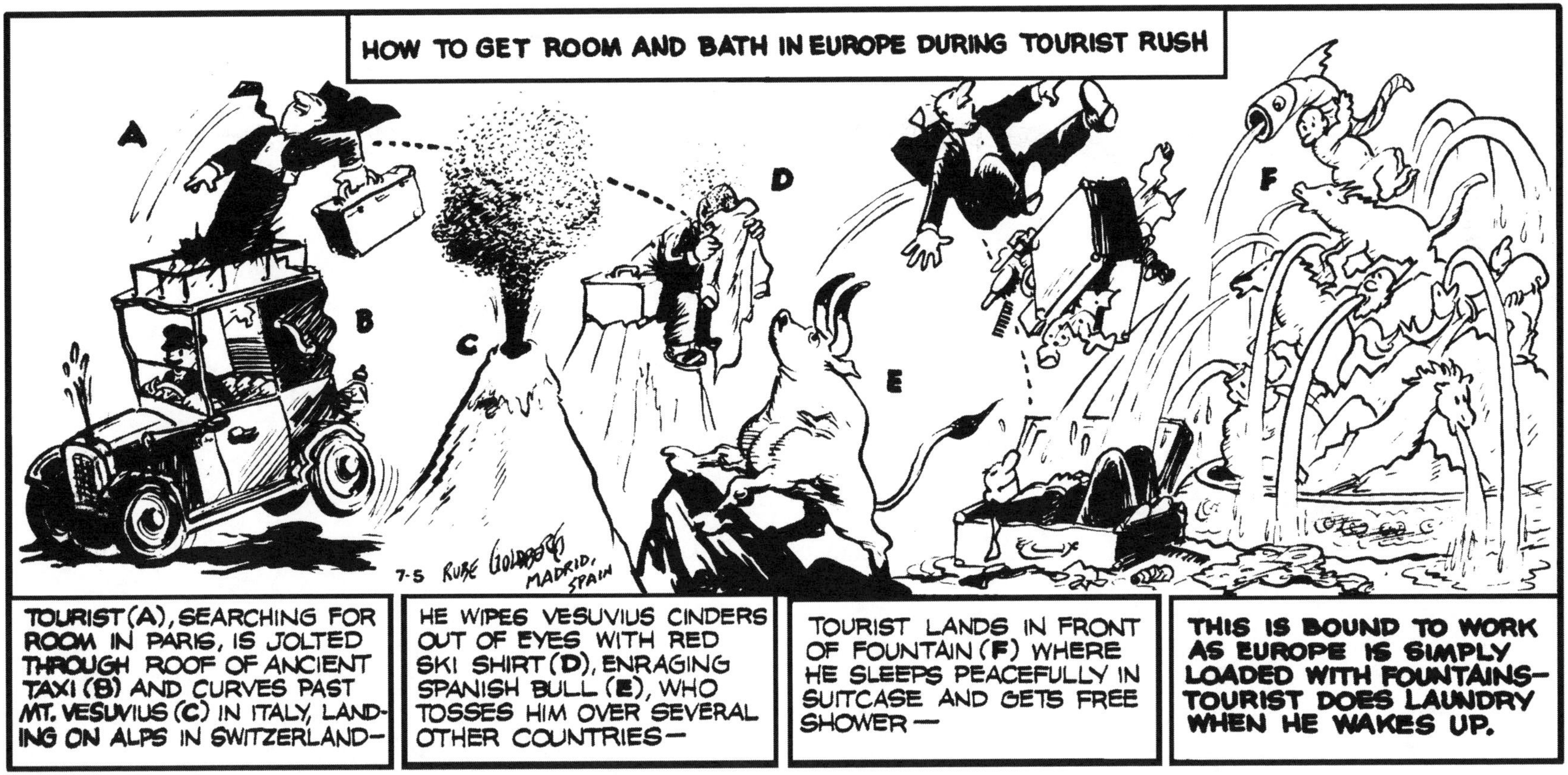
HOW TO GET ROOM AND BATH IN EUROPE DURING TOURIST RUSH
A
B
C
D
E
F
7-5 RUBE GOLDBERG MADRID, SPAIN
TOURIST (A), SEARCHING FOR ROOM IN PARIS, IS JOLTED THROUGH ROOF OF ANCIENT TAXI (B) AND CURVES PAST MT. VESUVIUS (C) IN ITALY, LANDING ON ALPS IN SWITZERLAND—
HE WIPES VESUVIUS CINDERS OUT OF EYES WITH RED SKI SHIRT (D), ENRAGING SPANISH BULL (E), WHO TOSSES HIM OVER SEVERAL OTHER COUNTRIES—
TOURIST LANDS IN FRONT OF FOUNTAIN (F) WHERE HE SLEEPS PEACEFULLY IN SUITCASE AND GETS FREE SHOWER—
THIS IS BOUND TO WORK AS EUROPE IS SIMPLY LOADED WITH FOUNTAINS—TOURIST DOES LAUNDRY WHEN HE WAKES UP.

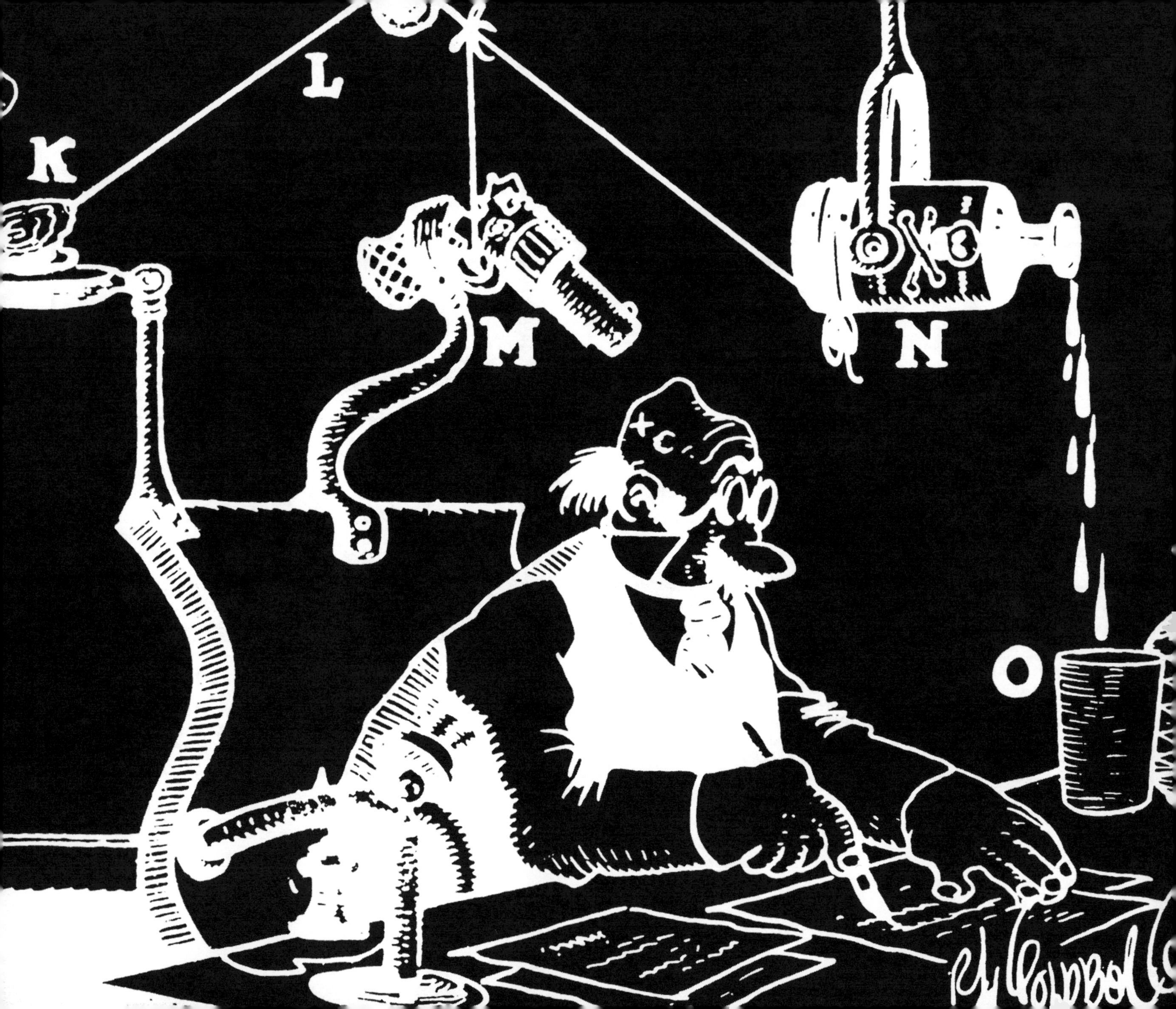
K
L
M
N
O

Work & Money

Rube was more than an illustrator; he was a highly successful entrepreneur with an unflagging interest in the workaday world. His ideas for outwitting bosses earned him a large personal fortune as well as the affection of millions of workers.

Rube's Inventions lightheartedly gave the office worker foolproof methods for avoiding people asking for loans, for appearing busy though idle, and other office protocols. But Rube was also a survivor of depressions, Great and otherwise, and the highs and lows of the stock market; his harsh comments about the market's brokers and speculators have a decidedly sardonic feel. Rube's Inventions not only offered suggestions for dodging bill collectors but also honorable "ways out" when the speculators had lost all of their client's money.

How to Succeed in Business

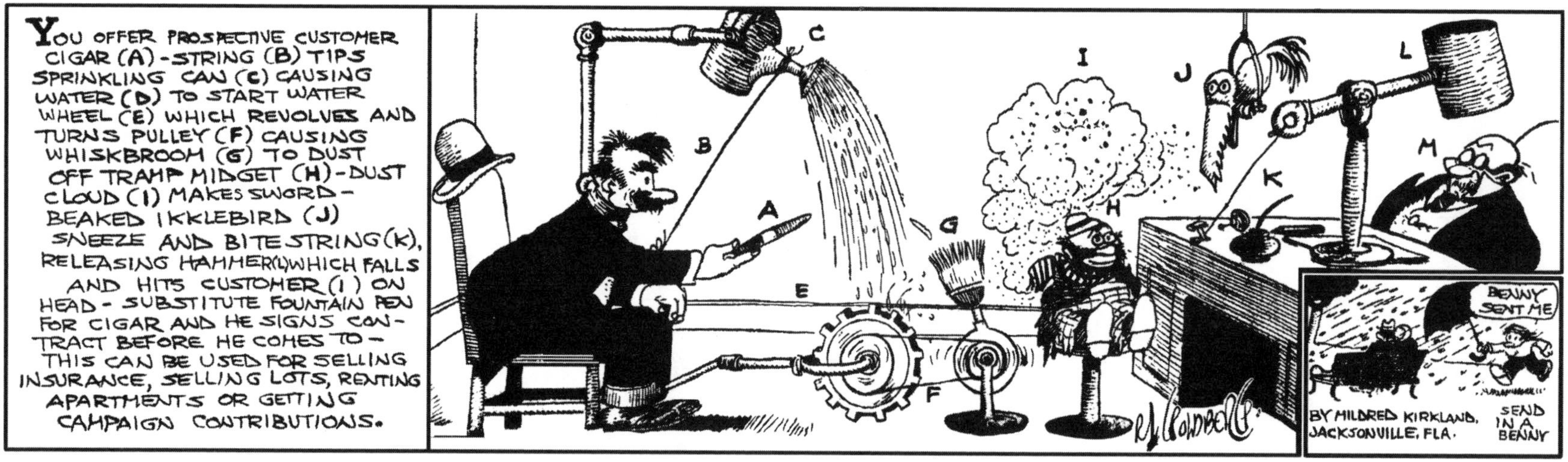
YOU OFFER PROSPECTIVE CUSTOMER CIGAR (A) - STRING (B) TIPS SPRINKLING CAN (C) CAUSING WATER (D) TO START WATER WHEEL (E) WHICH REVOLVES AND TURNS PULLEY (F) CAUSING WHISKBROOM (G) TO DUST OFF TRAMP MIDGET (H) - DUST CLOUD (I) MAKES SWORD-BEAKED IKKLEBIRD (J) SNEEZE AND BITE STRING (K), RELEASING HAMMER (L) WHICH FALLS AND HITS CUSTOMER (I) ON HEAD - SUBSTITUTE FOUNTAIN PEN FOR CIGAR AND HE SIGNS CONTRACT BEFORE HE COMES TO - THIS CAN BE USED FOR SELLING INSURANCE, SELLING LOTS, RENTING APARTMENTS OR GETTING CAMPAIGN CONTRIBUTIONS.
A
B
C
E
F
G
H
I
J
K
L
M
BENNY SENT ME
BY MILDRED KIRKLAND, JACKSONVILLE, FLA.
SEND IN A BENNY

Silencing the Stock Talker

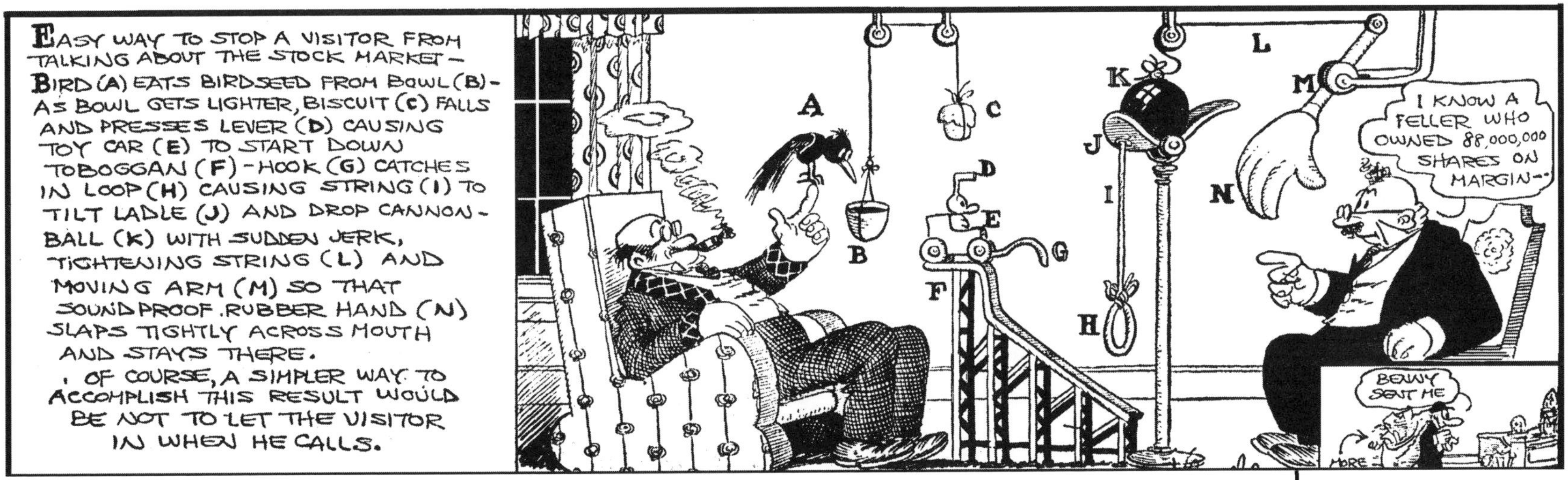
EASY WAY TO STOP A VISITOR FROM TALKING ABOUT THE STOCK MARKET - BIRD (A) EATS BIRDSEED FROM BOWL (B) - AS BOWL GETS LIGHTER, BISCUIT (C) FALLS AND PRESSES LEVER (D) CAUSING TOY CAR (E) TO START DOWN TOBOGGAN (F) - HOOK (G) CATCHES IN LOOP (H) CAUSING STRING (I) TO TILT LADLE (J) AND DROP CANNON-BALL (K) WITH SUDDEN JERK, TIGHTENING STRING (L) AND MOVING ARM (M) SO THAT SOUNDPROOF RUBBER HAND (N) SLAPS TIGHTLY ACROSS MOUTH AND STAYS THERE.
OF COURSE, A SIMPLER WAY TO ACCOMPLISH THIS RESULT WOULD BE NOT TO LET THE VISITOR IN WHEN HE CALLS.
A
B
C
D
E
F
G
H
I
J
K
L
M
N
I KNOW A FELLER WHO OWNED 88,000,000 SHARES ON MARGIN--
BENNY SENT ME
MORE

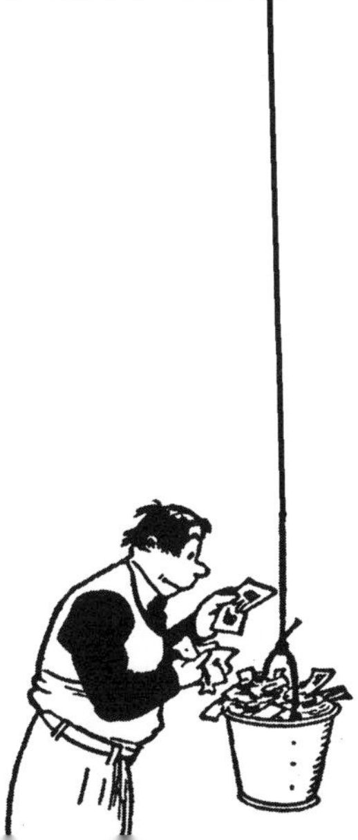

Automatic Suicide Device for Unlucky Stock Speculators

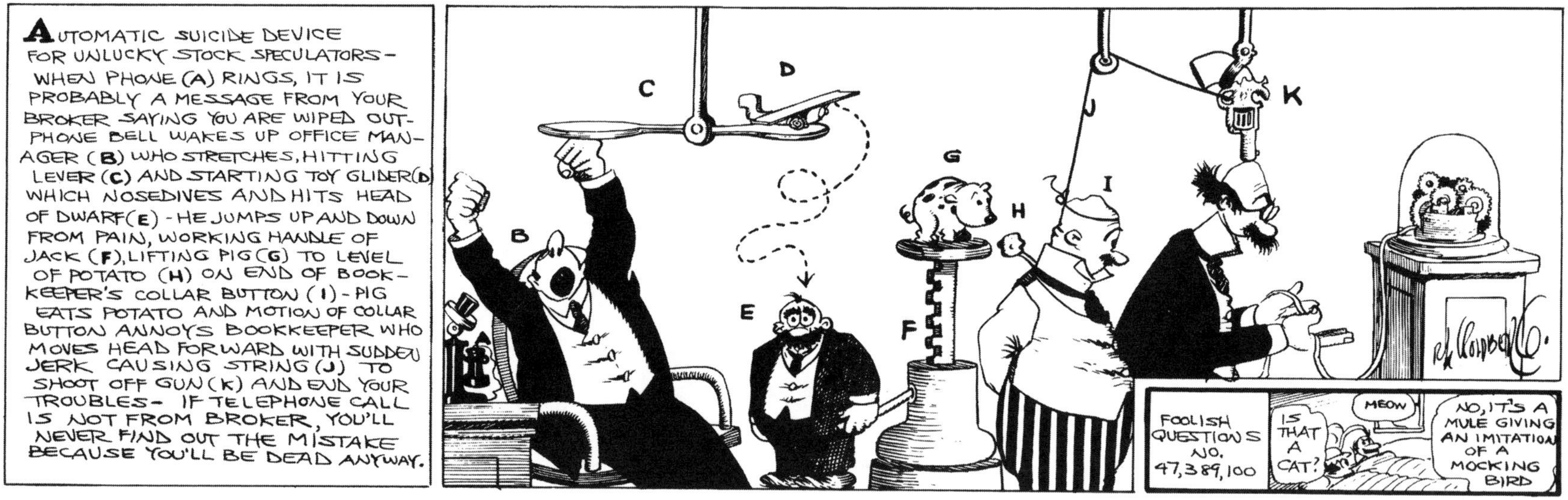
AUTOMATIC SUICIDE DEVICE FOR UNLUCKY STOCK SPECULATORS - WHEN PHONE (A) RINGS, IT IS PROBABLY A MESSAGE FROM YOUR BROKER SAYING YOU ARE WIPED OUT - PHONE BELL WAKES UP OFFICE MANAGER (B) WHO STRETCHES, HITTING LEVER (C) AND STARTING TOY GLIDER (D) WHICH NOSEDIVES AND HITS HEAD OF DWARF (E) - HE JUMPS UP AND DOWN FROM PAIN, WORKING HANDLE OF JACK (F), LIFTING PIG (G) TO LEVEL OF POTATO (H) ON END OF BOOKKEEPER'S COLLAR BUTTON (I) - PIG EATS POTATO AND MOTION OF COLLAR BUTTON ANNOYS BOOKKEEPER WHO MOVES HEAD FORWARD WITH SUDDEN JERK CAUSING STRING (J) TO SHOOT OFF GUN (K) AND END YOUR TROUBLES - IF TELEPHONE CALL IS NOT FROM BROKER, YOU'LL NEVER FIND OUT THE MISTAKE BECAUSE YOU'LL BE DEAD ANYWAY.
C
D
B
E
F
G
H
I
J
K
FOOLISH QUESTIONS NO. 47,389,100
IS THAT A CAT?
MEOW
NO, IT'S A MULE GIVING AN IMITATION OF A MOCKING BIRD

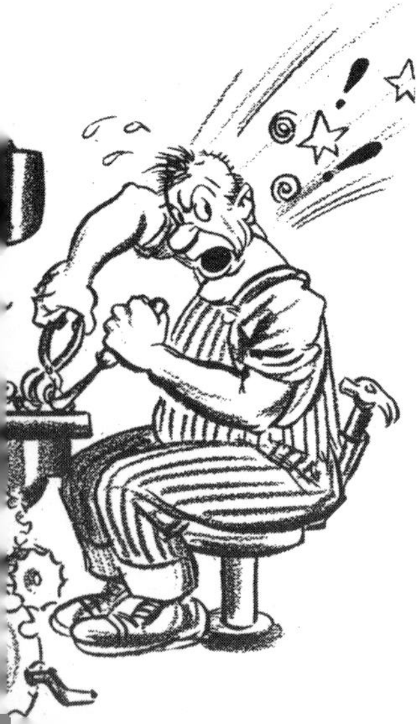

Killer Stock Market Share Price Indicator

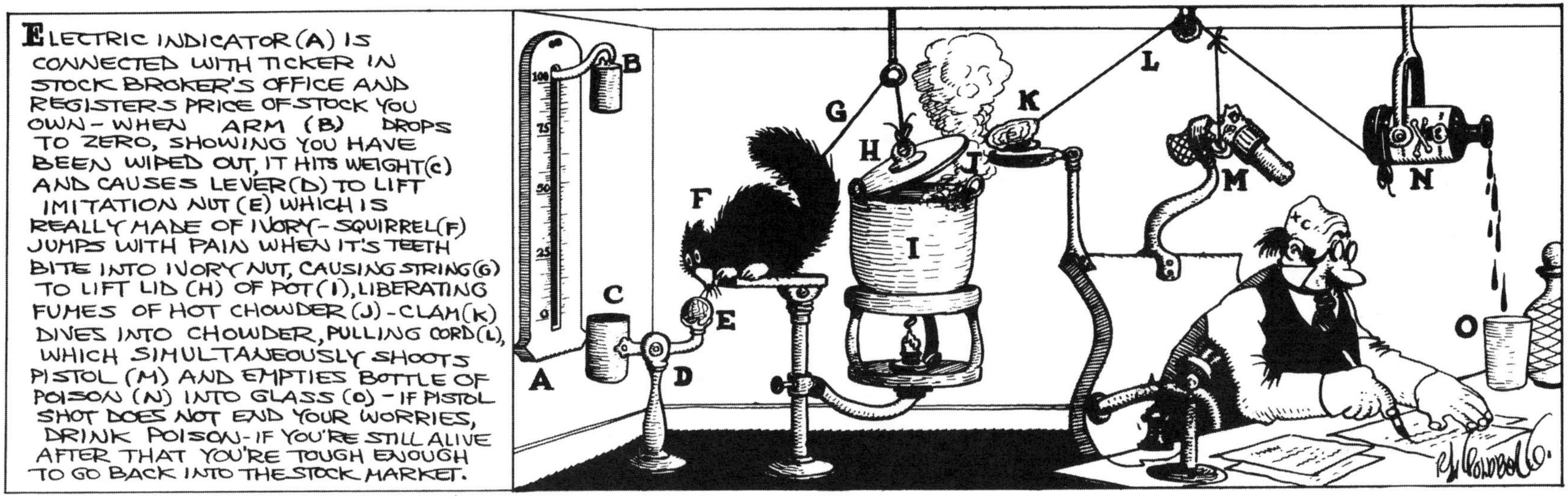
ELECTRIC INDICATOR (A) IS CONNECTED WITH TICKER IN STOCK BROKER'S OFFICE AND REGISTERS PRICE OF STOCK YOU OWN – WHEN ARM (B) DROPS TO ZERO, SHOWING YOU HAVE BEEN WIPED OUT, IT HITS WEIGHT (C) AND CAUSES LEVER (D) TO LIFT IMITATION NUT (E) WHICH IS REALLY MADE OF IVORY – SQUIRREL (F) JUMPS WITH PAIN WHEN IT'S TEETH BITE INTO IVORY NUT, CAUSING STRING (G) TO LIFT LID (H) OF POT (I), LIBERATING FUMES OF HOT CHOWDER (J) – CLAM (K) DIVES INTO CHOWDER, PULLING CORD (L), WHICH SIMULTANEOUSLY SHOOTS PISTOL (M) AND EMPTIES BOTTLE OF POISON (N) INTO GLASS (O) – IF PISTOL SHOT DOES NOT END YOUR WORRIES, DRINK POISON – IF YOU'RE STILL ALIVE AFTER THAT YOU'RE TOUGH ENOUGH TO GO BACK INTO THE STOCK MARKET.
A
B
C
D
E
F
G
H
I
J
K
L
M
N
O

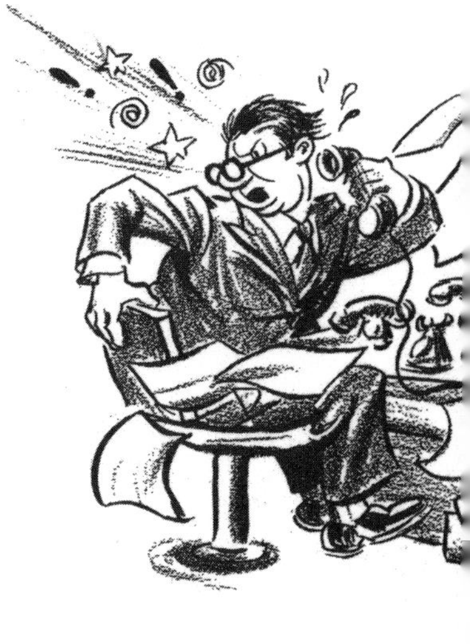

The Professor's Simple Touch Avoider

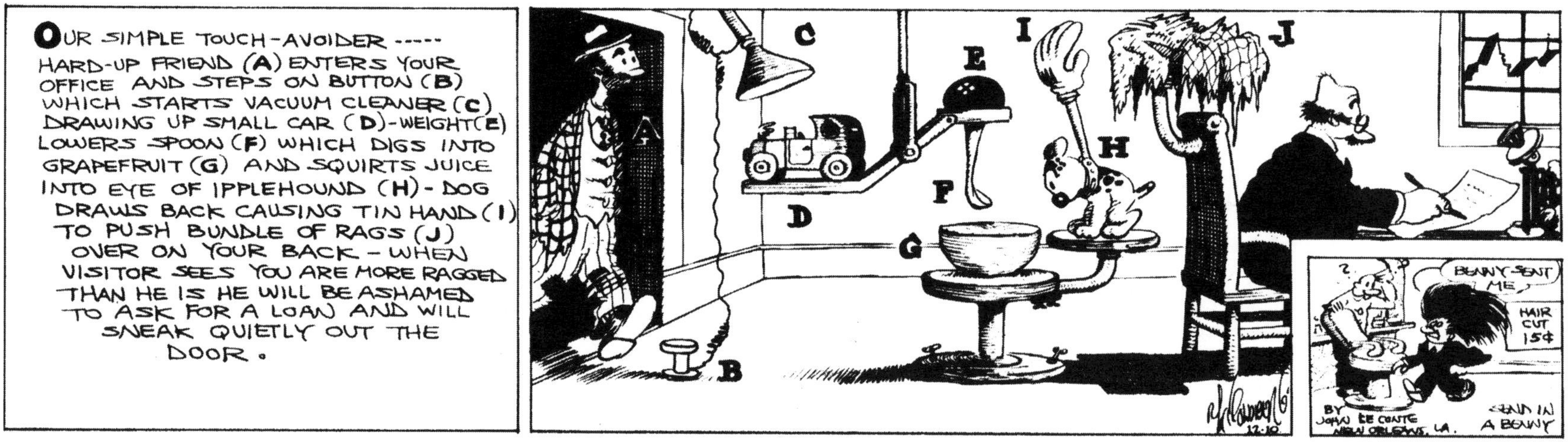
OUR SIMPLE TOUCH-AVOIDER ----- HARD-UP FRIEND (A) ENTERS YOUR OFFICE AND STEPS ON BUTTON (B) WHICH STARTS VACUUM CLEANER (C) DRAWING UP SMALL CAR (D)-WEIGHT (E) LOWERS SPOON (F) WHICH DIGS INTO GRAPEFRUIT (G) AND SQUIRTS JUICE INTO EYE OF IPPLEHOUND (H)- DOG DRAWS BACK CAUSING TIN HAND (I) TO PUSH BUNDLE OF RAGS (J) OVER ON YOUR BACK - WHEN VISITOR SEES YOU ARE MORE RAGGED THAN HE IS HE WILL BE ASHAMED TO ASK FOR A LOAN AND WILL SNEAK QUIETLY OUT THE DOOR.
A
B
C
D
E
F
G
H
I
J
?
BENNY SENT ME
HAIR CUT 15¢
BY JOHN LE CONTE NEW ORLEANS, LA.
SEND IN A BENNY

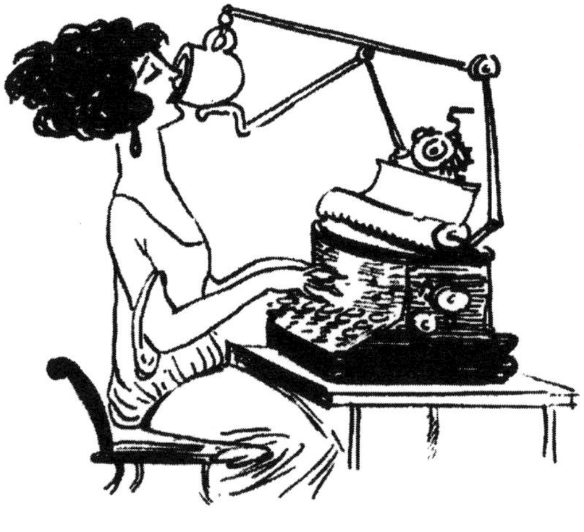

Idea for Dodging Bill Collectors

PROFESSOR BUTTS MISTAKES A LOT OF BROKEN GLASS FOR BATH SALTS AND WHEN THEY PULL HIM OUT OF THE TUB HE MUMBLES AN IDEA FOR DODGING BILL COLLECTORS.
AS TAILOR (A) FITS CUSTOMER (B) AND CALLS OU MEASUREMENTS, COLLEGE BOY (C) MISTAKES THEM FOR FOOTBALL SIGNALS AND MAKES A FLYING TACKLE AT CLOTHING DUMMY (D). DUMMY BUMPS HEAD AGAINST PADDLE (E) CAUSING IT TO PULL HOOK (F) AND THROW BOTTLE (G) ON END OF FOLDING HATRACK (H) WHICH SPREADS AND PUSHES HEAD OF CABBAGE (I) INTO NET (J). WEIGHT OF CABBAGE PULLS CORD (K) CAUSING SHEARS (L) TO CUT STRING (M). BAG OF SAND (N) DROPS ON SCALE (O) AND PUSHES BROOM (P) AGAINST PAIL OF WHITEWASH (Q) WHICH UPSETS ALL OVER YOU CAUSING YOU TO LOOK LIKE A MARBLE STATUE AND MAKING IT IMPOSSIBLE FOR YOU TO BE RECOGNIZED BY BILL COLLECTORS.
DON'T WORRY ABOUT POSING AS ANY PARTICULAR HISTORICAL STATUE BECAUSE BILL COLLECTORS DON'T KNOW MUCH ABOUT ART

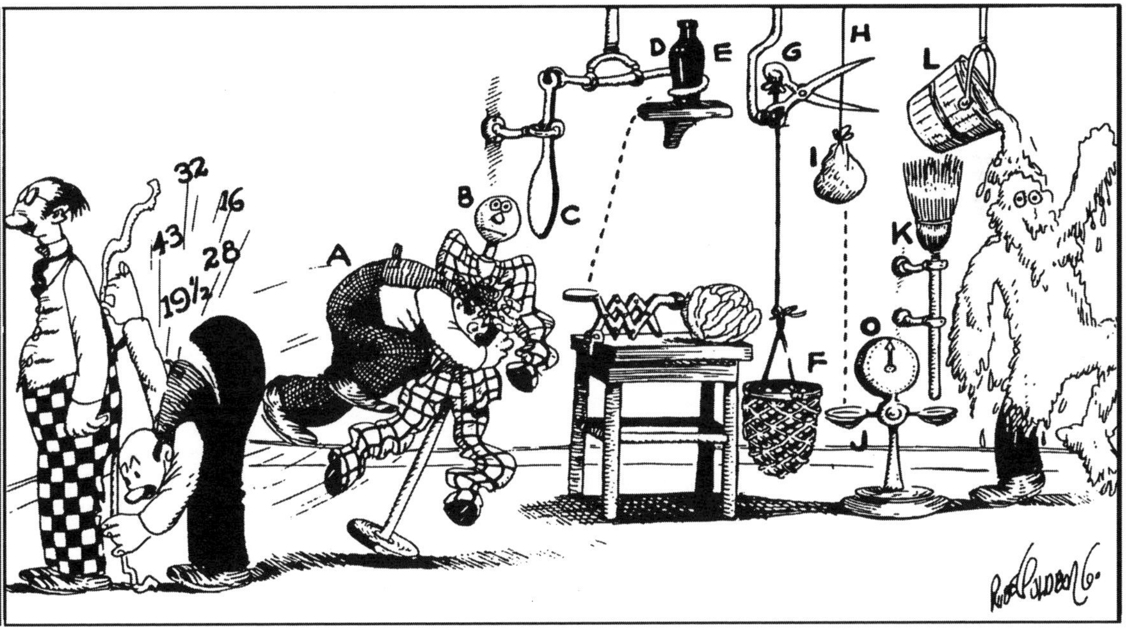
32
16
43
28
19½
A
B
C
D
E
G
H
I
L
K
O
F
J

Simple Appliance for Putting Postage Stamps on Envelopes

THE MASSIVE INTELLECT OF PROFESSOR BUTTS EVOLVES A SIMPLE APPLIANCE FOR PUTTING POSTAGE STAMPS ON ENVELOPES

BOSS (A) SNEEZES. SNOZZLEHOUND (B), FRIGHTENED OUT OF A SOUND SLUMBER, RUNS OUT OF THE OFFICE, UPSETTING HATRACK (C) AND BREAKING ICE WATER CONTAINER (D). WATER (E) IS SPILLED INTO TROUGH (F) AND IS THEN CONVEYED TO BUCKET (G).

THE WEIGHT OF THE WATER IN BUCKET CAUSES STRING (H) TO COMPRESS NUT-CRACKER (I) WHICH SQUEEZES BULB ON MEDICINE-DROPPER (J) AND MOISTENS POSTAGE STAMP (K)

STENOGRAPHER (L), ABOUT TO GO OUT TO LUNCH, HEARS THE SPLASHING OF WATER ON SEVERAL OCCASIONS DURING THE OPERATION OF THE APPARATUS. SHE THINKS IT IS RAINING AND PICKS UP HER UMBRELLA (M), WHICH PULLS BACK SMALL HOOK (N), CAUSING SPRING (P) TO THROW PADDLE (O) OVER ON ENVELOPE (Q) AND PRESS MOISTENED STAMP IN PLACE.

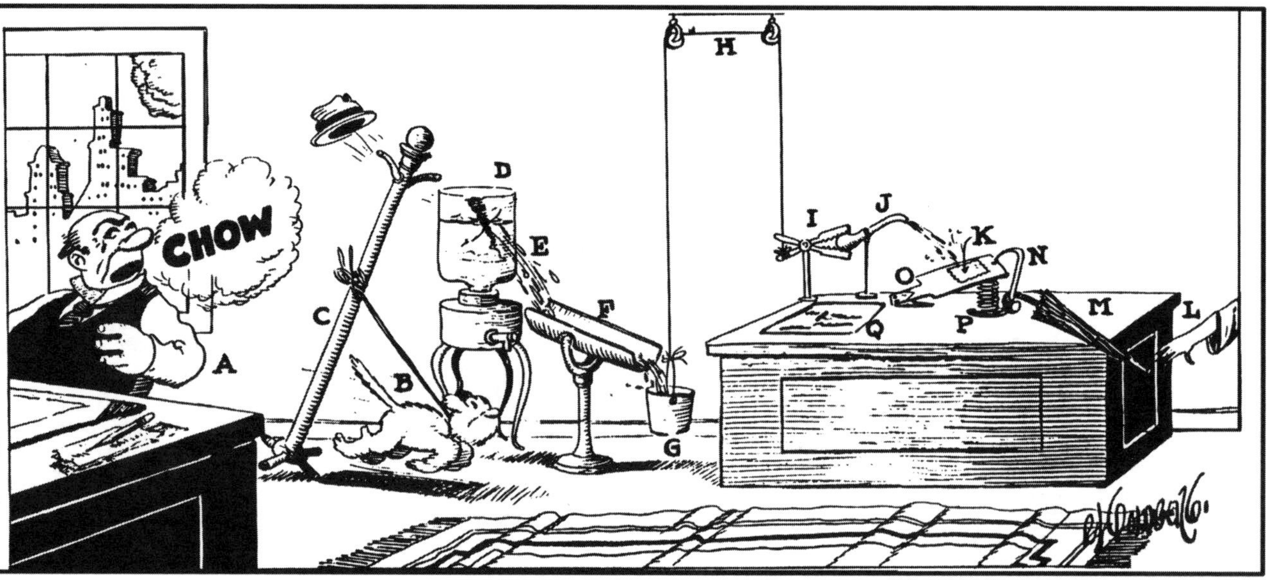
CHOW
A
B
C
D
E
F
G
H
I
J
K
L
M
N
O
P
Q

Efficient Way to Tie a Knot in String

WINTRY WIND (A) TURNS PINWHEEL (B) WHICH REVOLVES PULLEYS (C) AND TURNS ON HEAT IN RADIATOR (D) - CAT (E) IS SCALDED AND JUMPS ON CAKE OF ICE (F) WHICH CAUSES KNIFE (G) TO CUT BOLOGNA (H) IN HALF - PIECE OF BOLOGNA FALLS OFF PLATFORM (I), CAUSING STRING (J) TO OPEN CAGE (K) AND LET OUT MOSQUITO (L) WHICH BITES UNCLE RUFUS IN NECK (M) - HE LIFTS HEAD IN PAIN AND HITS DISC (N) WHICH CAUSES WALKING-BEAM (O) TO MOVE AND PRESS FINGER ON WOODEN HAND (P) AGAINST KNOT (Q) ALLOWING YOU TO TIE STRING TIGHTLY!

DON'T WASTE TOO MUCH TIME ON THIS BECAUSE NO MATTER WHERE OR HOW YOU SEND THE PACKAGE IT WILL BE SMASHED WHEN IT GETS THERE, ANYWAY.

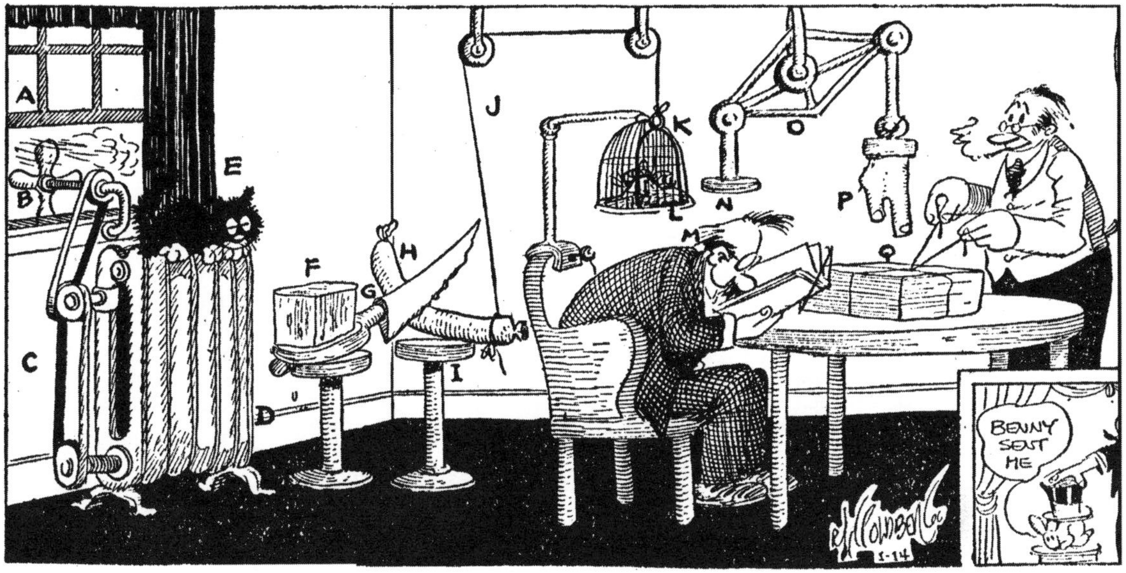
A
B
C
D
E
F
G
H
I
J
K
L
M
N
O
P
Q
BENNY SENT ME

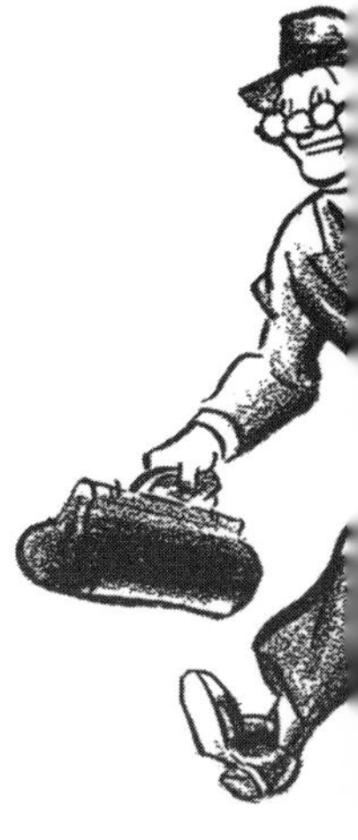

How to Keep from Dozing Off During Business Hours

HOT SUN (A) SHINES THROUGH MAGNIFYING GLASS (B), BURNS HOLE IN STRING (C) CAUSING MASSAGE BRUSH (D) TO FALL AND RUB ALONG NECK OF UFFLEDUFF (E) — UFFLEDUFF MOVES HEAD UP AND DOWN WITH GLEE CAUSING ROD (F) TO TURN PULLEY (G) AND START COFFEE MILL (H) — GROUND COFFEE (I) FALLS INTO CUP (J) LIFTING END OF LEVER (K) AND MAKING MATCH (L) STRIKE ON SAND-PAPER (M), SETTING OFF ROCKET (N) — STRING (O) SETS OFF CANNON (P) WITH LOUD REPORT WAKING YOU FOR THE TIME BEING — CANNON BALL (Q) HITS DEEP-VOICED POOVLEDIK AND STARTS HIM CRYING SO LONG AND LOUD YOU'VE GOT TO STAY AWAKE — DON'T ASK US WHERE TO GET AN UFFLEDUFF OR A POOVLEDIK — WE CAN'T KNOW EVERYTHING!

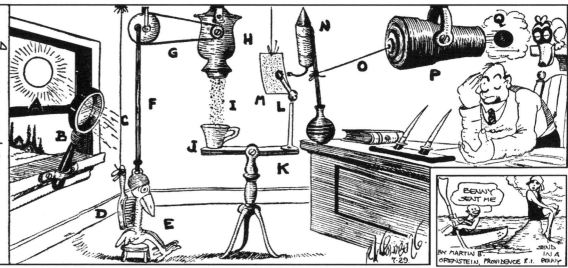

BENNY SENT ME

SEND IN A PENNY

BY MARTIN B. ORENSTEIN, PROVIDENCE R.I.

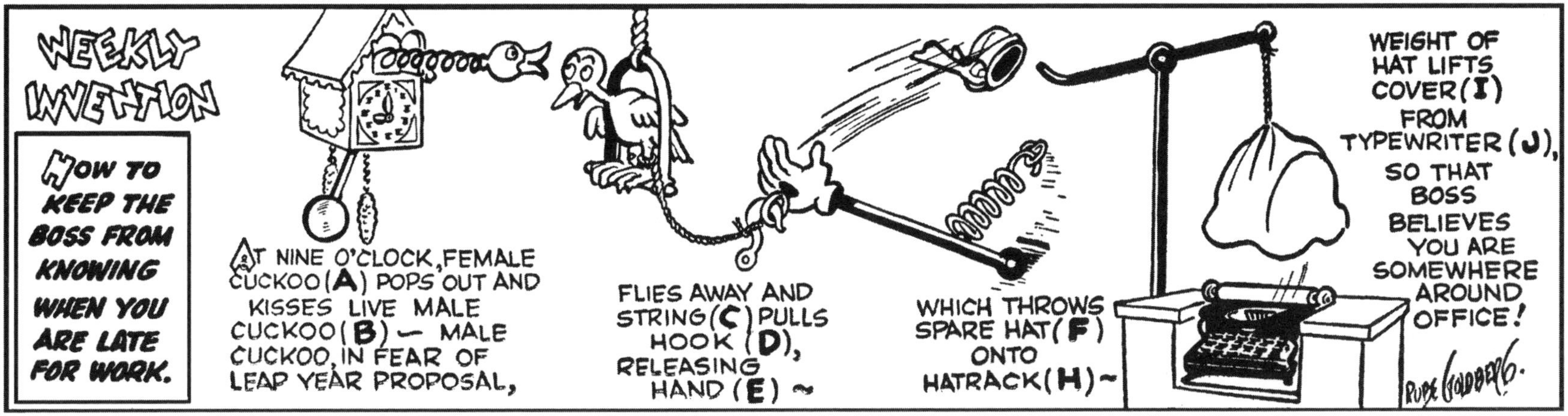
WEEKLY INVENTION
HOW TO KEEP THE BOSS FROM KNOWING WHEN YOU ARE LATE FOR WORK.
AT NINE O'CLOCK, FEMALE CUCKOO (A) POPS OUT AND KISSES LIVE MALE CUCKOO (B) — MALE CUCKOO, IN FEAR OF LEAP YEAR PROPOSAL,
FLIES AWAY AND STRING (C) PULLS HOOK (D), RELEASING HAND (E) ~
WHICH THROWS SPARE HAT (F) ONTO HATRACK (H) ~
WEIGHT OF HAT LIFTS COVER (I) FROM TYPEWRITER (J), SO THAT BOSS BELIEVES YOU ARE SOMEWHERE AROUND OFFICE!
RUBE GOLDBERG.

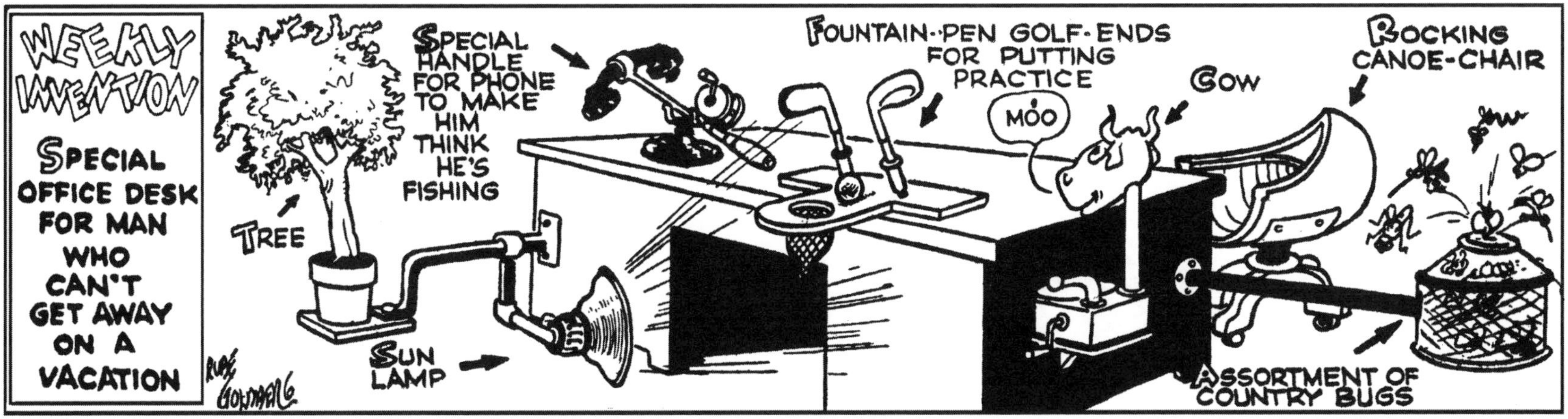
WEEKLY INVENTION
SPECIAL OFFICE DESK FOR MAN WHO CAN'T GET AWAY ON A VACATION
TREE
SPECIAL HANDLE FOR PHONE TO MAKE HIM THINK HE'S FISHING
FOUNTAIN-PEN GOLF-ENDS FOR PUTTING PRACTICE
MOO
COW
ROCKING CANOE-CHAIR
SUN LAMP
ASSORTMENT OF COUNTRY BUGS
RUBE GOLDBERG

How to Save Money

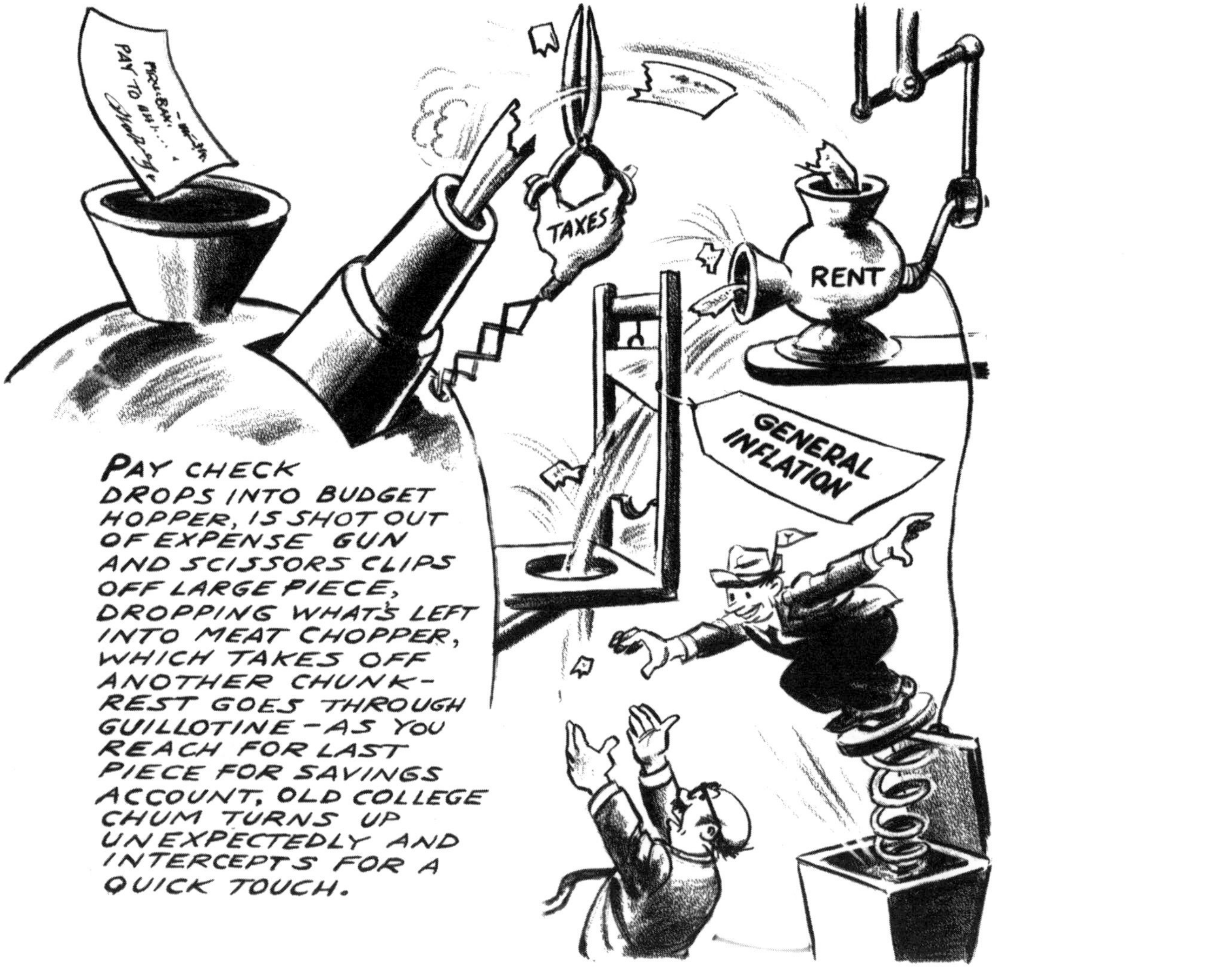
TAXES
RENT
GENERAL INFLATION
PAY CHECK DROPS INTO BUDGET HOPPER, IS SHOT OUT OF EXPENSE GUN AND SCISSORS CLIPS OFF LARGE PIECE, DROPPING WHAT'S LEFT INTO MEAT CHOPPER, WHICH TAKES OFF ANOTHER CHUNK- REST GOES THROUGH GUILLOTINE-AS YOU REACH FOR LAST PIECE FOR SAVINGS ACCOUNT, OLD COLLEGE CHUM TURNS UP UNEXPECTEDLY AND INTERCEPTS FOR A QUICK TOUCH.

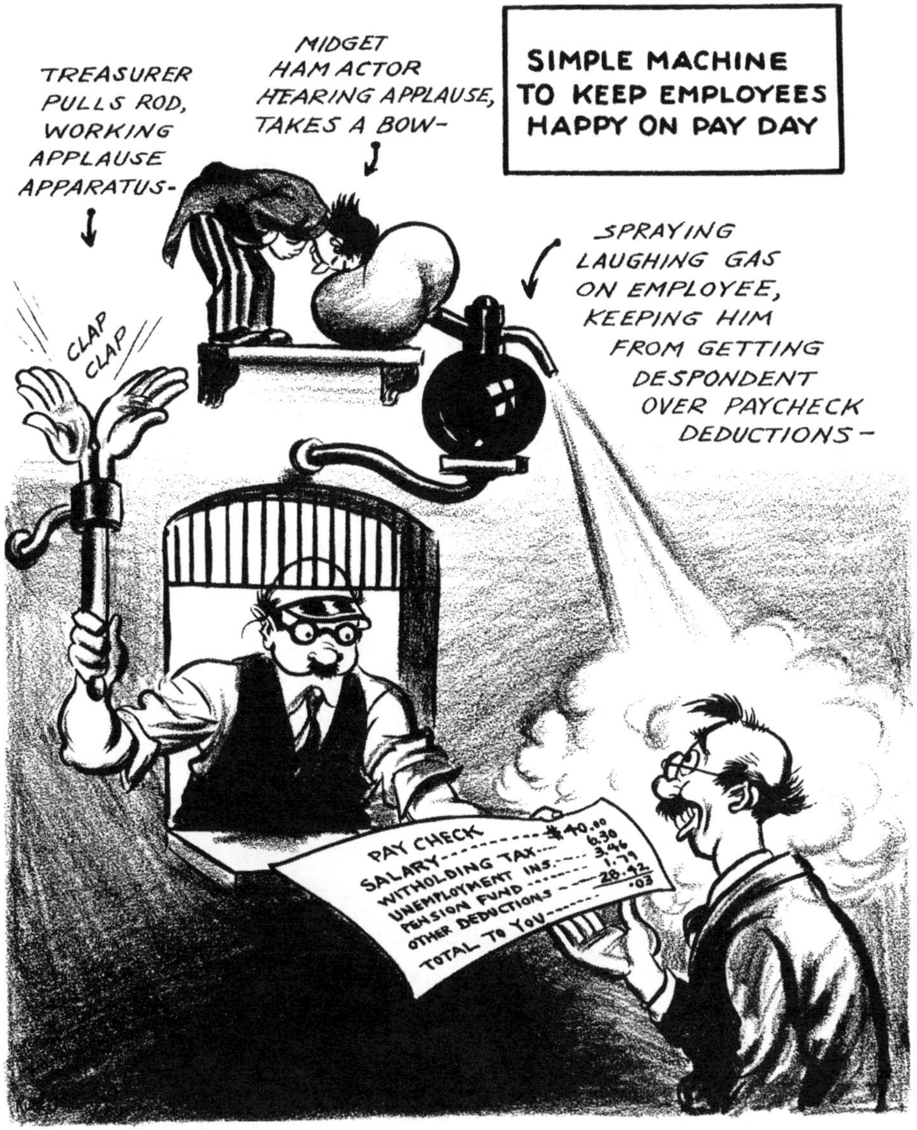
SIMPLE MACHINE
TO KEEP EMPLOYEES
HAPPY ON PAY DAY
TREASURER PULLS ROD, WORKING APPLAUSE APPARATUS-
MIDGET HAM ACTOR HEARING APPLAUSE, TAKES A BOW-
SPRAYING LAUGHING GAS ON EMPLOYEE, KEEPING HIM FROM GETTING DESPONDENT OVER PAYCHECK DEDUCTIONS-
CLAP CLAP
PAY CHECK
SALARY---------- $40.00
WITHOLDING TAX---- 6.30
UNEMPLOYMENT INS.---- 3.46
PENSION FUND ------ 1.79
OTHER DEDUCTIONS ---- 28.42
TOTAL TO YOU-------- .03

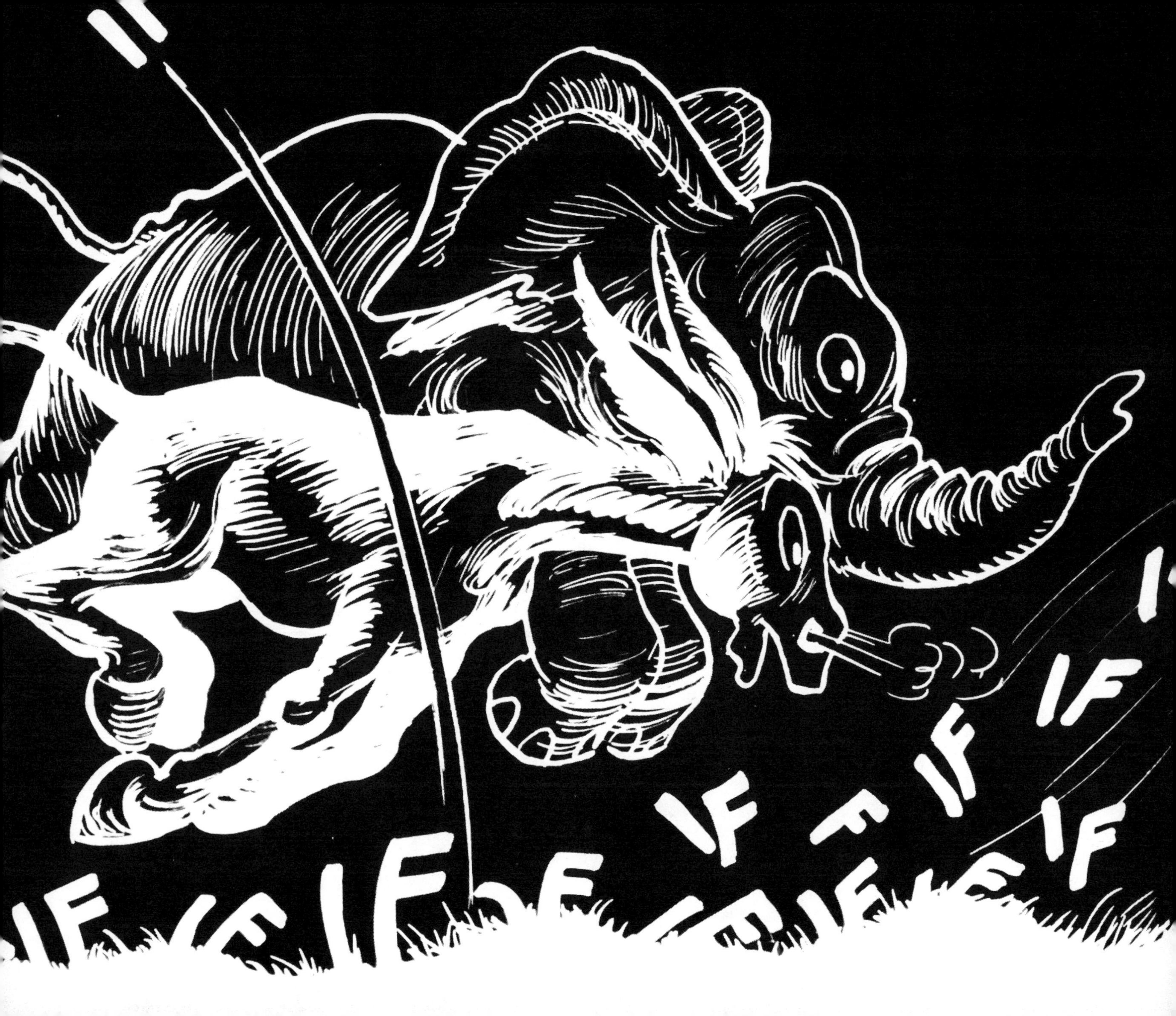
IF IF IF IF IF IF IF IF

Political Life

Politics and politicians were part of Rube's growing up. His father, Max, played host at home every Friday night to his politician cronies at a weekly poker game. This gave Rube an early introduction to the smoke-filled rooms where political deals were made. "To this day," Rube wrote, "politics to me seems so shackled in personal involvements that there is little room left for real dedication."

Rube never forgot those early childhood visions, and throughout his career his Invention cartoons came complete with sleepy and sleazy politicians, new-style voting machines, and the ripple effect of "deals" that affected his much-put-upon hero, the taxpayer.

Rube's editorial cartoons used his Inventions to show current personalities as part of a chain of connections that still resulted in stripping the shirt off the back of the middle-class taxpayer…Rube's subject as well as his audience.

Simple Way to Find the Name of the Next President

PROFESSOR BUTTS INVENTS A SURE AND SIMPLE WAY TO FIND THE NAME OF THE NEXT PRESIDENT-MAN (A) CATCHES COLD FROM OPEN WINDOW (B)-HE SNEEZES AND BLOWS ELECTRIC BULB (C) AGAINST DISC (D), CAUSING IT TO BREAK WITH LOUD REPORT-DWARF FLAGPOLE-SITTER (E), THINKING HE IS SHOT, FALLS ON HANDLE OF BICYCLE PUMP (F), CAUSING BUGLE (G) TO TOOT- MARCHING-CROW (H) STARTS MARCHING-WEIGHT ON END OF LEVER (I) CAUSES STRING (J) TO PULL DOWN END (K), RELEASING DOUGHNUT (L), WHICH DUNKS IT-SELF IN CUP OF COFFEE (M) -

AS COFFEE SPLASHES - OH, WELL, WHY GO ANY FURTHER? THIS IS APRIL FIRST!

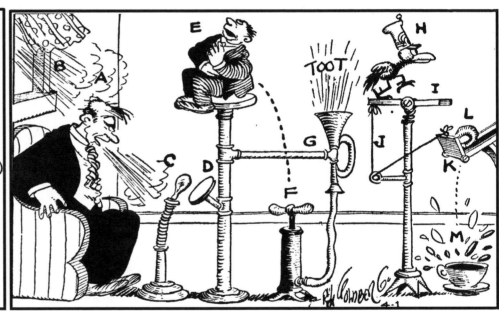

Automatic Vote-Counting Machine

FIRST, LOOK AT BOARD (A) AND RECOGNIZE PICTURE OF YOUR CANDIDATE (NO.1) TURN CLOCK (B) TO CORRESPONDING NUMBER AND PRESS ELECTRIC BUTTON (C) – THIS CAUSES CUCKOO (D) TO DUCK HEAD WITH THE EXACT FORCE TO MAKE MALLET (E) HIT PADDLE (F) AND TOSS BALL (G) THROUGH HOLE IN CANDIDATE'S HAT (NO.1) BALL HITS CLERK (H) WHO AWAKENS AND MARKS DOWN VOTE FOR YOUR CANDIDATE, TO WHOM HE HAS BEEN ASSIGNED – WHEN ALL CLERKS ARE UNCONSCIOUS, ELECTION IS OVER.

TALLY!

DON'T MIND ME – I'M A CANCELLED VOTE

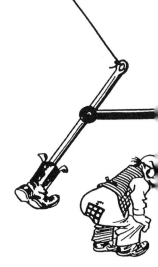

Our Latest Simple Alarm Clock

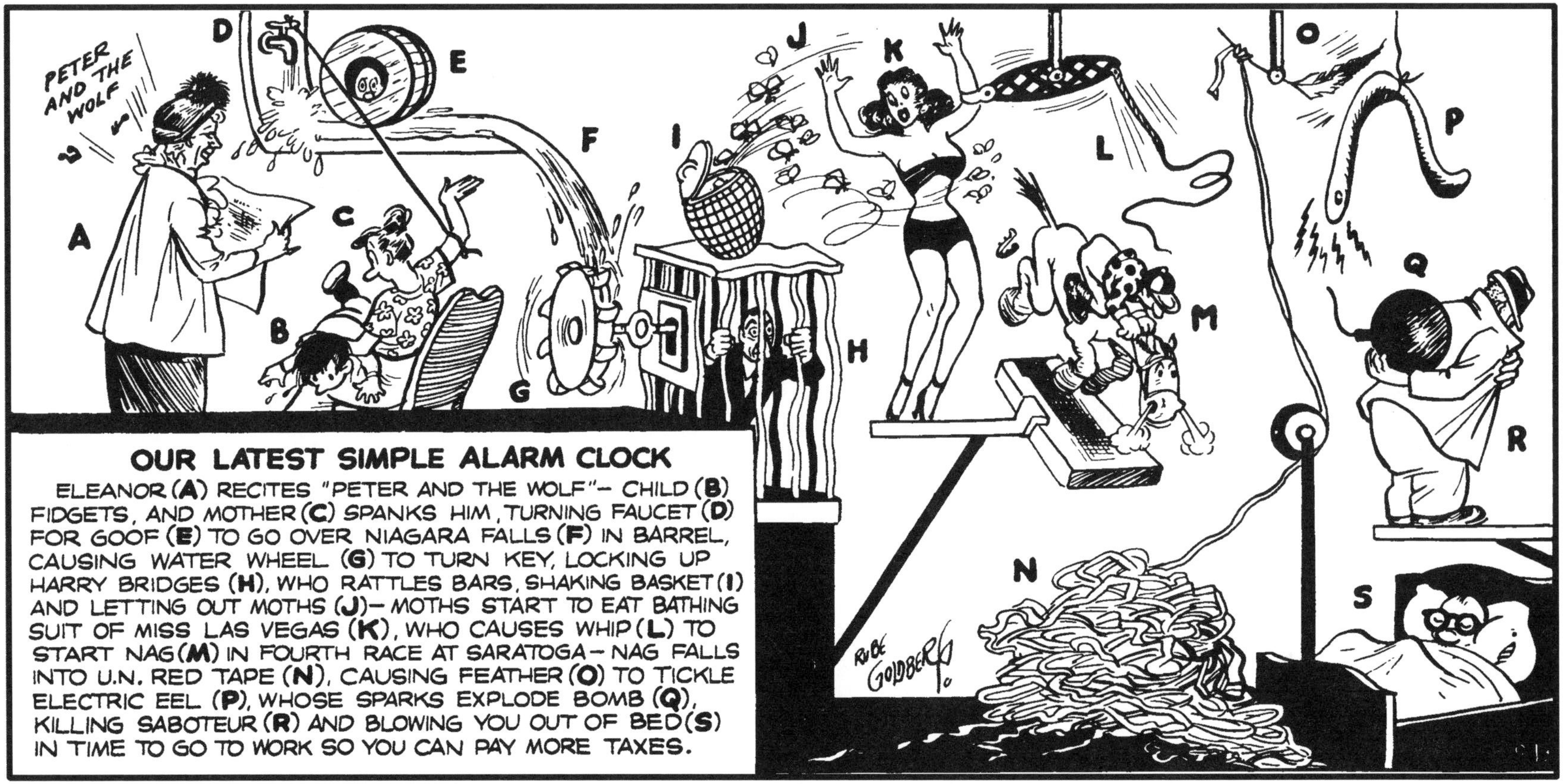
PETER AND THE WOLF
A
B
C
D
E
F
G
H
I
J
K
L
M
N
O
P
Q
R
S
OUR LATEST SIMPLE ALARM CLOCK
ELEANOR (A) RECITES "PETER AND THE WOLF"– CHILD (B) FIDGETS, AND MOTHER (C) SPANKS HIM, TURNING FAUCET (D) FOR GOOF (E) TO GO OVER NIAGARA FALLS (F) IN BARREL, CAUSING WATER WHEEL (G) TO TURN KEY, LOCKING UP HARRY BRIDGES (H), WHO RATTLES BARS, SHAKING BASKET (I) AND LETTING OUT MOTHS (J)– MOTHS START TO EAT BATHING SUIT OF MISS LAS VEGAS (K), WHO CAUSES WHIP (L) TO START NAG (M) IN FOURTH RACE AT SARATOGA – NAG FALLS INTO U.N. RED TAPE (N), CAUSING FEATHER (O) TO TICKLE ELECTRIC EEL (P), WHOSE SPARKS EXPLODE BOMB (Q), KILLING SABOTEUR (R) AND BLOWING YOU OUT OF BED (S) IN TIME TO GO TO WORK SO YOU CAN PAY MORE TAXES.
RUBE GOLDBERG

Taking the Shirt off the Taxpayer's Back

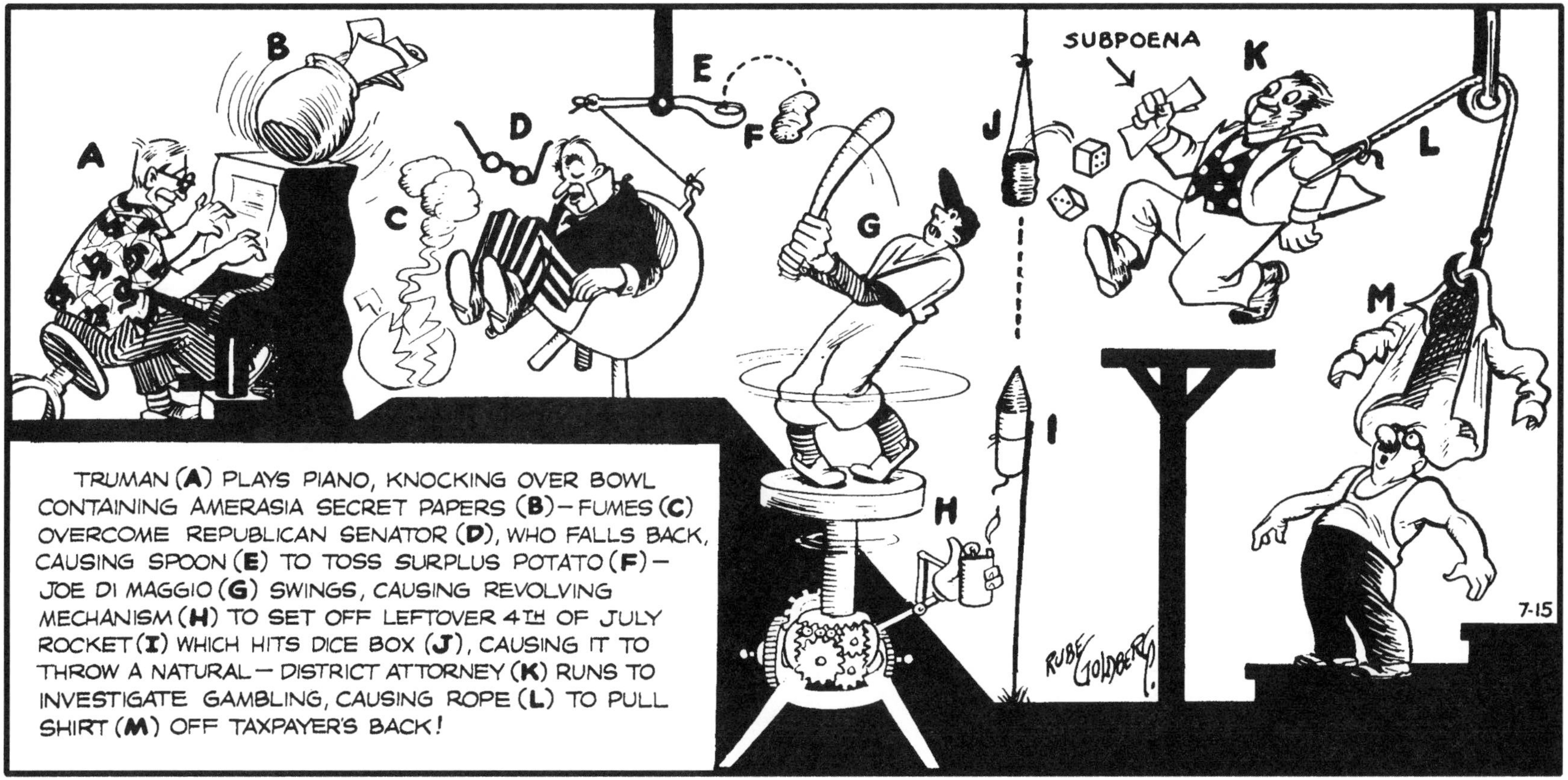
B
A
E
D
F
C
G
SUBPOENA
K
J
L
M
I
H
TRUMAN (A) PLAYS PIANO, KNOCKING OVER BOWL CONTAINING AMERASIA SECRET PAPERS (B) – FUMES (C) OVERCOME REPUBLICAN SENATOR (D), WHO FALLS BACK, CAUSING SPOON (E) TO TOSS SURPLUS POTATO (F) – JOE DI MAGGIO (G) SWINGS, CAUSING REVOLVING MECHANISM (H) TO SET OFF LEFTOVER 4TH OF JULY ROCKET (I) WHICH HITS DICE BOX (J), CAUSING IT TO THROW A NATURAL – DISTRICT ATTORNEY (K) RUNS TO INVESTIGATE GAMBLING, CAUSING ROPE (L) TO PULL SHIRT (M) OFF TAXPAYER'S BACK!
7-15
RUBE GOLDBERG

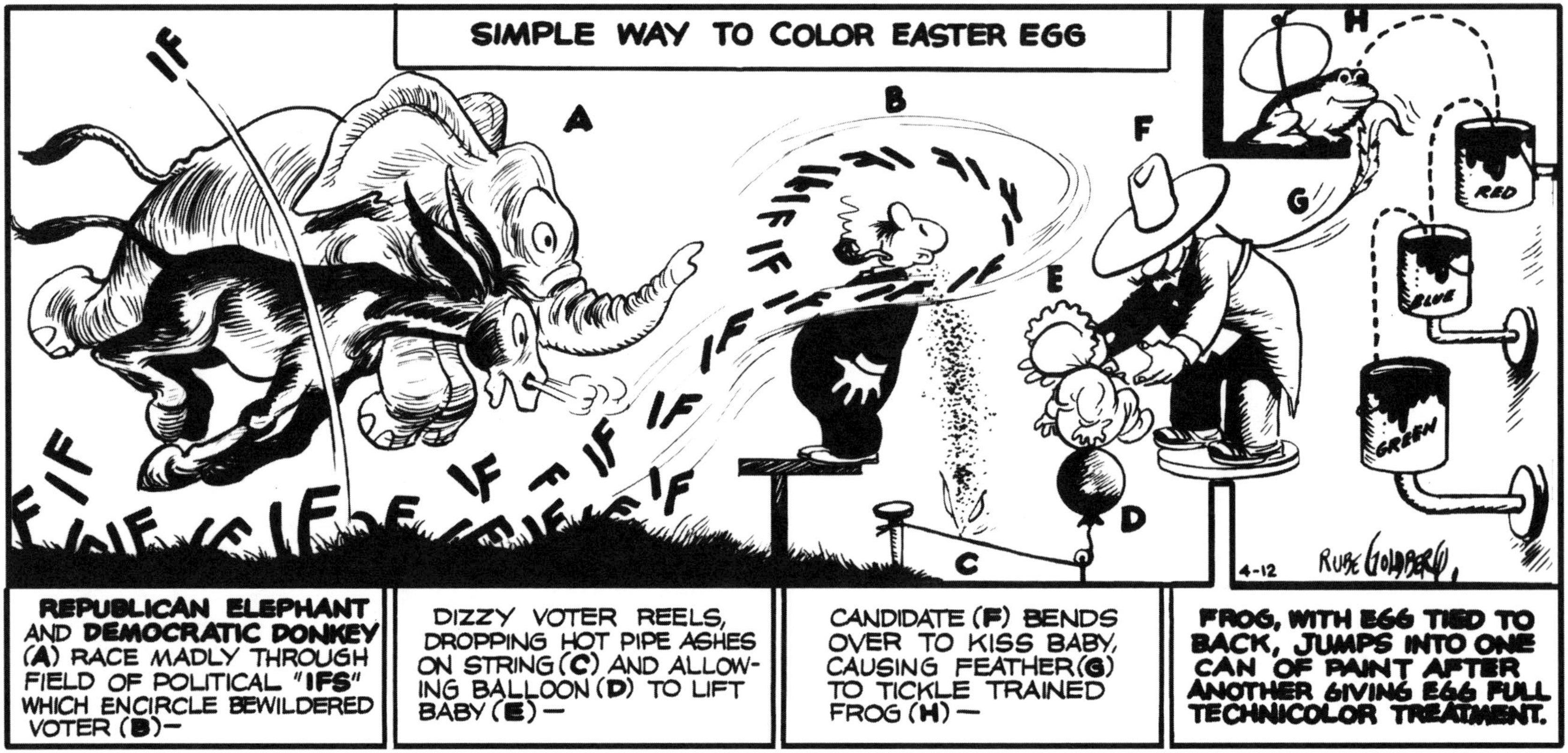
SIMPLE WAY TO COLOR EASTER EGG
A
B
C
D
E
F
G
H
RED
BLUE
GREEN
4-12
RUBE GOLDBERG
REPUBLICAN ELEPHANT AND DEMOCRATIC DONKEY (A) RACE MADLY THROUGH FIELD OF POLITICAL "IFS" WHICH ENCIRCLE BEWILDERED VOTER (B)—
DIZZY VOTER REELS, DROPPING HOT PIPE ASHES ON STRING (C) AND ALLOWING BALLOON (D) TO LIFT BABY (E)—
CANDIDATE (F) BENDS OVER TO KISS BABY, CAUSING FEATHER (G) TO TICKLE TRAINED FROG (H)—
FROG, WITH EGG TIED TO BACK, JUMPS INTO ONE CAN OF PAINT AFTER ANOTHER GIVING EGG FULL TECHNICOLOR TREATMENT.

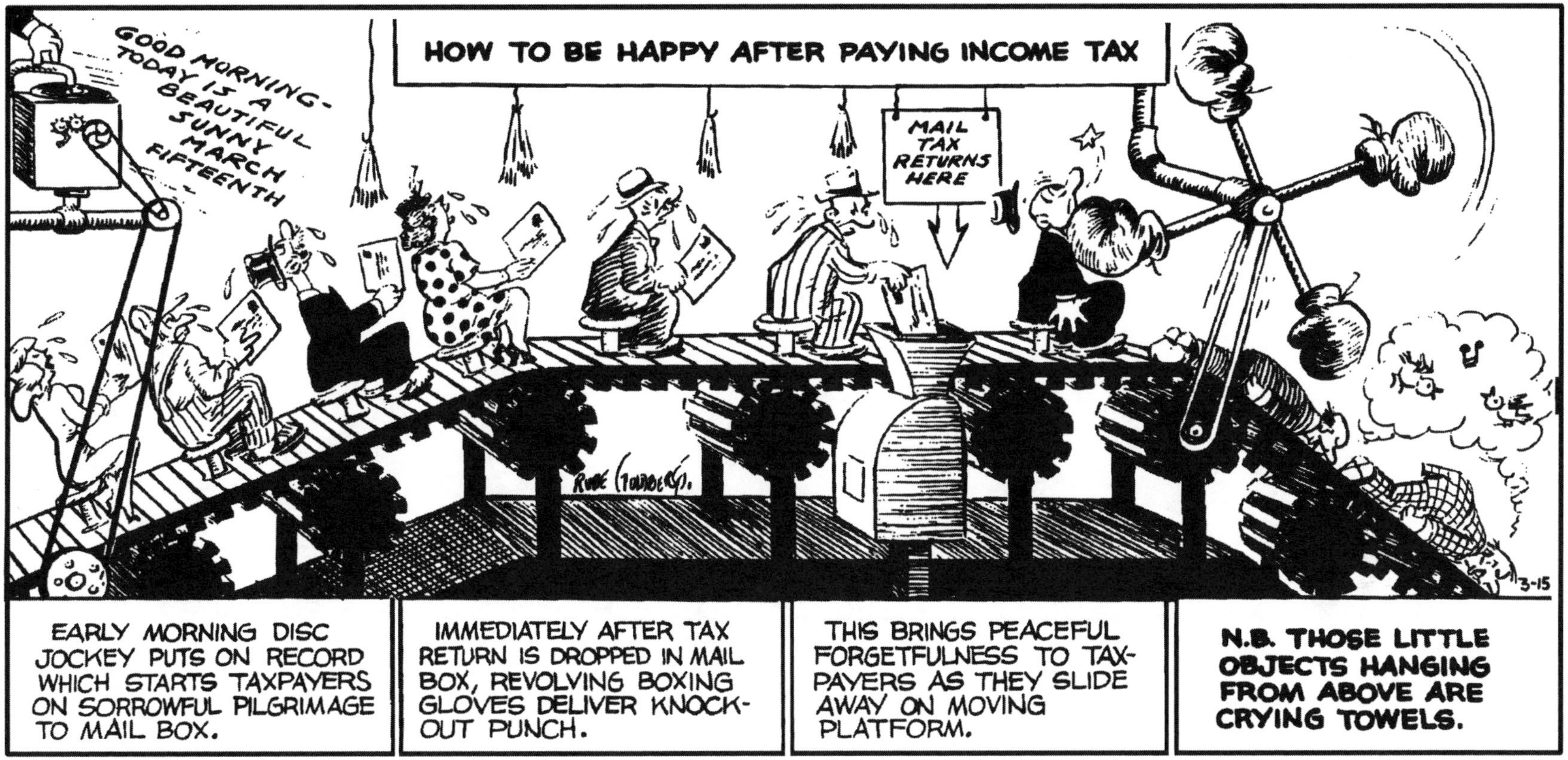
HOW TO BE HAPPY AFTER PAYING INCOME TAX
GOOD MORNING- TODAY IS A BEAUTIFUL SUNNY MARCH FIFTEENTH
MAIL TAX RETURNS HERE
RUBE GOLDBERG.
3-15
EARLY MORNING DISC JOCKEY PUTS ON RECORD WHICH STARTS TAXPAYERS ON SORROWFUL PILGRIMAGE TO MAIL BOX.
IMMEDIATELY AFTER TAX RETURN IS DROPPED IN MAIL BOX, REVOLVING BOXING GLOVES DELIVER KNOCK-OUT PUNCH.
THIS BRINGS PEACEFUL FORGETFULNESS TO TAX-PAYERS AS THEY SLIDE AWAY ON MOVING PLATFORM.
N.B. THOSE LITTLE OBJECTS HANGING FROM ABOVE ARE CRYING TOWELS.

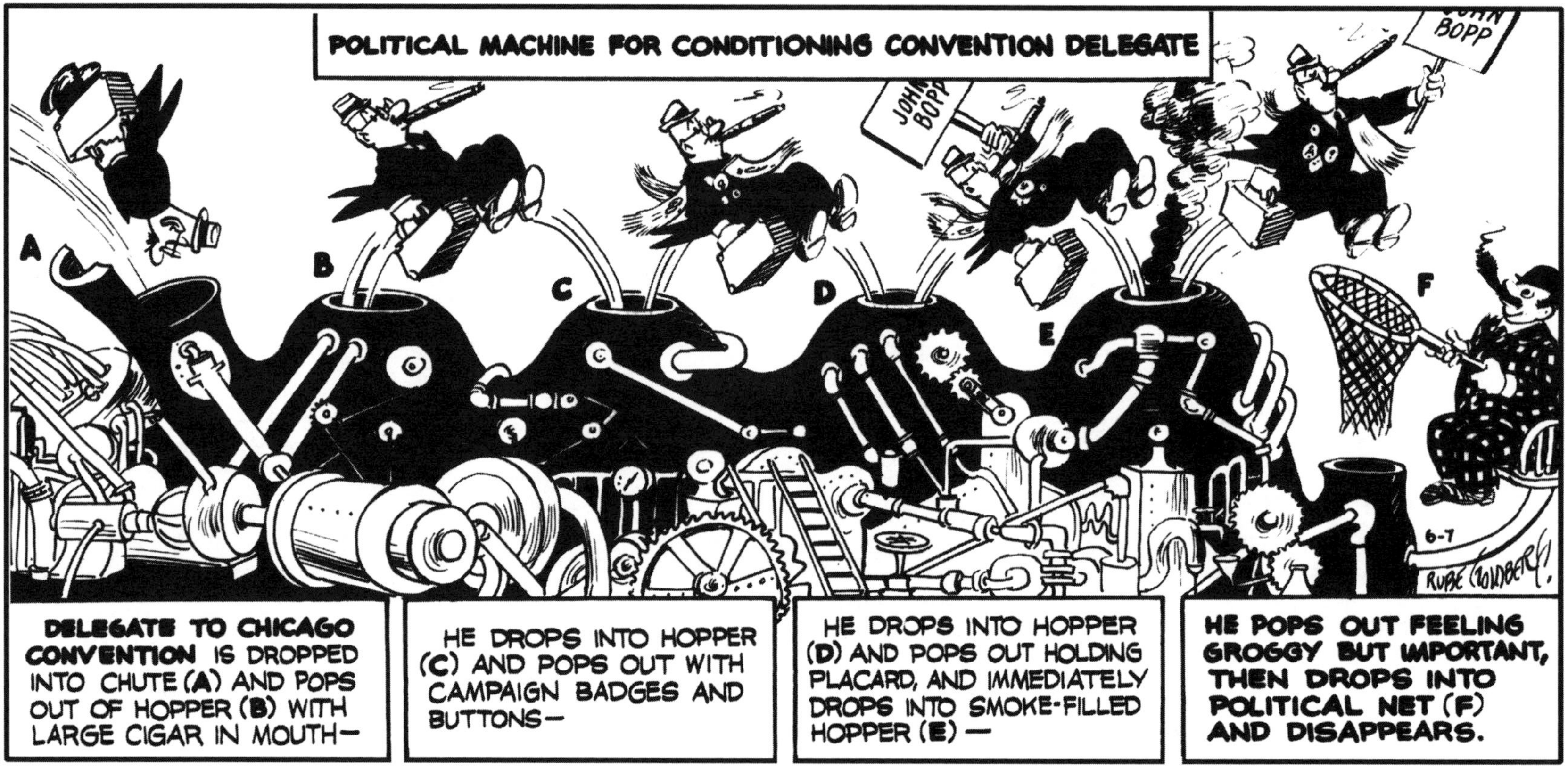
POLITICAL MACHINE FOR CONDITIONING CONVENTION DELEGATE
A
B
C
D
E
F
JOHN BOPP
6-7
RUBE GOLDBERG
DELEGATE TO CHICAGO CONVENTION IS DROPPED INTO CHUTE (A) AND POPS OUT OF HOPPER (B) WITH LARGE CIGAR IN MOUTH—
HE DROPS INTO HOPPER (C) AND POPS OUT WITH CAMPAIGN BADGES AND BUTTONS—
HE DROPS INTO HOPPER (D) AND POPS OUT HOLDING PLACARD, AND IMMEDIATELY DROPS INTO SMOKE-FILLED HOPPER (E) —
HE POPS OUT FEELING GROGGY BUT IMPORTANT, THEN DROPS INTO POLITICAL NET (F) AND DISAPPEARS.

Goofy Contraption

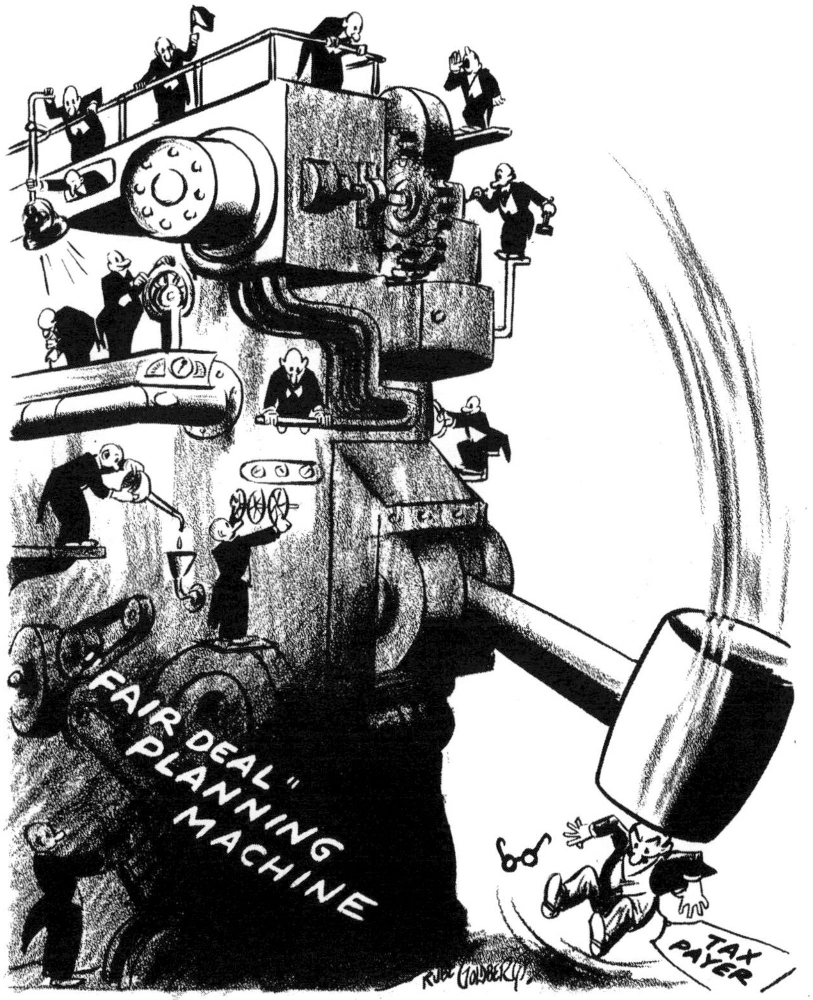
"FAIR DEAL" PLANNING MACHINE
TAX PAYER
RUBE GOLDBERG

Simplified Income Tax Return

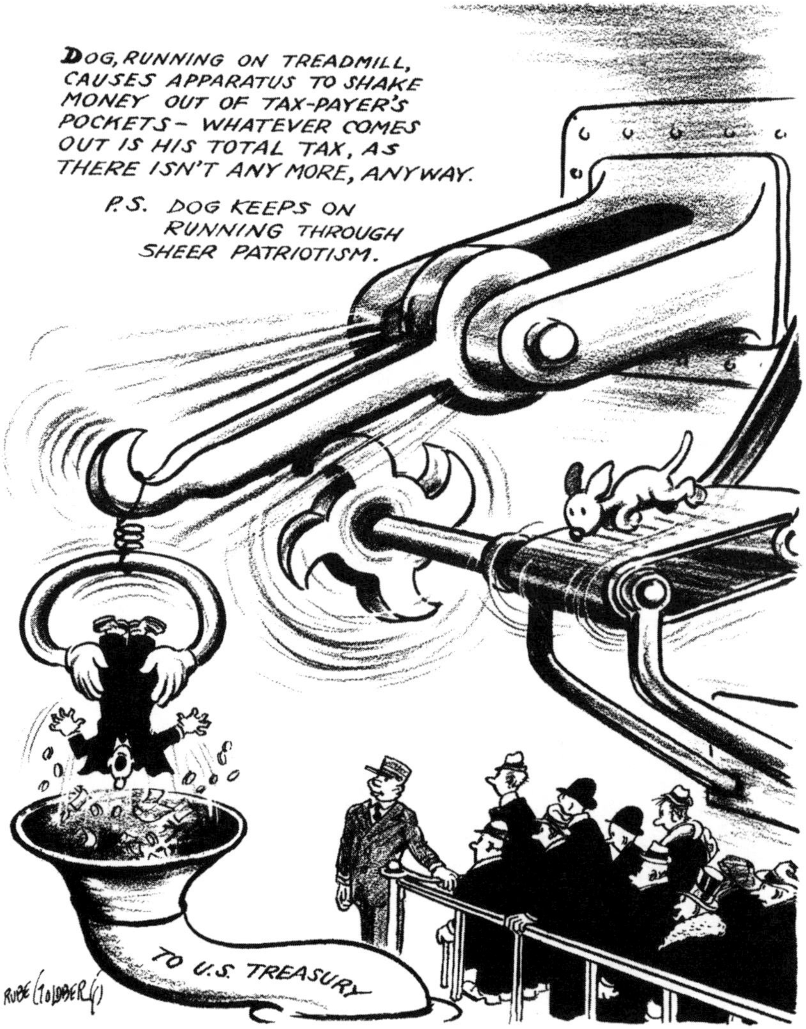
DOG, RUNNING ON TREADMILL, CAUSES APPARATUS TO SHAKE MONEY OUT OF TAX-PAYER'S POCKETS - WHATEVER COMES OUT IS HIS TOTAL TAX, AS THERE ISN'T ANY MORE, ANYWAY.
P.S. DOG KEEPS ON RUNNING THROUGH SHEER PATRIOTISM.
TO U.S. TREASURY
RUBE GOLDBERG

Why a Primary?

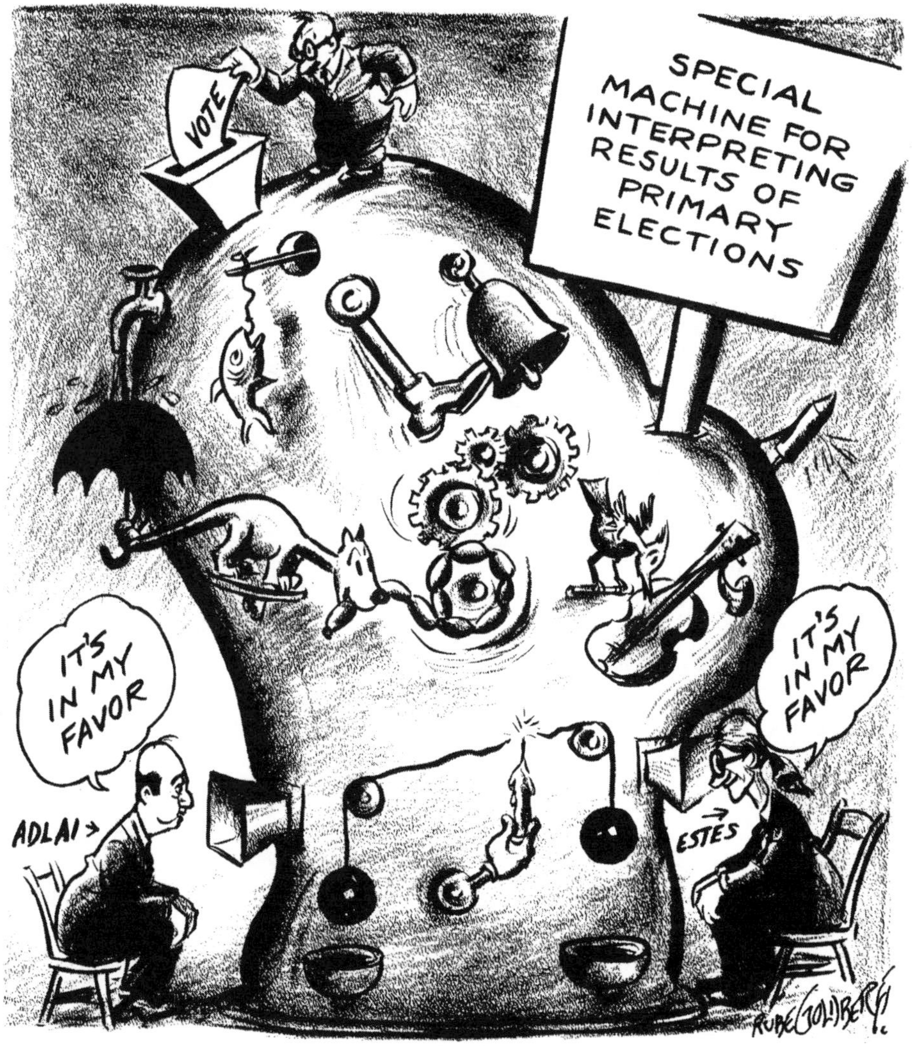
SPECIAL MACHINE FOR INTERPRETING RESULTS OF PRIMARY ELECTIONS
VOTE
IT'S IN MY FAVOR
IT'S IN MY FAVOR
ADLAI
ESTES
RUBE GOLDBERG

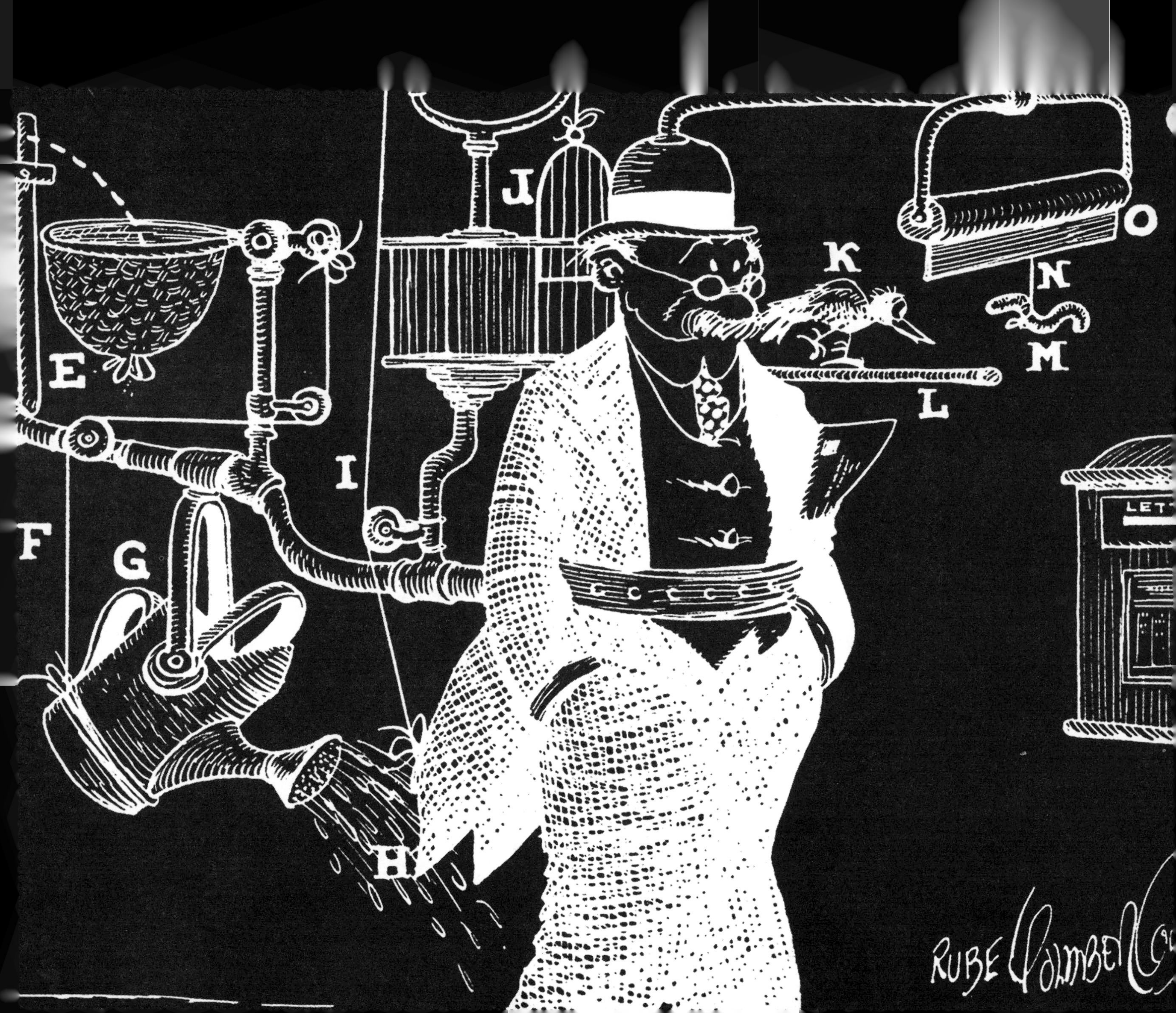
J
E
K
O
N
M
L
I
F
G
H
LETT
RUBE GOLDBER

&, Et Cetera

The diversity of the inventions created by Rube Goldberg—who modestly used the pen name "Professor Lucifer Gorgonzola Butts"—sometimes clouds our perception of the manner in which Goldbergian technology freed mankind from those mind-numbing day-to-day tasks that chained humankind to the lockstep of routine.

Rube shows that when we give up the simple for the complex, even at the cost of considerable time (and some patience), the rewards are great. Eliminating hungry moths bent on the destruction of a favorite sweater or suit, killing a disease-carrying housefly whose presence on your food could mean that this was your last meal, stopping a wall of rainwater pouring into your home through an open window while you were out—these are just a few of the life-easing inventions that came from the mind of that genius Reuben Lucius Goldberg.

A Simple Way to Take Your Own Picture

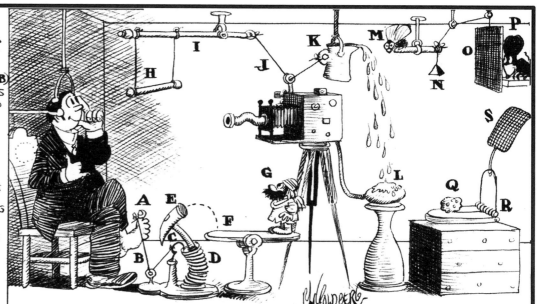

PROFESSOR BUTTS GOES OVER NIAGARA FALLS IN A COLLAPSIBLE ASH-CAN AND HITS UPON AN IDEA FOR A SIMPLE WAY TO TAKE YOUR OWN PICTURE.

WIGGLE BIG TOE (A), PULLING STRING (B) AND RAISING HOOK (C), WHICH RELEASES SPRING (D) AND CAUSES HAMMER (E) TO STRIKE PLATFORM (F) AND CATAPULT ARABIAN MIDGET (G) TO TRAPEZE (H). WEIGHT OF ARAB CAUSES BAR (I) TO TILT AND PULL CORD (J), WHICH UPSETS PITCHER OF SYRUP (K). SYRUP DRIPS ON CAMERA-BULB (L) ATTRACTING HUNGRY FLY (M) WHICH SWOOPS DOWN, ALLOWING WEIGHTED END OF BAR (N) TO LIFT SCREEN (O) WHICH HAS BEEN SHUTTING OFF VISION OF MOUSE (P). MOUSE SEES CHEESE (Q) AND JUMPS. TRAP (R) SNAPS, CAUSING SWATTER (S) TO SWAT FLY THEREBY SQUEEZING BULB & TAKING PICTURE. IF PICTURE IS NO GOOD DON'T BLAME IT ON INVENTION. IT'S THE WAY YOU LOOK.

Simple Idea to Keep You from Forgetting to Mail Your Wife's Letter

PROFESSOR BUTTS GETS CAUGHT IN A REVOLVING DOOR AND BECOMES DIZZY ENOUGH TO DOPE OUT AN IDEA TO KEEP YOU FROM FORGETTING TO MAIL YOUR WIFE'S LETTER.

AS YOU WALK PAST COBBLER SHOP, HOOK(A) STRIKES SUSPENDED BOOT(B) CAUSING IT TO KICK FOOTBALL(C) THROUGH GOAL POSTS(D). FOOTBALL DROPS INTO BASKET(E) AND STRING(F) TILTS SPRINKLING CAN(G) CAUSING WATER TO SOAK COAT TAILS(H). AS COAT SHRINKS CORD(I) OPENS DOOR(J) OF CAGE ALLOWING BIRD(K) TO WALK OUT ON PERCH(L) AND GRAB WORM(M) WHICH IS ATTACHED TO STRING(N). THIS PULLS DOWN WINDOW SHADE(O) ON WHICH IS WRITTEN, "YOU SAP, MAIL THAT LETTER." A SIMPLE WAY TO AVOID ALL THIS TROUBLE IS TO MARRY A WIFE WHO CAN'T WRITE.

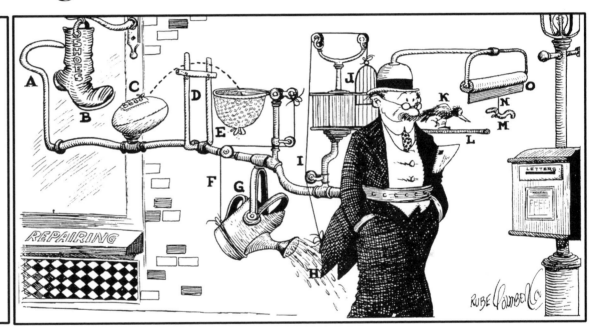

RUBE GOLDBERG Co.

Neat Little Fire Extinguisher

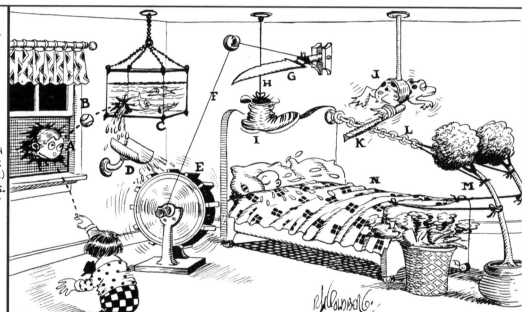

PROFESSOR BUTTS, TRAINING FOR THE OLYMIC GAMES, BROAD JUMPS INTO THE GRAND GANYON BY MISTAKE AND, BEFORE HE REACHES BOTTOM, HAS PLENTY OF TIME TO INVENT A NEAT LITTLE FIRE EXTINGUISHER.

PORTER (A) SMELLS SMOKE COMING FROM ROOM AND IN THE EXCITEMENT STICKS HIS HEAD THROUGH WINDOW SCREEN TO INVESTIGATE. LITTLE, BOY REMEMBERING CARNIVAL, THROWS BASEBALL (B) WHICH BOUNCES OFF PORTER'S HEAD AND BREAKS GLASS IN AQUARIUM (C), CAUSING WATER TO RUN INTO TROUGH (D) AND REVOLVE PADDLE WHEEL (E) WHICH WINDS ROPE (F), PULLING KNIFE (G) AND CUTTING CORD (H). SHOE (I) FALLS ON BABY'S FACE, BABY SHEDS COPIOUS TEARS. SPLASHING OF TEARS MAKES BULL FROG (J) THINK OF BABBLING BROOK AND HE STARTS SWIMMING CAUSING FILE (K) TO CUT CHAIN (L) WHICH BREAKS AND ALLOWS TREES (M) TO SNAP UPRIGHT AND PULL WET BLANKET (N) OVER BURNING WASTE BASKET, THEREBY EXTINGUISHING FIRE.

IF THE FIRE DOESN'T HAPPEN TO BE IN THE WASTE BASKET, CALL OUT THE FIRE DEPARTMENT.

The Latest Cigar Lighter

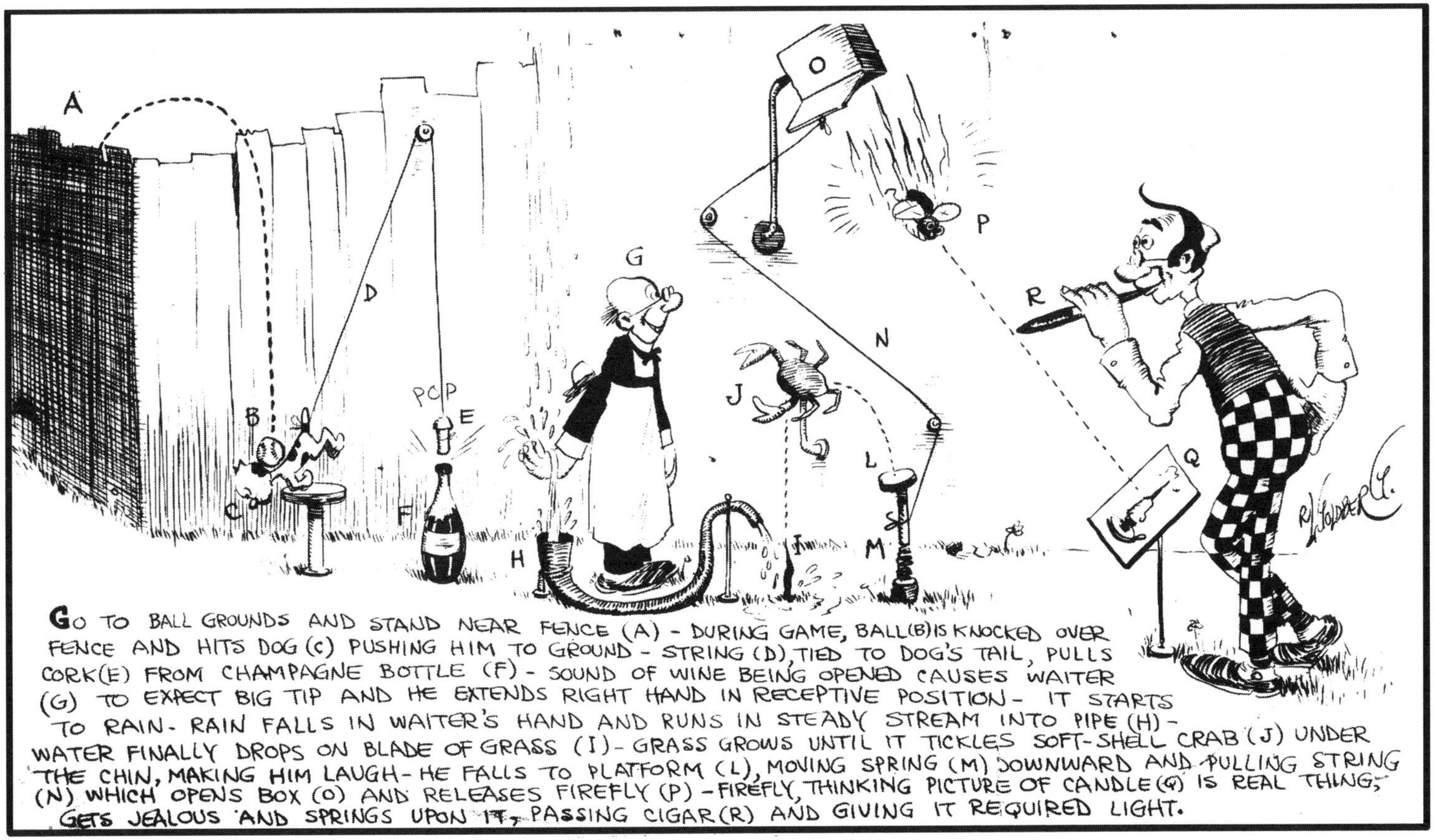
A
D
B
C
POP
E
F
G
H
J
I
L
M
N
O
P
R
Q
GO TO BALL GROUNDS AND STAND NEAR FENCE (A) - DURING GAME, BALL(B) IS KNOCKED OVER
FENCE AND HITS DOG (C) PUSHING HIM TO GROUND - STRING (D), TIED TO DOG'S TAIL, PULLS
CORK(E) FROM CHAMPAGNE BOTTLE (F) - SOUND OF WINE BEING OPENED CAUSES WAITER
(G) TO EXPECT BIG TIP AND HE EXTENDS RIGHT HAND IN RECEPTIVE POSITION - IT STARTS
TO RAIN - RAIN FALLS IN WAITER'S HAND AND RUNS IN STEADY STREAM INTO PIPE (H) -
WATER FINALLY DROPS ON BLADE OF GRASS (I) - GRASS GROWS UNTIL IT TICKLES SOFT-SHELL CRAB (J) UNDER
THE CHIN, MAKING HIM LAUGH - HE FALLS TO PLATFORM (L), MOVING SPRING (M) DOWNWARD AND PULLING STRING
(N) WHICH OPENS BOX (O) AND RELEASES FIREFLY (P) - FIREFLY, THINKING PICTURE OF CANDLE (Q) IS REAL THING,
GETS JEALOUS AND SPRINGS UPON IT, PASSING CIGAR (R) AND GIVING IT REQUIRED LIGHT.

Opening Windows

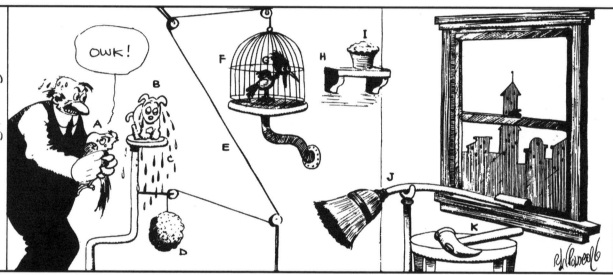

AFTER TRYING UNSUCCESSFULLY TO OPEN WINDOW FOR HALF AN HOUR, YOU RELIEVE YOUR ANGER BY CHOKING PARROT(A) - DOG (B) HEARS PARROT'S GROANS AND WEEPS OUT OF SYMPATHY- TEARS (C) SOAK SPONGE (D), CAUSING ITS WEIGHT TO PULL STRING (E) WHICH LIFTS TOP OFF CAGE (F) AND RELEASES WOODPECKER (G)- WOODPECKER CHEWS AWAY SHELF (H) AND HEAVY BISCUIT (I) FALLS ON BROOM-HANDLE (J), CAUSING IT TO ACT AS LEVER IN RAISING WINDOW - AFTER REPEATING THIS OPERATION SIX TIMES WITHOUT SUCCESS, TAKE HAMMER (K) AND BREAK GLASS IN WINDOW, ALLOWING FRESH AIR TO ENTER ROOM.

OWK!

HO HUM

Device for Closing the Window in Case of Rain

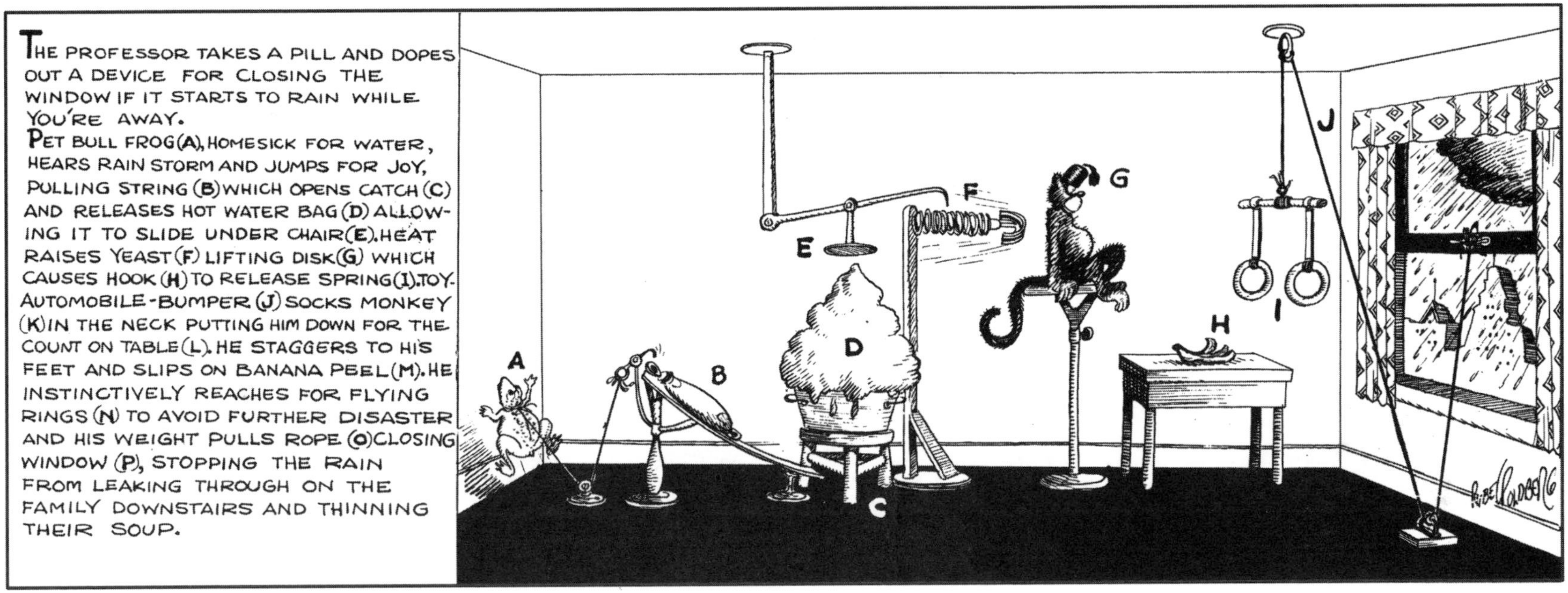
THE PROFESSOR TAKES A PILL AND DOPES OUT A DEVICE FOR CLOSING THE WINDOW IF IT STARTS TO RAIN WHILE YOU'RE AWAY.
PET BULL FROG (A), HOMESICK FOR WATER, HEARS RAIN STORM AND JUMPS FOR JOY, PULLING STRING (B) WHICH OPENS CATCH (C) AND RELEASES HOT WATER BAG (D) ALLOWING IT TO SLIDE UNDER CHAIR (E). HEAT RAISES YEAST (F) LIFTING DISK (G) WHICH CAUSES HOOK (H) TO RELEASE SPRING (I). TOY AUTOMOBILE-BUMPER (J) SOCKS MONKEY (K) IN THE NECK PUTTING HIM DOWN FOR THE COUNT ON TABLE (L). HE STAGGERS TO HIS FEET AND SLIPS ON BANANA PEEL (M). HE INSTINCTIVELY REACHES FOR FLYING RINGS (N) TO AVOID FURTHER DISASTER AND HIS WEIGHT PULLS ROPE (O) CLOSING WINDOW (P), STOPPING THE RAIN FROM LEAKING THROUGH ON THE FAMILY DOWNSTAIRS AND THINNING THEIR SOUP.
A
B
C
D
E
F
G
H
I
J

The Professor's Moth Exterminator

A
B
C
D
E
F
G
H
I
J
K
L
M
N
O
P
Q
R
S
T

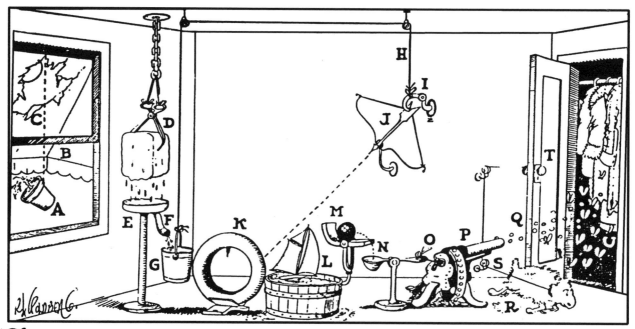

THE PROFESSOR EMERGES FROM THE GOOFY BOOTH WITH A DEVICE FOR THE EXTERMINATION OF MOTHS.

START SINGING. LADY UPSTAIRS, WHEN SUFFICIENTLY ANNOYED, THROWS FLOWER POT (A) THROUGH AWNING (B). HOLE (C) ALLOWS SUN TO COME THROUGH AND MELT CAKE OF ICE (D). WATER DRIPS INTO PAN (E) RUNNING THROUGH PIPE (F) INTO PAIL (G). WEIGHT OF PAIL CAUSES CORD (H) TO RELEASE HOOK (I) AND ALLOW ARROW (J) TO SHOOT INTO TIRE (K). ESCAPING AIR BLOWS AGAINST TOY SAILBOAT (L) DRIVING IT AGAINST LEVER (M) AND CAUSING BALL TO ROLL INTO SPOON (N) AND PULL STRING (O) WHICH SETS OFF MACHINE GUN (P) DISCHARGING CAMPHOR BALLS (Q). REPORT OF GUN FRIGHTENS LAMB (R) WHICH RUNS AND PULLS CORD (S), OPENING CLOSET DOOR (T). AS MOTHS (U) FLY OUT TO EAT WOOL FROM LAMB'S BACK THEY ARE KILLED BY THE BARRAGE OF MOTH BALLS.

IF ANY OF THE MOTHS ESCAPE AND THERE IS DANGER OF THEIR RETURNING, YOU CAN FOOL THEM BY MOVING.

Simple Way to Keep Shop Windows Clean

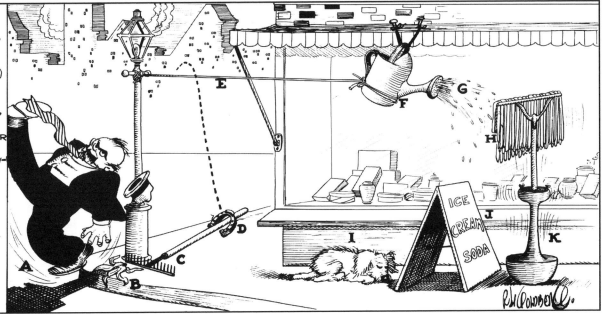

PROFESSOR BUTTS STANDS IN FRONT OF AN X-RAY AND SEES AN IDEA INSIDE HIS HEAD SHOWING HOW TO KEEP SHOP WINDOWS CLEAN.
PASSING MAN (A) SLIPS ON BANANA PEEL (B) CAUSING HIM TO FALL ON RAKE (C). AS HANDLE OF RAKE RISES IT THROWS HORSESHOE (D) ONTO ROPE (E) WHICH SAGS, THEREBY TILTING SPRINKLING CAN (F). WATER (G) SATURATES MOP (H). PICKLE TERRIER (I) THINKS IT IS RAINING, GETS UP TO RUN INTO HOUSE AND UPSETS SIGN (J) THROWING IT AGAINST NON-TIPPING CIGAR ASH RECEIVER (K) WHICH CAUSES IT TO SWING BACK AND FORTH AND SWISH THE MOP AGAINST WINDOW PANE, WIPING IT CLEAN.
IF MAN BREAKS HIS NECK BY FALL MOVE AWAY BEFORE COP ARRIVES.
A
B
C
D
E
F
G
H
I
J
K
ICE
CREAM
SODA

Invention for Turning on the Steam Heat

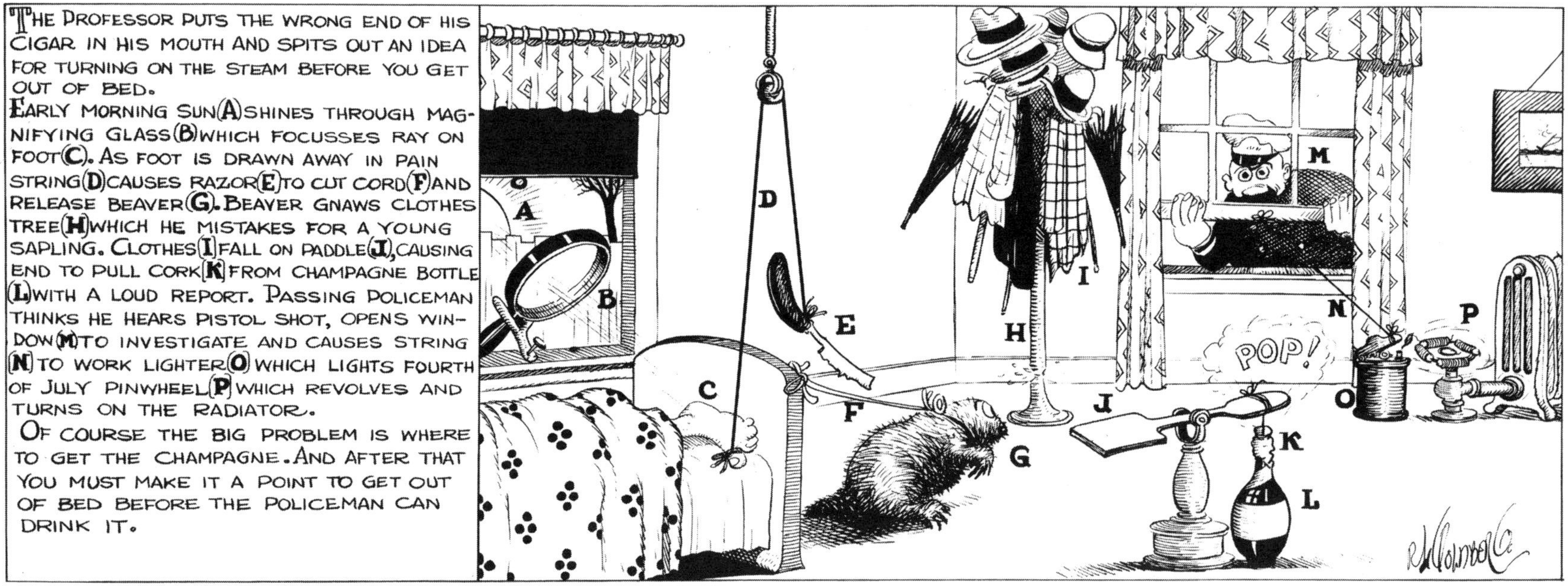
THE PROFESSOR PUTS THE WRONG END OF HIS CIGAR IN HIS MOUTH AND SPITS OUT AN IDEA FOR TURNING ON THE STEAM BEFORE YOU GET OUT OF BED.
EARLY MORNING SUN (A) SHINES THROUGH MAGNIFYING GLASS (B) WHICH FOCUSSES RAY ON FOOT (C). AS FOOT IS DRAWN AWAY IN PAIN STRING (D) CAUSES RAZOR (E) TO CUT CORD (F) AND RELEASE BEAVER (G). BEAVER GNAWS CLOTHES TREE (H) WHICH HE MISTAKES FOR A YOUNG SAPLING. CLOTHES (I) FALL ON PADDLE (J), CAUSING END TO PULL CORK (K) FROM CHAMPAGNE BOTTLE (L) WITH A LOUD REPORT. PASSING POLICEMAN THINKS HE HEARS PISTOL SHOT, OPENS WINDOW (M) TO INVESTIGATE AND CAUSES STRING (N) TO WORK LIGHTER (O) WHICH LIGHTS FOURTH OF JULY PINWHEEL (P) WHICH REVOLVES AND TURNS ON THE RADIATOR.
OF COURSE THE BIG PROBLEM IS WHERE TO GET THE CHAMPAGNE. AND AFTER THAT YOU MUST MAKE IT A POINT TO GET OUT OF BED BEFORE THE POLICEMAN CAN DRINK IT.
A
B
C
D
E
F
G
H
I
J
K
L
M
N
O
P
POP!

Idea for a New Scientific Barometer

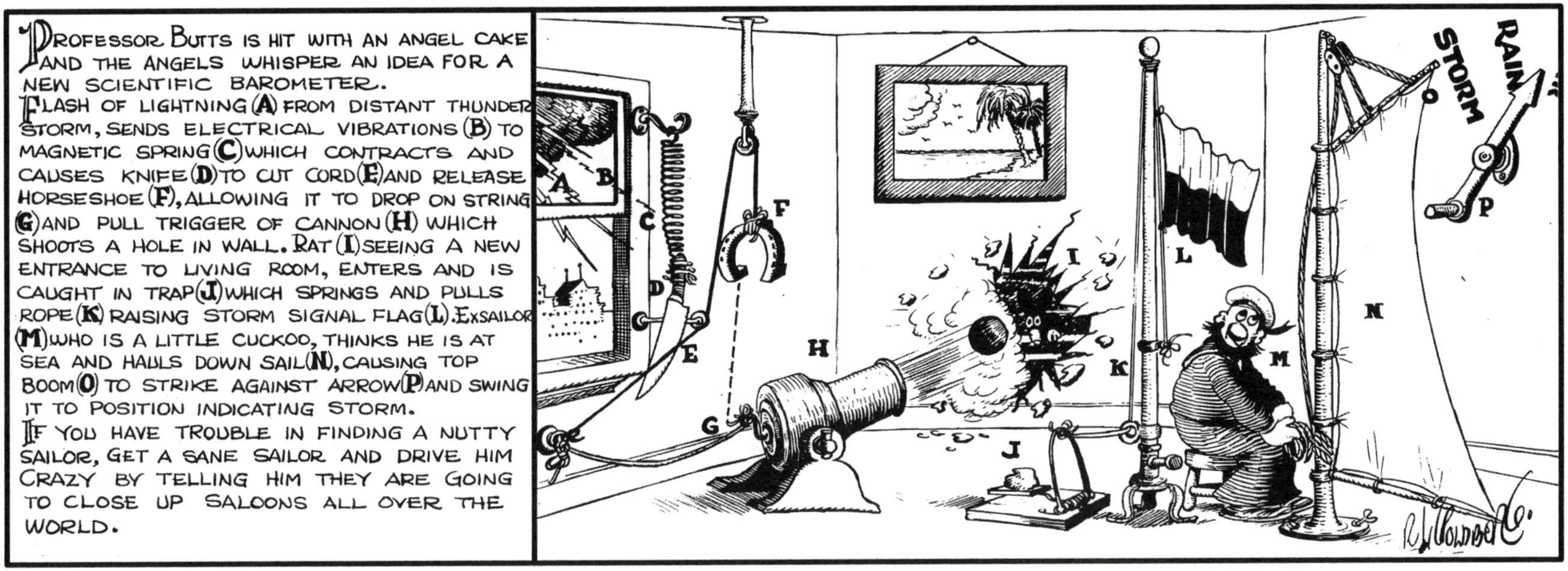
PROFESSOR BUTTS IS HIT WITH AN ANGEL CAKE AND THE ANGELS WHISPER AN IDEA FOR A NEW SCIENTIFIC BAROMETER.
FLASH OF LIGHTNING (A) FROM DISTANT THUNDERSTORM, SENDS ELECTRICAL VIBRATIONS (B) TO MAGNETIC SPRING (C) WHICH CONTRACTS AND CAUSES KNIFE (D) TO CUT CORD (E) AND RELEASE HORSESHOE (F), ALLOWING IT TO DROP ON STRING (G) AND PULL TRIGGER OF CANNON (H) WHICH SHOOTS A HOLE IN WALL. RAT (I) SEEING A NEW ENTRANCE TO LIVING ROOM, ENTERS AND IS CAUGHT IN TRAP (J) WHICH SPRINGS AND PULLS ROPE (K) RAISING STORM SIGNAL FLAG (L). EXSAILOR (M) WHO IS A LITTLE CUCKOO, THINKS HE IS AT SEA AND HAULS DOWN SAIL (N), CAUSING TOP BOOM (O) TO STRIKE AGAINST ARROW (P) AND SWING IT TO POSITION INDICATING STORM.
IF YOU HAVE TROUBLE IN FINDING A NUTTY SAILOR, GET A SANE SAILOR AND DRIVE HIM CRAZY BY TELLING HIM THEY ARE GOING TO CLOSE UP SALOONS ALL OVER THE WORLD.
STORM
RAIN

Invention to Shut Off the Radio to Answer the Telephone

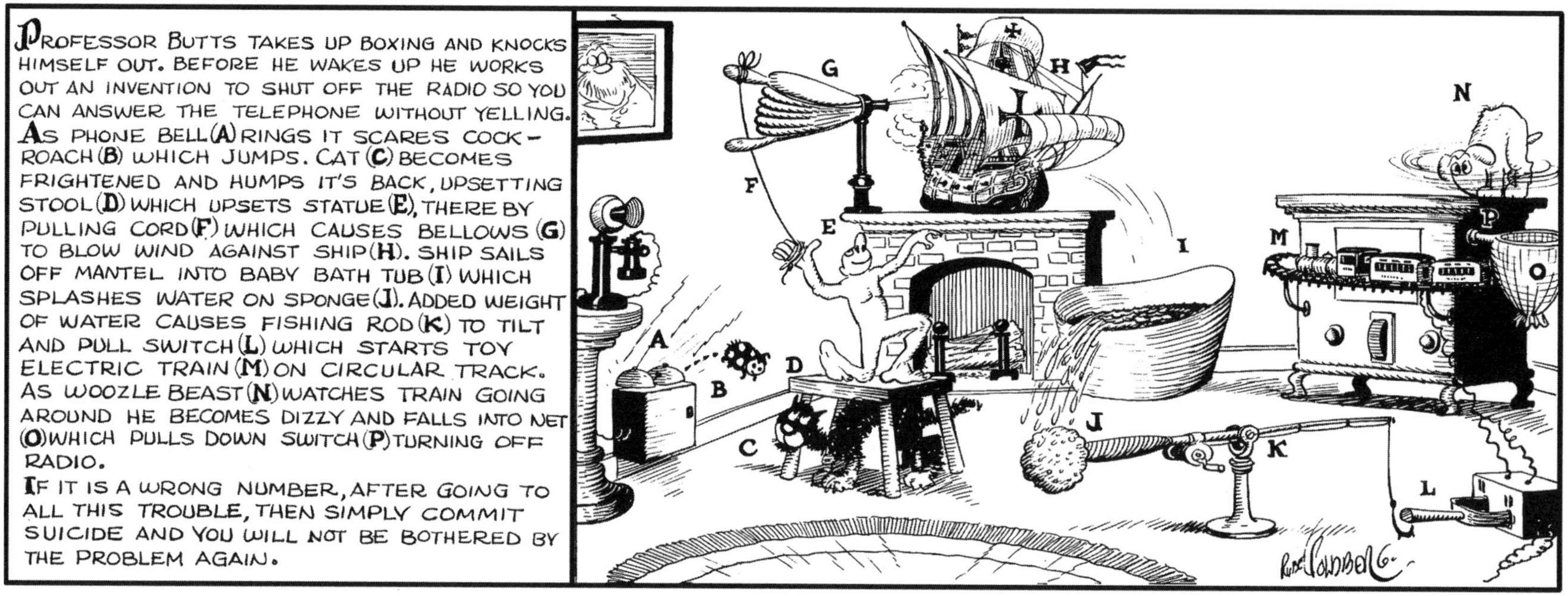
PROFESSOR BUTTS TAKES UP BOXING AND KNOCKS HIMSELF OUT. BEFORE HE WAKES UP HE WORKS OUT AN INVENTION TO SHUT OFF THE RADIO SO YOU CAN ANSWER THE TELEPHONE WITHOUT YELLING.
AS PHONE BELL (A) RINGS IT SCARES COCK-ROACH (B) WHICH JUMPS. CAT (C) BECOMES FRIGHTENED AND HUMPS IT'S BACK, UPSETTING STOOL (D) WHICH UPSETS STATUE (E), THERE BY PULLING CORD (F) WHICH CAUSES BELLOWS (G) TO BLOW WIND AGAINST SHIP (H). SHIP SAILS OFF MANTEL INTO BABY BATH TUB (I) WHICH SPLASHES WATER ON SPONGE (J). ADDED WEIGHT OF WATER CAUSES FISHING ROD (K) TO TILT AND PULL SWITCH (L) WHICH STARTS TOY ELECTRIC TRAIN (M) ON CIRCULAR TRACK. AS WOOZLE BEAST (N) WATCHES TRAIN GOING AROUND HE BECOMES DIZZY AND FALLS INTO NET (O) WHICH PULLS DOWN SWITCH (P) TURNING OFF RADIO.
IF IT IS A WRONG NUMBER, AFTER GOING TO ALL THIS TROUBLE, THEN SIMPLY COMMIT SUICIDE AND YOU WILL NOT BE BOTHERED BY THE PROBLEM AGAIN.
Rube Goldberg

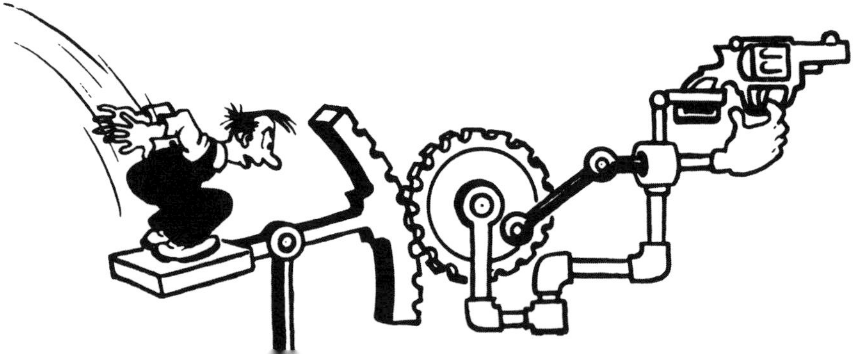

Idea for a Self-Rolling Rug

PROFESSOR BUTTS FLIES THROUGH THE WIND-
SHIELD OF HIS CAR AND WHEN THEY PICK
OUT THE BROKEN GLASS THEY FIND AN IDEA
FOR A SELF-ROLLING RUG.

PLACE FRESH PIE(A) ON WINDOW SILL(B) TO COOL.
WHEN TRAMP(C) SNEAKS UP TO STEAL IT, HOUSE-
MAID(D) FALLS BACK WITH FRIGHT INTO ROCK-
ING CHAIR(E) WHICH TILTS PEDESTAL(F), CAUS-
ING MARBLE STATUE OF DIVING VENUS(G) TO
DIVE INTO GOLDFISH BOWL(H) AND SPLASH WATER
ON PLANT(I) WHICH GROWS AND TURNS ON SWITCH(J)
OF RADIO(K) WHICH PLAYS OLD TUNE CALLED
"OCEANA ROLL". LITTLE TRICK ROLLING CIRCUS
ELEPHANT(L), HEARING TUNE, DOES HIS STUFF
AND KEEPS ROLLING OVER AND OVER UNTIL
RUG(M) IS COMPLETELY WRAPPED AROUND HIM
AND FLOOR IS CLEARED FOR DANCING.

RUG WRAPPED AROUND DELICATE
LITTLE ELEPHANT ALSO KEEPS HIM FROM
CATCHING COLD FROM DRAFT COMING
THROUGH OPEN WINDOW.

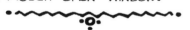

Self-Watering Palm Tree

PROFESSOR BUTT'S BRAIN TAKES A NOSEDIVE AND OUT COMES HIS SELF-WATERING PALM TREE.

STRING (A) WORKS JUMPING JACK (B), FRIGHTENING CAT (C) WHICH RAISES BACK AND LIFTS TROUGH (D), CAUSING BALL (E) TO FALL INTO TEACUP (F). SPRING (G) MAKES BALL REBOUND INTO CUP (H) PULLING ON STRING (I) WHICH RELEASES STICK (J), CAUSING SHELF (K) TO 'COLLAPSE. MILK CAN (L) DROPS ON LADLE (M) AND TENSION ON STRING (N) TILTS SHOE (O) AGAINST JIGGER ON SELTZER BOTTLE (P). SQUIRTING SELTZER ON ASH-CAN SPANIEL WHO HASN'T HAD A BATH IN FOUR YEARS SURPRISE CAUSES HIM TO TURN THREE SOMERSAULTS OVER APPARATUS (R) AND WATER SPLASHES NATURALLY INTO BOWLS, RUNNING THROUGH SPRAY (S) WATERING PALM (T), AND SAVING YOURSELF A TRIP TO HAVANA FOR TROPICAL ATMOSPHERE.

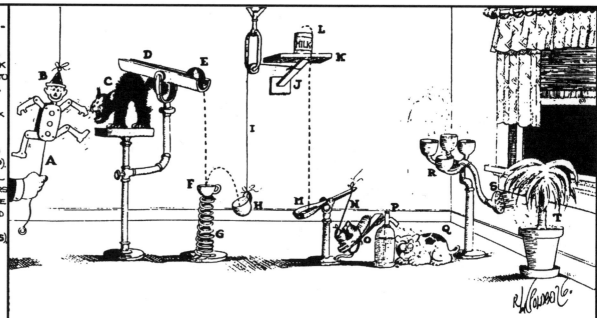

The Latest Simple Flyswatter

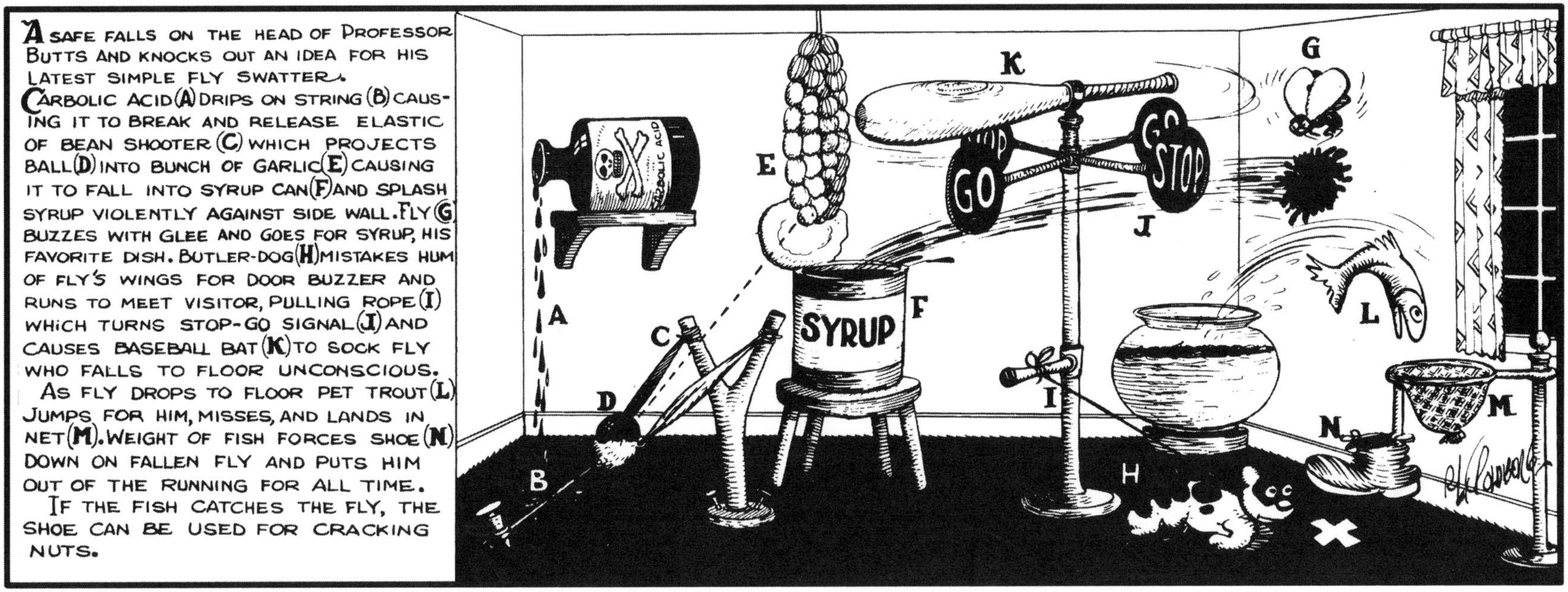
A SAFE FALLS ON THE HEAD OF PROFESSOR BUTTS AND KNOCKS OUT AN IDEA FOR HIS LATEST SIMPLE FLY SWATTER.
CARBOLIC ACID (A) DRIPS ON STRING (B) CAUSING IT TO BREAK AND RELEASE ELASTIC OF BEAN SHOOTER (C) WHICH PROJECTS BALL (D) INTO BUNCH OF GARLIC (E) CAUSING IT TO FALL INTO SYRUP CAN (F) AND SPLASH SYRUP VIOLENTLY AGAINST SIDE WALL. FLY (G) BUZZES WITH GLEE AND GOES FOR SYRUP, HIS FAVORITE DISH. BUTLER-DOG (H) MISTAKES HUM OF FLY'S WINGS FOR DOOR BUZZER AND RUNS TO MEET VISITOR, PULLING ROPE (I) WHICH TURNS STOP-GO SIGNAL (J) AND CAUSES BASEBALL BAT (K) TO SOCK FLY WHO FALLS TO FLOOR UNCONSCIOUS.
AS FLY DROPS TO FLOOR PET TROUT (L) JUMPS FOR HIM, MISSES, AND LANDS IN NET (M). WEIGHT OF FISH FORCES SHOE (N) DOWN ON FALLEN FLY AND PUTS HIM OUT OF THE RUNNING FOR ALL TIME.
IF THE FISH CATCHES THE FLY, THE SHOE CAN BE USED FOR CRACKING NUTS.
CARBOLIC ACID
SYRUP
GO
STOP
A
B
C
D
E
F
G
H
I
J
K
L
M
N

Invention to Put Out the Light After You Fall Asleep

PROFESSOR LUCIFER GORGONZOLA BUTTS
A.K. INVENTS A SIMPLE WAY TO PUT OUT
THE LIGHT AFTER YOU FALL ASLEEP-
SNORES (A) GO THROUGH TUBE (B)-BAR-
FLY (C) THINKS SOMEONE IS SAWING
WOOD AND FLIES TO TUBE LOOKING
FOR SAWDUST, CAUSING LEVER (D)
TO DROP AND LET BALL (E) ROLL OFF-
STRING (F) SHOOTS PISTOL (G)-
BULLET (H) KNOCKS OVER STRAP-
HANGER DOLL (I), PULLING
CORD (J) AND PUTTING OUT
LIGHT (K) - THEREBY SAVING
ELECTRICITY AND GETTING RID
OF BAR-FLY WHEN HE
STUMBLES AND BREAKS
HIS NECK IN THE DARK.
RUBE GOLDBERG
11-20.
A
B
C
D
E
F
G
H
I
J
K

A
B
C
D
E
F
G
H
I
J
K

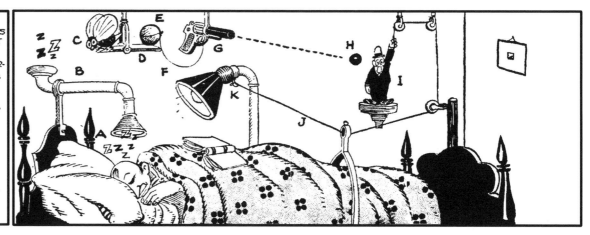

Be Your Own Dentist

BE YOUR OWN DENTIST!

FIRST TIE YOURSELF SECURELY TO CHAIR (A) AND WIGGLE FOOT (B). FEATHER (C) TICKLES BIRD (D) – AS BIRD SHAKES WITH LAUGHTER, IT MIXES COCKTAIL IN SHAKER (E) – BIRD FALLS FORWARD, SPILLING COCKTAIL, AND SQUIRREL (F) GETS SOUSED – IN HIS DRUNKEN EXCITEMENT, SQUIRREL REVOLVES CAGE (G), WHICH TURNS CRANK (H) AND PLAYS PHONOGRAPH RECORD (I). SONG (J) GETS DWARF (K) HOT UNDER COLLAR AND FLAMES (L) IGNITE FUSE (M) WHICH SETS OFF CANNON (N), SHOOTING OUT CANNON BALL (O), CAUSING STRING (P) TO PULL TOOTH!

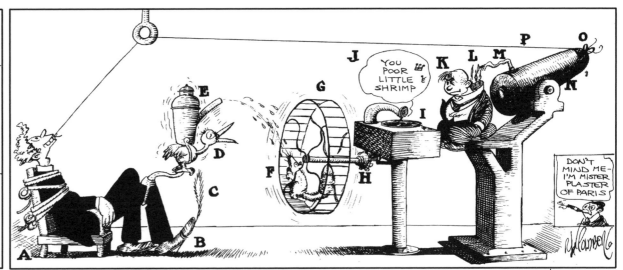

YOU POOR LITTLE SHRIMP

DON'T MIND ME – I'M MISTER PLASTER OF PARIS

173

The New Automatic Lawn Sprinkler

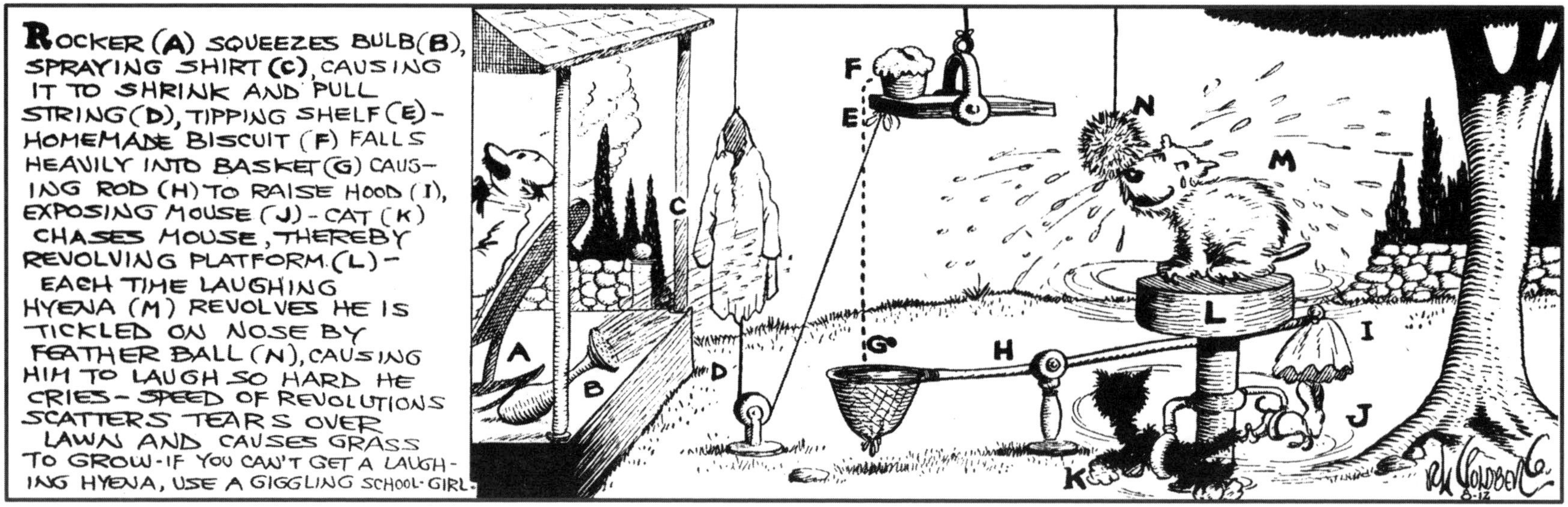
ROCKER (A) SQUEEZES BULB (B), SPRAYING SHIRT (C), CAUSING IT TO SHRINK AND PULL STRING (D), TIPPING SHELF (E) - HOMEMADE BISCUIT (F) FALLS HEAVILY INTO BASKET (G) CAUSING ROD (H) TO RAISE HOOD (I), EXPOSING MOUSE (J) - CAT (K) CHASES MOUSE, THEREBY REVOLVING PLATFORM (L) - EACH TIME LAUGHING HYENA (M) REVOLVES HE IS TICKLED ON NOSE BY FEATHER BALL (N), CAUSING HIM TO LAUGH SO HARD HE CRIES - SPEED OF REVOLUTIONS SCATTERS TEARS OVER LAWN AND CAUSES GRASS TO GROW - IF YOU CAN'T GET A LAUGHING HYENA, USE A GIGGLING SCHOOL-GIRL.
A
B
C
D
E
F
G
H
I
J
K
L
M
N

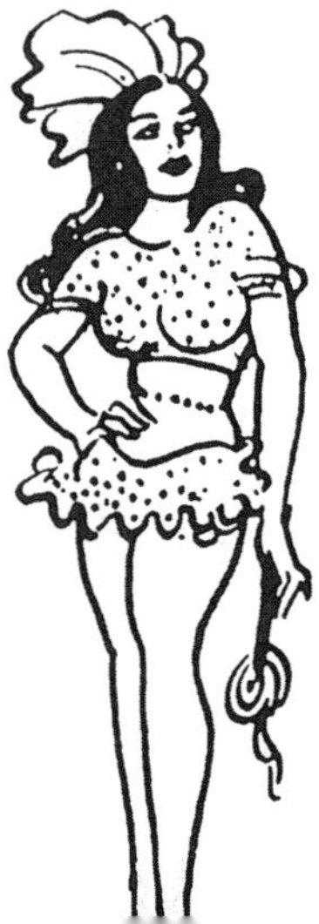

Slicing Bread for the Picnic Sandwich

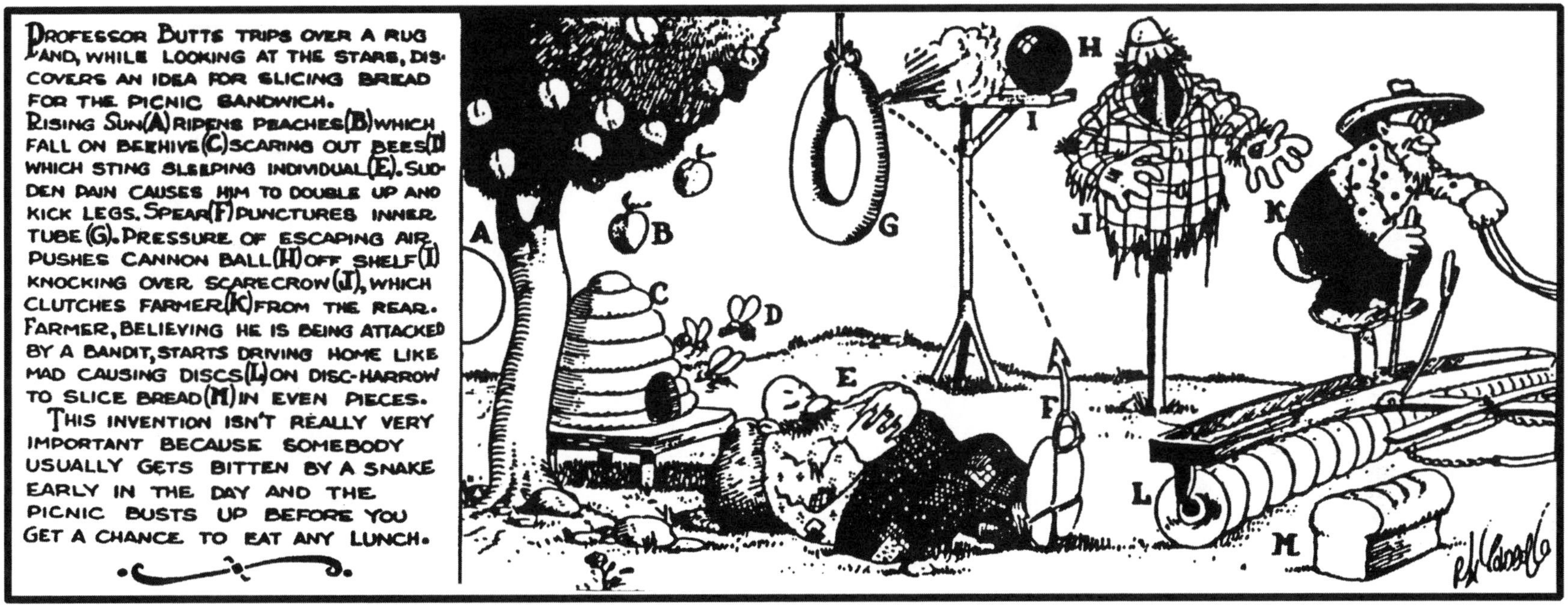
PROFESSOR BUTTS TRIPS OVER A RUG AND, WHILE LOOKING AT THE STARS, DISCOVERS AN IDEA FOR SLICING BREAD FOR THE PICNIC SANDWICH.
RISING SUN (A) RIPENS PEACHES (B) WHICH FALL ON BEEHIVE (C) SCARING OUT BEES (D) WHICH STING SLEEPING INDIVIDUAL (E). SUDDEN PAIN CAUSES HIM TO DOUBLE UP AND KICK LEGS. SPEAR (F) PUNCTURES INNER TUBE (G). PRESSURE OF ESCAPING AIR PUSHES CANNON BALL (H) OFF SHELF (I) KNOCKING OVER SCARECROW (J), WHICH CLUTCHES FARMER (K) FROM THE REAR. FARMER, BELIEVING HE IS BEING ATTACKED BY A BANDIT, STARTS DRIVING HOME LIKE MAD CAUSING DISCS (L) ON DISC-HARROW TO SLICE BREAD (M) IN EVEN PIECES.
THIS INVENTION ISN'T REALLY VERY IMPORTANT BECAUSE SOMEBODY USUALLY GETS BITTEN BY A SNAKE EARLY IN THE DAY AND THE PICNIC BUSTS UP BEFORE YOU GET A CHANCE TO EAT ANY LUNCH.
A
B
C
D
E
F
G
H
I
J
K
L
M

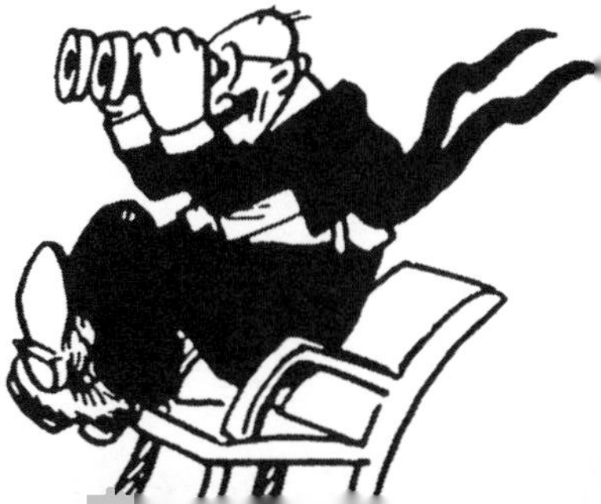

Handy Self-Working Sunshade

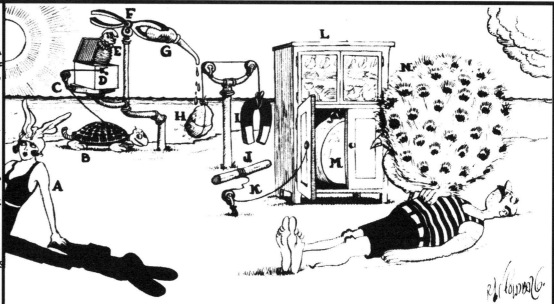

PROFESSOR BUTTS IS OPERATED ON FOR FALLEN ARCHES AND, WHILE UNDER THE ETHER, THINKS OF A HANDY, SELF-WORKING SUNSHADE. SHADOW OF BATHING GIRL(A) CLOSELY RESEMBLES A RABBIT. TORTOISE(B) REMEMBERING THE FABLE OF THE TORTOISE AND THE HARE STARTS TO RACE AND PULLS STRING(C) OPENING HOOK(D) WHICH ALLOWS JACK-IN-THE-BOX(E) TO JUMP AGAINST PLIERS(F) AND SQUEEZE BULB OF EYE-DROPPER(G) WHICH DRIPS WATER ON STONE(H) AS DROPS OF WATER WEAR AWAY STONE CAUSING IT TO BECOME LIGHTER IT RISES ALLOWING MAGNET(I) TO DESCEND. MAGNET ATTRACTS STEEL BAR(J) WHICH LEAVES THE GROUND WITH A SUDDEN JUMP PULLING CORD (K) OPENING DOOR OF CUPBOARD(L) EXPOSING HIGHLY POLISHED POT(M). AS CONCEITED PEACOCK (N) SEES HIS REFLECTION HIS VANITY PROMPTS HIM TO SPREAD HIS BEAUTIFUL TAIL THEREBY SHIELDING BATHER AND PROTECTING HIM FROM SUNBURN — EACH MORNING YOU CAN WRITE THE PEACOCK A LOT OF ADMIRING FAN LETTERS TO MAKE SURE HE IS GOOD AND CONCEITED BY THE TIME YOU NEED HIM.

Automatic Sheet Music Turner

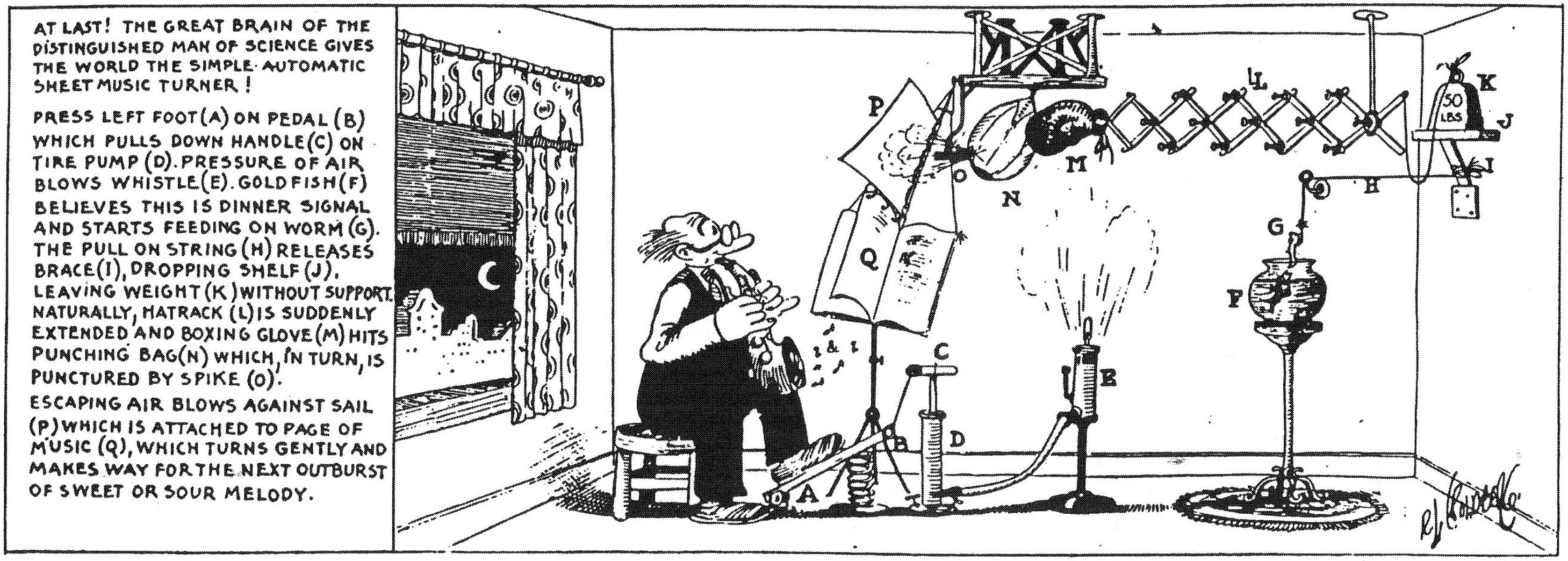
AT LAST! THE GREAT BRAIN OF THE DISTINGUISHED MAN OF SCIENCE GIVES THE WORLD THE SIMPLE AUTOMATIC SHEET MUSIC TURNER!
PRESS LEFT FOOT (A) ON PEDAL (B) WHICH PULLS DOWN HANDLE (C) ON TIRE PUMP (D). PRESSURE OF AIR BLOWS WHISTLE (E). GOLDFISH (F) BELIEVES THIS IS DINNER SIGNAL AND STARTS FEEDING ON WORM (G). THE PULL ON STRING (H) RELEASES BRACE (I), DROPPING SHELF (J), LEAVING WEIGHT (K) WITHOUT SUPPORT. NATURALLY, HATRACK (L) IS SUDDENLY EXTENDED AND BOXING GLOVE (M) HITS PUNCHING BAG (N) WHICH, IN TURN, IS PUNCTURED BY SPIKE (O).
ESCAPING AIR BLOWS AGAINST SAIL (P) WHICH IS ATTACHED TO PAGE OF MUSIC (Q), WHICH TURNS GENTLY AND MAKES WAY FOR THE NEXT OUTBURST OF SWEET OR SOUR MELODY.
50 LBS

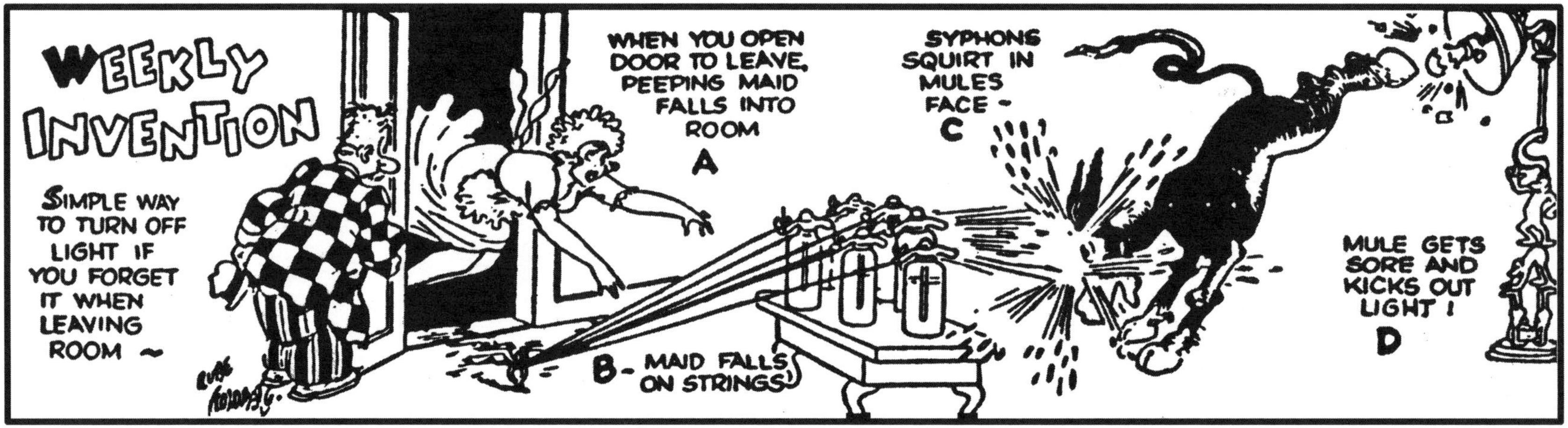
WEEKLY INVENTION
SIMPLE WAY TO TURN OFF LIGHT IF YOU FORGET IT WHEN LEAVING ROOM ~
WHEN YOU OPEN DOOR TO LEAVE, PEEPING MAID FALLS INTO ROOM A
B - MAID FALLS ON STRINGS
SYPHONS SQUIRT IN MULES FACE - C
MULE GETS SORE AND KICKS OUT LIGHT! D

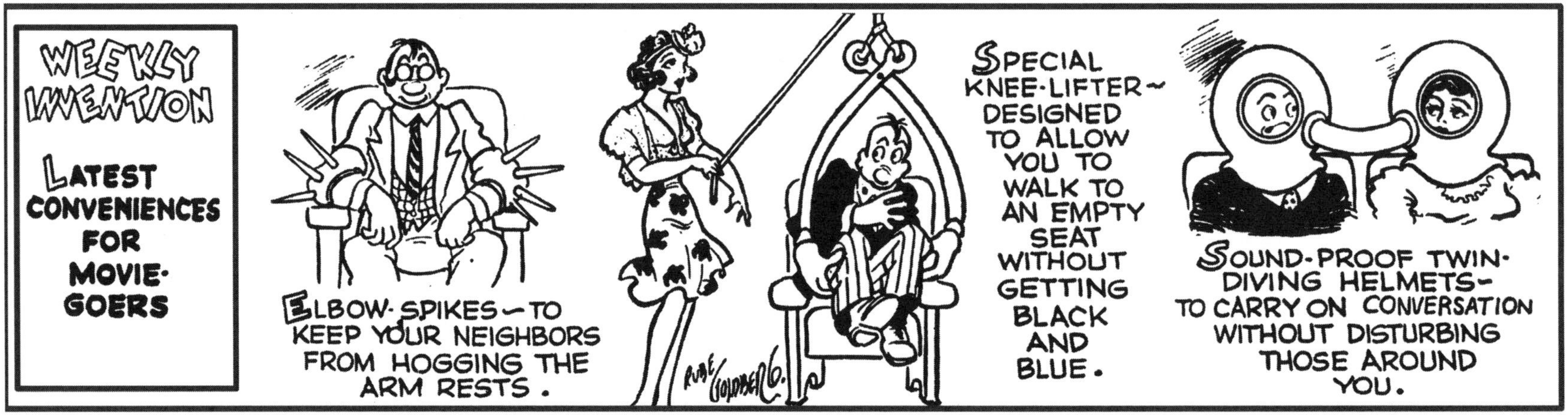
WEEKLY INVENTION
LATEST CONVENIENCES FOR MOVIE-GOERS
ELBOW-SPIKES—TO KEEP YOUR NEIGHBORS FROM HOGGING THE ARM RESTS.
RUBE GOLDBERG.
SPECIAL KNEE-LIFTER~ DESIGNED TO ALLOW YOU TO WALK TO AN EMPTY SEAT WITHOUT GETTING BLACK AND BLUE.
SOUND-PROOF TWIN-DIVING HELMETS- TO CARRY ON CONVERSATION WITHOUT DISTURBING THOSE AROUND YOU.

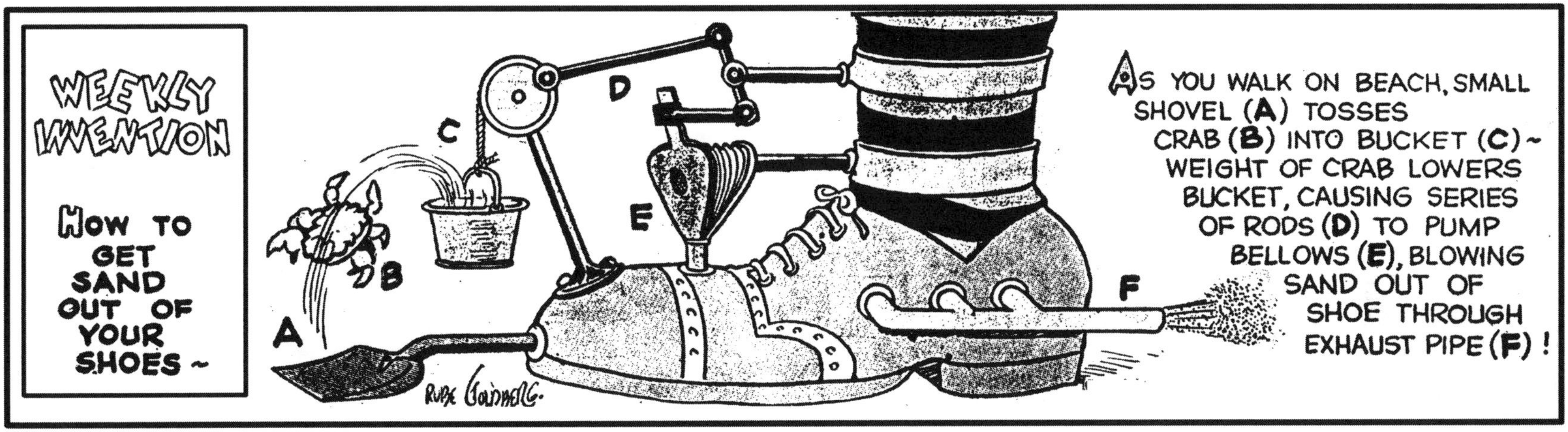
WEEKLY INVENTION
HOW TO GET SAND OUT OF YOUR SHOES ~
A
B
C
D
E
F
AS YOU WALK ON BEACH, SMALL SHOVEL (A) TOSSES CRAB (B) INTO BUCKET (C) ~ WEIGHT OF CRAB LOWERS BUCKET, CAUSING SERIES OF RODS (D) TO PUMP BELLOWS (E), BLOWING SAND OUT OF SHOE THROUGH EXHAUST PIPE (F) !
RUBE GOLDBERG

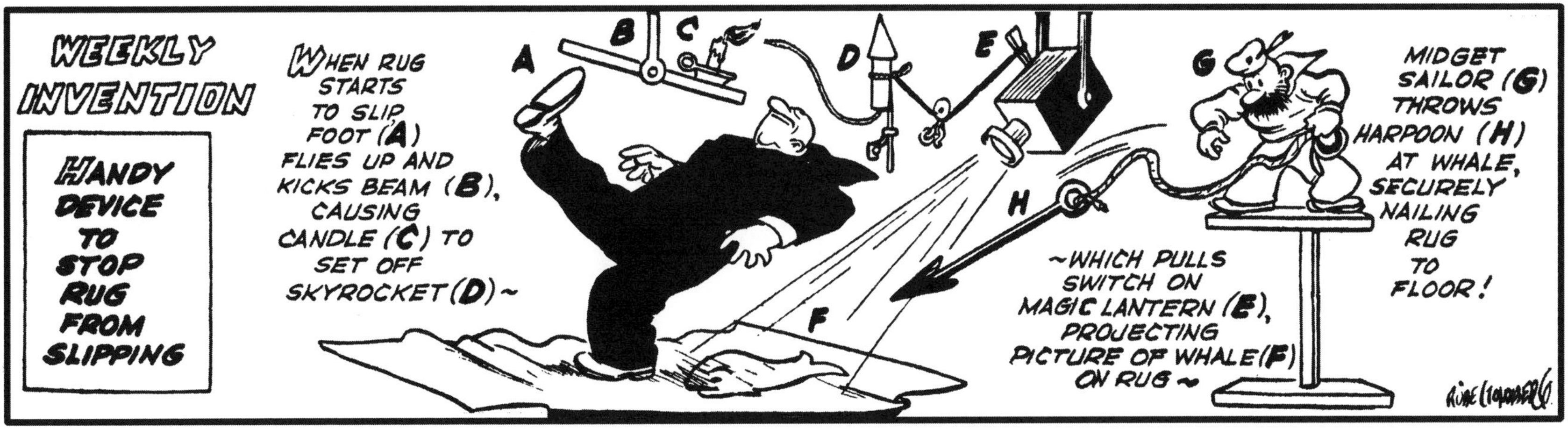
WEEKLY INVENTION
HANDY DEVICE TO STOP RUG FROM SLIPPING
WHEN RUG STARTS TO SLIP FOOT (A) FLIES UP AND KICKS BEAM (B), CAUSING CANDLE (C) TO SET OFF SKYROCKET (D) ~
A
B
C
D
E
F
G
H
~ WHICH PULLS SWITCH ON MAGIC LANTERN (E), PROJECTING PICTURE OF WHALE (F) ON RUG ~
MIDGET SAILOR (G) THROWS HARPOON (H) AT WHALE, SECURELY NAILING RUG TO FLOOR!
RUBE GOLDBERG

C
G
A
D
I
J
N
TRUE
FALSE
B
E
F
M
K
H
L
O
P
RUBE GOLDBERG

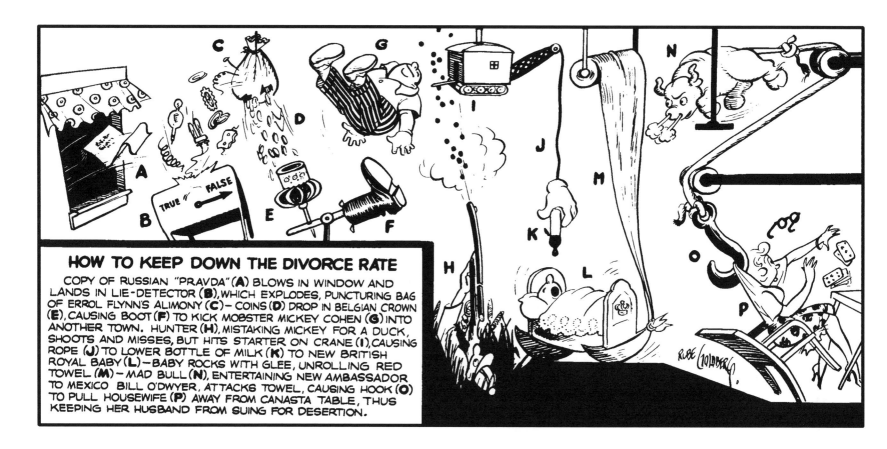

HOW TO KEEP DOWN THE DIVORCE RATE

COPY OF RUSSIAN "PRAVDA" (A) BLOWS IN WINDOW AND LANDS IN LIE-DETECTOR (B), WHICH EXPLODES, PUNCTURING BAG OF ERROL FLYNN'S ALIMONY (C) – COINS (D) DROP IN BELGIAN CROWN (E), CAUSING BOOT (F) TO KICK MOBSTER MICKEY COHEN (G) INTO ANOTHER TOWN. HUNTER (H), MISTAKING MICKEY FOR A DUCK, SHOOTS AND MISSES, BUT HITS STARTER ON CRANE (I), CAUSING ROPE (J) TO LOWER BOTTLE OF MILK (K) TO NEW BRITISH ROYAL BABY (L) – BABY ROCKS WITH GLEE, UNROLLING RED TOWEL (M) – MAD BULL (N), ENTERTAINING NEW AMBASSADOR TO MEXICO BILL O'DWYER, ATTACKS TOWEL, CAUSING HOOK (O) TO PULL HOUSEWIFE (P) AWAY FROM CANASTA TABLE, THUS KEEPING HER HUSBAND FROM SUING FOR DESERTION.

-NO MORE OVERSLEEPING -
WHEN SUN COMES UP, MAGNIFYING GLASS (A) BURNS HOLE IN PAPER BAG (B), DROPPING WATER INTO LADLE (C) AND LIFTING GATE (D), WHICH ALLOWS HEAVY BALL (E) TO ROLL DOWN CHUTE (F) - ROPE (G) LIFTS BED (H) INTO VERTICAL POSITION AND DROPS YOU INTO YOUR SHOES (I) -
A
B
C
D
E
F
G
H
P.S.- YOU CAN'T GO BACK AND SNEAK A FEW WINKS BECAUSE THERE'S NO PLACE TO LIE DOWN!
RUBE GOLDBERG

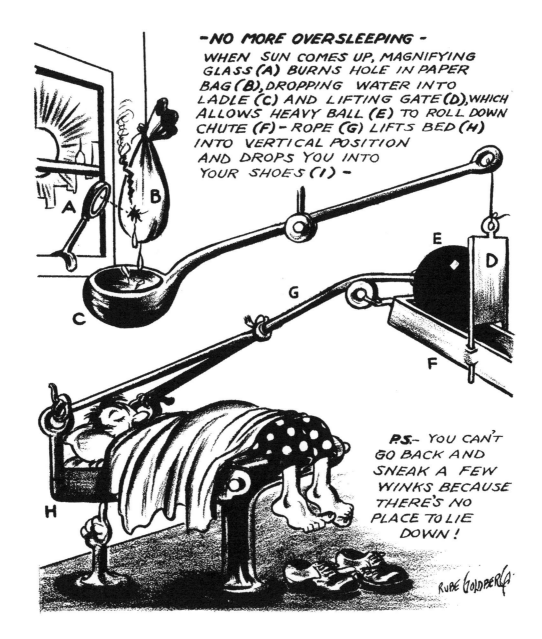

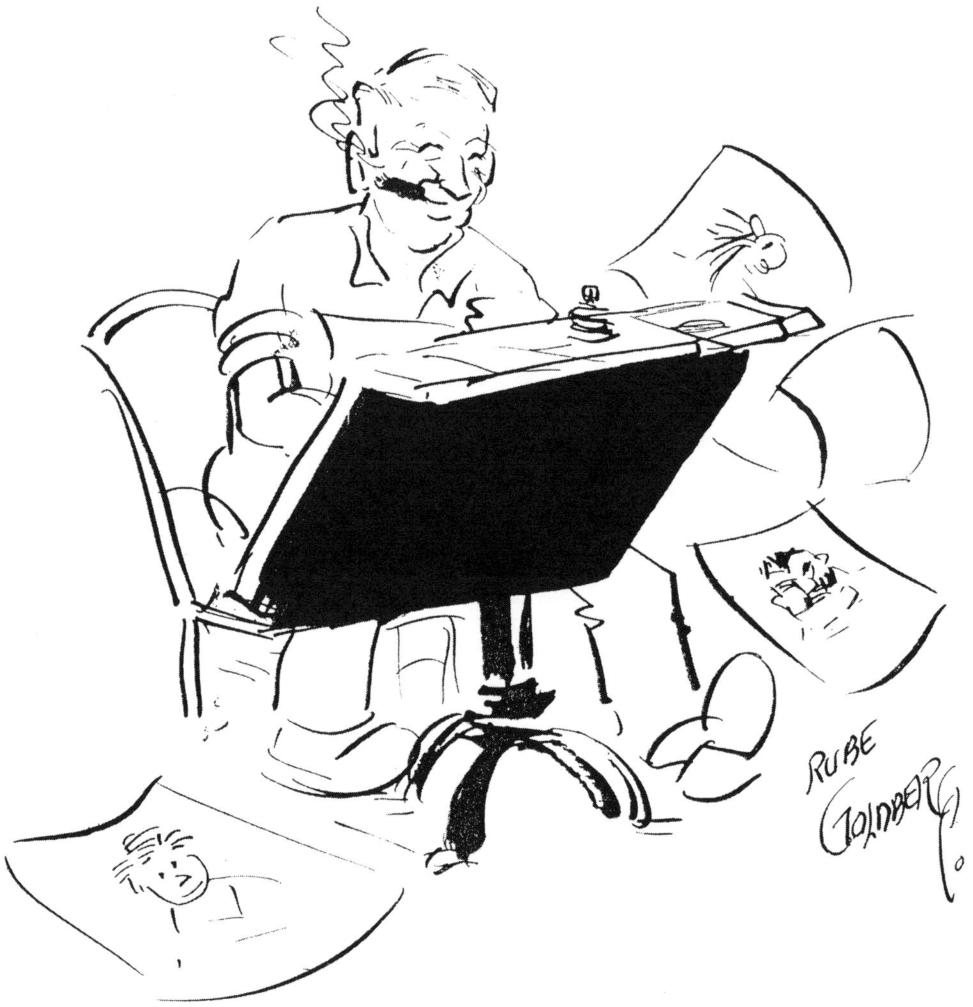
RUBE GOLDBERG

Sketches

Rube Goldberg Inventions combined pictures and words in a unique blend of both mediums. While the art was detailed, it was the words that led you through a series of steps to get to the answer. Part of Rube's genius was his ability to move you through those steps so that you got his message.

While Rube certainly did his share of continuity strips (*Boob McNutt, Bobo Baxter, Lala Palooza*, etc.), his main interest was to develop a complete thought, a complete statement, in his daily panel. His Inventions are complicated but complete. You are told the story in a single panel, using the words as a guide until you are given the answers.

Rube was a quick and skilled artist. His sketches quickly tell the story, the roughs look like finished art, and his finished art shows the detail that make his drawings come alive. Two examples are the roughs from "Simple Way to Keep a Fighter from Being Knocked Out" and "Keeping the Screen Door Closed," coupled with the finished cartoons that were published.

Rube developed his Inventions in four stages:

First, like most artists and writers he was experienced in listening to and at looking at people. He often made quick notes to help him remember what struck him as unusual and interesting about them. Rube was an avid newspaper reader, and he scanned the dailies looking for stories about people, situations, and ideas that he could use for his work.

Published patent specifications from the United States Patent Office that are part of an "idea" file in the Rube Goldberg archives held in the Bancroft Library at the University of California, Berkeley.

A. ZUKOR.
BURGLAR ALARM.
1,046,533.
Patented Dec. 10, 1912.
Fig. 1
Fig. 2
Fig. 3

A. M. LOUGHNEY.
ABDOMINAL FAT REDUCING APPLIANCE.
951,648.
Patented Mar. 8, 1910.
FIG. 1
FIG. 2
FIG. 3
FIG. 4

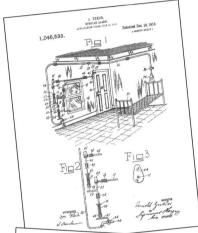

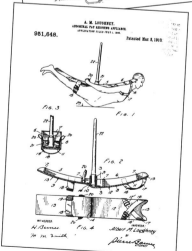

However, the Inventions also needed another factor, something that continuity comic strips didn't need. The Inventions needed a reason or problem to solve that would result in a definite and complete action—all in one panel. Also, since that one panel was supposed to be funny, it also had to make you laugh, or at least shake your head in wonderment that somebody could think of it.

One source of ideas for Rube's Inventions was the U.S. Patent Office, since it has more inventions and inventors than any other place. Some of the ideas people come up with are very unusual. Rube's archives had a collection of such clippings and patent specifications. One was for a burglar alarm with a showerhead instead of a loud noise system. The showerhead

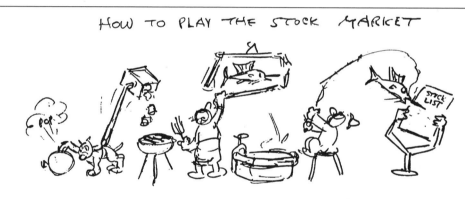

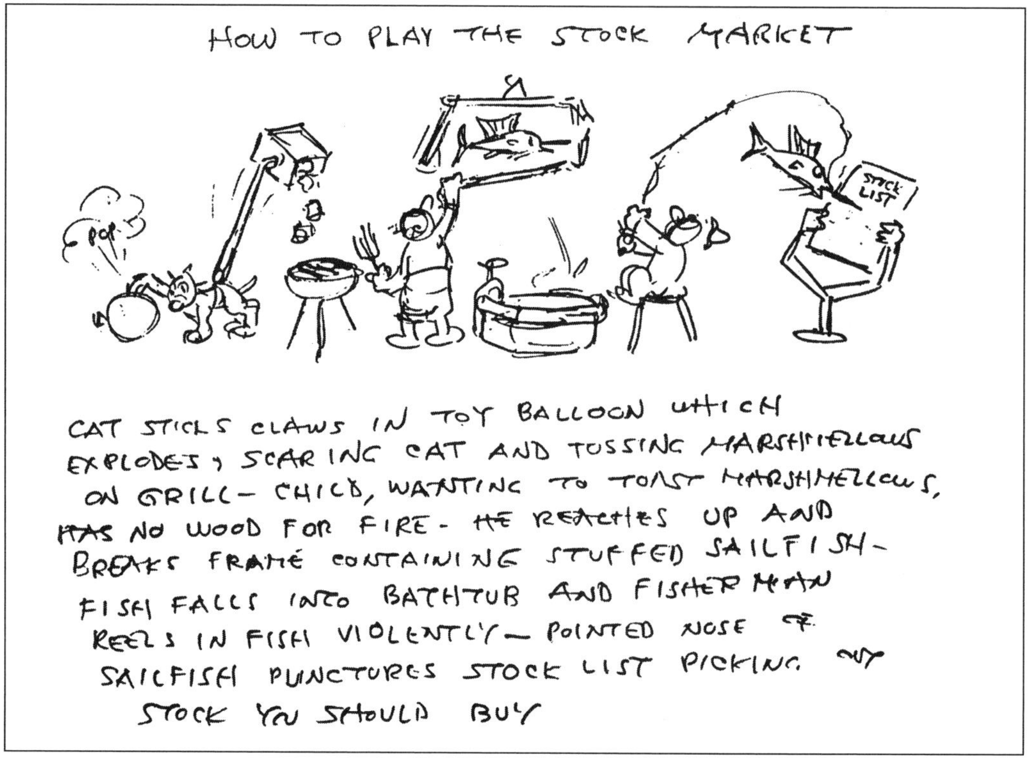

HOW TO PLAY THE STOCK MARKET
POP
STOCK LIST
CAT STICKS CLAWS IN TOY BALLOON WHICH EXPLODES, SCARING CAT AND TOSSING MARSHMELLOWS ON GRILL - CHICK, WANTING TO TOAST MARSHMELLOWS, HAS NO WOOD FOR FIRE - HE REACHES UP AND BREAKS FRAME CONTAINING STUFFED SAILFISH - FISH FALLS INTO BATHTUB AND FISHERMAN REELS IN FISH VIOLENTLY - POINTED NOSE OF SAILFISH PUNCTURES STOCK LIST PICKING OUT STOCK YOU SHOULD BUY

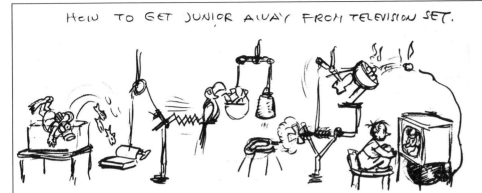

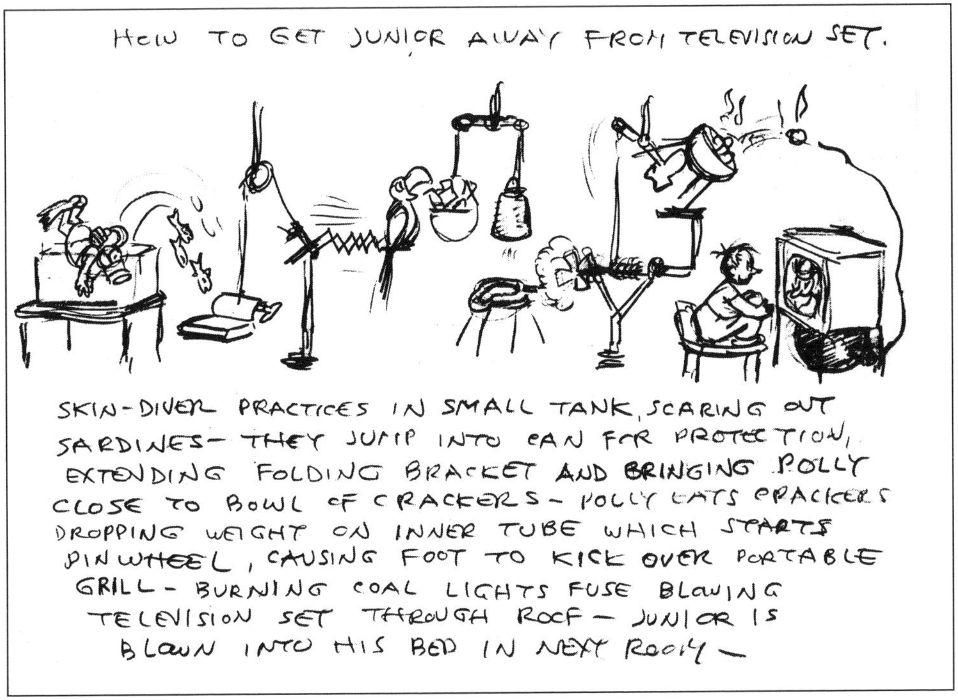

HOW TO GET JUNIOR AWAY FROM TELEVISION SET.
SKIN-DIVER PRACTICES IN SMALL TANK, SCARING OUT SARDINES— THEY JUMP INTO CAN FOR PROTECTION, EXTENDING FOLDING BRACKET AND BRINGING POLLY CLOSE TO BOWL OF CRACKERS— POLLY EATS CRACKERS DROPPING WEIGHT ON INNER TUBE WHICH STARTS PINWHEEL, CAUSING FOOT TO KICK OVER PORTABLE GRILL— BURNING COAL LIGHTS FUSE BLOWING TELEVISION SET THROUGH ROOF— JUNIOR IS BLOWN INTO HIS BED IN NEXT ROOM—

was positioned over your bed and drenched you with water to wake you up when a burglar was trying to break in. Another was a stomach or belly reducer that strapped you (belly side down) to something that looked like an oversized blotter. Then you got your wife or friend to rock you back and forth, exercising your belly and squashing it smaller. These patents were actually granted and were a gold mine of ideas for Rube and the Inventions of Professor Butts.

The second stage of creating an Invention was a "doodle" to get the basic idea down on paper. This was a pencil sketch that illustrated the idea and all its steps. Rube would bring in the animals, flowers, and other parts and props that made the invention happen. Then he would add the words that explained everything, and gave you the answers—not forgetting the laugh, or at least a "Gee whiz."

First rough sketch followed by a more finished version of the idea with Rube's typed draft caption.

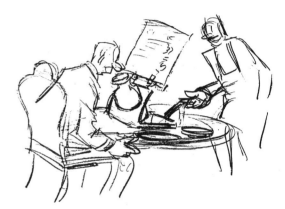

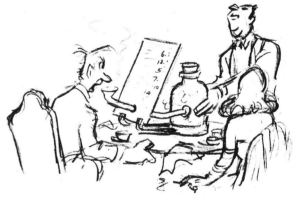

Simple tube for administering smelling salts when waiter brings check in night club.

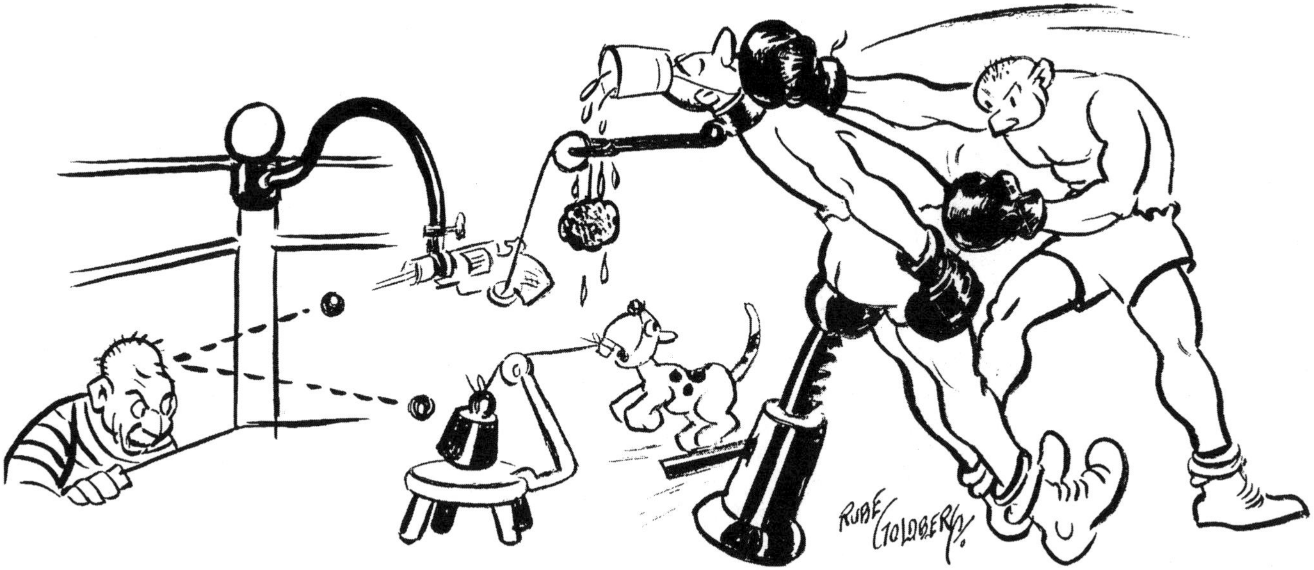

The top drawing shows Rube's last concept drawing before the finished art complete with captions was done, as shown in the bottom drawing.

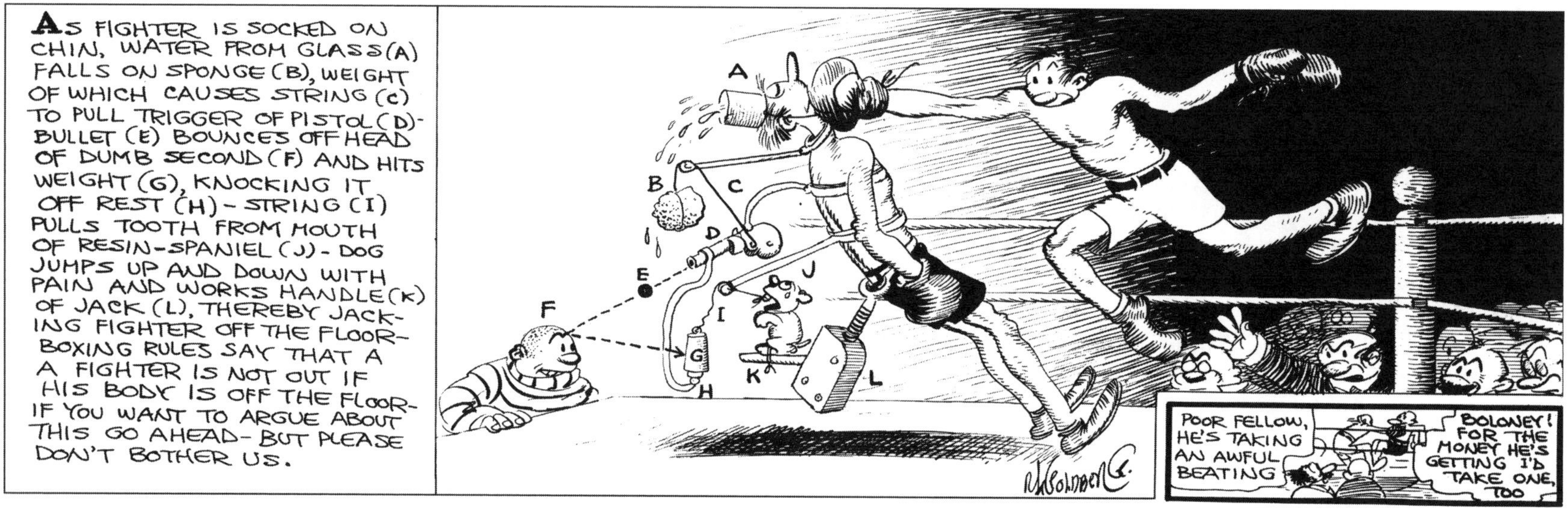
AS FIGHTER IS SOCKED ON CHIN, WATER FROM GLASS (A) FALLS ON SPONGE (B), WEIGHT OF WHICH CAUSES STRING (C) TO PULL TRIGGER OF PISTOL (D)- BULLET (E) BOUNCES OFF HEAD OF DUMB SECOND (F) AND HITS WEIGHT (G), KNOCKING IT OFF REST (H) - STRING (I) PULLS TOOTH FROM MOUTH OF RESIN-SPANIEL (J) - DOG JUMPS UP AND DOWN WITH PAIN AND WORKS HANDLE (K) OF JACK (L), THEREBY JACKING FIGHTER OFF THE FLOOR- BOXING RULES SAY THAT A A FIGHTER IS NOT OUT IF HIS BODY IS OFF THE FLOOR- IF YOU WANT TO ARGUE ABOUT THIS GO AHEAD- BUT PLEASE DON'T BOTHER US.
POOR FELLOW, HE'S TAKING AN AWFUL BEATING
BOLONEY! FOR THE MONEY HE'S GETTING I'D TAKE ONE, TOO

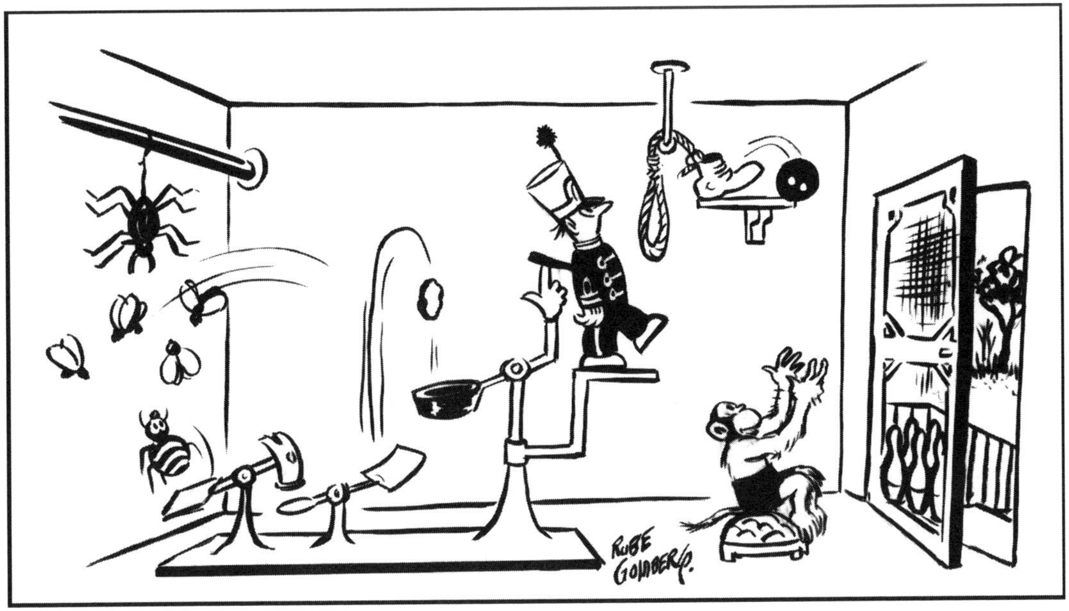
RUBE GOLDBERG

Rube's concept drawing for this Invention, when compared to the final drawing, illustrates the changes made between what's almost finished and the final drawing itself.

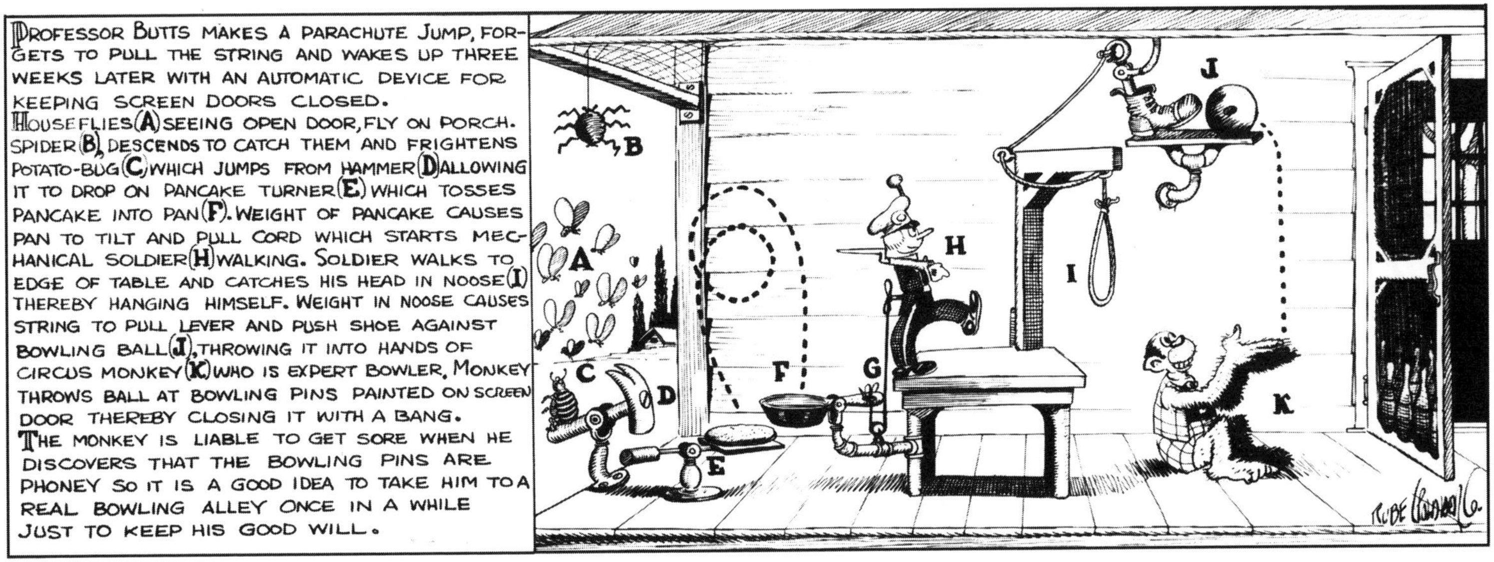
PROFESSOR BUTTS MAKES A PARACHUTE JUMP, FORGETS TO PULL THE STRING AND WAKES UP THREE WEEKS LATER WITH AN AUTOMATIC DEVICE FOR KEEPING SCREEN DOORS CLOSED.
HOUSEFLIES (A) SEEING OPEN DOOR, FLY ON PORCH. SPIDER (B), DESCENDS TO CATCH THEM AND FRIGHTENS POTATO-BUG (C) WHICH JUMPS FROM HAMMER (D) ALLOWING IT TO DROP ON PANCAKE TURNER (E) WHICH TOSSES PANCAKE INTO PAN (F). WEIGHT OF PANCAKE CAUSES PAN TO TILT AND PULL CORD WHICH STARTS MECHANICAL SOLDIER (H) WALKING. SOLDIER WALKS TO EDGE OF TABLE AND CATCHES HIS HEAD IN NOOSE (I) THEREBY HANGING HIMSELF. WEIGHT IN NOOSE CAUSES STRING TO PULL LEVER AND PUSH SHOE AGAINST BOWLING BALL (J), THROWING IT INTO HANDS OF CIRCUS MONKEY (K) WHO IS EXPERT BOWLER. MONKEY THROWS BALL AT BOWLING PINS PAINTED ON SCREEN DOOR THEREBY CLOSING IT WITH A BANG.
THE MONKEY IS LIABLE TO GET SORE WHEN HE DISCOVERS THAT THE BOWLING PINS ARE PHONEY SO IT IS A GOOD IDEA TO TAKE HIM TO A REAL BOWLING ALLEY ONCE IN A WHILE JUST TO KEEP HIS GOOD WILL.
J
B
H
A
I
C
F
G
D
K
E
RUBE GOLDBERG

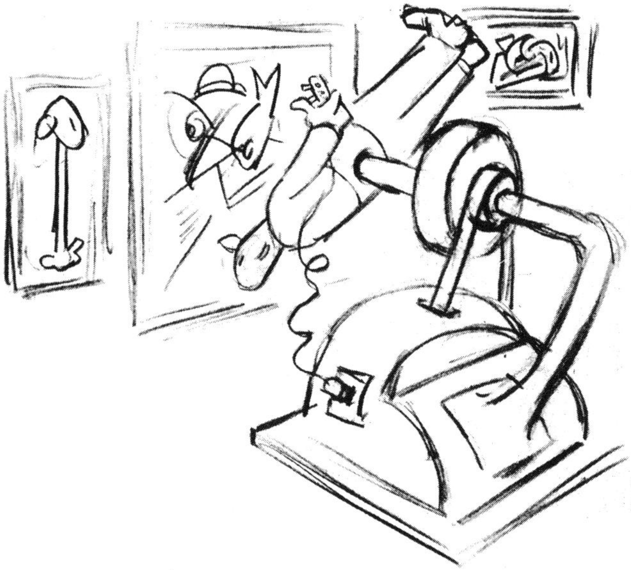

Revolvometer for looking at modernistic art.You press the electric button and stop yourself in any position in whsich the painting looks best.

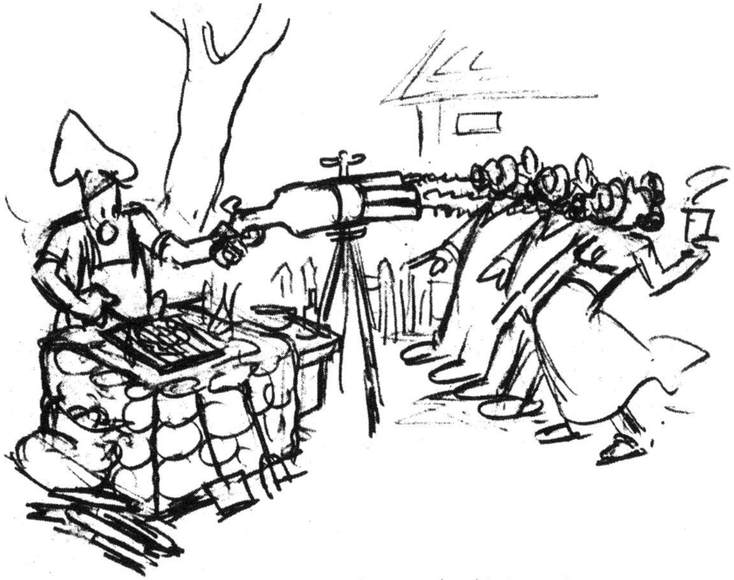

Quick-action gun to quiet guests who insist on tàlling you how to broil steak on outdoor grill.Boxing gloves land directly on button knocking guests unsconscious in which condition they remain until steak is served.

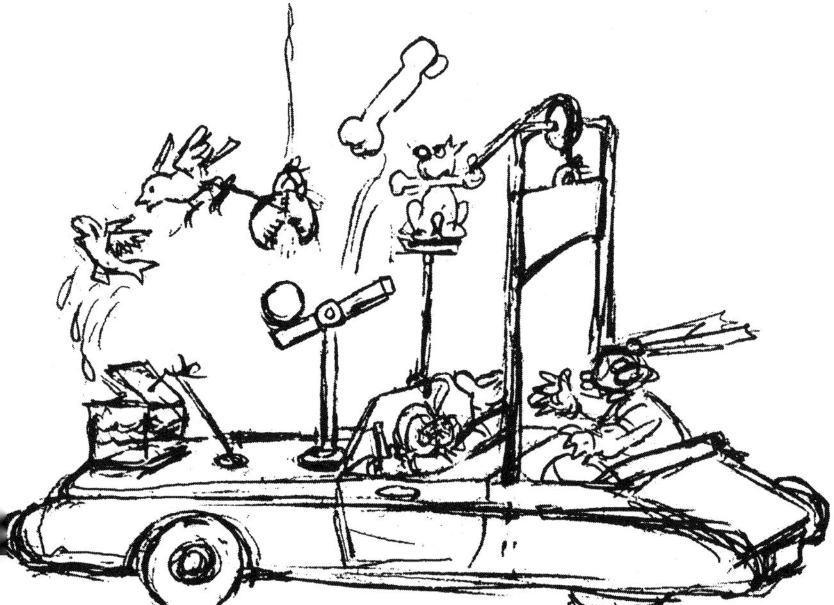

The third stage was the "rough." Here he developed the visual part of the Invention in clear and concise drawings. He could check the invention drawing to make sure it worked (according to Goldbergian engineering and the laws of physics), so that he could then write the words in the correct sequence and readers wouldn't lose their way through the complexity of the Invention.

The last stage was the finished art, when Rube added the background and the details that brought the drawing to life. Here is where he hand-lettered the words, making sure that in drawing the words he emphasized the action in a way that he felt regular typeset letters couldn't do. He wanted to make sure you quickly got what he was trying to say.

The sketches in this section have not been published before except for the screen-door closing sketch. The sketches were not only used for finished art but were also stored as ideas for future drawings. They give us a unique opportunity to look into Rube's mind while he was first putting his ideas down on paper.

Rube did what great creative artists do best. He took 50 percent reality, 50 percent imagination, shook, stirred, and cooked up a wonderful illustrated guidebook to help humanity deal with both life and technology.

Simple one-shift bouncer for free-loaders who crash your television set.

Bibliography

Rube Goldberg's best-remembered cartoon series was *The Inventions of Professor Lucifer Gorgonzola Butts* (1914-64), but *I'm the Guy* and *Foolish Questions* also were published for more than fifty years. Rube created over sixty different cartoon titles; some ran only two or three years, others for more than ten, and the three listed above for fifty. Rube would run different daily main cartoons with another two or three as side panels.

Some titles have been omitted from this list because they only ran one or two times either in newspapers or magazines. However, this list represents the main body of Rube's newspaper humor cartoons from 1904 through 1964. The bibliography includes ten books written in whole or in part by Rube with five more books written about Rube. Animated cartoons, a screenplay, a theatrical play, a television show, sculpture shows, and popular songs were also all part of Rube's creative output. About forty-eight magazine feature and short stories that Rube wrote and the numerous newspaper and magazine stories, radio and television broadcasts, and even a musical written about Rube are not listed here, but a search on Web sites or in a library reference files will lead the interested reader to the their sources.

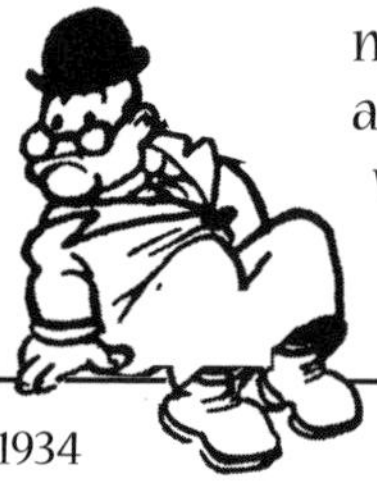

Cartoon Series

Alphabetical Soup	1934
Are You Saving Jokers?	1934
Benny Sent Me	1914–34
Bill	1931–34
Bill and Professor Butts	1934
Blame It on Wilber	1920–26
Blind Boobs	1921
Bobo Baxter	1927–28
Boob McNutt	1915–34
Boob McNutt's Ark	1933–34
Boob McNutt's Geography	1934
Boob News	1916
Boobs Abroad	1913–14, 1918
Bozo Butts—They Drive Him Nuts	1923–28
Brad and Dad	1923
Breaking Even	1913–19
The Candy Kid	1908–11
Cartoon Follies of 1926	1926
Doc Wright	1934–35
Father Was Right	1912–24
Fifty-Fifty	1913–34
Foolish Questions	1909–34
History in a Modern Picture Frame	1910–19
If Plays Were Only True to Life	1909–13
I'm Cured	1913–21
I'm the Guy	1911–34
I Never Thought of That	1910–20
Inventions of Professor Butts	1914–64
It All Depends on the Point of View	1909–13
It Costs Too Much to Live and You Can't Afford to Die	1911–26
It's All Wrong . . . It's All Wrong	1914–29
. . . Sweep Out the Padded Cell . . .	1913–30
Lala Palooza	1936–38
Life's Little Jokes	1911–35
Little Butch	1928–31